Blackstone's Statutes on

CRIMINAL LAW

GW00506025

Blackstone's Statutes on
CRIMINAL LAW

Eighth Edition

P. R. Glazebrook
Fellow of Jesus College
Cambridge

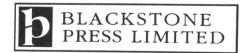

BLACKSTONE
PRESS LIMITED

This edition published in Great Britain 1997 by Blackstone Press Limited,
Aldine Place, London W12 8AA. Telephone 0181-740 2277

© P. R. Glazebrook, 1989

ISBN: 1 85431 794 6

First edition, 1989
Second edition, 1991
Reprinted, 1992
Third edition, 1993
Reprinted, 1993
Fourth edition, 1994
Reprinted, 1994
Fifth edition, 1995
Sixth edition, 1996
Seventh edition, 1997
Eighth edition, 1998

British Library Cataloguing in Publication Data
A CIP catalogue record for this book is available from the British Library

Typeset by Style Photosetting Limited, Mayfield, East Sussex
Printed by Bell & Bain Limited, Glasgow

CONTENTS

9 OFFENSIVE CONDUCT 201

10 INTERFERENCE WITH THE ADMINISTRATION OF JUSTICE OR THE POLICE 227

11   INTERFERENCE WITH GOVERNMENTAL OR PUBLIC SERVICES 240

12   PRELIMINARY OFFENCES 254

APPENDIX   'LEGISLATING THE CRIMINAL CODE' 270

PREFACE

England is one of only a handful of jurisdictions among the developed countries of the world which is still without a Criminal Code: most of the under-developed countries are, in this respect at least, better provided for. The Law Commission's declared aim is to make good this lack of a single, comprehensive enactment specifying both the conduct which is prohibited under threat of imprisonment and other severe penalties, and the conditions which must be satisfied before a person who has engaged in such conduct may be convicted and punished. In 1989, after many years' work, the Commission published a Report (Law Com. No. 177; HC Paper (1988–89) 299) which included a Draft Criminal Code Bill. The Draft Code, though very much better than nothing, was in many respects a disappointing document. It was not based on any clearly identified or consistent principles, and suffered from many of the defects proverbially attributed to buildings designed by a committee (in this case several committees) rather than an architect. It combined an eclectic choice of reforms with the all-too-faithful reproduction of many of the unprincipled quirks and anomalies of the present law. This law, enshrined in two centuries of statutory draftsmanship of very uneven quality and in judicial pronouncements often hastily rendered or poorly considered (or both), is itself the product of changing views of morality and of when and how penal measures should be used in the hope of protecting the community against the violent, the lustful, the avaricious, the selfish and the careless. So a good deal more work is needed before there is a Draft Code that will be worthy of Parliament's attention.

The Commission is now publishing a series of consultation papers and reports, under the general title 'Legislating the Criminal Code', containing bills in the style of the Draft Code. These draft bills deal with areas of the law where the need for reform is particularly urgent, and they show that the Commission has been having second — or third — thoughts about its 1989 Draft. Only time will tell whether such very limited bills (the Appendix prints three of them) represent, as the Commission hopes, the first stages in implementing the Code project, or the fatal first steps towards its abandonment, and a return to merely piecemeal reform of the criminal law. At present the Commission appears to be running around in ever diminishing circles, while the Home Office, reckless of the shape and intelligibility of the law, continues to add new offences and heavier penalties to the statute book in a manner reminiscent of the late eighteenth century. The crime of intimidating witnesses, jurors and others created by section 51 of the Criminal Justice and Public Order Act 1994 was expressly stated to be 'in addition to, and not in derogation of, any offences subsisting at common law' (s. 1(11)). That, being translated, can only mean that the Home Office was quite uncertain about the pre-existing law on the matter, but hoped that it was wider and vaguer than that for which it sought Parliament's approval. The deplorably vague provisions of the Protection from Harassment Act 1997 have likewise been added to the statute book without regard to either the common law of assault or to the numerous offences of harassment already there. Sections 28–33 of the Crime and Disorder Act 1998 are open to similar criticisms.

Students and teachers of criminal law (not to mention policemen, magistrates, jurors, lawyers and judges) have therefore to continue to confront a great jumble of statutory provisions, exhibiting many different drafting styles, which are replete with detail, but short on principle. There are believed to be close on 8,000 different criminal offences on the statute-book. This present selection, which is intended to be no more than a convenient means of reference to the main statutory framework of the substantive criminal law, is inevitably a personal and, to a degree, an arbitrary one. But it is hoped that it is extensive and varied enough to meet the needs both of those students following criminal law courses of a traditional sort, which involve a detailed study of the principal offences of personal violence and fraud (who will learn much about their inadequacies by studying the less familiar legislation designed to supplement them) and of those whose courses place more emphasis on the use of the criminal law to regulate less obvious, yet often equally harmful, forms of antisocial behaviour. Considerations of space and cost have, however, demanded the excision of most of the procedural, evidentiary, and administrative provisions of these statutes, as also of almost all penalty provisions where these are separate from the offence-creating ones.

In general the statutory provisions selected are printed in the form in which they were law on 31 July 1998 (amending legislation being incorporated silently).

P R Glazebrook

1 GENERAL RULES

(a) LIABILITY

INTERPRETATION ACT 1978

5. Definitions
In any Act, unless the contrary intention appears, words and expressions listed in Schedule 1 to this Act are to be construed according to that Schedule.

SCHEDULE 1
'Person' includes a body of persons corporate or unincorporate.
In relation to England and Wales—
    (a) 'indictable offence' means an offence which, if committed by an adult, is triable on indictment, whether it is exclusively so triable or triable either way;
    (b) 'summary offence' means an offence which, if committed by an adult, is triable only summarily;
    (c) 'offence triable either way' means an offence which, if committed by an adult, is triable either on indictment or summarily;
and the terms 'indictable', 'summary' and 'triable either way', in their application to offences, are to be construed accordingly.
In the above definitions references to the way or ways in which an offence is triable are to be construed without regard to the effect, if any, of section 22 of the Magistrates' Courts Act 1980 on the mode of trial in a particular case.

6. Gender and number
In any Act, unless the contrary intention appears,—
    (a) words importing the masculine gender include the feminine;
    (b) words importing the feminine gender include the masculine;
    (c) words in the singular include the plural and words in the plural include the singular.

15. Repeal of repeal
Where an Act repeals a repealing enactment, the repeal does not revive any enactment previously repealed unless words are added reviving it.

16. General savings
    (1) Without prejudice to section 15, where an Act repeals an enactment, the repeal does not, unless the contrary intention appears,—
    (a) revive anything not in force or existing at the time at which the repeal takes effect;
    (b) affect the previous operation of the enactment repealed or anything duly done or suffered under that enactment;

    (c) affect any right, privilege, obligation or liability acquired, accrued, or incurred under that enactment;

    (e) affect any investigation, legal proceeding or remedy in respect of any such right, privilege, obligation, liability, penalty, forfeiture or punishment;

and any such investigation, legal proceeding or remedy may be instituted, continued or enforced, and any such penalty, forefeiture or punishment may be imposed, as if the repealing Act had not been passed.

    (2) This section applies to the expiry of a temporary enactment as if it were repealed by an Act.

18. Duplicated offences

Where an act or omission constitutes an offence under two or more Acts, or both under an Act and at common law, the offender shall, unless the contrary intention appears, be liable to be prosecuted and punished under either or any of those Acts or at common law, but shall not be liable to be punished more than once for the same offence.

CRIMINAL LAW ACT 1967

1. Abolition of distinction between felony and misdemeanour

    (1) All distinctions between felony and misdemeanour are hereby abolished.

    (2) Subject to the provisions of this Act, on all matters on which a distinction has previously been made between felony and misdemeanour, including mode of trial, the law and practice in relation to all offences cognisable under the law of England and Wales (including piracy) shall be the law and practice applicable at the commencement of this Act in relation to misdemeanour.

6. Trial of offences

    (1) Where a person is arraigned on an indictment—

    (a) he shall in all cases be entitled to make a plea of not guilty in addition to any demurrer or special plea;

    (b) he may plead not guilty of the offence specifically charged in the indictment but guilty of another offence of which he might be found guilty on that indictment;

    (c) if he stands mute of malice or will not answer directly to the indictment, the court may order a plea of not guilty to be entered on his behalf, and he shall then be treated as having pleaded not guilty.

    (2) On an indictment for murder a person found not guilty of murder may be found guilty—

    (a) of manslaughter, or of causing grievous bodily harm with intent to do so; or

    (b) of any offence of which he may be found guilty under an enactment specifically so providing, or under section 4(2) of this Act; or

    (c) of any attempt to commit murder, or an attempt to commit any other offence of which he might be found guilty;

but may not be found guilty of any offence not included above.

    (3) Where, on a person's trial on indictment for any offence except treason or murder, the jury find him not guilty of the offence specifically charged in the indictment, but the allegations in the indictment amount to or include (expressly or by implication) an allegation of another offence falling within the jurisdiction of the court of trial, the jury may find him guilty of that other offence or of an offence of which he could be found guilty on an indictment specifically charging that other offence.

    (4) For purposes of subsection (3) above any allegation of an offence shall be taken as including an allegation of attempting to commit that offence; and where a person is charged on an indictment with attempting to commit an offence or with any assault or other act preliminary to an offence, but not with the completed offence, then

(subject to the discretion of the court to discharge the jury with a view to the preferment of an indictment for the completed offence) he may be convicted of the offence charged notwithstanding that he is shown to be guilty of the completed offence.

(5) Where a person arraigned on an indictment pleads not guilty of an offence charged in the indictment but guilty of some other offence of which he might be found guilty on that charge, and he is convicted on that plea of guilty without trial for the offence of which he has pleaded not guilty, then (whether or not the two offences are separately charged in distinct counts) his conviction of the one offence shall be an acquittal of the other.

CHILDREN AND YOUNG PERSONS ACT 1933

50. Age of criminal responsbility
It shall be conclusively presumed that no child under the age of ten years can be guilty of any offence.

55. Power to order fine or compensation to be paid by parent or guardian
(1) Where—
(a) a child or young person is convicted or found guilty of any offence for the commission of which a fine or costs may be imposed or a compensation order may be made under section 35 of the Powers of Criminal Courts Act 1973; and
(b) the court is of the opinion that the case would best be met by the imposition of a fine or costs or the making of such an order, whether with or without any other punishment,
it shall be the duty of the court to order that the fine, compensation or costs awarded be paid by the parent or guardian of the child or young person instead of by the child or young person himself, unless the court is satisfied—
(i) that the parent or guardian cannot be found; or
(ii) that it would be unreasonable to make an order for payment, having regard to the circumstances of the case.

CRIME AND DISORDER ACT 1998

34. Abolition of rebuttable presumption that a child is doli incapax
The rebuttable presumption of criminal law that a child aged 10 or over is incapable of committing an offence is hereby abolished.

THEFT ACT 1968

30. Husband and wife
(2) Subject to subsection (4) below, a person shall have the same right to bring proceedings against that person's wife or husband for any offence (whether under this Act or otherwise) as if they were not married, and a person bringing any such proceedings shall be competent to give evidence for the prosecution at every stage of the proceedings.

(4) Proceedings shall not be instituted against a person for any offence of stealing or doing unlawful damage to property which at the time of the offence belongs to that person's wife or husband, or for any attempt, incitement or conspiracy to commit such an offence, unless the proceedings are instituted by or with the consent of the Director of Public Prosecutions:
Provided that—
(a) this subsection shall not apply to proceedings against a person for an offence—

(i)   if that person is charged with committing the offence jointly with the wife or husband; or

(ii)   if by virtue of any judicial decree or order (wherever made) that person and the wife or husband are at the time of the offence under no obligation to cohabit.

CRIMINAL JUSTICE ACT 1967

8.   Proof of criminal intent

A court or jury, in determining whether a person has committed an offence,—

(a)   shall not be bound in law to infer that he intended or foresaw a result of his actions by reason only of its being a natural and probable consequence of those actions; but

(b)   shall decide whether he did intend or foresee that result by reference to all the evidence, drawing such inferences from the evidence as appear proper in the circumstances.

ACCESSORIES AND ABETTORS ACT 1861

8.   Abettors

Whosoever shall aid, abet, counsel, or procure the commission of any indictable offence, whether the same be an offence at common law or by virtue of any Act passed or to be passed, shall be liable to be tried, indicted, and punished as a principal offender.

MAGISTRATES' COURTS ACT 1980

44.   Aiders and abettors

(1)   A person who aids, abets, counsels or procures the commission by another person of a summary offence shall be guilty of the like offence and may be tried (whether or not he is charged as a principal) either by a court having jurisdiction to try that other person or by a court having by virtue of his own offence jurisdiction to try him.

(2)   Any offence consisting in aiding, abetting, counselling or procuring the commission of an offence triable either way (other than an offence listed in Schedule 1 to this Act) shall by virtue of this subsection be triable either way.

CRIMINAL JUSTICE ACT 1948

31.   Jurisdiction and procedure in respect of certain indictable offences committed in foreign countries

(1)   Any British subject employed under His Majesty's Government in the United Kingdom in the service of the Crown who commits in a foreign country, when acting or purporting to act in the course of his employment, any offence which, if committed in England, would be punishable on indictment, shall be guilty of an offence . . . and subject to the same punishment, as if the offence had been committed in England.

CIVIL AVIATION ACT 1982

92.   Application of criminal law to aircraft

(1)   Any act or omission taking place on board a British-controlled aircraft while in flight elsewhere than in or over the United Kingdom which, if taking place in, or in a part of, the United Kingdom, would constitute an offence under the law in force

in, or in that part of, the United Kingdom shall constitute that offence; but this subsection shall not apply to any act or omission which is expressly or impliedly authorised by or under that law when taking place outside the United Kingdom.

(4) For the purposes of this section the period during which an aircraft is in flight shall be deemed to include any period from the moment when power is applied for the purpose of the aircraft taking off on a flight until the moment when the landing run (if any) at the termination of that flight ends; and any reference in this section to an aircraft in flight shall include a reference to an aircraft during any period when it is on the surface of the sea or land but not within the territorial limits of any country.

(5) In this section, except where the context otherwise requires—
'aircraft' means any aircraft, whether or not a British-controlled aircraft, other than—

(a) a military aircraft; or

(b) subject to section 101(1)(b) below, an aircraft which, not being a military aircraft, belongs to or is exclusively employed in the service of Her Majesty in right of the United Kingdom;

'British-controlled aircraft' means an aircraft—

(a) which is for the time being registered in the United Kingdom; or

(b) which is not for the time being registered in any country but in the case of which either the operator of the aircraft or each person entitled as owner to any legal or beneficial interest in it satisfies the following requirements, namely—

(i) that he is a person qualified to be the owner of a legal or beneficial interest in an aircraft registered in the United Kingdom; and

(ii) that he resides or has his principal place of business in the United Kingdom; or

(c) which, being for the time being registered in some other country, is for the time being chartered by demise to a person who, or to persons each of whom, satisfies the requirements aforesaid; . . .

CRIMINAL JUSTICE ACT 1993

5. Extended jurisdiction over conspiracies to defraud
[See page 189]

6. Relevance of external law
[See page 190]

SEX OFFENDERS ACT 1997

7. Extension of jurisdiction
[See page 28]

(b) DEFENCES

CRIMINAL LAW ACT 1967

3. Use of force in making arrest, etc.
(1) A person may use such force as is reasonable in the circumstances in the prevention of crime, or in effecting or assisting in the lawful arrest of offenders or suspected offenders or of persons unlawfully at large.

(2) Subsection (1) above shall replace the rules of the common law on the question when force used for a purpose mentioned in the subsection is justified by that purpose.

POLICE AND CRIMINAL EVIDENCE ACT 1984

24. Arrest without warrant for arrestable offences

(1) The powers of summary arrest conferred by the following subsections shall apply—

(a) to offences for which the sentence is fixed by law;

(b) to offences for which a person of 21 years of age or over (not previously convicted) may be sentenced to imprisonment for a term of five years (or might be so sentenced but for the restrictions imposed by section 33 of the Magistrates' Courts Act 1980); and

(c) to the offences to which subsection (2) below applies,

and in this Act 'arrestable offence' means any such offence.

(2) The offences to which this subsection applies are—

(a) offences for which a person may be arrested under the Customs and Excise Acts, as defined in section 1(1) of the Customs and Excise Management Act 1979;

(b) offences under the Official Secrets Act 1920 that are not arrestable offences by virtue of the term of imprisonment for which a person may be sentenced in respect of them;

(bb) offences under any provision of the Official Secrets Act 1989 except section 8(1), (4) or (5);

(c) offences under section . . . 22 (causing prostitution of women) or 23 (procuration of girl under 21) of the Sexual Offences Act 1956;

(d) offences under section 12(1) (taking motor vehicle or other conveyance without authority etc.) or 25(1) (going equipped for stealing, etc.) of the Theft Act 1968;

(e) any offence under the Football (Offences) Act 1991;

(f) an offence under section 2 of the Obscene Publications Act 1959 (publication of obscene matter);

(g) an offence under section 1 of the Protection of Children Act 1978 (indecent photographs and pseudo-photographs of children);

(h) an offence under section 166 of the Criminal Justice and Public Order Act 1994 (sale of tickets by unauthorised persons);

(i) an offence under section 19 of the Public Order Act 1986 (publishing, etc. material intended or likely to stir up racial hatred);

(j) an offence under section 167 of the Criminal Justice and Public Order Act 1994 (touting for hire car services) . . .

(n) an offence under section 2 of the Protection from Harassment Act 1997 (harassment).

(3) Without prejudice to section 2 of the Criminal Attempts Act 1981, the powers of summary arrest conferred by the following subsections shall also apply to the offences of—

(a) conspiracy to commit any of the offences mentioned in subsection (2) above;

(b) attempting to commit any such offence (other than an offence under section 12(1) of the Theft Act 1968);

(c) inciting, aiding, abetting, counselling or procuring the commission of any such offence;

and such offences are also arrestable offences for the purposes of this Act.

(4) Any person may arrest without a warrant—

(a) anyone who is in the act of committing an arrestable offence;

(b) anyone whom he has reasonable grounds for suspecting to be committing such an offence.

(5) Where an arrestable offence has been committed, any person may arrest without a warrant—

(a)   anyone who is guilty of the offence;

(b)   anyone whom he has reasonable grounds for suspecting to be guilty of it.

(6)   Where a constable has reasonable grounds for suspecting that an arrestable offence has been committed, he may arrest without a warrant anyone whom he has reasonable grounds for suspecting to be guilty of the offence.

(7)   A constable may arrest without a warrant—

(a)   anyone who is about to commit an arrestable offence;

(b)   anyone whom he has reasonable grounds for suspecting to be about to commit an arrestable offence.

25.   General arrest conditions

(1)   Where a constable has reasonable grounds for suspecting that any offence which is not an arrestable offence has been committed or attempted, or is being committed or attempted, he may arrest the relevant person if it appears to him that service of a summons is impracticable or inappropriate because any of the general arrest conditions is satisfied.

(2)   In this section 'the relevant person' means any person whom the constable has reasonable grounds to suspect of having committed or having attempted to commit the offence or of being in the course of committing or attempting to commit it.

(3)   The general arrest conditions are—

(a)   that the name of the relevant person is unknown to, and cannot be ascertained by, the constable;

(b)   that the constable has reasonable grounds for doubting whether a name furnished by the relevant person as his name is his real name;

(c)   that—

(i)   the relevant person has failed to furnish a satisfactory address for service; or

(ii)   the constable has reasonable grounds for doubting whether an address furnished by the relevant person is a satisfactory address for service;

(d)   that the constable has reasonable grounds for believing that arrest is necessary to prevent the relevant person—

(i)   causing physical harm to himself or any other person;

(ii)   suffering physical injury;

(iii)   causing loss of or damage to property;

(iv)   committing an offence against public decency;

(v)   causing an unlawful obstruction of the highway;

(e)   that the constable has reasonable grounds for believing that arrest is necessary to protect a child or other vulnerable person from the relevant person.

(4)   For the purposes of subsection (3) above an address is a satisfactory address for service if it appears to the constable—

(a)   that the relevant person will be at it for a sufficiently long period for it to be possible to serve him with a summons; or

(b)   that some other person specified by the relevant person will accept service of a summons for the relevant person at it.

(5)   Nothing in subsection (3)(d) above authorises the arrest of a person under subparagraph (iv) of that paragraph except where members of the public going about their normal business cannot reasonably be expected to avoid the person to be arrested.

(6)   This section shall not prejudice any power of arrest conferred apart from this section.

117.   Power of constable to use reasonable force

Where any provision of this Act—

(a)   confers a power on a constable; and

(b)   does not provide that the power may only be exercised with the consent of some person, other than a police officer, the officer may use reasonable force, if necessary, in the exercise of the power.

FIRE SERVICES ACT 1947

30.   Powers of firemen and police in extinguishing fires
[See page 137]

EDUCATION ACT 1996

550A.   Power of members of staff to restrain pupils
[See page 46]

550B.   Detention outside school hours lawful despite absence of parental consent
[See pages 47]

CRIMINAL JUSTICE ACT 1925

47.   Abolition of presumption of coercion of married woman by husband
Any presumption of law that an offence committed by a wife in the presence of her husband is committed under the coercion of the husband is hereby abolished, but on a charge against a wife for any offence other than treason or murder it shall be a good defence to prove that the offence was committed in the presence of, and under the coercion of, the husband.

STATUTORY INSTRUMENTS ACT 1946

3.   Supplementary provisions as to publication
(1)   Regulations made for the purposes of this Act shall make provision for the publication by His Majesty's Stationery Office of lists showing the date upon which every statutory instrument printed and sold by or under the authority of the King's printer of Acts of Parliament was first issued by or under the authority of that office; and in any legal proceedings a copy of any list so published shall be received in evidence as a true copy, and an entry therein shall be conclusive evidence of the date on which any statutory instrument was first issued by or under the authority of His Majesty's Stationery Office.
(2)   In any proceedings against any person for an offence consisting of a contravention of any such statutory instrument, it shall be a defence to prove that the instrument had not been issued by or under the authority of His Majesty's Stationery Office at the date of the alleged contravention unless it is proved that at that date reasonable steps had been taken for the purpose of bringing the purport of the instrument to the notice of the public, or of persons likely to be affected by it, or of the person charged.

MAGISTRATES' COURTS ACT 1980

101.   Onus of proving exceptions, etc.
Where the defendant to an information or complaint relies for his defence on any exception, exemption, proviso, excuse or qualification, whether or not it accompanies the description of the offence or matter of complaint in the enactment creating the offence or on which the complaint is founded, the burden of proving the exception,

exemption, proviso, excuse or qualification shall be on him; and this notwithstanding that the information or complaint contains an allegation negativing the exception, exemption, proviso, excuse or qualification.

TRIAL OF LUNATICS ACT 1883

2. Special verdict where accused found guilty, but insane at date of act or omission charged, and orders thereupon

(1) Where in any indictment or information any act or omission is charged against any person as an offence, and it is given in evidence on the trial of such person for that offence that he was insane, so as not to be responsible, according to law, for his actions at the time when the act was done or omission made, then, if it appears to the jury before whom such person is tried that he did the act or made the omission charged, but was insane as aforesaid at the time when he did or made the same, the jury shall return a special verdict that the accused is not guilty by reason of insanity.

CRIMINAL PROCEDURE (INSANITY AND UNFITNESS TO PLEAD) ACT 1991

1. Acquittals on grounds of insanity

(1) A jury shall not return a special verdict under section 2 of the Trial of Lunatics Act 1883 (acquittal on ground of insanity) except on the written or oral evidence of two or more registered medical practitioners at least one of whom is duly approved.

6. Interpretation etc

(1) In this Act—

'duly approved', in relation to a registered medical practitioner, means approved for the purposes of section 12 of the 1983 Act by the Secretary of State as having special experience in the diagnosis or treatment of mental disorder.

CRIMINAL PROCEDURE (INSANITY) ACT 1964

5. Powers to deal with persons not guilty by reason of insanity or unfit to plead etc

(1) This section applies where—

(a) a special verdict is returned that the accused is not guilty by reason of insanity; or

(b) findings are recorded that the accused is under a disability and that he did the act or made the omission charged against him.

(2) Subject to subsection (3) below, the court shall either—

(a) make an order that the accused be admitted, in accordance with the provisions of Schedule 1 to the Criminal Procedure (Insanity and Unfitness to Plead) Act 1991, to such hospital as may be specified by the Secretary of State; or

(b) where they have the power to do so by virtue of section 5 of that Act, make in respect of the accused such one of the following orders as they think most suitable in all the circumstances of the case, namely—

(i) a guardianship order within the meaning of the Mental Health Act 1983;

(ii) a supervision and treatment order within the meaning of Schedule 2 to the said Act of 1991; and

(iii) an order for his absolute discharge.

(3) Paragraph (b) of subsection (2) above shall not apply where the offence to which the special verdict or findings relate is an offence the sentence for which is fixed by law.

(c) APPEALS

CRIMINAL APPEAL ACT 1968

3. Power to substitute conviction of alternative offence

(1) This section applies on an appeal against conviction, where the appellant has been convicted of an offence and the jury could on the indictment have found him guilty of some other offence, and on the finding of the jury it appears to the Court of Appeal that the jury must have been satisfied of facts which proved him guilty of the other offence.

(2) The Court may, instead of allowing or dismissing the appeal, substitute for the verdict found by the jury a verdict of guilty of the other offence, and pass such sentence in substitution for the sentence passed at the trial as may be authorised by law for the other offence, not being a sentence of greater severity.

8. Grounds for allowing and dismissing appeals

(1) Subject to the provisions of this Act, the Court of Appeal—

(a) shall allow an appeal against conviction if they think that the conviction is unsafe; and

(b) shall dismiss such an appeal in any other case.

12. Appeal against verdict of not guilty by reason of insanity

Subject to the provisions of this section, the Court of Appeal—

(a) shall allow an appeal under section 12 of this Act if they think that the verdict is unsafe; and shall dismiss such an appeal in any other case.

MAGISTRATES' COURTS ACT 1980

108. Right of appeal to the Crown Court

(1) A person convicted by a magistrates' court may appeal to the Crown Court—

(a) if he pleaded guilty, against his sentence;

(b) if he did not, against the conviction or sentence.

111. Statement of case by magistrates' court

(1) Any person who was a party to any proceeding before a magistrates' court or is aggrieved by the conviction, order, determination or other proceeding of the court may question the proceeding on the ground that it is wrong in law or is in excess of jurisdiction by applying to the justices composing the court to state a case for the opinion of the High Court on the question of law or jurisdiction involved; but a person shall not make an application under this section in respect of a decision against which he has a right of appeal to the High Court or which by virtue of any enactment passed after 31st December 1879 is final.

(4) On the making of an application under this section in respect of a decision any right of the applicant to appeal against the decision to the Crown Court shall cease.

(5) If the justices are of opinion that an application under this section is frivolous, they may refuse to state a case, and, if the applicant so requires, shall give him a certificate stating that the application has been refused; but the justices shall not refuse to state a case if the application is made by or under the direction of the Attorney General.

(6) Where justices refuse to state a case, the High Court may, on the application of the person who applied for the case to be stated, make an order of mandamus requiring the justices to state a case.

2 HOMICIDE AND FOETICIDE

HOMICIDE ACT 1957

1. Abolition of 'constructive malice'

(1) Where a person kills another in the course or furtherance of some other offence, the killing shall not amount to murder unless done with the same malice aforethought (express or implied) as is required for a killing to amount to murder when not done in the course or furtherance of another offence.

(2) For the purposes of the foregoing subsection, a killing done in the course or for the purpose of resisting an officer of justice, or of resisting or avoiding or preventing a lawful arrest, or of effecting or assisting an escape or rescue from legal custody, shall be treated as a killing in the course or furtherance of an offence.

2. Persons suffering from diminished responsibility

(1) Where a person kills or is a party to the killing of another, he shall not be convicted of murder if he was suffering from such abnormality of mind (whether arising from a condition of arrested or retarded development of mind or any inherent causes or induced by disease or injury) as substantially impaired his mental responsibility for his acts and omissions in doing or being a party to the killing.

(2) On a charge of murder, it shall be for the defence to prove that the person charged is by virtue of this section not liable to be convicted of murder.

(3) A person who but for this section would be liable, whether as a principal or as accessory, to be convicted of murder shall be liable instead to be convicted of manslaughter.

(4) The fact that one party to a killing is by virtue of this section not liable to be convicted of murder shall not affect the question whether the killing amounted to murder in the case of any other party to it.

3. Provocation

Where on a charge of murder there is evidence on which the jury can find that the person charged was provoked (whether by things done or by things said or by both together) to lose his self-control, the question whether the provocation was enough to make a reasonable man do as he did shall be left to be determined by the jury; and in determining that question the jury shall take into account everything both done and said according to the effect which, in their opinion, it would have on a reasonable man.

4. Suicide pacts

(1) It shall be manslaughter, and shall not be murder, for a person acting in pursuance of a suicide pact between him and another to kill the other or be a party to the other . . . being killed by a third person.

(2) Where it is shown that a person charged with the murder of another killed the other or was a party to his . . . being killed, it shall be for the defence to prove that the person charged was acting in pursuance of a suicide pact between him and the other.

(3) For the purposes of this section 'suicide pact' means a common agreement between two or more persons having for its object the death of all of them, whether or not each is to take his own life, but nothing done by a person who enters into a suicide pact shall be treated as done by him in pursuance of the pact unless it is done while he has the settled intention of dying in pursuance of the pact.

CRIMINAL PROCEDURE (INSANITY) ACT 1964

6. Evidence by prosecution of insanity or diminished responsibility
Where on a trial for murder the accused contends—
(a) that at the time of the alleged offence he was insane so as not to be responsible according to law for his actions; or
(b) that at that time he was suffering from such abnormality of mind as is specified in subsection (1) of section 2 of the Homicide Act 1957 (diminished responsibility),
the court shall allow the prosecution to adduce or elicit evidence tending to prove the other of those contentions, and may give directions as to the stage of the proceedings at which the prosecution may adduce such evidence.

INFANTICIDE ACT 1938

1. Offence of infanticide
(1) Where a woman by any wilful act or omission causes the death of her child being a child under the age of twelve months, but at the time of the act or omission the balance of her mind was disturbed by reason of her not having fully recovered from the effect of giving birth to the child or by reason of the effect of lactation consequent upon the birth of the child, then, notwithstanding that the circumstances were such that but for this Act the offence would have amounted to murder, she shall be guilty of felony, to wit of infanticide, and may for such offence be dealt with and punished as if she had been guilty of the offence of manslaughter of the child.
(2) Where upon the trial of a woman for the murder of her child, being a child under the age of twelve months, the jury are of opinion that she by any wilful act or omission caused its death, but that at the time of the act or omission the balance of her mind was disturbed by reason of her not having fully recovered from the effect of giving birth to the child or by reason of the effect of lactation consequent upon the birth of the child, then the jury may, notwithstanding that the circumstances were such that but for the provisions of this Act they might have returned a verdict of murder, return in lieu thereof a verdict of infanticide.
(3) Nothing in this Act shall affect the power of the jury upon an indictment for the murder of a child to return a verdict of manslaughter, or a verdict of guilty but insane . . .

LAW REFORM (YEAR AND A DAY RULE) ACT 1996

1. Abolition of 'year and a day rule'
The rule known as the 'year and a day rule' (that is, the rule that, for the purposes of offences involving death and of suicide, an act or omission is conclusively presumed not to have caused a person's death if more than a year and a day elapsed before he died) is abolished for all purposes.

2. Restriction on institution of proceedings for a fatal offence
(1) Proceedings to which this section applies may only be instituted by or with the consent of the Attorney General.

(2) This section applies to proceedings against a person for a fatal offence if—

(a) the injury alleged to have caused the death was sustained more than three years before the death occurred, or

(b) the person has previously been convicted of an offence committed in circumstances alleged to be connected with the death.

(3) In subsection (2) 'fatal offence' means—

(a) murder, manslaughter, infanticide or any other offence of which one of the elements is causing a person's death, or

(b) the offence of aiding, abetting, counselling or procuring a person's suicide.

3. Commencement etc

(2) Section 1 does not affect the continued application of the rule referred to in that section to a case where the act or omission (or the last of the acts or omissions) which caused the death occurred before the day on which this Act is passed.

OFFENCES AGAINST THE PERSON ACT 1861

9. Murder or manslaughter abroad

Where any murder or manslaughter shall be committed on land out of the United Kingdom, whether within the Queen's dominions or without, and whether the person killed were a subject of Her Majesty or not, every offence committed by any subject of Her Majesty in respect of any such case, whether the same shall amount to the offence of murder or of manslaughter, . . . may be dealt with, inquired of, tried, determined, and punished . . . in England or Ireland . . .

10. Provision for the trial of murder and manslaughter where the death or cause of death only happens in England or Ireland

Where any person being criminally stricken, poisoned, or otherwise hurt upon the sea, or at any place out of England or Ireland, shall die of such stroke, poisoning, or hurt in England or Ireland, or, being criminally stricken, poisoned or otherwise hurt in any place in England or Ireland, shall die of such stroke, poisoning, or hurt upon the sea, or at any place out of England or Ireland, every offence committed in respect of any such case, whether the same shall amount to the offence of murder or of manslaughter, . . . may be dealt with, inquired of, tried, determined, and punished . . . in England or Ireland . . .

WAR CRIMES ACT 1991

1. Jurisdiction over certain war crimes

(1) Subject to the provisions of this section, proceedings for murder, manslaughter or culpable homicide may be brought against a person in the United Kingdom irrespective of his nationality at the time of the alleged offence if that offence—

(a) was committed during the period beginning with 1st September 1939 and ending with 5th June 1945 in a place which at the time was part of Germany or under German occupation; and

(b) constituted a violation of the laws and customs of war.

(2) No proceedings shall by virtue of this section be brought against any person unless he was on 8th March 1990, or has subsequently become, a British citizen or resident in the United Kingdom, the Isle of Man or any of the Channel Islands.

CRIMINAL LAW ACT 1967

6(2) [Trial for murder]

[See page 2]

SUICIDE ACT 1961

1. Suicide to cease to be a crime
The rule of law whereby it is a crime for a person to commit suicide is hereby abrogated.

2. Criminal liability for complicity in another's suicide
(1) A person who aids, abets, counsels or procures the suicide of another, or an attempt by another to commit suicide shall be liable on conviction on indictment to imprisonment for a term not exceeding fourteen years.

(2) If on the trial of an indictment for murder or manslaughter it is proved that the accused aided, abetted, counselled or procured the suicide of the person in question, the jury may find him guilty of that offence.

(4) . . . no proceedings shall be instituted for an offence under this section except by or with the consent of the Director of Public Prosecutions.

ROAD TRAFFIC ACT 1988

1. Causing death by dangerous driving
[See page 57]

3A. Causing death by careless driving when under influence of drink or drugs
[See pages 57]

THEFT ACT 1968

12A(4) Aggravated vehicle taking causing death
[See pages 146]

GENOCIDE ACT 1969

1. Genocide
(1) A person commits an offence of genocide if he commits any act falling within the definition of 'genocide' in Article II of the Genocide Convention as set out in the Schedule to this Act.

(2) A person guilty of an offence of genocide shall on conviction on indictment—

(a) if the offence consists of the killing of any person, be sentenced to imprisonment for life;

(b) in any other case, be liable to imprisonment for a term not exceeding fourteen years.

(3) Proceedings for an offence of genocide shall not be instituted in England or Wales except by or with the consent of the Attorney-General and shall not be instituted in Northern Ireland except by or with the consent of the Attorney-General for Northern Ireland.

4. Short title and interpretation
(2) In this Act 'the Genocide Convention' means the Convention on the Prevention and Punishment of the Crime of Genocide approved by the General Assembly of the United Nations on 9th December 1948.

SCHEDULE

ARTICLE II OF GENOCIDE CONVENTION

In the present Convention, genocide means any of the following acts committed with intent to destroy, in whole or in part, a national, ethnical, racial or religious group, as such:

(a)   Killing members of the group;
(b)   Causing serious bodily or mental harm to members of the group;
(c)   Deliberately inflicting on the group conditions of life calculated to bring about its physical destruction in whole or in part;
(d)   Imposing measures intended to prevent births within the group;
(e)   Forcibly transferring children of the group to another group.

OFFENCES AGAINST THE PERSON ACT 1861

60.   Concealing the birth of a child

If any woman shall be delivered of a child, every person who shall, by any secret disposition of the dead body of the said child, whether such child died before, at, or after its birth, endeavour to conceal the birth thereof, shall be guilty of a misdemeanour, and being convicted thereof shall be liable, at the discretion of the court, to be imprisoned for any term not exceeding two years.

INFANT LIFE (PRESERVATION) ACT 1929

1.   Punishment for child destruction

(1)   Subject as hereinafter in this subsection provided, any person who, with intent to destroy the life of a child capable of being born alive, by any wilful act causes a child to die before it has an existence independent of its mother, shall be guilty of felony, to wit, of child destruction, and shall be liable on conviction thereof on indictment to penal servitude for life:

Provided that no person shall be found guilty of an offence under this section unless it is proved that the act which caused the death of the child was not done in good faith for the purpose only of preserving the life of the mother.

(2)   For the purposes of this Act, evidence that a woman had at any material time been pregnant for a period of twenty-eight weeks or more shall be a prima facie proof that she was at that time pregnant of a child capable of being born alive.

2.   Prosecution of offences

(2)   Where upon the trial of any person for the murder or manslaughter of any child, or for infanticide, or for an offence under section fifty-eight of the Offences against the Person Act, 1861 (which relates to administering drugs or using instruments to procure abortion), the jury are of opinion that the person charged is not guilty of murder, manslaughter or infanticide, or of an offence under the said section fifty-eight, as the case may be, but that he is shown by the evidence to be guilty of the felony of child destruction, the jury may find him guilty of that felony, and thereupon the person convicted shall be liable to be punished as if he had been convicted upon an indictment for child destruction.

(3)   Where upon the trial of any person for the felony of child destruction the jury are of opinion that the person charged is not guilty of any felony, but that he is shown by the evidence to be guilty of an offence under the said section fifty-eight of the Offences against the Person Act, 1861, the jury may find him guilty of that offence, and thereupon the person convicted shall be liable to be punished as if he had been convicted upon an indictment under that section.

OFFENCES AGAINST THE PERSON ACT 1861

58.   Administering drugs or using instruments to procure abortion

Every woman, being with child, who, with intent to procure her own miscarriage, shall unlawfully administer to herself any poison or other noxious thing, or shall unlawfully use any instrument or other means whatsoever with the like intent, and whosoever, with intent to procure the miscarriage of any woman, whether she be or be not with child, shall unlawfully administer to her or cause to be taken by her any poison or other noxious thing, or shall unlawfully use any instrument or other means whatsoever with the like intent, shall be guilty of felony, and being convicted thereof shall be liable . . . to be kept in penal servitude for life . . .

59. Procuring drugs, etc., to cause abortion
Whosoever shall unlawfully supply or procure any poison or other noxious thing, or any instrument or thing whatsoever, knowing that the same is intended to be unlawfully used or employed with intent to procure the miscarriage of any woman, whether she be or be not with child, shall be guilty of a misdemeanour, and being convicted thereof shall be liable . . . to be kept in penal servitude . . .

ABORTION ACT 1967

1. Medical termination of pregnancy
(1)   Subject to the provisions of this section, a person shall not be guilty of any offence under the law relating to abortion when a pregnancy is terminated by a registered medical practitioner if two medical practitioners are of the opinion, formed in good faith—

(a)   that the pregnancy has not exceeded its twenty-fourth week and that the continuance of the pregnancy would involve risk, greater than if the pregnancy were terminated, of injury to the physical or mental health of the pregnant woman or any existing children of her family; or

(b)   that the termination is necessary to prevent grave permanent injury to the physical or mental health of the pregnant woman; or

(c)   that the continuance of the pregnancy would involve risk to the life of the pregnant woman, greater than if the pregnancy were terminated; or

(d)   that there is a substantial risk that if the child were born it would suffer from such physical or mental abnormalities as to be seriously handicapped.

(2)   In determining whether the continuance of a pregnancy would involve such risk of injury to health as is mentioned in paragraph (a) or (b) of subsection (1) of this section, account may be taken of the pregnant woman's actual or reasonably foreseeable environment.

(3)   Except as provided by subsection (4) of this section, any treatment for the termination of pregnancy must be carried out in a hospital vested in the Secretary of State for the purpose of his functions under the National Health Service Act 1977 or the National Health Service (Scotland) Act 1978 or in a hospital vested in a National Health Service trust, or in a place for the time being approved for the purposes of this section by the Secretary of State.

(4)   Subsection (3) of this section, and so much of subsection (1) as relates to the opinion of two registered medical practitioners, shall not apply to the termination of a pregnancy by a registered practitioner in a case where he is of the opinion, formed in good faith, that the termination is immediately necessary to save the life or to prevent grave permanent injury to the physical or mental health of the pregnant woman.

2. Notification
(1)   The Minister of Health in respect of England and Wales, and the Secretary of State in respect of Scotland, shall by statutory instrument make regulations to provide—

(a)   for requiring any such opinion as is referred to in section 1 of this Act to be certified by the practitioners or practitioner concerned in such form and at such time as may be prescribed by the regulations, and for requiring the preservation and disposal of certificates made for the purposes of the regulations;

(b) for requiring any registered medical practitioner who terminates a pregnancy to give notice of the termination and such other information relating to the termination as may be so prescribed;

(c) for prohibiting the disclosure, except to such persons or for such purposes as may be so prescribed, of notices given or information furnished pursuant to the regulations.

(3) Any person who wilfully contravenes or wilfully fails to comply with the requirements of regulations under subsection (1) of this section shall be liable on summary conviction to a fine not exceeding level 5 on the standard scale.

4. Conscientious objection to participation in treatment

(1) Subject to subsection (2) of this section, no person shall be under any duty, whether by contract or by any statutory or other legal requirement, to participate in any treatment authorised by this Act to which he has a conscientious objection: Provided that in any legal proceedings the burden of proof of conscientious objection shall rest on the person claiming to rely on it.

(2) Nothing in subsection (1) of this section shall affect any duty to participate in treatment which is necessary to save the life or to prevent grave permanent injury to the physical or mental health of a pregnant woman.

5. Supplementary provisions

(1) No offence under the Infant Life (Preservation) Act 1929 shall be committed by a registered medical practitioner who terminates a pregnancy in accordance with the provisions of this Act.

(2) For the purposes of the law relating to abortion, anything done with intent to procure a woman's miscarriage (or, in the case of a woman carrying more than one foetus, her miscarriage of any foetus) is unlawfully done unless authorised by section 1 of this Act and, in the case of a woman carrying more than one foetus, anything done with intent to procure her miscarriage of any foetus is authorised by that section if—

(a) the ground for termination of the pregnancy specified in subsection (1)(d) of that section applies in relation to any foetus and the thing is done for the purpose of procuring the miscarriage of that foetus, or

(b) any of the other grounds for termination of the pregnancy specified in that section applies.

6. Interpretation

In this Act, the following expressions have meanings hereby assigned to them:—

'the law relating to abortion' means sections 58 and 59 of the Offences against the Person Act 1861, and any rule of law relating to the procurement of abortion.

NURSES, MIDWIVES AND HEALTH VISITORS ACT 1997

16. Attendance by unqualified persons at childbirth

(1) A person other than a registered midwife or a registered medical practitioner shall not attend a woman in childbirth.

(2) Subsection (1) does not apply—

(a) where the attention is given in a case of sudden or urgent necessity; or

(b) in the case of a person who, while undergoing training with a view to becoming a medical practitioner or to becoming a midwife, attends a woman in childbirth as part of a course of practical instruction in midwifery recognised by the General Medical Council or one of the National Boards.

(3) A person who contravenes subsection (1) shall be liable on summary conviction to a fine not exceeding level 4 on the standard scale.

3 PERSONAL INJURY, MOLESTATION AND HARASSMENT

(a) PERSONAL INJURY

OFFENCES AGAINST THE PERSON ACT 1861

4. Soliciting to commit murder
[See page 261]

16. Threats to kill
[See page 24]

17. Impeding a person endeavouring to save himself or another from shipwreck
[See page 24]

18. Wounding, or causing grievous bodily harm with intent to do grievous bodily harm, or to resist apprehension
Whosoever shall unlawfully and maliciously by any means whatsoever wound or cause any grievous bodily harm to any person . . . with intent . . . to do some . . . grievous bodily harm to any person, or with intent to resist or prevent the lawful apprehension or detainer of any person, shall be guilty of an offence, and being convicted thereof shall be liable, . . . to imprisonment for life . . .

20. Wounding or inflicting grievous bodily harm
Whosoever shall unlawfully and maliciously wound or inflict any grievous bodily harm upon any other person, either with or without any weapon or instrument, shall be guilty of an offence, and being convicted thereof shall be liable . . . to imprisonment for a term not exceeding five years.

21. Attempting to choke, etc., in order to commit or assist in the committing of any indictable offence
Whosoever shall, by any means whatsoever, attempt to choke, suffocate, or strangle any other person, or shall by any means calculated to choke, suffocate, or strangle, attempt to render any other person insensible, unconscious, or incapable of resistance, with intent in any of such cases thereby to enable himself or any other person to commit, or with intent in any of such cases thereby to assist any other person in committing any indictable offence, shall be guilty of an offence, and being convicted thereof shall be liable . . . to imprisonment for life . . .

22. Using chloroform, etc., to commit or assist in the committing of any indictable offence
Whosoever shall unlawfully apply or administer to or cause to be taken by, or attempt to apply or administer to or attempt to cause to be administered to or taken by, any person, any chloroform, laudanum, or other stupefying or overpowering drug, matter,

or thing, with intent in any of such cases thereby to enable himself or any other person to commit, or with intent in any of such cases thereby to assist any other person in committing any indictable offence, shall be guilty of an offence, and being convicted thereof shall be liable . . . to imprisonment for life . . .

23. Maliciously administering poison, etc., so as to endanger life or inflict grievous bodily harm

Whosoever shall unlawfully and maliciously administer to or cause to be administered to or taken by any other person any poison or other destructive or noxious thing, so as thereby to endanger the life of such person, or so as thereby to inflict upon such person any grievous bodily harm, shall be guilty of an offence, and being convicted thereof shall be liable . . . to imprisonment for any term not exceeding ten years . . .

24. Maliciously administering poison, etc., with intent to injure, aggrieve, or annoy any other person

[See page ??]

26. Not providing apprentices or servants with food, etc., or doing bodily harm, whereby life is endangered, or health permanently injured

Whosoever, being legally liable, either as a master or mistress, to provide for any apprentice or servant necessary food, clothing, or lodging, shall wilfully and without lawful excuse refuse or neglect to provide the same, or shall unlawfully and maliciously do or cause to be done any bodily harm to any such apprentice or servant, so that the life of such apprentice or servant shall be endangered, or the health of such apprentice or servant shall be likely to be permanently injured, shall be guilty of an offence, and being convicted thereof shall be liable . . . to imprisonment for a term not exceeding five years.

28. Causing bodily injury by gunpowder

Whosoever shall unlawfully and maliciously, by the explosion of gunpowder or other explosive substance, burn, maim, disfigure, disable, or do any grievous bodily harm to any person, shall be guilty of an offence, and being convicted thereof shall be liable, at the discretion of the court, to imprisonment for life.

29. Causing gunpowder to explode, or sending to any person an explosive substance, or throwing corrosive fluid on a person, with intent to do grievous bodily harm

[See page 261]

30. Placing gunpowder near a building etc., with intent to do bodily injury to any person

[See page 261]

31. Setting or allowing to remain spring guns, etc., with intent to inflict grievous bodily harm

[See page 96]

32. Placing wood, etc., on railway, taking up rails, showing or hiding signals, etc., with intent to endanger passengers

[See page 77]

33. Casting stone, etc., upon a railway carriage, with intent to endanger the safety of any person therein, or in any part of the same train

[See page 78]

34. Doing or omitting anything so as to endanger passengers by railway

[See page 78]

35.   Drivers of carriages injuring persons by furious driving

Whosoever, having the charge of any carriage or vehicle, shall by wanton or furious driving or racing, or other wilful misconduct, or by wilful neglect, do or cause to be done any bodily harm to any person whatsoever, shall be guilty of an offence, and being convicted thereof shall be liable, at the discretion of the court, to be imprisoned for any term not exceeding two years.

38.   Assault with intent to resist arrest

[See pages 24–5]

47.   Assault occasioning bodily harm

Whosoever shall be convicted upon an indictment of any assault occasioning actual bodily harm shall be liable . . . to be imprisoned for any term not exceeding five years.

64.   Making or having anything with intent to commit an offence in this Act

Whosoever shall knowingly have in his possession, or make or manufacture, any gunpowder, explosive substance, or any dangerous or noxious thing, or any machine, engine, instrument, or thing, with intent by means thereof to commit, or for the purpose of enabling any other person to commit, any of the offences in this Act mentioned shall be guilty of a misdemeanour, and being convicted thereof shall be liable, at the discretion of the court, to be imprisoned for any term not exceeding two years . . .

CRIME AND DISORDER ACT 1998

29.   Racially-aggravated assaults

[See pages 35–36]

CONSPIRACY AND PROTECTION OF PROPERTY ACT 1875

5.   Breach of contract involving injury to persons or property

Where any person wilfully and maliciously breaks a contract of service or of hiring, knowing or having reasonable cause to believe that the probable consequences of his so doing, either alone or in combination with others, will be to endanger human life, or cause serious bodily injury, or to expose valuable property whether real or personal to destruction or serious injury, he shall on conviction thereof by a court of summary jurisdiction, be liable either to pay a penalty not exceeding level 2 on the standard scale or to be imprisoned for a term not exceeding three months.

6.   Penalty for neglect by master to provide food, clothing, etc., for servant or apprentice

Where a master, being legally liable to provide for his servant or apprentice necessary food, clothing, medical aid, or lodging, wilfully and without lawful excuse refuses or neglects to provide the same, whereby the health of the servant or apprentice is or is likely to be seriously or permanently injured, he shall on summary conviction be liable either to pay a penalty not exceeding level 2 on the standard scale or to be imprisoned for a term not exceeding six months.

CRIMINAL DAMAGE ACT 1971

1.   Endangering life by destroying or damaging property

(2)   [See page 135]

PROHIBITION OF FEMALE CIRCUMCISION ACT 1985

1.   Prohibition of female circumcision

(1)   Subject to section 2 below, it shall be an offence for any person—

(a)   to excise, infibulate or otherwise mutilate the whole or any part of the labia majora or labia minora or clitoris of another person; or

(b)   to aid, abet, counsel or procure the performance by another person of any of those acts on that other person's own body.

2.   Saving for necessary surgical operations

(1)   Subsection (1)(a) of section 1 shall not render unlawful the performance of a surgical operation if that operation—

(a)   is necessary for the physical or mental health of the person on whom it is performed and is performed by a registered medical practitioner; or

(b)   is performed on a person who is in any stage of labour or has just given birth and is so performed for purposes connected with that labour or birth by—

(i)   a registered medical practitioner or a registered midwife; or

(ii)   a person undergoing a course of training with a view to becoming a registered medical practitioner or a registered midwife.

(2)   In determining for the purposes of this section whether an operation is necessary for the mental health of a person, no account shall be taken of the effect on that person of any belief on the part of that or any other person that the operation is required as a matter of custom or ritual.

MENTAL HEALTH ACT 1983

PART IV

56.   Patients to whom Part IV applies

(1)   This Part of this Act applies to any patient liable to be detained under this Act except—

(a)   a patient who is liable to be detained by virtue of an emergency application and in respect of whom the second medical recommendation referred to in section 4(4)(a) above has not been given and received;

(b)   a patient who is liable to be detained by virtue of section 5(2) or (4) or 35 above or section 135 or 136 below or by virtue of a direction under section 37(4) above; and

(c)   a patient who has been conditionally discharged under section 42(2) above or section 73 or 74 below and has not been recalled to hospital.

(2)   Section 57 and, so far as relevant to that section, sections 59, 60 and 62 below, apply also to any patient who is not liable to be detained under this Act.

57.   Treatment requiring consent and a second opinion

(1)   This section applies to the following forms of medical treatment for mental disorder—

(a)   any surgical operation for destroying brain tissue or for destroying the functioning of brain tissue; and

(b)   such other forms of treatment as may be specified for the purposes of this section by regulations made by the Secretary of State.

(2)   Subject to section 62 below, a patient shall not be given any form of treatment to which this section applies unless he has consented to it and—

(a)   a registered medical practitioner appointed for the purposes of this Part of this Act by the Secretary of State (not being the responsible medical officer) and two other persons appointed for the purposes of this paragraph by the Secretary of State (not being registered medical practitioners) have certified in writing that the patient is capable of understanding the nature, purpose and likely effects of the treatment in question and has consented to it; and

(b)   the registered medical practitioner referred to in paragraph (a) above has certified in writing that, having regard to the likelihood of the treatment alleviating or preventing a deterioration of the patient's condition, the treatment should be given.

(3)   Before giving a certificate under subsection (2)(b) above the registered medical practitioner concerned shall consult two other persons who have been professionally concerned with the patient's medical treatment, and of those persons one shall be a nurse and the other shall be neither a nurse nor a registered medical practitioner.

58. Treatment requiring consent or a second opinion

(1)   This section applies to the following forms of medical treatment for mental disorder—

(a)   such forms of treatment as may be specified for the purposes of this section by regulations made by the Secretary of State;

(b)   the administration of medicine to a patient by any means (not being a form of treatment specified under paragraph (a) above or section 57 above) at any time during a period for which he is liable to be detained as a patient to whom this Part of this Act applies if three months or more have elapsed since the first occasion in that period when medicine was administered to him by any means for his mental disorder.

(3)   Subject to section 62 below, a patient shall not be given any form of treatment to which this section applies unless—

(a)   he has consented to that treatment and either the responsible medical officer or a registered medical practitioner appointed for the purposes of this Part of this Act by the Secretary of State has certified in writing that the patient is capable of understanding its nature, purpose and likely effects and has consented to it; or

(b)   a registered medical practitioner appointed as aforesaid (not being the responsible medical officer) has certified in writing that the patient is not capable of understanding the nature, purpose and likely effects of that treatment or has not consented to it but that, having regard to the likelihood of its alleviating or preventing a deterioration of his condition, the treatment should be given.

(4)   Before giving a certificate under subsection (3)(b) above the registered medical practitioner concerned shall consult two other persons who have been professionally concerned with the patient's medical treatment, and of those persons one shall be a nurse and the other shall be neither a nurse nor a registered medical practitioner.

59. Plans of treatment

Any consent or certificate under section 57 or 58 above may relate to a plan of treatment under which the patient is to be given (whether within a specified period or otherwise) one or more of the forms of treatment to which that section applies.

60. Withdrawal of consent

(1)   Where the consent of a patient to any treatment has been given for the purposes of section 57 or 58 above, the patient may, subject to section 62 below, at any time before the completion of the treatment withdraw his consent, and those sections shall then apply as if the remainder of the treatment were a separate form of treatment.

(2)   Without prejudice to the application of subsection (1) above to any treatment given under the plan of treatment to which a patient has consented, a patient who has consented to such a plan may, subject to section 62 below, at any time withdraw his consent to further treatment, or to further treatment of any description, under the plan.

62. Urgent treatment

(1)   Sections 57 and 58 above shall not apply to any treatment—

(a)   which is immediately necessary to save the patient's life; or

(b)   which (not being irreversible) is immediately necessary to prevent a serious deterioration of his condition; or

(c)   which (not being irreversible or hazardous) is immediately necessary to alleviate serious suffering by the patient; or

(d)   which (not being irreversible or hazardous) is immediately necessary and represents the minimum interference necessary to prevent the patient from behaving violently or being a danger to himself or to others.

(2)   Sections 60 and 61(3) above shall not preclude the continuation of any treatment or of treatment under any plan pending compliance with section 57 or 58 above if the responsible medical officer considers that the discontinuance of the treatment or of treatment under the plan would cause serious suffering to the patient.

(3)   For the purposes of this section treatment is irreversible if it has unfavourable irreversible physical or psychological consequences and hazardous if it entails significant physical hazard.

63.   Treatment not requiring consent

The consent of a patient shall not be required for any medical treatment given to him for the mental disorder from which he is suffering, not being treatment falling within section 57 or 58 above, if the treatment is given by or under the direction of the responsible medical officer.

PART IX

127.   Ill-treatment of patients

(1)   It shall be an offence for any person who is an officer on the staff of or otherwise employed in, or who is one of the managers of, a hospital or mental nursing home—

(a)   to ill-treat or wilfully to neglect a patient for the time being receiving treatment for mental disorder as an in-patient in that hospital or home; or

(b)   to ill-treat or wilfully to neglect, on the premises of which the hospital or home forms part, a patient for the time being receiving such treatment there as an out-patient.

(2)   It shall be an offence for any individual to ill-treat or wilfully to neglect a mentally disordered patient who is for the time being subject to his guardianship under this Act or otherwise in his custody or care (whether by virtue of a legal or moral obligation or otherwise).

CRIMINAL JUSTICE ACT 1988

134.   Torture

(1)   A public official or person acting in an official capacity, whatever his nationality, commits the offence of torture if in the United Kingdom or elsewhere he intentionally inflicts severe pain or suffering on another in the performance or purported performance of his official duties.

(2)   A person not falling within subsection (1) above commits the offence of torture, whatever his nationality, if—

(a)   in the United Kingdom or elsewhere he intentionally inflicts severe pain or suffering on another at the instigation or with the consent or acquiescence—

(i)   of a public official; or

(ii)   of a person acting in an official capacity; and

(b)   the official or other person is performing or purporting to perform his official duties when he instigates the commission of the offence or consents to or acquiesces in it.

(3)   It is immaterial whether the pain or suffering is physical or mental and whether it is caused by an act or an omission.

(4)   It shall be a defence for a person charged with an offence under this section in respect of any conduct of his to prove that he had lawful authority, justification or excuse for that conduct.

(5)   For the purposes of this section 'lawful authority, justification or excuse' means—

(a)   in relation to pain or suffering inflicted in the United Kingdom, lawful authority, justification or excuse under the law of the part of the United Kingdom where it was inflicted;

(b)   in relation to pain or suffering inflicted outside the United Kingdom—

(i)   if it was inflicted by a United Kingdom official acting under the law of the United Kingdom or by a person acting in an official capacity under that law, lawful authority, justification or excuse under that law;

(ii)   if it was inflicted by a United Kingdom official acting under the law of any part of the United Kingdom or by a person acting in an official capacity under such law, lawful authority, justification or excuse under the law of the part of the United Kingdom under whose law he was acting; and

(iii)   in any other case, lawful authority, justification or excuse under the law of the place where it was inflicted.

(6)   A person who commits the offence of torture shall be liable on conviction on indictment to imprisonment for life.

(b)   MOLESTATION AND HARASSMENT

✗ CRIMINAL JUSTICE ACT 1988

✗ 39.   Common assault and battery to be summary offences

Common assault and battery shall be summary offences and a person guilty of either of them shall be liable to a fine not exceeding level 5 on the standard scale, to imprisonment for a term not exceeding six months, or to both.

OFFENCES AGAINST THE PERSON ACT 1861

16.   Threats to kill

A person who without lawful excuse makes to another a threat, intending that that other would fear it would be carried out, to kill that other or a third person, shall be guilty of an offence and liable on conviction on indictment to imprisonment for a term not exceeding ten years.

17.   Impeding a person endeavouring to save himself or another from shipwreck

Whosoever shall unlawfully and maliciously prevent or impede any person, being on board of or having quitted any ship or vessel which shall be in distress, or wrecked, stranded, or cast on shore, in his endeavour to save his life, or shall unlawfully and maliciously prevent or impede any person in his endeavour to save the life of any such person as in this section first aforesaid, shall be guilty of an offence, and being convicted thereof shall be liable . . . to imprisonment for life.

24.   Maliciously administering poison, etc., with intent to injure, aggrieve, or annoy any other person

Whosoever shall unlawfully and maliciously administer to or cause to be administered to or taken by any other person any poison or other destructive or noxious thing, with intent to injure, aggrieve, or annoy such person, shall be guilty of an offence, and being . . . convicted thereof shall be liable to imprisonment for a term not exceeding five years.

38.   Assault with intent to resist arrest

Whosoever . . . shall assault any person with intent to resist or prevent the lawful apprehension or detainer of himself or of any other person for any offence, shall be guilty of an offence, and being convicted thereof shall be liable, at the discretion of the court, to be imprisoned for any term not exceeding two years.

44. If the magistrates shall dismiss any complaint of assault or battery, they shall make out a certificate to that effect

If the justices, upon the hearing of any case of assault or battery upon the merits, where the complaint was preferred by or on behalf of the party aggrieved, shall deem the offence to be proved, or shall find the assault or battery to have been justified, or so trifling as not to merit any punishment, and shall accordingly dismiss the complaint, they shall forthwith make out a certificate under their hands stating the fact of such dismissal, and shall deliver such certificate to the party against whom the complaint was preferred.

45. Certificate or conviction shall be a bar to any other proceedings

If any person against whom any such complaint as in either of the last three preceding sections mentioned shall have been preferred by or on the behalf of the party aggrieved shall have obtained such certificate, or, having been convicted, shall have paid the whole amount adjudged to be paid, or shall have suffered the imprisonment awarded, in every such case he shall be released from all further or other proceedings, civil or criminal, for the same cause.

POLICE ACT 1996

89. Assaults on constables
[See page 238]

SEXUAL OFFENCES ACT 1956

1. Rape of woman or man
(1) It is an offence for a man to rape a woman or another man.

(2) A man commits rape if—

(a) he has sexual intercourse with a person (whether vaginal or anal) who at the time of the intercourse does not consent to it; and

(b) at the time he knows that the person does not consent to the intercourse or is reckless as to whether that person consents to it.

(3) A man also commits rape if he induces a married woman to have sexual intercourse with him by impersonating her husband.

(4) Subsection (2) applies for the purposes of any enactment.

SEXUAL OFFENCES (AMENDMENT) ACT 1976

1. Meaning of 'rape', etc.
(2) It is hereby declared that, if at a trial for a rape offence the jury has to consider whether a man believed that a woman or man was consenting to sexual intercourse, the presence or absence of reasonable grounds for such a belief is a matter to which the jury is to have regard, in conjunction with any other relevant matters, in considering whether he so believed.

SEXUAL OFFENCES ACT 1956

2. Procurement of woman by threats
(1) It is an offence for a person to procure a woman, by threats or intimidation, to have sexual intercourse in any part of the world.

3. Procurement of woman by false pretences
(1) It is an offence for a person to procure a woman, by false pretences or false representations, to have sexual intercourse in any part of the world.

4. Administering drugs to obtain or facilitate intercourse

(1) It is an offence for a person to apply or administer to, or cause to be taken by, a woman any drug, matter or thing with intent to stupefy or overpower her so as thereby to enable any man to have unlawful sexual intercourse with her.

5. Intercourse with a girl under thirteen
[See page 45]

6. Intercourse with a girl under sixteen
[See page 46]

7. Intercourse with defective

(1) It is an offence, subject to the exception mentioned in this section, for a man to have unlawful sexual intercourse with a woman who is a defective.

(2) A man is not guilty of an offence under this section because he has unlawful sexual intercourse with a woman if he does not know and has no reason to suspect her to be a defective.

9. Procurement of defective

(1) It is an offence, subject to the exception mentioned in this section, for a person to procure a woman who is a defective to have unlawful sexual intercourse in any part of the world.

(2) A person is not guilty of an offence under this section because he procures a defective to have unlawful sexual intercourse, if he does not know and has no reason to suspect her to be a defective.

10. Incest by a man
[See page 208]

11. Incest by a woman
[See page 208]

12. Buggery
[see page 208]

14. Indecent assault on a woman

(1) It is an offence, subject to the exception mentioned in subsection (3) of this section, for a person to make an indecent assault on a woman.

(2) A girl under the age of sixteen cannot in law give any consent which would prevent an act being an assault for the purposes of this section.

(3) Where a marriage is invalid under section two of the Marriage Act, 1949, or section one of the Age of Marriage Act, 1929 (the wife being a girl under the age of sixteen), the invalidity does not make the husband guilty of any offence under this section by reason of her incapacity to consent while under that age, if he believes her to be his wife and has reasonable cause for the belief.

(4) A woman who is a defective cannot in law give any consent which would prevent an act being an assault for the purposes of this section, but a person is only to be treated as guilty of an indecent assault on a defective by reason of that incapacity to consent, if that person knew or had reason to suspect her to be a defective.

15. Indecent assault on a man

(1) It is an offence for a person to make an indecent assault on a man.

(2) A boy under the age of sixteen cannot in law give any consent which would prevent an act being an assault for the purposes of this section.

(3) A man who is a defective cannot in law give any consent which would prevent an act being an assault for the purposes of this section, but a person is only to be treated as guilty of an indecent assault on a defective by reason of that incapacity to consent, if that person knew or had reason to suspect him to be a defective.

16. Assault with intent to commit buggery

(1) It is an offence for a person to assault another person with intent to commit buggery.

17. Abduction of woman by force or for the sake of her property

(1) It is felony for a person to take away or detain a woman against her will with the intention that she shall marry or have unlawful sexual intercourse with that or any other person, if she is so taken away or detained either by force or for the sake of her property or expectations of property.

(2) In the foregoing subsection, the reference to a woman's expectations of property relates only to property of a person to whom she is next of kin or one of the next of kin, and 'property' includes any interest in property.

21. Abduction of defective from parent or guardian

(1) It is an offence, subject to the exception mentioned in this section, for a person to take a woman who is a defective out of the possession of her parent or guardian against his will, if she is so taken with the intention that she shall have unlawful sexual intercourse with men or with a particular man.

(2) A person is not guilty of an offence under this section because he takes such a woman out of the possession of her parent or guardian as mentioned above, if he does not know and has no reason to suspect her to be a defective.

(3) In this section 'guardian' means any person having parental responsibility for or care of the woman.

24. Detention of woman in brothel or other premises

(1) It is an offence for a person to detain a woman against her will on any premises with the intention that she shall have unlawful sexual intercourse with men or with a particular man, or to detain a woman against her will in a brothel.

(2) Where a woman is on any premises for the purposes of having unlawful sexual intercourse or is in a brothel, a person shall be deemed for the purpose of the foregoing subsection to detain her there if, with the intention of compelling or inducing her to remain there, he either withholds from her her clothes or any other property belonging to her or theatens her with legal proceedings in the event of her taking away clothes provided for her by him or on his directions.

(3) A woman shall not be liable to any legal proceedings, whether civil or criminal, for taking away or being found in possession of any clothes she needed to enable her to leave premises on which she was for the purpose of having unlawful sexual intercourse or to leave a brothel.

27. Permitting defective to use premises for intercourse

(1) It is an offence, subject to the exception mentioned in this section, for a person who is the owner or occupier of any premises, or who has, or acts or assists in, the management or control of any premises, to induce or knowingly suffer a woman who is a defective to resort to or be on those premises for the purpose of having unlawful sexual intercourse with men or with a particular man.

(2) A person is not guilty of an offence under this section because he induces or knowingly suffers a defective to resort to or be on any premises for the purpose mentioned, if he does not know and has no reason to suspect her to be a defective.

44. Meaning of 'sexual intercourse'

Where, on the trial of any offence under this Act, it is necessary to prove sexual intercourse (whether natural or unnatural), it shall not be necessary to prove the completion of the intercourse by the emission of seed, but the intercourse shall be deemed complete upon proof of penetration only.

45. Meaning of defective
In this Act 'defective' means a person suffering from a state of arrested or incomplete development of mind which includes severe impairment of intelligence and social functioning.

46. Use of words 'man', 'boy', 'woman' and 'girl'
The use in any provision of this Act of the word 'man' without the addition of the word 'boy', or vice versa, shall not prevent the provision applying to any person to whom it would have applied if both words had been used, and similarly with the words 'woman' and 'girl'.

46A. Meaning of 'parental responsibility'
In this Act 'parental responsibility' has the same meaning as in the Children Act 1989.

47. Proof of exceptions
Where in any of the foregoing sections the description of an offence is expressed to be subject to exceptions mentioned in the section, proof of the exception is to lie on the person relying on it.

SEXUAL OFFENCES ACT 1993

1. Abolition of presumption of sexual incapacity
The presumption of criminal law that a boy under the age of fourteen is incapable of sexual intercourse is hereby abolished.

SEX OFFENDERS ACT 1997

7. Extension of jurisdiction: England and Wales and Northern Ireland
(1) Subject to subsection (2) below, any act done by a person in a country or territory outside the United Kingdom which—
    (a) constituted an offence under the law in force in that country or territory, and
    (b) would constitute a sexual offence to which this section applies if it had been done in England and Wales, or in Northern Ireland,
shall constitute that sexual offence under the law of that part of the United Kingdom.
(2) No proceedings shall by virtue of this section be brought against any person unless he was at the commencement of this section, or has subsequently become, a British citizen or resident in the United Kingdom.
(3) An act punishable under the law in force in any country or territory constitutes an offence under that law for the purposes of this section, however it is described in that law.
(7) Schedule 2 to this Act (which lists the sexual offences to which this section applies) shall have effect.

SCHEDULE 2

1.—(1) In relation to England and Wales, the following are sexual offences to which section 7 of this Act applies, namely—
    (a) offences under the following provisions of the Sexual Offences Act 1956—
        (i)   section 1 (rape);
        (ii)   section 5 (intercourse with girl under 13);
        (iii)   section 6 (intercourse with girl between 13 and 16);
        (iv)   section 12 (buggery);
        (v)   section 14 (indecent assault on a girl);
        (vi)   section 15 (indecent assault on a boy); and
        (vii) section 16 (assault with intent to commit buggery);

(b)   an offence under section 1 of the Indecency with Children Act 1960 (indecent conduct towards young child); and

(c)   an offence under section 1 of the Protection of Children Act 1978 (indecent photographs of children).

(2)   In sub-paragraph (1)(a) above, sub-paragraphs (i) and (iv) to (vii) do not apply where the victim of the offence was 16 or over at the time of the offence.

3.   Any reference in paragraph 1(1) . . . above to an offence includes—

(a)   a reference to any attempt, conspiracy or incitement to commit that offence; and

(b)   a reference to aiding and abetting, counselling or procuring the commission of that offence.

SEXUAL OFFENCES (CONSPIRACY AND INCITEMENT) ACT 1996

1.   Conspiracy to commit certain sexual acts outside the United Kingdom

(1)   Where each of the following conditions is satisfied in the case of any agreement, Part I of the Criminal Law Act 1977 (conspiracy) has effect in relation to the agreement falling within section 1(1) of that Act.

(2)   The first condition is that the pursuit of the agreed course of conduct would at some stage involve—

(a)   an act by one or more of the parties, or

(b)   the happening of some other event,

intended to take place in a country or territory outside the United Kingdom.

(3)   The second condition is that that act or other event constitutes an offence under the law in force in that country or territory.

(4)   The third condition is that the agreement would fall within section 1(1) of that Act as an agreement relating to the commission of a listed sexual offence but for the fact that the offence would not be an offence triable in England and Wales if committed in accordance with the parties' intentions.

(5)   The fourth condition is that—

(a)   a party to the agreement, or a party's agent, did anything in England and Wales in relation to the agreement before its formation, or

(b)   a party to the agreement became a party in England and Wales (by joining it either in person or through an agent), or

(c)   a party to the agreement, or a party's agent, did or omitted anything in England and Wales in pursuance of the agreement.

(6)   In the application of Part I of that Act to such an agreement, any reference to an offence is to be read as a reference to what would be the listed sexual offence in question but for the fact that it is not an offence triable in England and Wales.

2.   Incitement to commit certain sexual acts outside the United Kingdom

(1)   This section applies where—

(a)   any act done by a person in England and Wales would amount to the offence of incitement to commit a listed sexual offence but for the fact that what he had in view would not be an offence triable in England and Wales,

(b)   the whole or part of what he had in view was intended to take place in a country or territory outside the United Kingdom, and

(c)   what he had in view would involve the commission of an offence under the law in force in that country or territory.

(2)   Where this section applies—

(a)   what he had in view is to be treated as that listed sexual offence for the purposes of any charge of incitement brought in respect of that act, and

(b)   any such charge is accordingly triable in England and Wales.

(3)   Any act of incitement by means of a message (however communicated) is to be treated as done in England and Wales if the message is sent or received in England and Wales.

3.   Sections 1 and 2: supplementary

(1)   Conduct punishable under the law in force in any country or territory is an offence under that law for the purposes of sections 1 and 2, however it is described in that law.

(6)   In any proceedings in respect of any offence triable by virtue of section 1 or 2, it is immaterial to guilt whether or not the accused was a British citizen at the time of any act or other event proof of which is required for conviction of the offence.

(7)   References to an offence of conspiracy to commit a listed sexual offence include an offence triable in England and Wales as such a conspiracy by virtue of section 1 (without prejudice to subsection (6) of that section).

(8)   References to an offence of incitement to commit a listed sexual offence include an offence triable in England and Wales as such an incitement by virtue of section 2 (without prejudice to subsection (2) of that section).

(9)   Subsections (7) and (8) apply to references in any enactment, instrument or document (except those in sections 1 and 2 of this Act and in Part I of the Criminal Law Act 1977).

5.   Interpretation

In this Act 'listed sexual offence' has the meaning given by the Schedule.

SCHEDULE
LISTED SEXUAL OFFENCES

(1)   In relation to England and Wales, the following are listed sexual offences:
  (a)   offences under the following provisions of the Sexual Offences Act 1956—
    (i)   section 1 (rape),
    (ii)   section 5 (intercourse with girl under the age of thirteen),
    (iii) section 6 (intercourse with girl under the age of sixteen),
    (iv) section 12 (buggery),
    (v)   section 14 (indecent assault on a girl), and
    (vi) section 15 (indecent assault on a boy),
  (b)   an offence under section 1 of the Indecency with Children Act 1960 (indecent conduct towards young child).

(2)   In sub-paragraph (1)(a), sub-paragraphs (i), (iv), (v) and (vi) do not apply where the victim of the offence has attained the age of sixteen years.

MENTAL HEALTH ACT 1959

128.   Sexual intercourse with patients

(1)   Without prejudice to section seven of the Sexual Offences Act, 1956, it shall be an offence, subject to the exception mentioned in this section,—

  (a)   for a man who is an officer on the staff of or is otherwise employed in, or is one of the managers of, a hospital or mental nursing home to have unlawful sexual intercourse with a woman who is for the time being receiving treatment for mental disorder in that hospital or home, or to have such intercourse on the premises of which the hospital or home forms part with a woman who is for the time being receiving such treatment there as an out-patient;

  (b)   for a man to have unlawful sexual intercourse with a woman who is a mentally disordered patient and who is subject to his guardianship under the Mental Health Act 1983 or is otherwise in his custody or care under the Mental Health Act 1983 or in pursuance of arrangements under Part III of the National Assistance Act,

1948, or the National Health Service Act 1977 or as a resident in a residential care home within the meaning of Part I of the Registered Homes Act 1984.

(2) It shall not be an offence under this section for a man to have sexual intercourse with a woman if he does not know and has no reason to suspect her to be a mentally disordered patient.

(3) Any person guilty of an offence under this section shall be liable on conviction on indictment to imprisonment for a term not exceeding two years.

(5) This section shall be construed as one with the Sexual Offences Act, 1956; and section forty-seven of that Act (which relates to the proof of exceptions) shall apply to the exception mentioned in this section.

TAKING OF HOSTAGES ACT 1982

1. Hostage-taking

(1) A person, whatever his nationality, who, in the United Kingdom or elsewhere,—

(a) detains any other person ('the hostage'), and

(b) in order to compel a State, international governmental organisation or person to do or abstain from doing any act, threatens to kill, injure or continue to detain the hostage,

commits an offence.

(2) A person guilty of an offence under this Act shall be liable, on conviction or indictment, to imprisonment for life.

PUBLIC ORDER ACT 1986

PART I

1. Riot

(1) Where 12 or more persons who are present together use or threaten unlawful violence for a common purpose and the conduct of them (taken together) is such as would cause a person of reasonable firmness present at the scene to fear for his personal safety, each of the persons using unlawful violence for the common purpose is guilty of riot.

(2) It is immaterial whether or not the 12 or more use or threaten unlawful violence simultaneously.

(3) The common purpose may be inferred from conduct.

(4) No person of reasonable firmness need actually be, or be likely to be, present at the scene.

(5) Riot may be committed in private as well as in public places.

(6) A person guilty of riot is liable on conviction on indictment to imprisonment for a term not exceeding ten years or a fine or both.

2. Violent disorder

(1) Where 3 or more persons who are present together use or threaten unlawful violence and the conduct of them (taken together) is such as would cause a person of reasonable firmness present at the scene to fear for his personal safety, each of the persons using or threatening unlawful violence is guilty of violent disorder.

(2) It is immaterial whether or not the 3 or more use or threaten unlawful violence simultaneously.

(3) No person of reasonable firmness need actually be, or be likely to be, present at the scene.

(4) Violent disorder may be committed in private as well as in public places.

(5) A person guilty of violent disorder is liable on conviction on indictment to imprisonment for a term not exceeding 5 years or a fine or both, or on summary

conviction to imprisonment for a term not exceeding 6 months or a fine not exceeding the statutory maximum or both.

3. Affray

(1) A person is guilty of affray if he uses or threatens unlawful violence towards another and his conduct is such as would cause a person of reasonable firmness present at the scene to fear for his personal safety.

(2) Where 2 or more persons use or threaten the unlawful violence, it is the conduct of them taken together that must be considered for the purposes of subsection (1).

(3) For the purposes of this section a threat cannot be made by the use of words alone.

(4) No person of reasonable firmness need actually be, or be likely to be, present at the scene.

(5) Affray may be committed in private as well as in public places.

(7) A person guilty of affray is liable on conviction on indictment to imprisonment for a term not exceeding 3 years or a fine or both, or on summary conviction to imprisonment for a term not exceeding 6 months or a fine not exceeding the statutory maximum or both.

4. Fear or provocation of violence

(1) A person is guilty of an offence if he—

(a) uses towards another person threatening, abusive or insulting words or behaviour; or

(b) distributes or displays to another person any writing, sign or other visible representation which is threatening, abusive or insulting,

with intent to cause that person to believe that immediate unlawful violence will be used against him or another by any person, or to provoke the immediate use of unlawful violence by that person or another, or whereby that person is likely to believe that such violence will be used or it is likely that such violence will be provoked.

(2) An offence under this section may be committed in a public or a private place, except that no offence is committed where the words or behaviour are used, or the writing, sign or other visible representation is distributed or displayed, by a person inside a dwelling and the other person is also inside that or another dwelling.

(4) A person guilty of an offence under this section is liable on summary conviction to imprisonment for a term not exceeding 6 months or a fine not exceeding level 5 on the standard scale or both.

4A Intentional harassment, alarm or distress

(1) A person is guilty of an offence if, with intent to cause a person harassment, alarm or distress, he—

(a) uses threatening, abusive or insulting words or behaviour, or disorderly behaviour, or

(b) displays any writing, sign or other visible representation which is threatening, abusive or insulting,

thereby causing that or another person harassment, alarm or distress.

(2) An offence under this section may be committed in a public or a private place, except that no offence is committed where the words or behaviour are used, or the writing, sign or other visible representation is displayed, by a person inside a dwelling and the person who is harassed, alarmed or distressed is also inside that or another dwelling.

(3) It is a defence for the accused to prove—

(a) that he was inside a dwelling and had no reason to believe that the words or behaviour used, or the writing, sign or other visible representation displayed would be heard or seen by a person outside that or any other dwelling, or

(b) that his conduct was reasonable.

(5) A person guilty of an offence under this section is liable on summary conviction to imprisonment for a term not exceeding 6 months or a fine not exceeding level 5 on the standard scale or both.

5. Harassment, alarm or distress

(1) A person is guilty of an offence if he—

(a) uses threatening, abusive or insulting words or behaviour, or disorderly behaviour, or

(b) displays any writing, sign or other visible representation which is threatening, abusive or insulting,

within the hearing or sight of a person likely to be caused harassment, alarm or distress thereby.

(2) An offence under this section may be committed in a public or a private place, except that no offence is committed where the words or behaviour are used, or the writing, sign or other visible representation is displayed, by a person inside a dwelling and the other person is also inside that or another dwelling.

(3) It is a defence for the accused to prove—

(a) that he had no reason to believe that there was any person within hearing or sight who was likely to be caused harassment, alarm or distress, or

(b) that he was inside a dwelling and had no reason to believe that the words or behaviour used, or the writing, sign or other visible representation displayed, would be heard or seen by a person outside that or any other dwelling, or

(c) that his conduct was reasonable.

(6) A person guilty of an offence under this section is liable on summary conviction to a fine not exceeding level 3 on the standard scale.

6. Mental element: miscellaneous

(1) A person is guilty of riot only if he intends to use violence or is aware that his conduct may be violent.

(2) A person is guilty of violent disorder or affray only if he intends to use or threaten violence or is aware that his conduct may be violent or threaten violence.

(3) A person is guilty of an offence under section 4 only if he intends his words or behaviour, or the writing, sign or other visible representation, to be threatening, abusive or insulting, or is aware that it may be threatening, abusive or insulting.

(4) A person is guilty of an offence under section 5 only if he intends his words or behaviour, or the writing, sign or other visible representation, to be threatening, abusive or insulting, or is aware that it may be threatening, abusive or insulting or (as the case may be) he intends his behaviour to be or is aware that it may be disorderly.

(5) For the purposes of this section a person whose awareness is impaired by intoxication shall be taken to be aware of that of which he would be aware if not intoxicated, unless he shows either that his intoxication was not self-induced or that it was caused solely by the taking or administration of a substance in the course of medical treatment.

(6) In subsection (5) 'intoxication' means any intoxication, whether caused by drink, drugs or other means, or by a combination of means.

(7) Subsections (1) and (2) do not affect the determination for the purposes of riot or violent disorder of the number of persons who use or threaten violence.

8. Interpretation

In this Part—

'dwelling' means any structure or part of a structure occupied as a person's home or as other living accommodation (whether the occupation is separate or shared with others) but does not include any part not so occupied, and for this purpose 'structure' includes a tent, caravan, vehicle, vessel or other temporary or movable structure;

'violence' means any violent conduct, so that—

(a)   except in the context of affray, it includes violent conduct towards property as well as violent conduct towards persons, and

(b)   it is not restricted to conduct causing or intended to cause injury or damage but includes any other violent conduct (for example, throwing at or towards a person a missile of a kind capable of causing injury which does not hit or falls short).

PART III

17.   Meaning of 'racial hatred'

In this Part 'racial hatred' means hatred against a group of persons in Great Britain defined by reference to colour, race, nationality (including citizenship) or ethnic or national origins.

18.   Use of words or behaviour or display of written material

(1)   A person who uses threatening, abusive or insulting words or behaviour, or displays any written material which is threatening, abusive or insulting, is guilty of an offence if—

(a)   he intends thereby to stir up racial hatred, or

(b)   having regard to all the circumstances racial hatred is likely to be stirred up thereby.

(2)   An offence under this section may be committed in a public or a private place, except that no offence is committed where the words or behaviour are used, or the written material is displayed, by a person inside a dwelling and are not heard or seen except by other persons in that or another dwelling.

(4)   In proceedings for an offence under this section it is a defence for the accused to prove that he was inside a dwelling and had no reason to believe that the words or behaviour used, or the written material displayed, would be heard or seen by a person outside that or any other dwelling.

(5)   A person who is not shown to have intended to stir up racial hatred is not guilty of an offence under this section if he did not intend his words or behaviour, or the written material, to be, and was not aware that it might be, threatening, abusive or insulting.

(6)   This section does not apply to words or behaviour used, or written material displayed, solely for the purpose of being included in a programme included in a programme service.

19.   Publishing or distributing written material

(1)   A person who publishes or distributes written material which is threatening, abusive or insulting is guilty of an offence if—

(a)   he intends thereby to stir up racial hatred, or

(b)   having regard to all the circumstances racial hatred is likely to be stirred up thereby.

(2)   In proceedings for an offence under this section it is a defence for an accused who is not shown to have intended to stir up racial hatred to prove that he was not aware of the content of the material and did not suspect, and had no reason to suspect, that it was threatening, abusive or insulting.

(3)   References in this Part to the publication or distribution of written material are to its publication or distribution to the public or a section of the public.

38.   Contamination of or interference with goods with intention of causing public alarm or anxiety, etc.

(1)   It is an offence for a person, with the intention—

(a)   of causing public alarm or anxiety, or

(b)   of causing injury to members of the public consuming or using the goods, or

(c)   of causing economic loss to any person by reason of the goods being shunned by members of the public, or

(d)   of causing economic loss to any person by reason of steps taken to avoid any such alarm or anxiety, injury or loss
to contaminate or interfere with goods, or make it appear that goods have been contaminated or interfered with, or to place goods which have been contaminated or interfered with, or which appear to have been contaminated and interfered with, in a place where goods of that description are consumed, used, sold or otherwise supplied.

(2)   It is also an offence for a person, with any such intention as is mentioned in paragraph (a), (c) or (d) of subsection (1), to threaten that he or another will do, or claim that he or another has done, any of the acts mentioned in that subsection.

(3)   It is an offence for a person to be in possession of any of the following articles with a view to the commission of an offence under subsection (1)—

(a)   materials to be used for contaminating or interfering with goods or making it appear that goods have been contaminated or interfered with, or

(b)   goods which have been contaminated or interfered with, or which appear to have been contaminated or interfered with.

(4)   A person guilty of an offence under this section is liable—

(a)   on conviction on indictment to imprisonment for a term not exceeding 10 years or a fine or both, or

(b)   on summary conviction to imprisonment for a term not exceeding six months or a fine not exceeding the statutory maximum or both.

(5)   In this section 'goods' includes substances whether natural or manufactured and whether or not incorporated in or mixed with other goods.

(6)   The reference in subsection (2) to a person claiming that certain acts have been committed does not include a person who in good faith reports or warns that such acts have been, or appear to have been, committed.

CRIME AND DISORDER ACT 1998

28.   Meaning of 'racially aggravated'

(1)   An offence is racially aggravated for the purposes of sections 29 to 32 below if—

(a)   at the time of committing the offence, or immediately before or after doing so, the offender demonstrates towards the victim of the offence hostility based on the victim's membership (or presumed membership) of a racial group; or

(b)   the offence is motivated (wholly or partly) by hostility towards members of a racial group based on their membership of that group.

(2)   In subsection (1)(a) above—
'membership', in relation to a racial group, includes association with members of that group;
'presumed' means presumed by the offender.

(3)   It is immaterial for the purposes of paragraph (a) or (b) of subsection (1) above whether or not the offender's hostility is also based, to any extent, on—

(a)   the fact or presumption that any person or group of persons belongs to any religious group; or

(b)   any other factor not mentioned in that paragraph.

(4)   In this section 'racial group' means a group of persons defined by reference to race, colour, nationality (including citizenship) or ethnic or national origins.

29.   Racially-aggravated assaults

(1)   A person is guilty of an offence under this section if he commits—

(a)   an offence under section 20 of the Offences Against the Person Act 1861 (malicious wounding or grievous bodily harm);

(b)   an offence under section 47 of that Act (actual bodily harm); or

(c)   common assault,
which is racially aggravated for the purposes of this section.

(2)   A person guilty of an offence failing within subsection (1)(a) or (b) above shall be liable—

(a)   on summary conviction, to imprisonment for a term not exceeding six months or to a fine not exceeding the statutory maximum, or to both;

(b)   on conviction on indictment, to imprisonment for a term not exceeding seven years or to a fine, or to both.

(3)   A person guilty of an offence falling within subsection (1)(c) above shall be liable—

(a)   on summary conviction, to imprisonment for a term not exceeding six months or to a fine not exceeding the statutory maximum, or to both;

(b)   on conviction on indictment, to imprisonment for a term not exceeding two years or to a fine, or to both.

30.   Racially-aggravated criminal damage

(1)   A person is guilty of an offence under this section if he commits an offence under section 1(1) of the Criminal Damage Act 1971 (destroying or damaging property belonging to another) which is racially aggravated for the purposes of this section.

(2)   A person guilty of an offence under this section shall be liable—

(a)   on summary conviction, to imprisonment for a term not exceeding six months or to a fine not exceeding the statutory maximum, or to both;

(b)   on conviction on indictment, to imprisonment for a term not exceeding fourteen years or to a fine, or to both.

(3)   For the purposes of this section, section 28(1)(a) above shall have effect as if the person to whom the property belongs or is treated as belonging for the purposes of that Act were the victim of the offence.

31.   Racially-aggravated public order offences

(1)   A person is guilty of an offence under this section if he commits—

(a)   an offence under section 4 of the Public Order Act 1986 (fear or provocation of violence);

(b)   an offence under section 4A of that Act (intentional harassment, alarm or distress); or

(c)   an offence under section 5 of that Act (harassment, alarm or distress), which is racially aggravated for the purposes of this section.

(4)   A person guilty of an offence failing within subsection (1)(a) or (b) above shall be liable—

(a)   on summary conviction, to imprisonment for a term not exceeding six months or to a fine not exceeding the statutory maximum, or to both;

(b)   on conviction on indictment, to imprisonment for a term not exceeding two years or to a fine, or to both.

(5)   A person guilty of an offence failing within subsection (1)(c) above shall be liable on summary conviction to a fine not exceeding level 4 on the standard scale.

(6)   If, on the trial on indictment of a person charged with an offence falling within subsection (1)(a) or (b) above, the jury find him not guilty of the offence charged, they may find him guilty of the basic offence mentioned in that provision.

(7)   For the purposes of subsection (1)(c) above, section 28(1)(a) above shall have effect as if the person likely to be caused harassment, alarm or distress were the victim of the offence.

32.   Racially-aggravated harassment etc.

(1)   A person is guilty of an offence under this section if he commits—

(a)   an offence under section 2 of the Protection from Harassment Act 1997 (offence of harassment); or

(b)   an offence under section 4 of that Act (putting people in fear of violence), which is racially aggravated for the purposes of this section.

(3)   A person guilty of an offence falling within subsection (1)(a) above shall be liable—

(a)   on summary conviction, to imprisonment for a term not exceeding six months or to a fine not exceeding the statutory maximum, or to both;

(b)   on conviction on indictment, to imprisonment for a term not exceeding two years or to a fine, or to both.

(4)   A person guilty of an offence falling within subsection (1)(b) above shall be liable—

(a)   on summary conviction, to imprisonment for a term not exceeding six months or to a fine not exceeding the statutory maximum, or to both;

(b)   on conviction on indictment, to imprisonment for a term not exceeding seven years or to a fine, or to both.

(5)   If, on the trial on indictment of a person charged with an offence failing within subsection (1)(a) above, the jury find him not guilty of the offence charged, they may find him guilty of the basic offence mentioned in that provision.

(6)   If, on the trial on indictment of a person charged with an offence falling within subsection (1)(b) above, the jury find him not guilty of the offence charged, they may find him guilty of an offence failing within subsection (1)(a) above.

FOOTBALL (OFFENCES) ACT 1991

1.   Designated football matches

(1)   In this Act a 'designated football match' means an association football match designated, or of a description designated, for the purposes of this Act by order of the Secretary of State.

Any such order shall be made by statutory instrument which shall be subject to annulment in pursuance of a resolution of either House of Parliament.

(2)   References in this Act to things done at a designated football match include anything done at the ground—

(a)   within the period beginning two hours before the start of the match or (if earlier) two hours before the time at which it is advertised to start and ending one hour after the end of the match; or

(b)   where the match is advertised to start at a particular time on a particular day but does not take place on that day, within the period beginning two hours before and ending one hour after the advertised starting time.

2.   Throwing of missiles

It is an offence for a person at a designated football match to throw anything at or towards—

(a)   the playing area, or any area adjacent to the playing area to which spectators are not generally admitted, or

(b)   any area in which spectators or other persons are or may be present, without lawful authority or lawful excuse (which shall be for him to prove).

3.   Indecent or racialist chanting

(1)   It is an offence to take part at a designated football match in chanting of an indecent or racialist nature.

(2)   For this purpose—

(a)   'chanting' means the repeated uttering of any words or sounds in concert with one or more others; and

(b)   'of a racialist nature' means consisting of or including matter which is threatening, abusive or insulting to a person by reason of his colour, race, nationality (including citizenship) or ethnic or national origins.

4. Going onto the playing area

It is an offence for a person at a designated football match to go onto the playing area, or any area adjacent to the playing area to which spectators are not generally admitted, without lawful authority or lawful excuse (which shall be for him to prove).

FIREARMS ACT 1968

16A Possession of firearm with intent to cause fear of violence
[See page 101]

THEFT ACT 1968

21. Blackmail
[See page 149]

CRIMINAL DAMAGE ACT 1971

2. Threats to destroy or damage property
[See page 135]

PROTECTION FROM HARASSMENT ACT 1997

1. Prohibition of harassment

(1) A person must not pursue a course of conduct—
    (a) which amounts to harassment of another, and
    (b) which he knows or ought to know amounts to harassment of the other.

(2) For the purposes of this section, the person whose course of conduct is in question ought to know that it amounts to harassment of another if a reasonable person in possession of the same information would think the course of conduct amounted to harassment of the other.

(3) Subsection (1) does not apply to a course of conduct if the person who pursued it shows—
    (a) that it was pursued for the purpose of preventing or detecting crime,
    (b) that it was pursued under any enactment or rule of law or to comply with any condition or requirement imposed by any person under any enactment, or
    (c) that in the particular circumstances the pursuit of the course of conduct was reasonable.

2. Offence of harassment

(1) A person who pursues a course of conduct in breach of section 1 is guilty of an offence.

(2) A person guilty of an offence under this section is liable on summary conviction to imprisonment for a term not exceeding six months, or a fine not exceeding level 5 on the standard scale, or both.

4. Putting people in fear of violence

(1) A person whose course of conduct causes another to fear, on at least two occasions, that violence will be used against him is guilty of an offence if he knows or ought to know that his course of conduct will cause the other so to fear on each of those occasions.

(2) For the purposes of this section, the person whose course of conduct is in question ought to know that it will cause another to fear that violence will be used against him on any occasion if a reasonable person in possession of the same information would think the course of conduct would cause the other so to fear on that occasion.

(3) It is a defence for a person charged with an offence under this section to show that—

(a) his course of conduct was pursued for the purpose of preventing or detecting crime,

(b) his course of conduct was pursued under any enactment or rule of law or to comply with any condition or requirement imposed by any person under any enactment, or

(c) the pursuit of his course of conduct was reasonable for the protection of himself or another or for the protection of his or another's property.

(4) A person guilty of an offence under this section is liable—

(a) on conviction on indictment, to imprisonment for a term not exceeding five years, or a fine, or both, or

(b) on summary conviction, to imprisonment for a term not exceeding six months, or a fine not exceeding the statutory maximum, or both.

(5) If on the trial on indictment of a person charged with an offence under this section the jury find him not guilty of the offence charged, they may find him guilty of an offence under section 2.

(6) The Crown Court has the same powers and duties in relation to a person who is by virtue of subsection (5) convicted before it of an offence under section 2 as a magistrates' court would have on convicting him of the offence.

5. Restraining orders

(1) A court sentencing or otherwise dealing with a person ('the defendant') convicted of an offence under section 2 or 4 may (as well as sentencing him or dealing with him in any other way) make an order under this section.

(2) The order may, for the purpose of protecting the victim of the offence, or any other person mentioned in the order, from further conduct which—

(a) amounts to harassment, or

(b) will cause a fear of violence,

prohibit the defendant from doing anything described in the order.

(3) The order may have effect for a specified period or until further order.

(4) The prosecutor, the defendant or any other person mentioned in the order may apply to the court which made the order for it to be varied or discharged by a further order.

(5) If without reasonable excuse the defendant does anything which he is prohibited from doing by an order under this section, he is guilty of an offence.

(6) A person guilty of an offence under this section is liable—

(a) on conviction on indictment, to imprisonment for a term not exceeding five years, or a fine, or both, or

(b) on summary conviction, to imprisonment for a term not exceeding six months, or a fine not exceeding the statutory maximum, or both.

7. Interpretation of this group of sections

(1) This section applies for the interpretation of sections 1 to 5.

(2) References to harassing a person include alarming the person or causing the person distress.

(3) A 'course of conduct' must involve conduct on at least two occasions.

(4) 'Conduct' includes speech.

12. National security, etc.

(1) If the Secretary of State certifies that in his opinion anything done by a specified person on a specified occasion related to—

(a) national security,

(b) the economic well-being of the United Kingdom, or

(c)   the prevention or detection of serious crime,
and was done on behalf of the Crown, the certificate is conclusive evidence that this
Act does not apply to any conduct of that person on that occasion.

(2)   In subsection (1), 'specified' means specified in the certificate in question.

CRIME AND DISORDER ACT 1998

32.   Racially-aggravated harassment, etc
[See pages 36–37]

TRADE UNION AND LABOUR RELATIONS (CONSOLIDATION) ACT 1992

241.   Intimidation or annoyance by violence or otherwise

(1)   A person commits an offence who, with a view to compelling another person
to abstain from doing or to do any act which that person has a legal right to do or
abstain from doing, wrongfully and without legal authority—

(a)   uses violence to or intimidates that person or his wife or children, or injures
his property

(b)   persistently follows that person about from place to place,

(c)   hides any tools, clothes or other property owned or used by that person, or
deprives him of or hinders him in the use thereof,

(d)   watches or besets the house or other place where that person resides, works,
carries on business or happens to be, or the approach to any such house or place, or

(e)   follows that person with two or more other persons in a disorderly manner
in or through any street or road.

TELECOMMUNICATIONS ACT 1984

43.   Improper use of public telecommunication system

(1)   A person who—

(a)   sends, by means of a public telecommunication system, a message or other
matter that is grossly offensive or of an indecent, obscene or menacing character; or

(b)   sends by those means, for the purpose of causing annoyance, inconvenience
or needless anxiety to another, a message that he knows to be false or persistently
makes use for that purpose of a public telecommunication system,
shall be guilty of an offence and liable on summary conviction to imprisonment for a
term not exceeding six months or a fine not exceeding level 5 on the standard scale
or both.

(2)   Subsection (1) above does not apply to anything done in the course of
providing a cable programme service . . .

MALICIOUS COMMUNICATIONS ACT 1988

1.   Offence of sending letters etc. with intent to cause distress or anxiety

(1)   Any person who sends to another person—

(a)   a letter or other article which conveys—

(i)   a message which is indecent or grossly offensive;

(ii)   a threat; or

(iii)   information which is false and known or believed to be false by the
sender; or

(b)   any other article which is, in whole or part, of an indecent or grossly
offensive nature,

is guilty of an offence if his purpose, or one of his purposes, in sending it is that it should, so far as falling within paragraph (a) or (b) above, cause distress or anxiety to the recipient or to any other person to whom he intends that it or its contents or nature should be communicated.

(2)   A person is not guilty of an offence by virtue of subsection (1)(a)(ii) above if he shows—

(a)   that the threat was used to reinforce a demand which he believed he had reasonable grounds for making; and

(b)   that he believed that the use of the threat was a proper means of reinforcing the demand.

(3)   In this section references to sending include references to delivering and to causing to be sent or delivered and 'sender' shall be construed accordingly.

(4)   A person guilty of an offence under this section shall be liable on summary conviction to a fine not exceeding level 4 on the standard scale.

ADMINISTRATION OF JUSTICE ACT 1970

40.   Punishment for unlawful harassment of debtors

(1)   A person commits an offence if, with the object of coercing another person to pay money claimed from the other as a debt due under a contract, he—

(a)   harasses the other with demands for payment which, in respect of their frequency or the manner or occasion of making any such demand, or of any threat or publicity by which any demand is accompanied, are calculated to subject him or members of his family or household to alarm, distress or humiliation;

(b)   falsely represents, in relation to the money claimed, that criminal proceedings lie for failure to pay it;

(c)   falsely represents himself to be authorised in some official capacity to claim or enforce payment; or

(d)   utters a document falsely represented by him to have some official character or purporting to have some official character which he knows it has not.

(2)   A person may be guilty of an offence by virtue of subsection 1 (a) above if he concerts with others in the taking of such action as is described in that paragraph, notwithstanding that his own course of conduct does not by itself amount to harassment.

(3)   Subsection 1 (a) above does not apply to anything done by a person which is reasonable (and otherwise permissible in law) for the purpose—

(a)   of securing the discharge of an obligation due, or believed by him to be due, to himself or to persons for whom he acts, or protecting himself or them from future loss; or

(b)   of the enforcement of any liability by legal process.

PROTECTION FROM EVICTION ACT 1977

1.   Unlawful eviction and harassment of occupier

(1)   In this section 'residential occupier', in relation to any premises, means a person occupying the premises as a residence, whether under a contract or by virtue of any enactment or rule of law giving him the right to remain in occupation or restricting the right of any person to recover possession of the premises.

(2)   If any person unlawfully deprives the residential occupier of any premises of his occupation of the premises or any part thereof, or attempts to do so, he shall be guilty of an offence unless he proves that he believed, and had reasonable cause to believe, that the residential occupier had ceased to reside in the premises.

(3)   If any person with intent to cause the residential occupier of any premises—

(a)   to give up the occupation of the premises or any part thereof; or

(b)   to refrain from exercising any right or pursuing any remedy in respect of the premises or part thereof;
does acts likely to interfere with the peace or comfort of the residential occupier or members of his household, or persistently withdraws or withholds services reasonably required for the occupation of the premises as a residence, he shall be guilty of an offence.

(3A)   Subject to subsection (3B) below, the landlord of a residential occupier or an agent of the landlord shall be guilty of an offence if—
(a)   he does acts likely to interfere with the peace or comfort of the residential occupier or members of his household, or
(b)   he persistently withdraws or withholds services reasonably required for the occupation of the premises in question as a residence,
and (in either case) he knows, or has reasonable cause to believe, that that conduct is likely to cause the residential occupier to give up the occupation of the whole or part of the premises or to refrain from exercising any right or pursuing any remedy in respect of the whole or part of the premises.

(3B)   A person shall not be guilty of an offence under subsection (3A) above if he proves that he had reasonable grounds for doing the acts or withdrawing or withholding the services in question.

(3C)   In subsection (3A) above 'landlord', in relation to a residential occupier of any premises, means the person who, but for—
(a)   the residential occupier's right to remain in occupation of the premises, or
(b)   a restriction on the person's right to recover possession of the premises,
would be entitled to occupation of the premises and any superior landlord under whom that person derives title.

CRIMINAL LAW ACT 1977

51. Bomb hoaxes

(1)   A person who—
(a)   places any article in any place whatever; or
(b)   dispatches any article by post, rail or any other means whatever of sending things from one place to another,
with the intention (in either case) of inducing in some other person a belief that it is likely to explode or ignite and thereby cause personal injury or damage to property is guilty of an offence.
In this subsection 'article' includes substance.

(2)   A person who communicates any information which he knows or believes to be false to another person with the intention of inducing in him or any other person a false belief that a bomb or other thing liable to explode or ignite is present in any place or location whatever is guilty of an offence.

(3)   For a person to be guilty of an offence under subsection (1) or (2) above it is not necessary for him to have any particular person in mind as the person in whom he intends to induce the belief mentioned in that subsection.

(c) PROTECTION OF CHILDREN AND MINORS

OFFENCES AGAINST THE PERSON ACT 1861

27.   Exposing child, whereby life is endangered, or health permanently injured

Whosoever shall unlawfully abandon or expose any child, being under the age of two years, whereby the life of such child shall be endangered, or the health of such child shall have been or shall be likely to be permanently injured, shall be guilty of an offence, and being convicted thereof shall be liable to imprisonment for a term not exceeding five years.

LICENSING ACT 1902

2. Penalty for being drunk while in charge of child

(1) If any person is found drunk in any highway or other public place, whether a building or not, or on any licensed premises, while having the charge of a child apparently under the age of seven years, he may be apprehended, and shall, if the child is under that age, be liable on summary conviction, to a fine not exceeding level 2 on the standard scale or to imprisonment for any period not exceeding one month.

(2) If the child appears to the court to be under the age of seven the child shall, for the purposes of this section, be deemed to be under that age unless the contrary is proved.

8. Interpretation of 'public place'

For the purposes of section twelve of the Licensing Act, 1872, and of sections one and two of this Act, the expression 'public place' shall include any place to which the public have access, whether on payment or otherwise.

CHILDREN AND YOUNG PERSONS ACT 1933

1. Cruelty to persons under sixteen

(1) If any person who has attained the age of sixteen years and has responsibility for any child or young person under that age, wilfully assaults, ill-treats, neglects, abandons, or exposes him, or causes or procures him to be assaulted, ill-treated, neglected, abandoned, or exposed, in a manner likely to cause him unnecessary suffering or injury to health (including injury to or loss of sight, or hearing, or limb, or organ of the body, and any mental derangement), that person shall be guilty of a misdemeanour, and shall be liable—

(a) on conviction on indictment, to a fine or alternatively, . . . or in addition thereto, to imprisonment for any term not exceeding ten years;

(b) on summary conviction, to a fine not exceeding the prescribed sum or alternatively, . . . or in addition thereto, to imprisonment for any term not exceeding six months.

(2) For the purposes of this section—

(a) a parent or other person legally liable to maintain a child or young person or the legal guardian of a child or young person shall be deemed to have neglected him in a manner likely to cause injury to his health if he has failed to provide adequate food, clothing, medical aid or lodging for him, or if, having been unable otherwise to provide such food, clothing, medical aid or lodging, he has failed to take steps to procure it to be provided under the enactments applicable in that behalf;

(b) where it is proved that the death of an infant under three years of age was caused by suffocation (not being suffocation caused by disease or the presence of any foreign body in the throat or air passages of the infant) while the infant was in bed with some other person who has attained the age of sixteen years, that other person shall, if he was, when he went to bed, under the influence of drink, be deemed to have neglected the infant in a manner likely to cause injury to its health.

(3) A person may be convicted of an offence under this section—

(a) notwithstanding that actual suffering or injury to health, or the likelihood of actual suffering or injury to health, was obviated by the action of another person;

(b) notwithstanding the death of the child or young person in question.

(7) Nothing in this section shall be construed as affecting the right of any parent, teacher, or other person having the lawful control or charge of a child or young person to administer punishment to him.

3. Allowing persons under sixteen to be in brothels

(1) If any person having responsibility for a child or young person who has attained the age of four years and is under the age of sixteen years, allows that child or young person to reside in or to frequent a brothel, he shall be liable on summary

conviction, to a fine not exceeding level 2 on the standard scale, or alternatively . . . or in addition thereto, to imprisonment for any term not exceeding six months.

5.   Giving intoxicating liquor to children under five

If any person gives, or causes to be given, to any child under the age of five years any intoxicating liquor, except upon the order of a duly qualified medical practitioner, or in case of sickness, apprehended sickness, or other urgent cause, he shall, on summary conviction, be liable to a fine not exceeding level 1 on the standard scale.

7.   Sale of tobacco, etc., to persons under sixteen

(1)   Any person who sells to a person under the age of sixteen years any tobacco or cigarette papers, whether for his own use or not, shall be liable on summary conviction to a fine not exceeding level 4 on the standard scale:
Provided that a person shall not be guilty of an offence under this section in respect of any sale of tobacco otherwise than in the form of cigarettes, if he did not know and had no reason to believe that the tobacco was for the use of the person to whom it was sold.

(1A)   It shall be a defence for a person charged with an offence under subsection (1) above to prove that he took all reasonable precautions and exercised all due diligence to avoid the commission of the offence.

(5)   For the purposes of this section the expression 'tobacco' includes cigarettes, any product containing tobacco and intended for oral or nasal use and smoking mixtures intended as a substitute for tobacco, and the expression 'cigarette' includes cut tobacco rolled up in papers, tobacco leaf, or other material in such form as to be capable of immediate use for smoking.

11.   Exposing children under twelve to risk of burning

If any person who has attained the age of sixteen years, having responsibility for any child under the age of twelve years, allows the child to be in any room containing an open fire grate or any heating appliance liable to cause injury to a person by contact therewith not sufficiently protected to guard against the risk of his being burnt or scalded without taking reasonable precautions against that risk, and by reason thereof the child is killed or suffers serious injury, he shall on summary conviction be liable to a fine not exceeding level 1 on the standard scale:
Provided that neither this section, nor any proceedings taken thereunder shall affect any liability of any such person to be proceeded against by indictment for any indictable offence.

17.   Interpretation of Part I

(1)   For the purposes of this Part of this Act, the following shall be presumed to have responsibility for a child or young person—
    (a)   Any person who—
      (i)   has parental responsibility for him (within the meaning of the Children Act 1989); or
      (ii)   is otherwise legally liable to maintain him; and
    (b)   any person who has care of him.

(2)   A person who is presumed to be responsible for a child or young person by virtue of subsection (1)(a) shall not be taken to have ceased to be responsible for him by reason only that he does not have care of him.

18.   Restrictions on employment of children

(1)   Subject to the provisions of this section and of any byelaws made thereunder no child shall be employed—
    (a)   so long as he is under the age of thirteen years; or
    (b)   before the close of school hours on any day on which he is required to attend school; or

(c)   before seven o'clock in the morning or after seven o'clock in the evening on any day; or

(d)   for more than two hours on any day on which he is required to attend school; or

(e)   for more than two hours on any Sunday; or

(f)   to lift, carry or move anything so heavy as to be likely to cause injury to him.

23.   Prohibition against persons under sixteen taking part in performances endangering life or limb

No child shall take part in any performance to which section 37 of the Children and Young Persons Act 1963 applies and in which his life or limbs are endangered and every person who causes or procures a child, or being his parent or guardian allows him, to take part in such a performance, shall be liable on summary conviction to a fine not exceeding level 3 on the standard scale;

Provided that no proceedings shall be taken under this subsection except by or with the authority of a chief officer of police.

24.   Restrictions on training for performances of a dangerous nature

(1)   No child under the age of twelve years shall be trained to take part in performances of a dangerous nature, and no child who has attained that age shall be trained to take part in such performances except under and in accordance with the terms of a licence granted and in force under this section; and every person who causes or procures a person, or being his parent or guardian allows him, to be trained to take part in performances of a dangerous nature in contravention of this section, shall be liable on summary conviction to a fine not exceeding level 3 on the standard scale.

(2)   A local authority may grant a licence for a child who has attained the age of twelve years but is under the age of sixteen years to be trained to take part in performances of a dangerous nature.

EDUCATION ACT 1996

548.   No right to give corporal punishment

(1)   Where, in any proceedings, it is shown that corporal punishment has been given to a pupil to whom this subsection applies by or on the authority of a member of the staff, giving the punishment cannot be justified on the ground that it was done in pursuance of a right exercisable by the member of the staff by virtue of his position as such.

(2)   Where in any proceedings, it is shown that corporal punishment has been given to a pupil by or on the authority of a member of the staff, giving the punishment cannot be justified if the punishment was inhuman or degrading.

(3)   Subsection (1) applies to—

(a)   any pupil for whom education is provided—

(i)   at a school maintained by a local education authority;

(ii)   at a special school not so maintained; or

(iii)   at a grant-maintained school;

(b)   any pupil for whom education is provided at an independent school—

(i)   which is maintained or assisted by a Minister of the Crown (including a school of which a government department is the proprietor) or assisted by a local education authority; and

(ii)   which falls within a prescribed class;

(c)   any pupil for whom education is provided by a local education authority otherwise than at a school; and

(d)   to whom subsection (5) below applies and for whom education is provided at an independent school not falling within paragraph (b) above.

(6)   A person does not commit an offence by reason of any conduct relating to a pupil which would, apart from this section, be justified on the ground that it is done in pursuance of a right exercisable by a member of the staff by virtue of his position as such.

549.   Interpretation of section 548

(1)   Subject to subsection (2) below, references in section 548 to giving corporal punishment are references to doing anything for the purposes of punishing the pupil concerned (whether or not there are also other reasons for doing it) which, apart from any justification, would constitute battery.

(2)   A person is not to be taken for the purpose of section 548 as giving corporal punishment by virtue of anything done for reasons that include averting an immediate danger of personal injury to, or an immediate danger to the property of, any person (including the pupil concerned).

(3)   In determining whether punishment is inhuman or degrading regard shall be had to all the circumstances of the case, including the reason for giving it, how soon after the event it is given, its nature, the manner and circumstances in which it is given, the persons involved and its mental and physical effects.

(4)   In section 548 'member of the staff' means—

(a)   in relation to a person who is a pupil by reason of the provision of education for him at any school, any teacher who works at the school and any other person who has lawful control or charge of the pupil and works there; and

(b)   in relation to a person who is a pupil by reason of the provision of education for him by a local education authority at a place other than a school, any teacher employed by the authority who works at that place and any other person employed by the authority who has lawful control or charge of the pupil and works there.

(5)   In section 548 and this section 'pupil' does not include any person who has attained the age of 18.

550A.   Power of members of staff to restrain pupils

(1)   A member of the staff of a school may use, in relation to any pupil at the school, such force as is reasonable in the circumstances for the purpose of preventing the pupil from doing (or continuing to do) any of the following, namely—

(a)   committing any offence,

(b)   causing personal injury to, or damage to the property of, any person (including the pupil himself), or

(c)   engaging in any behaviour prejudicial to the maintenance of good order and discipline at the school or among any of its pupils, whether that behaviour occurs during a teaching session or otherwise.

(2)   Subsection (1) applies where a member of the staff of a school is—

(a)   on the premises of the school, or

(b)   elsewhere at a time when, as a member of its staff, he has lawful control or charge of the pupil concerned;

but it does not authorise anything to be done in relation to a pupil which constitutes the giving of corporal punishment within the meaning of section 548.

(3)   Subsection (1) shall not be taken to prevent any person from relying on any defence available to him otherwise than by virtue of this section.

(4)   In this section—

'member of the staff', in relation to a school, means any teacher who works at the school and any other person who, with the authority of the head teacher, has lawful control or charge of pupils at the school;

'offence' includes anything that would be an offence but for the operation of any presumption that a person under a particular age is incapable of committing an offence.

550B. Detention outside school hours lawful despite absence of parental consent

(1)   Where a pupil to whom this section applies is required on disciplinary grounds to spend a period of time in detention at his school after the end of any school session, his detention shall not be rendered unlawful by virtue of the absence of his parent's consent to it if the conditions set out in subsection (3) are satisfied.

(2)   This section applies to any pupil who has not attained the age of 18 and is attending—

(a)   a school maintained by a local education authority;

(b)   a grant-maintained or grant-maintained special school; or

(c)   a city technology college or city college for the technology of the arts.

(3)   The conditions referred to in subsection (1) are as follows—

(a)   the head teacher of the school must have previously determined, and have—

(i)   made generally known within the school, and

(ii)   taken steps to bring to the attention of the parent of every person who is for the time being a registered pupil there, that the detention of pupils after the end of a school session is one of the measures that may be taken with a view to regulating the conduct of pupils;

(b)   the detention must be imposed by the head teacher or by another teacher at the school specifically or generally authorised by him for the purpose;

(c)   the detention must be reasonable in all the circumstances; and

(d)   the pupil's parent must have been given at least 24 hours' notice in writing that the detention was due to take place.

(4)   In determining for the purposes of subsection (3)(c) whether a pupil's detention is reasonable, the following matters in particular shall be taken into account—

(a)   whether the detention constitutes a proportionate punishment in the circumstances of the case; and

(b)   any special circumstances relevant to its imposition on the pupil which are known to the person imposing it (or of which he ought reasonably to be aware) including in particular—

(i)   the pupil's age,

(ii)   any special educational needs he may have,

(iii)   any religious requirements affecting him, and

(iv)   where arrangements have to be made for him to travel from the school to his home, whether suitable alternative arrangements can reasonably be made by his parent.

SEXUAL OFFENCES ACT 1956

5. Intercourse with girl under thirteen

It is felony for a man to have unlawful sexual intercourse with a girl under the age of thirteen.

6. Intercourse with girl under sixteen

(1)   It is an offence, subject to the exceptions mentioned in this section, for a man to have unlawful sexual intercourse with a girl . . . under the age of sixteen.

(2)   Where a marriage is invalid under section two of the Marriage Act, 1949, or section one of the Age of Marriage Act, 1929 (the wife being a girl under the age of sixteen), the invalidity does not make the husband guilty of an offence under this section because he has sexual intercourse with her, if he believes her to be his wife and has reasonable cause for the belief.

(3)   A man is not guilty of an offence under this section because he has unlawful sexual intercourse with a girl under the age of sixteen, if he is under the age of twenty

four and has not previously been charged with a like offence, and he believes her to be of the age of sixteen or over and has reasonable cause for the belief.

In this subsection 'a like offence' means an offence under this section or an attempt to commit one, or an offence under paragraph (1) of section five of the Criminal Law Amendment Act, 1885 (the provision replaced for England and Wales by this section).

14. Indecent assault on a girl under sixteen
(2) [See page 26]

15. Indecent assault on a boy under sixteen
(2) [See page 26]

19. Abduction of unmarried girl under eighteen from parent or guardian
(1) It is an offence, subject to the exception mentioned in this section, for a person to take an unmarried girl under the age of eighteen out of the possession of her parent or guardian against his will, if she is so taken with the intention that she shall have unlawful sexual intercourse with men or with a particular man.

(2) A person is not guilty of an offence under this section because he takes such a girl out of the possession of her parent or guardian as mentioned above, if he believes her to be of the age of eighteen or over and has reasonable cause for the belief.

(3) In this section 'guardian' means any person having parental responsibility for or care of the girl.

20. Abduction of unmarried girl under sixteen from parent or guardian
(1) It is an offence for a person acting without lawful authority or excuse to take an unmarried girl under the age of sixteen out of the possession of her parent or guardian against his will.

(2) In the foregoing subsection 'guardian' means any person having parental responsibility for or care of the girl.

25. Permitting girl under thirteen to use premises for intercourse
It is felony for a person who is the owner or occupier of any premises, or who has, or acts or assists in, the management or control of any premises, to induce or knowingly suffer a girl under the age of thirteen to resort to or be on those premises for the purpose of having unlawful sexual intercourse with men or with a particular man.

26. Permitting girl under sixteen to use premises for intercourse
It is an offence for a person who is the owner or occupier of any premises, or who has, or acts or assists in, the management or control of any premises, to induce or knowingly suffer a girl . . . under the age of sixteen, to resort to or be on those premises for the purpose of having unlawful sexual intercourse with men or with a particular man.

28. Causing or encouraging prostitution of, intercourse with, or indecent assault on, girl under sixteen
(1) It is an offence for a person to cause or encourage the prostitution of, or the commission of unlawful sexual intercourse with, or of an indecent assault on, a girl under the age of sixteen for whom he is responsible.

(2) Where a girl has become a prostitute, or has had unlawful sexual intercourse, or has been indecently assaulted, a person shall be deemed for the purposes of this section to have caused or encouraged it, if he knowingly allowed her to consort with, or to enter or continue in the employment of, any prostitute or person of known immoral character.

(3) The persons who are to be treated for the purposes of this section as responsible for a girl are (subject to subsection (4) of this section)—

(a)   other parents;

(b)   any person who is not a parent of hers but who has parental responsibility for her; and

(c)   any person who has care of her.

(4)   An individual falling within subsection (3)(a) or (b) of this section is not to be treated as responsible for a girl if—

(a)   a residence order under the Children Act 1989 is in force with respect to her and he is not named in the order as the person with whom she is to live; or

(b)   a care order under that Act is in force with respect to her.

(5)   If, on a charge of an offence against a girl under this section, the girl appears to the court to have been under the age of sixteen at the time of the offence charged, she shall be presumed for the purposes of this section to have been so, unless the contrary is proved.

44.   Meaning of 'sexual intercourse'
[See page 27]

46.   Use of words 'man', 'boy', 'woman' and 'girl'
[See page 28]

46A.   Meaning of 'parental responsibility'
[See page 28]

47.   Proof of exceptions
[See page 28]

INDECENCY WITH CHILDREN ACT 1960

1.   Indecent conduct towards young child
(1)   Any person who commits an act of gross indecency with or towards a child under the age of fourteen, or who incites a child that age to such an act with him or another, shall be liable on conviction on indictment to imprisonment for a term not exceeding ten years, or on summary conviction to imprisonment for a term not exceeding six months, to a fine not exceeding the prescribed sum, or to both.

CRIMINAL LAW ACT 1977

54.   Inciting girl under sixteen to have incestuous sexual intercourse
(1)   It is an offence for a man to incite to have sexual intercourse with him a girl under the age of sixteen whom he knows to be his grand-daughter, daughter or sister.

(2)   In the preceding subsection 'man' includes boy, 'sister' includes half-sister, and for the purposes of that subsection any expression importing a relationship between two people shall be taken to apply notwithstanding that the relationship is not traced through lawful wedlock.

PROTECTION OF CHILDREN ACT 1978

1.   Indecent photographs of children
(1)   It is an offence for a person—

(a)   to take, or permit to be taken, or to make any indecent photograph or psuedo-photograph of a child; or

(b)   to distribute or show such indecent photographs or psuedo-photographs; or

(c)   to have in his possession such indecent photographs, or psuedo-photographs with a view to their being distributed or shown by himself or others; or

(d)   to publish or cause to be published any advertisement likely to be understood as conveying that the advertiser distributes or shows such indecent photographs or psuedo-photographs, or intends to do so.

(2)   For purposes of this Act, a person is to be regarded as distributing an indecent photograph or psuedo-photograph if he parts with possession of it to, or exposes or offers it for acquisition by, another person.

(3)   Proceedings for an offence under this Act shall not be instituted except by or with the consent of the Director of Public Prosecutions.

(4)   Where a person is charged with an offence under subsection (1)(b) or (c), it shall be a defence for him to prove—

(a)   that he had a legitimate reason for distributing or showing the photographs or psuedo-photographs or (as the case may be) having them in his possession; or

(b)   that he had not himself seen the photographs or psuedo-photographs and did not know, nor had any cause to suspect, them to be indecent.

7. Interpretation

(1)   The following subsections apply for the interpretation of this Act.

(2)   References to an indecent photograph include an indecent film, a copy of an indecent photograph or film, and an indecent photograph comprised in a film.

(3)   Photographs (including those comprised in a film) shall, if they show children and are indecent, be treated for all purposes of this Act as indecent photographs of children, and so as respects pseudo-photographs.

(4)   References to a photograph include—

(a)   the negative as well as the positive version; and

(b)   data stored on a computer disc or by other electronic means which is capable of conversion into a photograph.

(5)   'Film' includes any form of video-recording.

(6)   'Child', subject to subsection (8), means a person under the age of 16.

(7)   'Pseudo-photograph' means an image, whether made by computer-graphics or otherwise howsoever, which appears to be a photograph.

(8)   If the impression conveyed by a pseudo-photograph is that the person shown is a child, the pseudo-photograph shall be treated for all purposes of this Act as showing a child and so shall a pseudo-photograph where the predominant impression conveyed is that the person shown is a child notwithstanding that some of the physical characteristics shown are those of an adult.

(9)   References to an indecent pseudo-photograph include—

(a)   a copy of an indecent pseudo-photograph; and

(b)   data stored on a computer disc or by other electronic means which is capable of conversion into a pseudo-photograph.

CRIMINAL JUSTICE ACT 1988

160.   Possession of indecent photograph of child

(1)   It is an offence for a person to have any indecent photograph of a child (meaning in this section a person under the age of 16) in his possession.

(2)   Where a person is charged with an offence under subsection (1) above, it shall be a defence for him to prove—

(a)   that he had a legitimate reason for having the photograph in his possession; or

(b)   that he had not himself seen the photograph and did not know, nor had any cause to suspect, it to be indecent; or

(c)   that the photograph was sent to him without any prior request made by him or on his behalf and that he did not keep it for an unreasonable time.

(3)   A person shall be liable on summary conviction of an offence under this section to a fine not exceeding level 5 on the standard scale.

(4)   Sections 1(3), 2(3), 3 and 7 of the Protection of Children Act 1978 shall have effect as if any reference in them to that Act included a reference to this section.

(5)   Possession before this section comes into force is not an offence.

EDUCATION ACT 1996

444.   Failure to secure regular attendance at school of registered pupil

(1)   If a child of compulsory school age who is a registered pupil at a school fails to attend regularly at the school, his parent is guilty of an offence.

(2)   Subsections (3) to (6) below apply in proceedings for an offence under this section in respect of a child who is not a boarder at the school at which he is a registered pupil.

(3)   The child shall not be taken to have failed to attend regularly at the school by reason of his absence from the school—

(a)   with leave,

(b)   at any time when he was prevented from attending by reason of sickness or any unavoidable cause, or

(c)   on any day exclusively set apart for religious observance by the religious body to which his parent belongs.

(4)   The child shall not be taken to have failed to attend regularly at the school if the parent proves—

(a)   that the school at which the child is a registered pupil is not within walking distance of the child's home, and

(b)   that no suitable arrangements have been made by the local education authority or the funding authority for any of the following—

(i)   his transport to and from the school,

(ii)   boarding accommodation for him at or near the school, and

(iii)   enabling him to become a registered pupil at a school nearer to his home.

(5)   In subsection (4) above, 'walking distance' means—

(a)   in relation to a child who is under the age of eight years, two miles, and

(b)   in relation to a child who has attained the age of eight years, three miles, in each case measured by the nearest available route.

(6)   If it is proved that the child has no fixed abode, subsection (4) above shall not apply, but the parent shall be acquitted if he proves—

(a)   that he is engaged in a trade or business of such a nature as to require him to travel from place to place,

(b)   that the child has attended at a school as a registered pupil as regularly as the nature of that trade or business permits, and

(c)   if the child has attained the age of six years, that he has made at least two hundred attendances during the period of twelve months ending with the date on which the proceedings were instituted.

(7)   In proceedings for an offence under this section in respect of a child who is a boarder at the school at which he is a registered pupil, the child shall be taken to have failed to attend regularly at the school if he is absent from it without leave during any part of the school term at a time when he was not prevented from being present by reason of sickness or any unavoidable cause.

(9)   In this section 'leave', in relation to a school, means leave granted by any person authorised to do so by the governing body or proprietor of the school.

HYPNOTISM ACT 1952

3.   Prohibition on hypnotising persons under eighteen

A person who gives an exhibition, demonstration or performance of hypnotism on a person who has not attained the age of [eighteen years] at or in connection with an entertainment to which the public are admitted, whether on payment or otherwise, shall, unless he had reasonable cause to believe that that person had attained that age, be liable on summary conviction to a fine not exceeding [level 3 on the standard scale].

CHILDREN AND YOUNG PERSONS (HARMFUL PUBLICATIONS) ACT 1955

1. Works to which this Act applies
This Act applies to any book, magazine or other like work which is of a kind likely to fall into the hands of children or young persons and consists wholly or mainly of stories told in pictures (with or without the addition of written matter), being stories portraying—
  (a)   the commission of crimes; or
  (b)   acts of violence or cruelty; or
  (c)   incidents of a repulsive or horrible nature;
in such a way that the work as a whole would tend to corrupt a child or young person into whose hands it might fall.

2. Penalty for printing, publishing, selling etc., works to which this Act applies
(1)   A person who prints, publishes, sells or lets on hire a work to which this Act applies, or has any such work in his possession for the purpose of selling it or letting it on hire, shall be guilty of an offence and liable, on summary conviction, to imprisonment for a term not exceeding four months or to a fine not exceeding one hundred pounds or to both:
Provided that, in any proceedings taken under this subsection against a person in respect of selling or letting on hire a work or of having it in his possession for the purpose of selling it or letting it on hire, it shall be a defence for him to prove that he had not examined the contents of the work and had no reasonable cause to suspect that it was one to which this Act applies.
(2)   A prosecution for an offence under this section shall not, in England or Wales, be instituted except by, or with the consent of, the Attorney-General.

4. Prohibition of importation of works to which this Act applies and articles for printing them
The importation of—
  (a)   any work to which this Act applies; and
  (b)   any plate prepared for the purpose of printing copies of any such work and any photographic film prepared for that purpose;
is hereby prohibited.

LICENSING ACT 1964

168. Children prohibited from bars
[See page 110]

169. Serving or delivering intoxicating liquor to or for consumption by persons under 18
[See pages 110–111]

TATTOOING OF MINORS ACT 1969

1. Prohibition of tattooing of minors
It shall be an offence to tattoo a person under the age of eighteen except when the tattoo is performed for medical reasons by a duly qualified medical practitioner or by

a person working under his direction, but it shall be a defence for a person charged to show that at the time the tattoo was performed he had reasonable cause to believe that the person tattooed was of or over the age of eighteen and did in fact so believe.

3. Definition
For the purposes of this Act 'tattoo' shall mean the insertion into the skin of any colouring material designed to leave a permanent mark.

CHILD ABDUCTION ACT 1984

1. Offence of abduction of child by parent, etc.
(1) Subject to subsections (5) and (8) below, a person connected with a child under the age of sixteen commits an offence if he takes or sends the child out of the United Kingdom without the appropriate consent.

(2) A person is connected with a child for the purposes of this section if—
  (a) he is a parent of the child; or
  (b) in the case of a child whose parents were not married to each other at the time of his birth, there are reasonable grounds for believing that he is the father of the child; or
  (c) he is a guardian of the child; or
  (d) he is a person in whose favour a residence order is in force with respect to the child; or
  (e) he has custody of the child.

(3) In this section 'the appropriate consent' in relation to a child, means—
  (a) the consent of each of the following—
    (i) the child's mother;
    (ii) the child's father, if he has parental responsibility for him;
    (iii) any guardian of the child;
    (iv) any person in whose favour a residence order is in force with respect to the child;
    (v) any person who has custody of the child; or
  (b) the leave of the court granted under or by virtue of any provision of Part II of the Children Act 1989; or
  (c) if any person has custody of the child, the leave of the court which awarded custody to him.

(4) A person does not commit an offence under this section by taking or sending a child out of the United Kingdom without obtaining the appropriate consent if—
  (a) he is a person in whose favour there is a residence order in force with respect to the child, and
  (b) he takes or sends him out of the United Kingdom for a period of less than one month.

(4A) Subsection (4) above does not apply if the person taking or sending the child out of the United Kingdom does so in breach of an order under Part II of the Children Act 1989.

(5) A person does not commit an offence under this section by doing anything without the consent of another person whose consent is required under the foregoing provisions if—
  (a) he does it in the belief that the other person—
    (i) has consented; or
    (ii) would consent if he was aware of all the relevant circumstances; or
  (b) he has taken all reasonable steps to communicate with the other person but has been unable to communicate with him; or
  (c) the other person has unreasonably refused to consent.

(5A)   Subsection (5)(c) above does not apply if—
    (a)   the person who refused to consent is a person—
        (i)   in whose favour there is a residence order in force with respect to the child; or
        (ii)   who has custody of the child; or
    (b)   the person taking or sending the child out of the United Kingdom is, by so acting, in breach of an order made by a court in the United Kingdom.

(6)   Where, in proceedings for an offence under this section, there is sufficient evidence to raise an issue as to the application of subsection (5) above, it shall be for the prosecution to prove that the subsection does not apply.

(7)   For the purposes of this section—
    (a)   'guardian of a child', 'residence order' and 'parental responsibility' have the same meaning as in the Children Act 1989; and
    (b)   a person shall be treated as having custody of a child if there is in force an order of a court in the United Kingdom awarding him (whether solely or jointly with another person) custody, legal custody or care and control of the child.

(8)   This section shall have effect subject to the provisions of the Schedule to this Act in relation to a child who is in the care of a local authority detained in a place of safety, remanded to a local authority accommodation or the subject of proceedings or an order relating to adoption.

2.   Offence of abduction of child by other persons

(1)   Subject to subsection (3) below, a person, other than one mentioned in subsection (2) below, commits an offence if, without lawful authority or reasonable excuse, he takes or detains a child under the age of sixteen—
    (a)   so as to remove him from the lawful control of any person having lawful control of the child; or
    (b)   so as to keep him out of the lawful control of any person entitled to lawful control of the child.

(2)   The persons are—
    (a)   where the father and mother of the child in question were married to each other at the time of his birth, the child's father and mother;
    (b)   where the father and mother of the child in question were not married to each other at the time of his birth, the child's mother; and
    (c)   any other person mentioned in section 1(2)(c) to (e) above.

(3)   In proceedings against any person for an offence under this section, it shall be a defence for that person to prove—
    (a)   where the father and mother of the child in question were not married to each other at the time of his birth—
        (i)   that he is the child's father; or
        (ii)   that, at the time of the alleged offence, he believed, on reasonable grounds, that he was the child's father; or
    (b)   that, at the time of the alleged offence, he believed that the child had attained the age of sixteen.

3.   Construction of references to taking, sending and detaining

For the purposes of this Part of this Act—
    (a)   a person shall be regarded as taking a child if he causes or induces the child to accompany him or any other person or causes the child to be taken;
    (b)   a person shall be regarded as sending a child if he causes the child to be sent;
    (c)   a person shall be regarded as detaining a child if he causes the child to be detained or induces the child to remain with him or any other person; and
    (d)   references to a child's parents and to a child whose parents were (or were not) married to each other at the time of his birth shall be construed in accordance with section 1 of the Family Law Reform Act 1987 (which extends their meaning).

INTOXICATING SUBSTANCES (SUPPLY) ACT 1985

1. Offence of supplying intoxicating substance
[See page 115]

HORSES (PROTECTIVE HEADGEAR FOR YOUNG RIDERS) ACT 1990

1. Causing or permitting child under 14 to ride on road without protective headgear

(1) Except as provided by regulations, it is an offence for any person to whom this subsection applies to cause or permit a child under the age of 14 years to ride a horse on a road unless the child is wearing protective headgear, of such description as may be specified in regulations, in such manner as may be so specified.

(2) Subsection (1) above applies to the following persons—

    (a) any person who—

        (i) for the purposes of Part I of the Children and Young Persons Act 1933, has responsibility for the child; or

        (ii) (*applies to Scotland only*);

    (b) any owner of the horse;

    (c) any person other than its owner who has custody of or is in possession of the horse immediately before the child rides it; and

    (d) where the child is employed, his employer and any other person to whose orders the child is subject in the course of his employment.

(3) A person guilty of an offence under subsection (1) above is liable on summary conviction to a fine not exceeding level 1 on the standard scale.

3. Interpretation

(1) In this Act—

'horse' includes pony, mule, donkey or other equine animal;

'regulations' means regulations under section 2 of this Act; and

'road' does not include a footpath or bridleway but, subject to that, has—

    (a) in England and Wales the meaning given by section 192(1) of the Road Traffic Act 1988 . . .

(2) For the purposes of the definition of 'road' in subsection (1) above—

    (a) 'footpath' means a way—

        (i) over which the public have a right of way or, in Scotland, of passage on foot only; and

        (ii) which is not associated with a carriageway; and

    (b) 'bridleway' means a way over which the public have the following, but no other, rights of way: a right of way on foot and a right of way on horseback or leading a horse, with or without a right to drive animals of any description along the way.

CHILDREN AND YOUNG PERSONS (PROTECTION FROM TOBACCO) ACT 1991

3. Sale of unpackaged cigarettes

(1) It shall be an offence for any person carrying on a retail business to sell cigarettes to any person other than in pre-packed quantities of 10 or more cigarettes in their original package.

(2) Any person guilty of an offence under subsection (1) above shall be liable on summary conviction to a fine not exceeding level 3 on the standard scale.

(3) In this section, 'original package' means the package in which the cigarettes were supplied for the purpose of retail sale by the manufacturer or importer; and 'package' means any box, carton or other container.

4. Display of warning statements in retail premises and on vending machines

(1)   A notice displaying the following statement—

'It is illegal to sell tobacco products to anyone under the age of 16'

shall be exhibited at every premises at which tobacco is sold by retail, and shall be so exhibited in a prominent position where the statement is readily visible to persons at the point of sale of the tobacco; and where—

(a)   any person carries on a business involving the sale of tobacco by retail at any premises, and

(b)   no notice is exhibited at those premises in accordance with this subsection, that person shall be guilty of an offence.

(2)   A notice displaying the following statement—

'This machine is only for the use of people aged 16 or over'

shall be exhibited on every automatic machine for the sale of tobacco which is kept available for use as such at any premises, and shall be so exhibited in such a way that the statement is readily visible to persons using the machine and where—

(a)   any person is the owner of any such machine which is so kept or the owner of the premises at which any such machine is so kept, and

(b)   no notice is exhibited on the machine in accordance with this subsection, that person shall be guilty of an offence.

(3)   The dimensions of the notice to be exhibited in accordance with subsection (1) or (2) above, and the size of the statement to be displayed on it, shall be such as may be prescribed by regulations made by the Secretary of State; and any such regulations may make different provision for different cases.

(4)   Any person guilty of an offence under subsection (1) or (2) above shall be liable on summary conviction to a fine not exceeding level 3 on the standard scale.

(5)   It shall be a defence for a person charged with any such offence to prove that he took all reasonable precautions and exercised all due diligence to avoid the commission of the offence.

(6)   Where any such offence is committed by a body corporate and is proved to have been committed with the consent or connivance of, or to be attributable to any neglect on the part of, any director, manager, secretary or other similar officer of the body corporate, or any person who was purporting to act in any such capacity, he as well as the body corporate shall be guilty of that offence and shall be liable to be proceeded against and punished accordingly.

In relation to a body corporate whose affairs are managed by its members, 'director' means a member of the body corporate.

(8)   In this section—

'premises' includes any place and any vehicle, vessel, aircraft, hovercraft, stall or moveable structure; and

'tobacco' (except where it appears in the statement required by subsection (1)) has the same meaning as in section 7 of the Children and Young Persons Act 1933.

4 DANGEROUS CONDUCT

(a) TRAFFIC

ROAD TRAFFIC ACT 1988

1. Causing death by dangerous driving

A person who causes the death of another person by driving a mechanically propelled vehicle dangerously on a road or other public place is guilty of an offence.

2. Dangerous driving

A person who drives a mechanically propelled vehicle dangerously on a road or other public place is guilty of an offence.

2A. Meaning of dangerous driving

(1) For the purposes of sections 1 and 2 above a person is to be regarded as driving dangerously if (and, subject to subsection (2) below, only if)—

(a) the way he drives falls far below what would be expected of a competent and careful driver, and

(b) it would be obvious to a competent and careful driver that driving in that way would be dangerous.

(2) A person is also to be regarded as driving dangerously for the purposes of sections 1 and 2 above if it would be obvious to a competent and careful driver that driving the vehicle in its current state would be dangerous.

(3) In subsections (1) and (2) above 'dangerous' refers to danger either of injury to any person or of serious damage to property; and in determining for the purposes of those subsections what would be expected of, or obvious to, a competent and careful driver in a particular case, regard shall be had not only to the circumstances of which he could be expected to be aware but also to any circumstances shown to have been within the knowledge of the accused.

(4) In determining for the purposes of subsection (2) above the state of a vehicle, regard may be had to anything attached to or carried on or in it and to the manner in which it is attached or carried.

3. Careless, and inconsiderate, driving

If a person drives a mechanically propelled vehicle on a road or other public place without due care and attention, or without reasonable consideration for other persons using the road or place, he is guilty of an offence.

3A. Causing death by careless driving when under influence of drink or drugs

(1) If a person causes the death of another person by driving a mechanically propelled vehicle on a road or other public place without due care and attention, or without reasonable consideration for other persons using the road or place, and—

(a) he is, at the time when he is driving, unfit to drive through drink or drugs, or

(b) he has consumed so much alcohol that the proportion of it in his breath, blood or urine at that time exceeds the prescribed limit, or

(c) he is, within 18 hours after that time, required to provide a specimen in pursuance of section 7 of this Act, but without reasonable excuse fails to provide it, he is guilty of an offence.

(2) For the purposes of this section a person shall be taken to be unfit to drive at any time when his ability to drive properly is impaired.

(3) Subsection (1)(b) and (c) above shall not apply in relation to a person driving a mechanically propelled vehicle other than a motor vehicle.

4. Driving, or being in charge, when under influence of drink or drugs

(1) A person who, when driving or attempting to drive a mechanically propelled vehicle on a road or other public place, is unfit to drive through drink or drugs is guilty of an offence.

(2) Without prejudice to subsection (1) above, a person who, when in charge of a mechanically propelled vehicle which is on a road or other public place, is unfit to drive through drink or drugs is guilty of an offence.

(3) For the purposes of subsection (2) above, a person shall be deemed not to have been in charge of a mechanically propelled vehicle if he proves that at the material time the circumstances were such that there was no likelihood of his driving it so long as he remained unfit to drive through drink or drugs.

(4) The court may, in determining whether there was such a likelihood as is mentioned in subsection (3) above, disregard any injury to him and any damage to the vehicle.

(5) For the purposes of this section, a person shall be taken to be unfit to drive if his ability to drive properly is for the time being impaired.

5. Driving or being in charge of a motor vehicle with alcohol concentration above prescribed limit

(1) If a person—

(a) drives or attempts to drive a motor vehicle on a road or other public place, or

(b) is in charge of a motor vehicle on a road or other public place,

after consuming so much alcohol that the proportion of it in his breath, blood or urine exceeds the prescribed limit he is guilty of an offence.

(2) It is a defence for a person charged with an offence under subsection (1)(b) above to prove that at the time he is alleged to have committed the offence the circumstances were such that there was no likelihood of his driving the vehicle whilst the proportion of alcohol in his breath, blood or urine remained likely to exceed the prescribed limit.

(3) The court may, in determining whether there was such a likelihood as is mentioned in subsection (2) above, disregard any injury to him and any damage to the vehicle.

6. Breath tests

(1) Where a constable in uniform has reasonable cause to suspect—

(a) that a person driving or attempting to drive or in charge of a motor vehicle on a road or other public place has alcohol in his body or has committed a traffic offence whilst the vehicle was in motion, or

(b) that a person has been driving or attempting to drive or been in charge of a motor vehicle on a road or other public place with alcohol in his body and that that person still has alcohol in his body, or

(c)   that a person has been driving or attempting to drive or been in charge of a motor vehicle on a road or other public place and has committed a traffic offence whilst the vehicle was in motion,

he may, subject to section 9 of this Act, require him to provide a specimen of breath for a breath test.

(2)   If an accident occurs owing to the presence of a motor vehicle on a road or other public place, a constable may, subject to section 9 of this Act, require any person who he has reasonable cause to believe was driving or attempting to drive or in charge of the vehicle at the time of the accident to provide a specimen of breath for a breath test.

(3)   A person may be required under subsection (1) or subsection (2) above to provide a specimen either at or near the place where the requirement is made or, if the requirement is made under subsection (2) above and the constable making the requirement thinks fit, at a police station specified by the constable.

(4)   A person who, without reasonable excuse, fails to provide a specimen of breath when required to do so in pursuance of this section is guilty of an offence.

(8)   In this section 'traffic offence' means an offence under—
  (a)   any provision of Part II of the Public Passenger Vehicles Act 1981,
  (b)   any provision of the Road Traffic Regulation Act 1984,
  (c)   any provision of the Road Traffic Offenders Act 1988 except Part III, or
  (d)   any provision of this Act except Part V.

7.   Provision of specimens for analysis

(1)   In the course of an investigation into whether a person has committed an offence under section 4 or 5 of this Act a constable may, subject to the following provisions of this section and section 9 of this Act, require him—
  (a)   to provide two specimens of breath for analysis by means of a device of a type approved by the Secretary of State, or
  (b)   to provide a specimen of blood or urine for a laboratory test.

(2)   A requirement under this section to provide specimens of breath can only be made at a police station.

(3)   A requirement under this section to provide a specimen of blood or urine can only be made at a police station or at a hospital; and it cannot be made at a police station unless—
  (a)   the constable making the requirement has reasonable cause to believe that for medical reasons a specimen of breath cannot be provided or should not be required, or
  (b)   at the time the requirement is made a device or a reliable device of the type mentioned in subsection (1)(a) above is not available at the police station or it is then for any other reason not practicable to use such a device there, or
  (c)   the suspected offence is one under section 4 of this Act and the constable making the requirement has been advised by a medical practitioner that the condition of the person required to provide the specimen might be due to some drug;

but may then be made notwithstanding that the person required to provide the specimen has already provided or been required to provide two specimens of breath.

(4)   If the provision of a specimen other than a specimen of breath may be required in pursuance of this section the question whether it is to be a specimen of blood or a specimen of urine shall be decided by the constable making the requirement, but if a medical practitioner is of the opinion that for medical reasons a specimen of blood cannot or should not be taken the specimen shall be a specimen of urine.

(5)   A specimen of urine shall be provided within one hour of the requirement for its provision being made and after the provision of a previous specimen of urine.

(6)   A person who, without reasonable excuse, fails to provide a specimen when required to do so in pursuance of this section is guilty of an offence.

(7) A constable must, on requiring any person to provide a specimen in pursuance of this section, warn him that a failure to provide it may render him liable to prosecution.

8. Choice of specimens of breath

(1) Subject to subsection (2) below, of any two specimens of breath provided by any person in pursuance of section 7 of this Act that with the lower proportion of alcohol in the breath shall be used and the other shall be disregarded.

(2) If the specimen with the lower proportion of alcohol contains no more than 50 microgrammes of alcohol in 100 millilitres of breath, the person who provided it may claim that it should be replaced by such specimen as may be required under section 7(4) of this Act and, if he then provides such a specimen, neither specimen of breath shall be used.

9. Protection for hospital patients

(1) While a person is at a hospital as a patient he shall not be required to provide a specimen of breath for a breath test or to provide a specimen for a laboratory test unless the medical practitioner in immediate charge of his case has been notified of the proposal to make the requirement; and—

(a) if the requirement is then made, it shall be for the provision of a specimen at the hospital, but

(b) if the medical practitioner objects on the ground specified in subsection (2) below, the requirement shall not be made.

(2) The ground on which the medical practitioner may object is that the requirement or the provision of a specimen or, in the case of a specimen of blood or urine, the warning required under section 7(7) of this Act, would be prejudicial to the proper care and treatment of the patient.

11. Interpretation of sections 4 to 10

(1) The following provisions apply for the interpretation of sections 4 to 10 of this Act.

(2) In those sections—

'breath test' means a preliminary test for the purpose of obtaining, by means of a device of a type approved by the Secretary of State, an indication whether the proportion of alcohol in a person's breath or blood is likely to exceed the prescribed limit,

'drug' includes any intoxicant other than alcohol,

'fail' includes refuse,

'hospital' means an institution which provides medical or surgical treatment for in-patients or out-patients,

'the prescribed limit' means, as the case may require—

(a) 35 microgrammes of alcohol in 100 millilitres of breath,

(b) 80 milligrammes of alcohol in 100 millilitres of blood, or

(c) 107 milligrammes of alcohol in 100 millilitres of urine,

or such other proportion as may be prescribed by regulations made by the Secretary of State.

(3) A person does not provide a specimen of breath for a breath test or for analysis unless the specimen—

(a) is sufficient to enable the test or the analysis to be carried out, and

(b) is provided in such a way as to enable the objective of the test or analysis to be satisfactorily achieved.

(4) A person provides a specimen of blood if and only if he consents to its being taken by a medical practitioner and it is so taken.

12. Motor racing on public ways

(1) A person who promotes or takes part in a race or trial of speed between motor vehicles on a public way is guilty of an offence.

(2) In this section 'public way' means, in England and Wales, a public highway . . .

13. Regulation of motoring events on public ways

(1) A person who promotes or takes part in a competition or trial (other than a race or trial of speed) involving the use of motor vehicles on a public way is guilty of an offence unless the competition or trial—

(a) is authorised, and

(b) is conducted in accordance with any conditions imposed,

by or under regulations under this section.

(4) In this section 'public way' means, in England and Wales, a public highway . . .

13A. Disapplication of sections 1 to 3 for authorised motoring events

(1) A person shall not be guilty of an offence under sections 1, 2 or 3 of this Act by virtue of driving a vehicle in a public place other than a road if he shows that he was driving in accordance with an authorisation for a motoring event given under regulations made by the Secretary of State.

14. Seat belts: adults

(1) The Secretary of State may make regulations requiring, subject to such exceptions as may be prescribed, persons who are driving or riding in motor vehicles on a road to wear seat belts of such description as may be prescribed.

(3) A person who drives or rides in a motor vehicle in contravention of regulations under this section is guilty of an offence; but, notwithstanding any enactment or rule of law, no person other than the person actually committing the contravention is guilty of an offence by reason of the contravention.

(6) Regulations under this section requiring the wearing of seat belts by persons riding in motor vehicles shall not apply to children under the age of fourteen years.

15. Restriction on carrying children not wearing seat belts in motor vehicles

(1) Except as provided by regulations, where a child under the age of fourteen years is in the front of a motor vehicle, a person must not without reasonable excuse drive the vehicle on a road unless the child is wearing a seat belt in conformity with regulations.

(2) It is an offence for a person to drive a motor vehicle in contravention of subsection (1) above.

(3) Except as provided by regulations, where a child under the age of fourteen years is in the rear of a motor vehicle and any seat belt is fitted in the rear of that vehicle, a person must not without reasonable excuse drive the vehicle on a road unless the child is wearing a seat belt in conformity with regulations.

(4) It is an offence for a person to drive a motor vehicle in contravention of subsection (3) above.

(9) In this section—

'regulations' means regulations made by the Secretary of State under this section, and

'seat belt' includes any description of restraining device for a child and any reference to wearing a seat belt is to be construed accordingly.

16. Wearing of protective headgear

(1) The Secretary of State may make regulations requiring, subject to such exceptions as may be specified in the regulations, persons driving or riding (otherwise than in side-cars) on motor cycles of any class specified in the regulations to wear protective headgear of such description as may be so specified.

(2) A requirement imposed by regulations under this section shall not apply to any follower of the Sikh religion while he is wearing a turban.

(4) A person who drives or rides a motor cycle in contravention of regulations under this section is guilty of an offence; but notwithstanding any enactment or rule of law no person other than the person actually committing the contravention is guilty of an offence by reason of the contravention unless the person actually committing the contravention is a child under the age of sixteen years.

18. Authorisation of head-worn appliances for use on motor cycles

(1) The Secretary of State may make regulations prescribing (by reference to shape, construction or any other quality) types of appliance of any description to which this section applies as authorised for use by persons driving or riding (otherwise than in sidecars) on motor cycles of any class specified in the regulations.

(3) If a person driving or riding on a motor cycle on a road uses an appliance of any description for which a type is prescribed under this section and that appliance—

(a) is not of a type so prescribed, or

(b) is otherwise used in contravention of regulations under this section,

he is guilty of an offence.

(4) If a person sells, or offers for sale, an appliance of any such description as authorised for use by persons on or in motor cycles, or motor cycles of any class, and that appliance is not of a type prescribed under this section as authorised for such use, he is, subject to subsection (5) below, guilty of an offence.

(5) A person shall not be convicted of an offence under this section in respect of the sale or offer for sale of an appliance if he proves that it was sold or, as the case may be, offered for sale for export from Great Britain.

(7) This section applies to appliances of any description designed or adapted for use—

(a) with any headgear, or

(b) by being attached to or placed upon the head,

(as, for example, eye protectors or earphones).

(8) References in this section to selling or offering for sale include respectively references to letting on hire and offering to let on hire.

22. Leaving vehicles in dangerous positions

If a person in charge of a vehicle causes or permits the vehicle or a trailer drawn by it to remain at rest on a road in such a position or in such condition or in such circumstances as to be likely to cause danger to other persons using the road, he is guilty of an offence.

22A. Causing danger to road-users

(1) A person is guilty of an offence if he intentionally and without lawful authority or reasonable cause—

(a) causes anything to be on or over a road, or

(b) interferes with a motor vehicle, trailer or cycle, or

(c) interferes (directly or indirectly) with traffic equipment,

in such circumstances that it would be obvious to a reasonable person that to do so would be dangerous.

(2) In subsection (1) above 'dangerous' refers to danger either of injury to any person while on or near a road, or of serious damage to property on or near a road; and in determining for the purposes of that subsection what would be obvious to a reasonable person in a particular case, regard shall be had not only to the circumstances of which he could be expected to be aware but also to any circumstances shown to have been within the knowledge of the accused.

(3) In subsection (1) above 'traffic equipment' means—

(a)   anything lawfully placed on or near a road by a highway authority;

(b)   a traffic sign lawfully placed on or near a road by a person other than a highway authority;

(c)   any fence, barrier or light lawfully placed on or near a road—

(i)   in pursuance of section 174 of the Highways Act 1980, section 8 of the Public Utilities Street Works Act 1950 or section 61 of the New Roads and Street Works Act 1991 (which provide for guarding, lighting and signing in streets where works are undertaken), or

(ii)   by a constable or a person acting under the instructions (whether general or specific) of a chief officer of police.

(4)   For the purposes of subsection (3) above anything placed on or near a road shall unless the contrary is proved be deemed to have been lawfully placed there.

(5)   In this section 'road' does not include a footpath or bridleway.

23.   Restriction of carriage of persons on motor cycles

(1)   Not more than one person in addition to the driver may be carried on a two-wheeled motor cycle.

(2)   No person in addition to the driver may be carried on a two-wheeled motor cycle otherwise than sitting astride the motor cycle and on a proper seat securely fixed to the motor cycle behind the driver's seat.

(3)   If a person is carried on a motor cycle in contravention of this section, the driver of the motor cycle is guilty of an offence.

24.   Restriction of carriage of persons on bicycles

(1)   Not more than one person may be carried on a road on a bicycle not propelled by mechanical power unless it is constructed or adapted for the carriage of more than one person.

(2)   In this section—

(a)   references to a person carried on a bicycle include references to a person riding the bicycle, and

(b)   'road' includes bridleway.

(3)   If a person is carried on a bicycle in contravention of subsection (1) above, each of the persons carried is guilty of an offence.

25.   Tampering with motor vehicles

If, while a motor vehicle is on a road or on a parking place provided by a local authority, a person—

(a)   gets on to the vehicle, or

(b)   tampers with the brake or other part of its mechanism,

without lawful authority or reasonable cause he is guilty of an offence.

26.   Holding or getting on to vehicle in order to be towed or carried

(1)   If, for the purpose of being carried, a person without lawful authority or reasonable cause takes or retains hold of, or gets on to, a motor vehicle or trailer while in motion on a road he is guilty of an offence.

(2)   If, for the purpose of being drawn, a person takes or retains hold of a motor vehicle or trailer while in motion on a road he is guilty of an offence.

27.   Control of dogs on roads

(1)   A person who causes or permits a dog to be on a designated road without the dog being held on a lead is guilty of an offence.

(2)   In this section 'designated road' means a length of road specified by an order in that behalf of the local authority in whose area the length of road is situated.

(4)   An order under this section may provide that subsection (1) above shall apply subject to such limitations or exceptions as may be specified in the order, and (without

prejudice to the generality of this subsection) subsection (1) above does not apply to dogs proved—

(a)   to be kept for driving or tending sheep or cattle in the course of a trade or business, or

(b)   to have been at the material time in use under proper control for sporting purposes.

28.   Dangerous cycling

(1)   A person who rides a cycle on a road dangerously is guilty of an offence.

(2)   For the purposes of subsection (1) above a person is to be regarded as riding dangerously if (and only if)—

(a)   the way he rides falls far below what would be expected of a competent and careful cyclist, and

(b)   it would be obvious to a competent and careful cyclist that riding in that way would be dangerous.

(3)   In subsection (2) above 'dangerous' refers to danger either of injury to any person or of serious damage to property; and in determining for the purposes of that subsection what would be obvious to a competent and careful cyclist in a particular case, regard shall be had not only to the circumstances of which he could be expected to be aware but also to any circumstances shown to have been within the knowledge of the accused.

29.   Careless, and inconsiderate, cycling

If a person rides a cycle on a road without due care and attention, or without reasonable consideration for other persons using the road, he is guilty of an offence.

In this section 'road' includes a bridleway.

30.   Cycling when under influence of drink or drugs

(1)   A person who, when riding a cycle on a road or other public place, is unfit to ride through drink or drugs (that is to say, is under the influence of drink or a drug to such an extent as to be incapable of having proper control of the cycle) is guilty of an offence.

(3)   In this section 'road' includes a bridleway.

31.   Regulation of cycle racing on public ways

(1)   A person who promotes or takes part in a race or trial of speed on a public way between cycles is guilty of an offence, unless the race or trial—

(a)   is authorised, and

(b)   is conducted in accordance with any conditions imposed,

by or under regulations under this section.

(6)   In this section 'public way' means, in England and Wales, a public highway . . .

34.   Prohibition of driving motor vehicles elsewhere than on roads

(1)   Subject to the provisions of this section, if without lawful authority a person drives a motor vehicle—

(a)   on to or upon any common land, moorland or land of any other description, not being land forming part of a road, or

(b)   on any road being a footpath or bridleway,

he is guilty of an offence.

(2)   It is not an offence under this section to drive a motor vehicle on any land within fifteen yards of a road, being a road on which a motor vehicle may lawfully be driven, for the purpose only of parking the vehicle on that land.

(3)   A person shall not be convicted of an offence under this section with respect to a vehicle if he proves to the satisfaction of the court that it was driven in contravention of this section for the purpose of saving life or extinguishing fire or meeting any other like emergency.

35. Drivers to comply with traffic directions

(1) Where a constable is for the time being engaged in the regulation of traffic in a road, a person driving or propelling a vehicle who neglects or refuses—

(a) to stop the vehicle, or

(b) to make it proceed in, or keep to, a particular line of traffic,

when directed to do so by the constable in the execution of his duty is guilty of an offence.

(2) Where—

(a) a traffic survey of any description is being carried out on or in the vicinity of a road, and

(b) a constable gives to a person driving or propelling a vehicle a direction—

(i) to stop the vehicle,

(ii) to make it proceed in, or keep to, a particular line of traffic, or

(iii) to proceed to a particular point on or near the road on which the vehicle is being driven or propelled,

being a direction given for the purposes of the survey (but not a direction requiring any person to provide any information for the purposes of a traffic survey),

the person is guilty of an offence if he neglects or refuses to comply with the direction.

36. Drivers to comply with traffic signs

(1) Where a traffic sign, being a sign—

(a) of the prescribed size, colour and type, or

(b) of another character authorised by the Secretary of State under the provisions in that behalf of the Road Traffic Regulation Act 1984,

has been lawfully placed on or near a road, a person driving or propelling a vehicle who fails to comply with the indication given by the sign is guilty of an offence.

(2) A traffic sign shall not be treated for the purposes of this section as having been lawfully placed unless either—

(a) the indication given by the sign is an indication of a statutory prohibition, restriction or requirement, or

(b) it is expressly provided by or under any provision of the Traffic Acts that this section shall apply to the sign or to signs of a type of which the sign is one;

and, where the indication mentioned in paragraph (a) of this subsection is of the general nature only of the prohibition, restriction or requirement to which the sign relates, a person shall not be convicted of failure to comply with the indication unless he has failed to comply with the prohibition, restriction or requirement to which the sign relates.

(3) For the purposes of this section a traffic sign placed on or near a road shall be deemed—

(a) to be of the prescribed size, colour and type, or of another character authorised by the Secretary of State under the provisions in that behalf of the Road Traffic Regulation Act 1984, and

(b) (subject to subsection (2) above) to have been lawfully so placed,

unless the contrary is proved.

(4) Where a traffic survey of any description is being carried out on or in the vicinity of a road, this section applies to a traffic sign by which a direction is given—

(a) to stop a vehicle,

(b) to make it proceed in, or keep to, a particular line of traffic, or

(c) to proceed to a particular point on or near the road on which the vehicle is being driven or propelled,

being a direction given for the purposes of the survey (but not a direction requiring any person to provide any information for the purposes of the survey).

37. Directions to pedestrians

Where a constable in uniform is for the time being engaged in the regulation of vehicular traffic in a road, a person on foot who proceeds across or along the carriageway in contravention of a direction to stop given by the constable in the execution of his duty, either to persons on foot or to persons on foot and other traffic, is guilty of an offence.

40A. Using vehicles in dangerous condition

A person is guilty of an offence if he uses, or causes or permits another to use, a motor vehicle or trailer on a road when—

(a) the condition of the motor vehicle or trailer, or of its accessories or equipment, or

(b) the purpose for which it is used, or

(c) the number of passengers carried by it or the manner in which they are carried, or

(d) the weight, position or distribution of its load, or the manner in which it is secured,

is such that the use of the motor vehicle or trailer involves a danger of injury to any person.

41A. Breach of requirement as to brakes, steering-gear or tyres

A person who—

(a) contravenes or fails to comply with a construction and use requirement as to brakes, steering-gear or tyres, or

(b) uses on a road a motor vehicle or trailer which does not comply with such a requirement, or causes or permits a motor vehicle or trailer to be so used, is guilty of an offence.

41B. Breach of requirement as to weight: goods and passenger vehicles

(1) A person who—

(a) contravenes or fails to comply with a construction and use requirement as to any description of weight applicable to—

(i) a goods vehicle, or

(ii) a motor vehicle or trailer adapted to carry more than eight passengers, or

(b) uses on a road a vehicle which does not comply with such a requirement, or causes or permits a vehicle to be so used,

is guilty of an offence.

(2) In any proceedings for an offence under this section in which there is alleged a contravention of or failure to comply with a construction and use requirement as to any description of weight applicable to a goods vehicle, it shall be a defence to prove either—

(a) that at the time when the vehicle was being used on the road—

(i) it was proceeding to a weighbridge which was the nearest available one to the place where the loading of the vehicle was completed for the purpose of being weighed, or

(ii) it was proceeding from a weighbridge after being weighed to the nearest point at which it was reasonably practicable to reduce the weight to the relevant limit, without causing an obstruction on any road, or

(b) in a case where the limit of that weight was not exceeded by more than 5 per cent.—

(i) that that limit was not exceeded at the time when the loading of the vehicle was originally completed, and

(ii) that since that time no person has made any addition to the load.

42. Breach of other construction and use requirements

A person who—

(a)   contravenes or fails to comply with any construction or use requirement other than one within section 41A(a) or 41B(1)(a) of this Act, or

(b)   uses on a road a motor vehicle or trailer which does not comply with such a requirement, or causes or permits a motor vehicle or trailer to be so used, is guilty of an offence.

75. Vehicles not to be sold in unroadworthy condition or altered so as to be unroadworthy

(1)   Subject to the provisions of this section no person shall supply a motor vehicle or trailer in an unroadworthy condition.

(2)   In this section references to supply include—

(a)   sell,

(b)   offer to sell or supply, and

(c)   expose for sale.

(3)   For the purposes of subsection (1) above a motor vehicle or trailer is in an unroadworthy condition if—

(a)   it is in such a condition that the use of it on a road in that condition would be unlawful by virtue of any provision made by regulations under section 41 of this Act as respects—

(i)   brakes, steering-gear or tyres, or

(ii)   the construction, weight or equipment of vehicles, or

(b)   it is in such a condition that its use on a road would involve a danger of injury to any person.

(4)   Subject to the provisions of this section no person shall alter a motor vehicle or trailer so as to render its condition such that the use of it on a road in that condition

(a)   would be unlawful by virtue of any provision made as respects the construction, weight or equipment of vehicles by regulations under section 41, or

(b)   would involve a danger of injury to any person.

(5)   A person who supplies or alters a motor vehicle or trailer in contravention of this section, or causes or permits it to be so supplied or altered, is guilty of an offence.

(6)   A person shall not be convicted of an offence under this section in respect of the supply or alteration of a motor vehicle or trailer if he proves—

(a)   that it was supplied or altered, as the case may be, for export from Great Britain, or

(b)   that he had reasonable cause to believe that the vehicle or trailer would not be used on a road in Great Britain, or would not be so used until it had been put into a condition in which it might lawfully be so used.

(6A)   Paragraph (b) of subsection (6) above shall not apply in relation to a person who, in the course of a trade or business—

(a)   exposes a vehicle or trailer for sale, unless he also proves that he took all reasonable steps to ensure that any prospective purchaser would be aware that its use in its current condition on a road in Great Britain would be unlawful, or

(b)   offers to sell a vehicle or trailer, unless he also proves that he took all reasonable steps to ensure that the person to whom the offer was made was aware of that fact.

76. Fitting and supply of defective or unsuitable vehicle parts

(1)   If any person—

(a)   fits a vehicle part to a vehicle, or

(b)   causes or permits a vehicle part to be fitted to a vehicle,

in such circumstances that the use of the vehicle on a road would, by reason of that part being fitted to the vehicle, constitute a contravention of or failure to comply with any of the construction and use requirements, he is guilty of an offence.

(2)   A person shall not be convicted of an offence under subsection (1) above if he proves—

(a)   that the vehicle to which the part was fitted was to be exported from Great Britain, or

(b)   that he had reasonable cause to believe that that vehicle—

(i)   would not be used on a road in Great Britain, or

(ii)   that it would not be so used until it had been put into a condition in which its use would not constitute a contravention of or a failure to comply with any of the construction and use requirements.

(3)   If a person—

(a)   supplies a vehicle part or causes or permits a vehicle part to be supplied, and

(b)   has reasonable cause to believe that the part is to be fitted to a motor vehicle, or to a vehicle of a particular class, or to a particular vehicle,

he is guilty of an offence if that part could not be fitted to a motor vehicle, or, as the case may require, to a vehicle of that class or of a class to which the particular vehicle belongs, except in such circumstances that the use of the vehicle on a road would, by reason of that part being fitted to the vehicle, constitute a contravention of or failure to comply with any of the construction and use requirements.

(4)   In this section references to supply include—

(a)   sell, and

(b)   offer to sell or supply.

(5)   A person shall not be convicted of an offence under subsection (3) above in respect of the supply of a vehicle part if he proves—

(a)   that the part was supplied for export from Great Britain, or

(b)   that he had reasonable cause to believe that—

(i)   it would not be fitted to a vehicle used on a road in Great Britain, or

(ii)   it would not be so fitted until it had been put into such a condition that it could be fitted otherwise than in such circumstances that the use of the vehicle on a road would, by reason of that part being fitted to the vehicle, constitute a contravention of or failure to comply with any of the construction and use requirements.

87.   Drivers of motor vehicles to have driving licences

(1)   It is an offence for a person to drive on a road a motor vehicle of any class otherwise than in accordance with a licence authorising him to drive a motor vehicle of that class.

(2)   It is an offence for a person to cause or permit another person to drive on a road a motor vehicle of any class otherwise than in accordance with a licence authorising that person to drive a motor vehicle of that class.

103.   Obtaining licence, or driving, while disqualified

(1)   A person is guilty of an offence if, while disqualified for holding or obtaining a licence, he—

(a)   obtains a licence, or

(b)   drives a motor vehicle on a road.

(2)   A licence obtained by a person who is disqualified is of no effect (or, where the disqualification relates only to vehicles of a particular class, is of no effect in relation to vehicles of that class).

143.   Users of motor vehicles to be insured or secured against third-party risks

(1)   Subject to the provisions of Part [VI] of this Act—

(a)   a person must not use a motor vehicle on a road unless there is in force in relation to the use of the vehicle by that person such a policy of insurance or such a security in respect of third party risks as complies with the requirements of Part [VI] of this Act, and

(b) a person must not cause or permit any other person to use a motor vehicle on a road unless there is in force in relation to the use of the vehicle by that other person such a policy of insurance or such a security in respect of third party risks as complies with the requirements of Part [VI] of this Act.

(2) If a person acts in contravention of subsection (1) above he is guilty of an offence.

(3) A person charged with using a motor vehicle in contravention of this section shall not be convicted if he proves—

(a) that the vehicle did not belong to him and was not in his possession under a contract of hiring or of loan,

(b) that he was using the vehicle in the course of his employment, and

(c) that he neither knew nor had reason to believe that there was not in force in relation to the vehicle such a policy of insurance of security as is mentioned in subsection (1) above.

(4) Part [VI] of this Act does not apply to invalid carriages.

168. Failure to give, or giving false, name and address in case of dangerous or careless or inconsiderate driving or cycling

Any of the following persons—

(a) the driver of a motor vehicle who is alleged to have committed an offence under section 2 or 3 of this Act, or

(b) the rider of a cycle who is alleged to have committed an offence under section 28 or 29 of this Act,

who refuses, on being so required by any person having reasonable ground for so requiring, to give his name or address, or gives a false name or address, is guilty of an offence.

169. Pedestrian contravening constable's direction to stop to give name and address

A constable may require a person committing an offence under section 37 of this Act to give his name and address, and if that person fails to do so he is guilty of an offence.

170. Duty of driver to stop, report accident and give information or documents

(1) This section applies in a case where, owing to the presence of a mechanically propelled vehicle on a road, an accident occurs by which—

(a) personal injury is caused to a person other than the driver of that mechanically propelled vehicle, or

(b) damage is caused—

(i) to a vehicle other than that mechanically propelled vehicle or a trailer drawn by that mechanically propelled vehicle, or

(ii) to an animal other than an animal in or on that mechanically propelled vehicle or a trailer drawn by that mechanically propelled vehicle, or

(iii) to any other property constructed on, fixed to, growing in or otherwise forming part of the land on which the road in question is situated or land adjacent to such land.

(2) The driver of the motor vehicle must stop and, if required to do so by any person having reasonable grounds for so requiring, give his name and address and also the name and address of the owner and the identification marks of the vehicle.

(3) If for any reason the driver of the motor vehicle does not give his name and address under subsection (2) above, he must report the accident.

(4) A person who fails to comply with subsection (2) or (3) above is guilty of an offence.

(5)   If, in a case where this section applies by virtue of subsection (1)(a) above, the driver of a motor vehicle does not at the time of the accident produce such a certificate of insurance or security, or other evidence, as is mentioned in section 165(2)(a) of this Act—

(a)   to a constable, or

(b)   to some person who, having reasonable grounds for so doing, has required him to produce it,

the driver must report the accident and produce such a certificate or other evidence.

This subsection does not apply to the driver of an invalid carriage.

(6)   To comply with a duty under this section to report an accident or to produce such a certificate of insurance or security, or other evidence, as is mentioned in section 165(2)(a) of this Act, the driver—

(a)   must do so at a police station or to a constable, and

(b)   must do so as soon as is reasonably practicable and, in any case, within twenty-four hours of the occurrence of the accident.

(7)   A person who fails to comply with a duty under subsection (5) above is guilty of an offence, but he shall not be convicted by reason only of a failure to produce a certificate or other evidence if, within five days after the occurrence of the accident, the certificate or other evidence is produced at a police station that was specified by him at the time when the accident was reported.

(8)   In this section 'animal' means horse, cattle, ass, mule, sheep, pig, goat or dog.

171.   Duty of owner of motor vehicle to give information for verifying compliance with requirement of compulsory insurance or security

(1)   For the purpose of determining whether a motor vehicle was or was not being driven in contravention of section 143 of this Act on any occasion when the driver was required under section 165(1) or 170 of this Act to produce such a certificate of insurance or security, or other evidence, as is mentioned in section 165(2)(a) of this Act, the owner of the vehicle must give such information as he may be required, by or on behalf of a chief officer of police, to give.

(2)   A person who fails to comply with the requirement of subsection (1) above is guilty of an offence.

(3)   In this section 'owner', in relation to a vehicle which is the subject of a hiring agreement, includes each party to the agreement.

172.   Duty to give information as to identity of driver etc., in certain circumstances

(1)   This section applies—

(a)   to any offence under the preceding provisions of this Act except—

(i)   an offence under Part V, or

(ii)   an offence under section 13, 16, 51(2), 61(4), 67(9), 68(4), 96 or 120, and to an offence under section 178 of this Act,

(b)   to any offence under sections 25, 26 or 27 of the Road Traffic Offenders Act 1988,

(c)   to any offence against any other enactment relating to the use of vehicles on roads, except an offence under paragraph 8 of Schedule 1 to the Road Traffic (Driver Licensing and Information Systems) Act 1989, and

(d)   to manslaughter . . . by the driver of a motor vehicle.

(2)   Where the driver of a vehicle is alleged to be guilty of an offence to which this section applies—

(a)   the person keeping the vehicle shall give such information as to the identity of the driver as he may be required to give by or on behalf of a chief officer of police, and

(b)   any other person shall if required as stated above give any information which it is in his power to give and may lead to identification of the driver.

(3)   Subject to the following provisions, a person who fails to comply with a requirement under subsection (2) above shall be guilty of an offence.

(4)   A person shall not be guilty of an offence by virtue of paragraph (a) of subsection (2) above if he shows that he did not know and could not with reasonable diligence have ascertained who the driver of the vehicle was.

(5)   Where a body corporate is guilty of an offence under this section and the offence is proved to have been committed with the consent or connivance of, or to be attributable to neglect on the part of, a director, manager, secretary or other similar officer of the body corporate, or a person who was purporting to act in any such capacity, he, as well as the body corporate, is guilty of that offence and liable to be proceeded against and punished accordingly.

(6)   Where the alleged offender is a body corporate, . . . or the proceedings are brought against him by virtue of subsection (5) above or subsection (11) below, subsection (4) above shall not apply unless, in addition to the matters there mentioned, the alleged offender shows that no record was kept of the persons who drove the vehicle and that the failure to keep a record was reasonable.

(7)   A requirement under subsection (2) may be made by written notice served by post; and where it is so made—

(a)   it shall have effect as a requirement to give the information within the period of 28 days beginning with the day on which the notice is served, and

(b)   the person on whom the notice is served shall not be guilty of an offence under this section if he shows either that he gave the information as soon as reasonably practicable after the end of that period or that it has not been reasonably practicable for him to give it.

(8)   Where the person on whom a notice under subsection (7) above is to be served is a body corporate, the notice is duly served if it is served on the secretary or clerk of that body.

(9)   For the purposes of section 7 of the Interpretation Act 1978 as it applies for the purposes of this section the proper address of any person in relation to the service on him of a notice under subsection (7) above is—

(a)   in the case of the secretary or clerk of a body corporate, that of the registered or principal office of that body or (if the body corporate is the registered keeper of the vehicle concerned) the registered address, and

(b)   in any other case, his last known address at the time of service.

(10)   In this section—

'registered address', in relation to the registered keeper of a vehicle, means the address recorded in the record kept under the Vehicles (Excise) Act 1971 with respect to that vehicle as being that person's address, and

'registered keeper', in relation to a vehicle, means the person in whose name the vehicle is registered under that Act;

and references to the driver of a vehicle include references to the rider of a cycle.

185.   Meaning of 'motor vehicle' and other expressions relating to vehicles

(1)   In this Act—

. . .

'invalid carriage' means a mechanically propelled vehicle the weight of which unladen does not exceed 254 kilograms and which is specially designed and constructed, and not merely adapted, for the use of a person suffering from some physical defect or disability and is used solely by such a person,

. . .

'motor car' means a mechanically propelled vehicle, not being a motor cycle or an invalid carriage, which is constructed itself to carry a load or passengers and the weight of which unladen—

(a)   if it is constructed solely for the carriage of passengers and their effects, is adapted to carry not more than seven passengers exclusive of the driver and is fitted with tyres of such type as may be specified in regulations made by the Secretary of State, does not exceed 3050 kilograms,

(b)   if it is constructed or adapted for use for the conveyance of goods or burden of any description, does not exceed 3050 kilograms, or 3500 kilograms if the vehicle carries a container or containers for holding for the purposes of its propulsion any fuel which is wholly gaseous at 17.5 degrees Celsius under a pressure of 1.013 bar or plant and materials for producing such fuel,

(c)   does not exceed 2540 kilograms in a case not falling within sub-paragraph (a) or (b) above,

'motor cycle' means a mechanically propelled vehicle, not being an invalid carriage, with less than four wheels and the weight of which unladen does not exceed 410 kilograms,

. . .

'motor vehicle' means, subject to section 20 of the Chronically Sick and Disabled Persons Act 1970 (which makes special provision about invalid carriages, within the meaning of that Act), a mechanically propelled vehicle intended or adapted for use on roads, and

'trailer' means a vehicle drawn by a motor vehicle.

. . .

192.   General interpretation of Act

(1)   In this Act—

'bridleway' means a way over which the public have the following, but no other, rights of way: a right of way on foot and a right of way on horseback or leading a horse, with or without a right to drive animals of any description along the way,

'carriage of goods' includes the haulage of goods,

'cycle' means a bicycle, a tricycle, or a cycle having four or more wheels, not being in any case a motor vehicle,

'driver', where a separate person acts as a steersman of a motor vehicle, includes (except for the purposes of section 1 of this Act) that person as well as any other person engaged in the driving of the vehicle, and 'drive' is to be interpreted accordingly,

'footpath', in relation to England and Wales, means a way over which the public have a right of way on foot only,

'goods' includes goods or burden of any description,

'goods vehicle' means a motor vehicle constructed or adapted for use for the carriage of goods, or a trailer so constructed or adapted,

'highway authority', in relation to England and Wales, means—

(a)   in relation to a road other than a trunk road, the authority (being either the council of a county, metropolitan district or London borough or the Common Council of the City of London) which is responsible for the maintenance of the road, and

(b)   in relation to a trunk road, the Secretary of State.

. . .

'owner', in relation to a vehicle which is the subject of a hiring agreement or hire-purchase agreement, means the person in possession of the vehicle under that agreement,

'petty sessions area' has the same meaning as in the Magistrates' Courts Act 1980,

'prescribed' means prescribed by regulations made by the Secretary of State,

'road', in relation to England and Wales, means any highway and any other road to which the public has access, and includes bridges over which a road passes, 'the Road Traffic Acts' means the Road Traffic Offenders Act 1988, the Road Traffic (Consequential Provisions) Act 1988 (so far as it reproduces the effect of provisions repealed by that Act) and this Act,

'statutory', in relation to any prohibition, restriction, requirement or provision, means contained in, or having effect under, any enactment (including any enactment contained in this Act),

'the Traffic Acts' means the Road Traffic Acts and the Road Traffic Regulation Act 1984,

'traffic sign' has the meaning given by section 64(1) of the Road Traffic Regulation Act 1984,

'tramcar' includes any carriage used on any road by virtue of an order under the Light Railways Act 1896, and

'trolley vehicle' means a mechanically propelled vehicle adapted for use on roads without rails and moved by power transmitted to it from some external source.

. . .

(3)   References in this Act to a class of vehicles are to be interpreted as references to a class defined or described by reference to any characteristics of the vehicles or to any other circumstances whatsoever.

THEFT ACT 1968

12A.   Aggravated vehicle taking
[See pages 146–147]

HIGHWAYS ACT 1980

137.   Penalty for wilful obstruction
(1)   If a person, without lawful authority or excuse, in any way wilfully obstructs the free passage along a highway he is guilty of an offence and liable to a fine not exceeding level 3 on the standard scale.

161.   Penalties for causing certain kinds of danger or annoyance
(1)   If a person, without lawful authority or excuse, deposits any thing whatsoever on a highway in consequence of which a user of the highway is injured or endangered, that person is guilty of an offence and liable to a fine not exceeding level 3 on the standard scale.

(2)   If a person, without lawful authority or excuse, lights any fire, or discharges any firearm or firework, within fifty feet of the centre of a highway which consists of or comprises a carriageway, and in consequence a user of the highway is injured, interrupted or endangered, that person is guilty of an offence and liable to a fine not exceeding level 3 on the standard scale.

(3)   If a person plays at football or any other game on a highway to the annoyance of a user of the highway he is guilty of an offence and liable to a fine not exceeding level 1 on the standard scale.

(4)   If a person, without lawful authority or excuse, allows any filth, dirt, lime or other offensive matter or thing to run or flow on to a highway from any adjoining premises, he is guilty of an offence and liable to a fine not exceeding level 1 on the standard scale.

162.   Penalty for placing rope, etc., across highway
A person who for any purpose places any rope, wire or other apparatus across a highway in such a manner as to be likely to cause danger to persons using the highway is, unless he proves that he had taken all necessary means to give adequate warning of the danger, guilty of an offence and liable, to a fine not exceeding level 3 on the standard scale.

ROAD TRAFFIC REGULATION ACT 1984

81. General speed limit for restricted roads
(1) It shall not be lawful for a person to drive a motor vehicle on a restricted road at a speed exceeding 30 miles per hour.

(2) The Ministers acting jointly may by order made by statutory instrument and approved by a resolution of each House of Parliament increase or reduce the rate of speed fixed by subsection (1) above, either as originally enacted or as varied under this subsection.

82. What roads are restricted roads
(1) Subject to the provisions of this section and of section 84(3) of this Act, a road is a restricted road for the purposes of section 81 of this Act if there is provided on it a system of street lighting furnished by means of lamps placed not more than 200 yards apart.

(2) A direction may be given—

(a) that a specified road which is a restricted road for the purposes of section 81 of this Act shall cease to be a restricted road for those purposes, or

(b) that a specified road which is not a restricted road for those purposes shall become a restricted road for those purposes.

83. Provisions as to directions under s 82(2)
(1) Any direction under section 82(2) of this Act in respect of a trunk road shall be given by means of an order made by the Secretary of State after giving public notice of his intention to make an order.

(2) Any such direction in respect of a road which is not a trunk road shall, subject to Parts I to III of Schedule 9 to this Act, be given by means of an order made by the local authority.

84. Speed limits on roads other than restricted roads
(1) An order made under this subsection as respects any road may prohibit—

(a) the driving of motor vehicles on that road at a speed exceeding that specified in the order,

(b) the driving of motor vehicles on that road at a speed exceeding that specified in the order during periods specified in the order, or

(c) the driving of motor vehicles on that road at a speed exceeding the speed for the time being indicated by traffic signs in accordance with the order.

(1A) An order made by virtue of subsection (1)(c) above may—

(a) make provision restricting the speeds that may be indicated by traffic signs or the periods during which the indication may be given, and

(b) provide for the indications to be given only in such circumstances as may be determined by or under the order;

but any such order must comply with regulations made under subsection (1B) below, except where the Secretary of State authorises otherwise in a particular case.

(1B) The Secretary of State may make regulations governing the provision which may be made by orders of local authorities under subsection (1)(c) above, and any such regulations may in particular—

(a) prescribe the circumstances in which speed limits may have effect by virtue of an order,

(c) make transitional provision and different provision for different cases.

(2) The power to make an order under subsection (1) is exercisable by the traffic authority, who shall before exercising it in any case give public notice of their intention to do so.

(3)   While an order made by virtue of subsection (1)(a) above is in force as respects a road, that road shall not be a restricted road for the purposes of section 81 of this Act.

(4)   This section does not apply to any part of a special road which is open for use as a special road.

85.   Traffic signs for indicating speed restrictions

(4)   Where no such system of street or carriageway lighting as is mentioned in section 82(1) is provided on a road, but a limit of speed is to be observed on the road, a person shall not be convicted of driving a motor vehicle on the road at a speed exceeding the limit unless the limit is indicated by means of such traffic signs as are mentioned in subsection (1) or subsection (2) above.

(5)   In any proceedings for a contravention of section 81 of this Act, where the proceedings relate to driving on a road provided with such a system of street or carriageway lighting, evidence of the absence of traffic signs displayed in pursuance of this section to indicate that the road is not a restricted road for the purposes of that section shall be evidence that the road is a restricted road for those purposes.

86.   Speed limits for particular classes of vehicles

(1)   It shall not be lawful for a person to drive a motor vehicle of any class on a road at a speed greater than the speed specified in Schedule 6 to this Act as the maximum speed in relation to a vehicle of that class.

87.   Exemption of fire brigade, ambulance and police vehicles from speed limits

No statutory provision imposing a speed limit on motor vehicles shall apply to any vehicle on an occasion when it is being used for fire brigade, ambulance or police purposes, if the observance of that provision would be likely to hinder the use of the vehicle for the purpose for which it is being used on that occasion.

89.   Speeding offences generally

(1)   A person who drives a motor vehicle on a road at a speed exceeding a limit imposed by or under any enactment to which this section applies shall be guilty of an offence.

(4)   If a person who employs other persons to drive motor vehicles on roads publishes or issues any time-table or schedule, or gives any directions, under which any journey, or any stage or part of any journey, is to be completed within some specified time, and it is not practicable in the circumstances of the case for that journey (or that stage or part of it) to be completed in the specified time without the commission of such an offence as is mentioned in subsection (1) above, the publication or issue of the time-table or schedule, or the giving of the directions may be produced as prima facie evidence that the employer procured or (as the case may be) incited the persons employed by him to drive the vehicles to commit such an offence.

TOWN POLICE CLAUSES ACT 1847

28.   Penalty on persons committing any of the offences herein named

Every person who in any street, to the obstruction, annoyance, or danger of the residents or passengers, commits any of the following offences, shall be liable to a penalty not exceeding [level 3 on the standard scale] for each offence, or, in the discretion of the justice before whom he is convicted, may be committed to prison, there to remain for a period not exceeding fourteen days; . . . ; (that is to say,)

Every person who exposes for show, hire, or sale (except in a market or market place or fair lawfully appointed for that purpose) any horse or other animal, or exhibits in a caravan or otherwise any show or public entertainment, or shoes, bleeds, or farries any horse or animal (except in cases of accident), or cleans, dresses, exercises, trains, or breaks, or turns loose any horse or animal, or makes or repairs any part of any cart or carriage (except in cases of accident where repair on the spot is necessary):

Every person who suffers to be at large any unmuzzled ferocious dog, or sets on or urges any dog or other animal to attack, worry, or put in fear any person or animal:

Every person who slaughters or dresses any cattle, or any part thereof, except in the case of any cattle over-driven which may have met with any accident, and which for the public safety or other reasonable cause ought to be killed on the spot:

Every person having the care of any waggon, cart, or carriage who rides on the shafts thereof, or who without having reins, and holding the same, rides upon such waggon, cart, or carriage or on any animal drawing the same, or who is at such a distance from such waggon, cart, or carriage, as not to have due control over every animal drawing the same, or who does not, in meeting any other carriage, keep his waggon, cart, or carriage to the left or near side or who in passing any other carriage does not keep his waggon, cart, or carriage on the right or off side of the road, (except in cases of actual necessity, or some sufficient reason for deviation,) or who, by obstructing the street, wilfully prevents any person or carriage from passing him, or any waggon, cart, or carriage under his care:

Every person who rides or drives furiously any horse or carriage, or drives furiously any cattle:

Every person who causes any public carriage, sledge, truck, or barrow, with or without horses, or any beast of burden, to stand longer than is necessary for loading or unloading goods, or for taking up or setting down passengers, (except hackney carriages, and horses and other beasts of draught or burthen, standing for hire in any place appointed for that purpose by the commissioners or other lawful authority,) and every person who, by means of any cart, carriage, sledge, truck, or barrow, or any animal, or other means wilfully interrupts any public crossing, or wilfully causes any obstruction in any public footpath or other public thoroughfare:

Every person who causes any tree or timber or iron beam to be drawn in or upon any carriage, without having sufficient means of safely guiding the same:

Every person who leads or rides any horse or other animal, or draws or drives any cart or carriage, sledge, truck, or barrow, upon any footway of any street, or fastens any horse or other animal so that it stands across or upon any footway:

Every person who places or leaves any furniture, goods, wares, or merchandize, or any cask, tub, basket, pail, or bucket, or places or uses any standing-place, stool, bench, stall, or showboard, on any footway, or who places any blind, shade, covering, awning, or other projection over or along any such footway, unless such blind, shade, covering, awning, or other projection is eight feet in height at least in every part thereof from the ground:

Every person who places, hangs up, or otherwise exposes to sale any goods, wares, merchandize, matter, or thing whatsoever, so that the same project into or over any footway, or beyond the line of any house, shop, or building at which the same are so exposed, so as to obstruct or incommode the passage of any person over or along such footway:

Every person who rolls or carries any cask, tub, hoop, or wheel, or any ladder, plank, pole, timber, or log of wood, upon any footway, except for the purpose of loading or unloading any cart or carriage, or of crossing the footway:

Every person who places any line, cord, or pole across any street, or hangs or places any clothes thereon:

Every person who wilfully and indecently exposes his person:

Every person who publicly offers for sale or distribution, or exhibits to public view any profane . . . book, paper, print, drawing, painting, or representation, or sings any profane or obscene song or ballad, or uses any profane or obscene language:

Every person who wantonly discharges any firearm, or throws or discharges any stone or other missile, or makes any bonfire, or throws or sets fire to any firework:

Every person who wilfully and wantonly disturbs any inhabitant, by pulling or ringing any door bell, or knocking at any door, or who wilfully and unlawfully extinguishes the light of any lamp:

Every person who flies any kite, or who makes or uses any slide upon ice or snow:

Every person who cleanses, hoops, fires, washes, or scalds any cask or tub, or hews, saws, bores, or cuts any timber or stone, or slacks, sifts, or screens any lime:

Every person who throws or lays down any stones, coals, slate, shells, lime, bricks, timber, iron, or other materials (except building materials so inclosed as to prevent mischief to passengers):

Every person who beats or shakes any carpet, rug, or mat (except door mats beaten or shaken before the hour of eight in the morning):

Every person who fixes or places any flower-pot or box, or other heavy article, in any upper window, without sufficiently guarding the same against being blown down:

Every person who throws from the roof or any part of any house or other building any slate, brick, wood, rubbish, or other thing, except snow thrown so as not to fall on any passenger:

Every occupier of any house or other building, or other person, who orders or permits any person in his service to stand on the sill of any window, in order to clean, paint, or perform any other operation upon the outside of such window, or upon any house or other building within the said limits, unless such window be in the sunk or basement storey:

Every person who leaves open any vault or cellar, or the entrance from any street to any cellar or room underground, without a sufficient fence or handrail, or leaves defective the door, window, or other covering of any vault or cellar, or who does not sufficiently fence any area, pit, or sewer left open, or who leaves such open area, pit, or sewer, without a sufficient light after sunset to warn and prevent persons from falling thereinto:

Every person who throws or lays any dirt, litter, or ashes, or night-soil, or any carrion, fish, offal, or rubbish, on any street, or causes any offensive matter to run from any manufactory, brewery, slaughter-house, butcher's shop, or dunghill, into any street: Provided always, that it shall not be deemed an offence to lay sand or other materials in any street in time of frost, to prevent accidents, or litter or other suitable materials to prevent the freezing of water in pipes, or in the case of sickness to prevent noise, if the party laying any such things causes them to be removed as soon as the occasion for them ceases:

Every person who keeps any pigstye to the front of any street, not being shut out from such street by a sufficient wall or fence, or who keeps any swine in or near any street, so as to be a common nuisance.

OFFENCES AGAINST THE PERSON ACT 1861

32. Placing wood, etc., on railway, taking up rails, showing or hiding signals, etc., with intent to endanger passengers

Whosoever shall unlawfully and maliciously put or throw upon or across any railway any wood, stone, or other matter or thing, or shall unlawfully and maliciously take up, remove, or displace any rail, sleeper, or other matter or thing belonging to any railway, or shall unlawfully and maliciously turn, move or divert any points or other machinery belonging to any railway, or shall unlawfully and maliciously make or show, hide or remove, any signal or light upon or near to any railway, or shall unlawfully and maliciously do or cause to be done any other matter or thing, with intent, in any of the cases aforesaid, to endanger the safety of any person travelling or being upon such railway, shall be guilty of an offence, and being convicted thereof shall be liable, at the discretion of the court, to imprisonment for life.

33.   Casting stone, etc., upon a railway carriage, with intent to endanger the safety of any person therein, or in any part of the same train

Whosoever shall unlawfully and maliciously throw, or cause to fall or strike, at, against, into, or upon any engine, tender, carriage, or truck used upon any railway, any wood, stone, or other matter or thing, with intent to injure or endanger the safety of any person being in or upon such engine, tender, carriage, or truck, or in or upon any other any other engine, tender, carriage, or truck of any train of which such first-mentioned engine, tender, carriage, or truck shall form part, shall be guilty of an offence, and being convicted thereof shall be liable . . . to imprisonment for life.

34.   Doing or omitting anything so as to endanger passengers by railway

Whosoever, by any unlawful act, or by any wilful omission or neglect, shall endanger or cause to be endangered the safety of any person conveyed or being in or upon a railway, or shall aid or assist therein, shall be guilty of an offence, and being convicted thereof shall be liable, at the discretion of the court, to be imprisoned for any term not exceeding two years.

MALICIOUS DAMAGE ACT 1861

35.   Placing wood, etc, on railway, taking up rails, etc, turning points, showing or hiding signals, etc, with intent to obstruct or overthrow any engine, etc.

Whosoever shall unlawfully and maliciously put, place, cast, or throw upon or across any railway any wood, stone, or other matter or thing, or shall unlawfully and maliciously take up, remove, or displace any rail, sleeper, or other matter or thing belonging to any railway, or shall unlawfully and maliciously turn, move, or divert any points or other machinery belonging to any railway, or shall unlawfully and maliciously make or show, hide or remove, any signal or light upon or near to any railway, or shall unlawfully and maliciously do or cause to be done any other matter or thing, with intent, in any of the cases aforesaid, to obstruct, upset, overthrow, injure, or destroy any engine, tender, carriage, or truck using such railway, shall be guilty of felony, and being convicted thereof shall be liable, at the discretion of the court, to be kept in penal servitude for life . . . or to be imprisoned . . .

36.   Obstructing engines or carriages on railways

Whosoever, by any unlawful act, or by any wilful omission or neglect, shall obstruct or cause to be obstructed any engine or carriage using any railway, or shall aid or assist therein, shall be guilty of a misdemeanour, and being convicted thereof shall be liable, at the discretion of the court, to be imprisoned for any term not exceeding two years, with or without hard labour.

47.   Exhibiting false signals, etc.

Whosoever shall unlawfully mask, alter, or remove any light or signal, or unlawfully exhibit any false light or signal, with intent to bring any ship, vessel, or boat into danger, or shall, unlawfully and maliciously do anything tending to the immediate loss or destruction of any ship, vessel, or boat, and for which no punishment is hereinbefore provided, shall be guilty of felony, and being convicted thereof shall be liable, at the discretion of the court, to be kept in penal servitude for life . . . or to be imprisoned . . .

48.   Removing or concealing buoys and other sea marks

Whosoever shall unlawfully and maliciously cut away, cast adrift, remove, alter, deface, sink, or destroy, or shall unlawfully and maliciously do any act with intent to cut away, cast adrift, remove, alter, deface, sink, or destroy, or shall in any other manner unlawfully and maliciously injure or conceal any boat, buoy, buoy rope, perch, or mark used or intended for the guidance of seamen, or for the purpose of navigation, shall be guilty of felony, and being convicted thereof shall be liable, at the discretion of the court, to be kept in penal servitude for any term not exceeding seven years . . . or to be imprisoned . . .

58. Malice against owner of property unnecessary

Every punishment and forfeiture by this Act imposed on any person maliciously committing any offence, whether the same be punishable upon indictment or upon summary conviction, shall equally apply and be enforced, whether the offence shall be committed from malice conceived against the owner of the property in respect of which it shall be committed, or otherwise.

MERCHANT SHIPPING ACT 1894

422. Duty of vessel to assist the other in case of collision

(1)   In every case of collision between two vessels, it shall be the duty of the master or person in charge of each vessel, if and so far as he can do so without danger to his own vessel crew and passengers (if any),

(a)   to render to the other vessel her master crew and passengers (if any) such assistance as may be practicable, and may be necessary to save them from any danger caused by the collision, and to stay by the other vessel until he has ascertained that she has no need of further assistance, and also

(b)   to give to the master or person in charge of the other vessel the name of his own vessel and of the port to which she belongs, and also the names of the ports from which she comes and to which she is bound.

(2)   . . .

(3)   If the master or person in charge fails without reasonable cause to comply with this section, he shall be guilty of an offence and—

(a)   in the case of a failure to comply with subsection (1)(a) of this section, liable on conviction on indictment to a fine and imprisonment for a term not exceeding two years and on summary conviction to a fine not exceeding fifty thousand pounds and imprisonment for a term not exceeding six months; and

(b)   in the case of a failure to comply with subsection (1)(b) of this section, liable on conviction on indictment to a fine and on summary conviction to a fine not exceeding the statutory maximum,

and in either case if he is a certificated officer, an inquiry into his conduct may be held, and his certificate cancelled or suspended.

MERCHANT SHIPPING ACT 1970

27. Conduct endangering ships, structures or individuals

(1)   This section applies—

(a)   to the master of, or any seaman employed in, a ship registered in the United Kingdom; and

(b)   to the master of, or any seaman employed in, a ship which—

(i)   is registered under the law of any country outside the United Kingdom, and

(ii)   is in a port in the United Kingdom or within the seaward limits of the territorial sea of the United Kingdom while proceeding to or from any such port.

(2)   If a person to whom this section applies, while on board his ship or in its immediate vicinity—

(a)   does any act which causes or is likely to cause—

(i)   the loss or destruction of or serious damage to his ship or its machinery, navigational equipment or safety equipment, or

(ii)   the loss or destruction of or serious damage to any other ship or any structure, or

(iii)   the death of or serious injury to any person, or

(b)   omits to do anything required—

(i)   to preserve his ship or its machinery, navigational equipment or safety equipment from being lost, destroyed or seriously damaged, or

(ii)   to preserve any person on board his ship from death or serious injury, or

(iii)   to prevent his ship from causing the loss or destruction of or serious damage to any other ship or any structure, or the death of or serious injury to any person not on board his ship,

and either of the conditions sepcified in subsection (3) of this section is satisfied with respect to that act or omission, he shall (subject to subsections (6) and (7) of this section) be guilty of an offence.

(3)   Those conditions are—

(a)   that the act or omission was deliberate or amounted to a breach or neglect of duty;

(b)   that the master or seaman in question was under the influence of drink or a drug at the time of the act or omission.

(4)   If a person to whom this section applies—

(a)   discharges any of his duties, or performs any other function in relation to the operation of his ship or its machinery or equipment, in such a manner as to cause, or to be likely to cause, any such loss, destruction, death or injury as is mentioned in subsection (2)(a) of this section, or

(b)   fails to discharge any of his duties, or to perform any such function, properly to such an extent as to cause, or to be likely to cause, any of those things,

he shall (subject to subsections (6) and (7) of this section) be guilty of an offence.

(5)   A person guilty of an offence under this section shall be liable—

(a)   on summary conviction, to a fine not exceeding the statutory maximum;

(b)   on conviction on indictment, to imprisonment for a term not exceeding two years or a fine, or both.

(6)   In proceedings for an offence under this section it shall be a defence to prove—

(a)   in the case of an offence under subsection (2) of this section where the act or omission alleged against the defendant constituted a breach or neglect of duty, that the defendant took all reasonable steps to discharge that duty;

(b)   in the case of an offence under subsection (4) of this section, that the defendant took all reasonable precautions and exercised all due diligence to avoid committing the offence; or

(c)   in the case of an offence under either of those subsections—

(i)   that he could have avoided committing the offence only by disobeying a lawful command, or

(ii)   that in all the circumstances the loss, destruction, damage, death or injury in question, or (as the case may be) the likelihood of its being caused, either could not reasonably have been foreseen by the defendant or could not reasonably have been avoided by him.

(7)   In the application of this section to any person falling within subsection (1)(b) of this section, subsections (2) and (4) shall have effect as if paragraphs (a)(i) and (b)(i) of subsection (2) were omitted;

(8)   In this section—

'breach or neglect of duty', except in relation to a master, includes any disobedience to a lawful command;

'duty'—

(a)   in relation to a master or seaman, means any duty falling to be discharged by him in his capacity as such; and

(b)   in relation to a master, includes his duty with respect to the good management of his ship and his duty with respect to the safety of operation of his ship, its machinery and equipment; and

'structure' means any fixed or movable structure (of whatever description) other than a ship.

28.   Drunkenness, etc. on duty

If the skipper of or a seaman employed or engaged in a fishing vessel registered in the United Kingdom is, while on board the vessel, under the influence of drink or a drug to such an extent that his capacity to fulfil his responsibility for the vessel or, as the case may be, carry out the duties of his employment or engagement is impaired, he shall be liable on conviction on indictment to imprisonment for a term not exceeding two years and a fine and, on summary conviction, to a fine not exceeding the statutory maximum.

30.   Continued or concerted disobedience, neglect of duty, etc.

If a seaman employed in a ship registered in the United Kingdom—
    (a)   persistently and wilfully neglects his duty; or
    (b)   persistently and wilfully disobeys lawful commands; or
    [(c)   combines with other seamen employed in that ship—
        (i)   to disobey lawful commands which are required to be obeyed at a time while the ship is at sea;
        (ii)   to neglect any duty which is required to be discharged at such a time; or
        (iii)   to impede, at such a time, the progress of a voyage or the navigation of the ship;
he shall be liable on [conviction on indictment, to imprisonment for a term not exceeding two years and a fine and, on summary conviction, to a fine not exceeding [the statutory maximum]].

For the purposes of this section a ship shall be treated as being at sea at any time when it is not securely moored in a safe berth].

33.   Defence of drug taken for medical purposes

In proceedings for an offence under section 27 or section 28 of this Act it shall be a defence to prove that at the time of the act or omission alleged against the defendant he was under the influence of a drug taken by him for medical purposes and either that he took it on medical advice and complied with any directions given as part of that advice or that he had no reason to believe that the drug might have the influence it had.

MERCHANT SHIPPING ACT 1988

30.   Owner and master liable in respect of dangerously unsafe ship

    (1)   If, having regard to the nature of the service for which it is intended—
    (a)   a ship in a port in the United Kingdom, or
    (b)   a ship registered in the United Kingdom which is in any other port,
is, by reason of any of the matters mentioned in subsection (3), not fit to go to sea without serious danger to human life, then, subject to subsections (5) and (6), the master and the owner of the ship shall each be guilty of an offence.

    (2)   Where, at the time when a ship is not fit to go to sea as mentioned in subsection (1), any responsibilities of the owner with respect to the particular matters by reason of which the ship is not fit to go to sea have been assumed (whether wholly or in part) by any person or persons other than the owner, and have been so assumed by that person or (as the case may be) by each of those persons either—
    (a)   directly, under the terms of a charter-party or management agreement made with the owner, or

(b)   indirectly, under the terms of a series of charter-parties or management agreements,
the reference to the owner in subsection (1) shall be construed as including a reference to that other person or (as the case may be) to each of those other persons.

(3)   The matters referred to in subsection (1) are—

(a)   the condition, or the unsuitability for its purpose, of—

(i)   the ship or its machinery or equipment, or

(ii)   any part of the ship or its machinery or equipment;

(b)   undermanning;

(c)   overloading or unsafe or improper loading;

(d)   any other matter relevant to the safety of the ship.

(4)   A person guilty of an offence under this section shall be liable—

(a)   on summary conviction, to a fine not exceeding £50,000;

(b)   on conviction on indictment, to imprisonment for a term not exceeding two years or a fine, or both.

(5)   It shall be a defence in proceedings for an offence under this section to prove that at the time of the alleged offence—

(a)   arrangements had been made which were appropriate to ensure that before the ship went to sea it was made fit to do so without serious danger to human life by reason of the matters falling within subsection (3) which are specified in the charge; or

(b)   it was reasonable for such arrangements not to have been made.

(6)   It shall also be a defence in proceedings for an offence under this section to prove—

(a)   that, under the terms of one or more charter-parties or management agreements entered into by the defendant, the relevant responsibilities, namely—

(i)   where the defendant is the owner, his responsibilities with respect to the matters referred to in subsection (5)(a), or

(ii)   where the defendant is liable to proceedings under this section by virtue of subsection (2), so much of those responsibilities as had been assumed by him as mentioned in that subsection,
had at the time of the alleged offence been wholly assumed by some other person or persons party thereto; and

(b)   that in all the circumstances of the case the defendant had taken such steps as it was reasonable for him to take, and exercised such diligence as it was reasonable for him to exercise, to secure the proper discharge of the relevant responsibilities during the period during which they had been assumed by some other person or persons as mentioned in paragraph (a);
and, in determining whether the defendant had done so, regard shall be had in particular to the matters mentioned in subsection (7).

(7)   Those matters are—

(a)   whether prior to the time of the alleged offence the defendant was, or in all the circumstances ought reasonably to have been, aware of any deficiency in the discharge of the relevant responsibilities; and

(b)   the extent to which the defendant was or was not able, under the terms of any such charter-party or management agreement as is mentioned in subsection (6)(a)—

(i)   to terminate it, or

(ii)   to intervene in the management of the ship,
in the event of any such deficiency, and whether it was reasonable for the defendant to place himself in that position.

(9)   In this section—
'management agreement', in relation to a ship, means any agreement (other than a charter-party or a contract of employment) under which the ship is managed, either

wholly or in part, by a person other than the owner (whether on behalf of the owner or on behalf of some other person);

'relevant responsibilities' shall be construed in accordance with subsection (6);

and any reference in this section to going to sea shall, in a case where the service for which a ship is intended consists of going on voyages or excursions that do not involve going to sea, be construed as a reference to going on such a voyage or excursion.

(10)   References in this section to responsibilities being assumed by a person under the terms of a charter-party or management agreement are references to their being so assumed by him whether or not he has entered into a further charter-party or management agreement providing for them to be assumed by some other person.

31.   Owner liable for unsafe operation of ship

(1)   It shall be the duty of the owner of a ship to which this section applies to take all reasonable steps to secure that the ship is operated in a safe manner.

(2)   This section applies to—

(a)   any ship registered in the United Kingdom; and

(b)   any ship which—

(i)   is registered under the law of any country outside the United Kingdom, and

(ii)   is within the seaward limits of the territorial sea of the United Kingdom while proceeding to or from a port in the United Kingdom,

unless the ship would not be so proceeding but for weather conditions or any other unavoidable circumstances.

(3)   If the owner of a ship to which this section applies fails to discharge the duty imposed on him by subsection (1), he shall be guilty of an offence and liable—

(a)   on summary conviction, to a fine not exceeding £50,000;

(b)   on conviction on indictment, to imprisonment for a term not exceeding two years or a fine, or both.

(4)   Where any such ship—

(a)   is chartered by demise, or

(b)   is managed, either wholly or in part, by a person other than the owner under the terms of a management agreement within the meaning of section 30,

any reference to the owner of the ship in subsection (1) or (3) above shall be construed as including a reference—

(i)   to the charterer under the charter by demise, or

(ii)   to any such manager as is referred to in paragraph (b), or

(iii)   (if the ship is both chartered and managed as mentioned above) to both the charterer and any such manager,

and accordingly the reference in subsection (1) to the taking of all reasonable steps shall, in relation to the owner, the charterer or any such manager, be construed as a reference to the taking of all such steps as it is reasonable for him to take in the circumstances of the case.

AVIATION AND MARITIME SECURITY ACT 1990

9.   Hijacking of ships

(1)   A person who unlawfully, by the use of force or by threats of any kind, seizes a ship or exercises control of it, commits the offence of hijacking a ship, whatever his nationality and whether the ship is in the United Kingdom or elsewhere, but subject to subsection (2) below.

(2)   Subsection (1) above does not apply in relation to a warship or any other ship used as a naval auxiliary or in customs or police service unless—

(a)   the person seizing or exercising control of the ship is a United Kingdom national, or

(b)   his act is committed in the United Kingdom, or

(c)   the ship is used in the naval or customs service of the United Kingdom or in the service of any police force in the United Kingdom.

(3)   A person guilty of the offence of hijacking a ship is liable on conviction on indictment to imprisonment for life.

10.   Seizing or exercising control of fixed platforms

(1)   A person who unlawfully, by the use of force or by threats of any kind, seizes a fixed platform or exercises control of it, commits an offence, whatever his nationality and whether the fixed platform is in the United Kingdom or elsewhere.

(2)   A person guilty of an offence under this section is liable on conviction on indictment to imprisonment for life.

11.   Destroying ships or fixed platforms or endangering their safety

(1)   Subject to subsection (5) below, a person commits an offence if he unlawfully and intentionally—

(a)   destroys a ship or a fixed platform,

(b)   damages a ship, its cargo or a fixed platform so as to endanger, or to be likely to endanger, the safe navigation of the ship, or as the case may be, the safety of the platform, or

(c)   commits on board a ship or on a fixed platform an act of violence which is likely to endanger the safe navigation of the ship, or as the case may be, the safety of the platform.

(2)   Subject to subsection (5) below, a person commits an offence if he unlawfully and intentionally places, or causes to be placed, on a ship or fixed platform any device or substance which—

(a)   in the case of a ship, is likely to destroy the ship or is likely so to damage it or its cargo as to endanger its safe navigation, or

(b)   in the case of a fixed platform, is likely to destroy the fixed platform or so to damage it as to endanger its safety.

(3)   Nothing in subsection (2) above is to be construed as limiting the circumstances in which the commission of any act—

(a)   may constitute an offence under subsection (1) above, or

(b)   may constitute attempting or conspiring to commit, or aiding, abetting, counselling, procuring or inciting, or being art and part in, the commission of such an offence.

(4)   Except as provided by subsection (5) below, subsections (1) and (2) above apply whether any such act as is mentioned in those subsections is committed in the United Kingdom or elsewhere and whatever the nationality of the person committing the act.

(5)   Subsections (1) and (2) above do not apply in relation to any act committed in relation to a warship or any other ship used as a naval auxiliary or in customs or police service unless—

(a)   the person committing the act is a United Kingdom national, or

(b)   his act is committed in the United Kingdom, or

(c)   the ship is used in the naval or customs service of the United Kingdom or in the service of any police force in the United Kingdom.

(6)   A person guilty of an offence under this section is liable on conviction on indictment to imprisonment for life.

(7)   In this section—

'act of violence' means—

(a)   any act done in the United Kingdom which constitutes the offence of murder, attempted murder, manslaughter, culpable homicide or assault or an offence under section 18, 20, 21, 22, 23, 24, 28 or 29 of the Offences against the Person Act 1861 or under section 2 of the Explosive Substances Act 1883, and

(b)   any act done outside the United Kingdom which, if done in the United Kingdom, would constitute such an offence as is mentioned in paragraph (a) above, and

'unlawfully'—

(a)   in relation to the commission of an act in the United Kingdom, means so as (apart from this Act) to constitute an offence under the law of the part of the United Kingdom in which the act is committed, and

(b)   in relation to the commission of an act outside the United Kingdom means so that the commission of the act would (apart from this Act) have been an offence under the law of England and Wales if it had been committed in England and Wales . . .

12.   Other acts endangering or likely to endanger safe navigation

(1)   Subject to subsection (6) below, it is an offence for any person unlawfully and intentionally—

(a)   to destroy or damage any property to which this subsection applies, or

(b)   seriously to interfere with the operation of any such property,

where the destruction, damage or interference is likely to endanger the safe navigation of any ship.

(2)   Subsection (1) above applies to any property used for the provision of maritime navigation facilities, including any land, building or ship so used, and including any apparatus or equipment so used, whether it is on board a ship or elsewhere.

(3)   Subject to subsection (6) below, it is also an offence for any person intentionally to communicate any information which he knows to be false in a material particular, where the communication of the information endangers the safe navigation of any ship.

(4)   It is a defence for a person charged with an offence under subsection (3) above to prove that, when he communicated the information, he was lawfully employed to perform duties which consisted of or included the communication of information and that he communicated the information in good faith in performance of those duties.

(5)   Except as provided by subsection (6) below, subsections (1) and (3) above apply whether any such act as is mentioned in those subsections is committed in the United Kingdom or elsewhere and whatever the nationality of the person committing the act.

(6)   For the purposes of subsections (1) and (3) above any danger, or likelihood of danger, to the safe navigation of a warship or any other ship used as a naval auxiliary or in customs or police service is to be disregarded unless—

(a)   the person committing the act is a United Kingdom national, or

(b)   his act is committed in the United Kingdom, or

(c)   the ship is used in the naval or customs service of the United Kingdom or in the service of any police force in the United Kingdom.

(7)   A person guilty of an offence under this section is liable on conviction on indictment to imprisonment for life.

(8)   In this section 'unlawfully' has the same meaning as in section 11 of this Act.

13.   Offences involving threats

(1)   A person commits an offence if—

(a)   in order to compel any other person to do or abstain from doing any act, he threatens that he or some other person will do in relation to any ship or fixed platform an act which is an offence by virtue of section 11(1) of this Act, and

(b)   the making of that threat is likely to endanger the safe navigation of the ship or, as the case may be, the safety of the fixed platform.

(2)   Subject to subsection (4) below, a person commits an offence if—
(a)   in order to compel any other person to do or abstain from doing any act, he threatens that he or some other person will do an act which is an offence by virtue of section 12(1) of this Act, and
(b)   the making of that threat is likely to endanger the safe navigation of any ship.
(3)   Except as provided by subsection (4) below, subsections (1) and (2) above apply whether any such act as is mentioned in those subsections is committed in the United Kingdom or elsewhere and whatever the nationality of the person committing the act.
(4)   Section 12(6) of this Act applies for the purposes of subsection (2)(b) above as it applies for the purposes of section 12(1) and (3) of this Act.
(5)   A person guilty of an offence under this section is liable on conviction on indictment to imprisonment for life.

17.   Interpretation of Part II
(1)   In this Part of this Act—
'fixed platform' means—
(a)   any offshore installation, within the meaning of the Mineral Workings (Offshore Installations) Act 1971, which is not a ship, and
(b)   any other artificial island, installation or structure which—
(i)   permanently rests on, or is permanently attached to, the seabed,
(ii)i   is maintained for the purposes of the exploration or exploitation of resources or for other economic purposes, and
(iii)   is not connected with dry land by a permanent structure providing access at all times and for all purposes;
'naval service' includes military and air force service;
'ship' means any vessel (including hovercraft, submersible craft and other floating craft) other than one which—
(a)   permanently rests on, or is permanently attached to, the seabed, or
(b)   has been withdrawn from navigation or laid up; and
'United Kingdom national' means an individual who is—
(a)   a British citizen, a British Dependent Territories citizen, a British National (Overseas) or a British Overseas citizen,
(b)   a person who under the British Nationality Act 1981 is a British subject, or
(c)   a British protected person (within the meaning of that Act).
(2)   For the purposes of this Part of this Act the territorial waters adjacent to any part of the United Kingdom shall be treated as included in that part of the United Kingdom.

AVIATION SECURITY ACT 1982

1.   Hijacking
(1)   A person on board an aircraft in flight who unlawfully, by the use of force or by threats of any kind, seizes the aircraft or exercises control of it commits the offence of hijacking, whatever his nationality, whatever the State in which the aircraft is registered and whether the aircraft is in the United Kingdom or elsewhere, but subject to subsection (2) below.
(2)   If—
(a)   the aircraft is used in military, customs or police service, or
(b)   both the place of take-off and the place of landing are in the territory of the State in which the aircraft is registered,
subsection (1) above shall not apply unless—
(i)   the person seizing or exercising control of the aircraft is a United Kingdom national; or
(ii)   his act is committed in the United Kingdom; or

(iii)   the aircraft is registered in the United Kingdom or is used in the military or customs service of the United Kingdom or in the service of any police force in the United Kingdom.

(3)   A person who commits the offence of hijacking shall be liable, on conviction on indictment, to imprisonment for life.

(5)   For the purposes of this section the territorial waters of any State shall be treated as part of its territory.

2.   Destroying, damaging or endangering safety of aircraft

(1)   It shall, subject to subsection (4) below, be an offence for any person unlawfully and intentionally—

(a)   to destroy an aircraft in service or so to damage such an aircraft as to render it incapable of flight or as to be likely to endanger its safety in flight; or

(b)   to commit on board an aircraft in flight any act of violence which is likely to endanger the safety of the aircraft.

(2)   It shall also, subject to subsection (4) below, be an offence for any person unlawfully and intentionally to place, or cause to be placed, on an aircraft in service any device or substance which is likely to destroy the aircraft, or is likely so to damage it as to render it incapable of flight or as to be likely to endanger its safety in flight; but nothing in this subsection shall be construed as limiting the circumstances in which the commission of any act—

(a)   may constitute an offence under subsection (1) above, or

(b)   may constitute attempting or conspiring to commit, or aiding, abetting, counselling or procuring, or being art and part in, the commission of such an offence.

(3)   Except as provided by subsection (4) below, subsections (1) and (2) above shall apply whether any such act as is therein mentioned is committed in the United Kingdom or elsewhere, whatever the nationality of the person committing the act and whatever the State in which the aircraft is registered.

(4)   Subsections (1) and (2) above shall not apply to any act committed in relation to an aircraft used in military, customs or police service unless—

(a)   the act is committed in the United Kingdom, or

(b)   where the act is committed outside the United Kingdom, the person committing it is a United Kingdom national.

(5)   A person who commits an offence under this section shall be liable, on conviction on indictment, to imprisonment for life.

(6)   In this section 'unlawfully'—

(a)   in relation to the commission of an act in the United Kingdom, means so as (apart from this Act) to constitute an offence under the law of the part of the United Kingdom in which the act is committed, and

(b)   in relation to the commission of an act outside the United Kingdom, means so that the commission of the act would (apart from this Act) have been an offence under the law of England and Wales if it had been committed in England and Wales or of Scotland if it had been committed in Scotland.

(7)   In this section 'act of violence' means—

(a)   any act done in the United Kingdom which constitutes the offence of murder, attempted murder, manslaughter, culpable homicide or assault or an offence under section 18, 20, 21, 22, 23, 24, 28 or 29 of the Offences against the Person Act 1861 or under section 2 of the Explosive Substances Act 1883, and

(b)   any act done outside the United Kingdom which, if done in the United Kingdom, would constitute such an offence as is mentioned in paragraph (a) above.

3.   Other acts endangering or likely to endanger safety of aircraft

(1)   It shall, subject to subsections (5) and (6) below, be an offence for any person unlawfully and intentionally to destroy or damage any property to which this

subsection applies, or to interfere with the operation of any such property, where the destruction, damage or interference is likely to endanger the safety of aircraft in flight.

(2)   Subsection (1) above applies to any property used for the provision of air navigation facilities, including any land, building or ship so used, and including any apparatus or equipment so used, whether it is on board an aircraft or elsewhere.

(3)   It shall also, subject to subsections (4) and (5) below, be an offence for any person intentionally to communicate any information which is false, misleading or deceptive in a material particular, where the communication of the information endangers the safety of an aircraft in flight or is likely to endanger the safety of aircraft in flight.

(4)   It shall be a defence for a person charged with an offence under subsection (3) above to prove—

(a)   that he believed, and had reasonable grounds for believing, that the information was true; or

(b)   that, when he communicated the information, he was lawfully employed to perform duties which consisted of or included the communication of information and that he communicated the information in good faith in the performance of those duties.

(5)   Subsections (1) and (3) above shall not apply to the commission of any act unless either the act is committed in the United Kingdom, or, where it is committed outside the United Kingdom—

(a)   the person committing it is a United Kingdom national; or

(b)   the commission of the act endangers or is likely to endanger the safety in flight of a civil aircraft registered in the United Kingdom or chartered by demise to a lessee whose principal place of business, or (if he has no place of business) whose permanent residence, is in the United Kingdom; or

(c)   the act is committed on board a civil aircraft which is so registered or so chartered; or

(d)   the act is committed on board a civil aircraft which lands in the United Kingdom with the person who committed the act still on board.

(6)   Subsection (1) above shall also not apply to any act committed outside the United Kingdom and so committed in relation to property which is situated outside the United Kingdom and is not used for the provision of air navigation facilities in connection with international air navigation, unless the person committing the act is a United Kingdom national.

(7)   A person who commits an offence under this section shall be liable, on conviction on indictment, to imprisonment for life.

(8)   In this section 'civil aircraft' means any aircraft other than an aircraft used in military, customs or police service and 'unlawfully' has the same meaning as in section 2 of this Act.

4.   Offences in relation to certain dangerous articles

(1)   It shall be an offence for any person without lawful authority or reasonable excuse (the proof of which shall lie on him) to have with him—

(a)   in any aircraft registered in the United Kingdom, whether at a time when the aircraft is in the United Kingdom or not, or

(b)   in any other aircraft at a time when it is in, or in flight over, the United Kingdom, or

(c)   in any part of an aerodrome in the United Kingdom, or

(d)   in any air navigation installation in the United Kingdom which does not form part of an aerodrome,

any article to which this section applies.

(2)   This section applies to the following articles, that is to say—

(a)   any firearm, or any article having the appearance of being a firearm, whether capable of being discharged or not;

(b)   any explosive, any article manufactured or adapted (whether in the form of a bomb, grenade or otherwise) so as to have the appearance of being an explosive, whether it is capable of producing a practical effect by explosion or not, or any article marked or labelled so as to indicate that it is or contains an explosive; and

(c)   any article (not falling within either of the preceding paragraphs) made or adapted for use for causing injury to or incapacitating a person or for destroying or damaging property, or intended by the person having it with him for such use, whether by him or by any other person.

(3)   For the purposes of this section a person who is for the time being in an aircraft, or in part of an aerodrome, shall be treated as having with him in the aircraft, or in that part of the aerodrome, as the case may be, an article to which this section applies if—

(a)   where he is in an aircraft, the article, or an article in which it is contained, is in the aircraft and has been caused (whether by him or by any other person) to be brought there as being, or as forming part of, his baggage on a flight in the aircraft or has been caused by him to be brought there as being, or as forming part of, any other property to be carried on such a flight, or

(b)   where he is in part of an aerodrome (otherwise than in an aircraft), the article, or an article in which it is contained, is in that or any other part of the aerodrome and has been caused (whether by him or by any other person) to be brought into the aerodrome as being, or as forming part of, his baggage on a flight from that aerodrome or has been caused by him to be brought there as being, or as forming part of, any other property to be carried on such a flight on which he is also to be carried, notwithstanding that the circumstances may be such that (apart from this subsection) he would not be regarded as having the article with him in the aircraft or in a part of the aerodrome, as the case may be.

(4)   A person guilty of an offence under this section shall be liable—

(a)   on summary conviction, to a fine not exceeding the statutory maximum or to imprisonment for a term not exceeding three months or to both;

(b)   on conviction on indictment, to a fine or to imprisonment for a term not exceeding five years or to both.

(5)   Nothing in subsection (3) above shall be construed as limiting the circumstances in which a person would, apart from that subsection, be regarded as having an article with him as mentioned in subsection (1) above.

38.   Interpretation etc.

(1)   In this Act, except in so far as the context otherwise requires—

'aerodrome' means the aggregate of the land, buildings and works comprised in an aerodrome within the meaning of the Civil Aviation Act 1982 and (if and so far as not comprised in an aerodrome as defined in that Act) any land, building or works situated within the boundaries of an area designated, by an order made by the Secretary of State which is for the time being in force, as constituting the area of an aerodrome for the purposes of this Act;

'air navigation installation' means any building, works, apparatus or equipment used wholly or mainly for the purpose of assisting air traffic control or as an aid to air navigation, together with any land contiguous or adjacent to any such building, works, apparatus or equipment and used wholly or mainly for purposes connected therewith;

'aircraft registered or operating in the United Kingdom' means any aircraft which is either—

(a)   an aircraft registered in the United Kingdom, or

(b)   an aircraft not so registered which is for the time being allocated for use on flights which (otherwise than in exceptional circumstances) include landing at or taking off from one or more aerodromes in the United Kingdom;

'article' includes any substance, whether in solid or liquid form or in the form of a gas or vapour;

'constable' includes any person having the powers and privileges of a constable;

'explosive' means any article manufactured for the purpose of producing a practical effect by explosion, or intended for that purpose by a person having the article with him;

'firearm' includes an airgun or air pistol;

'manager', in relation to an aerodrome, means the person (whether . . . the Civil Aviation Authority, a local authority or any other person) by whom the aerodrome is managed;

'military service' includes naval and air force service;

'measures' (without prejudice to the generality of that expression) includes the construction, execution, alteration, demolition or removal of buildings or other works and also includes the institution or modification, and the supervision and enforcement, of any practice or procedure;

'operator' has the same meaning as in the Civil Aviation Act 1982;

'property' includes any land, buildings or works, any aircraft or vehicle and any baggage, cargo or other article of any description;

'United Kingdom national' means an individual who is—

(a)   a British citizen, a British Dependent Territories citizen [, a British National (Overseas)] or a British Overseas citizen;

(b)   a person who under the British Nationality Act 1981 is a British subject; or

(c)   a British protected person (within the meaning of that Act).

(2)   For the purposes of this Act—

(a)   in the case of an air navigation installation provided by, or used wholly or mainly by, the Civil Aviation Authority, that Authority, and

(b)   in the case of any other air navigation installation, the manager of an aerodrome by whom it is provided, or by whom it is wholly or mainly used,

shall be taken to be the authority responsible for that air navigation installation.

(3)   For the purposes of this Act—

(a)   the period during which an aircraft is in flight shall be deemed to include any period from the moment when all its external doors are closed following embarkation until the moment when any such door is opened for disembarkation, and, in the case of a forced landing, any period until the competent authorities take over responsibility for the aircraft and for persons and property on board; and

(b)   an aircraft shall be taken to be in service during the whole of the period which begins with the pre-flight preparation of the aircraft for a flight and ends 24 hours after the aircraft lands having completed that flight, and also at any time (not falling within that period) while, in accordance with the preceding paragraph, the aircraft is in flight, and anything done on board an aircraft while in flight over any part of the United Kingdom shall be treated as done in that part of the United Kingdom.

(4)   For the purposes of this Act the territorial waters adjacent to any part of the United Kingdom shall be treated as included in that part of the United Kingdom.

CIVIL AVIATION ACT 1982

81. Dangerous flying

(1)   Where an aircraft is flown in such a manner as to be the cause of unnecessary danger to any person or property on land or water, the pilot or the person in charge of the aircraft, and also the owner thereof, unless he proves to the satisfaction of the court that the aircraft was so flown without his actual fault or privity, shall be liable on summary conviction to a fine not exceeding [level 4 on the standard scale] or to imprisonment for a term not exceeding six months or to both.

(2)   In this section the expression 'owner' in relation to an aircraft includes any person by whom the aircraft is hired at the time of the offence.

AVIATION AND MARITIME SECURITY ACT 1990

1.   Endangering safety at aerodromes

(1)   It is an offence for any person by means of any device, substance or weapon intentionally to commit at an aerodrome serving international civil aviation any act of violence which—

(a)   causes or is likely to cause death or serious personal injury, and

(b)   endangers or is likely to endanger the safe operation of the aerodrome or the safety of persons at the aerodrome.

(2)   It is also, subject to subsection (4) below, an offence for any person by means of any device, substance or weapon unlawfully and intentionally—

(a)   to destroy or seriously to damage—

(i)   property used for the provision of any facilities at an aerodrome serving international civil aviation (including any apparatus or equipment so used), or

(ii)   any aircraft which is at such an aerodrome but is not in service, or

(b)   to disrupt the services of such an aerodrome,

in such a way as to endanger or be likely to endanger the safe operation of the aerodrome or the safety of persons at the aerodrome.

(3)   Except as provided by subsection (4) below, subsections (1) and (2) above apply whether any such act as is referred to in those subsections is committed in the United Kingdom or elsewhere and whatever the nationality of the person committing the act.

(4)   Subsection (2)(a)(ii) above does not apply to any act committed in relation to an aircraft used in military, customs or police service unless—

(a)   the act is committed in the United Kingdom, or

(b)   where the act is committed outside the United Kingdom, the person committing it is a United Kingdom national.

(5)   A person who commits an offence under this section is liable on conviction on indictment to imprisonment for life.

(9)   In this section—

'act of violence' means—

(a)   any act done in the United Kingdom which constitutes the offence of murder, attempted murder, manslaughter, culpable homicide or assault or an offence under section 18, 20, 21, 22, 23, 24, 28 or 29 of the Offences against the Person Act 1861 or under section 2 of the Explosive Substances Act 1883, and

(b)   any act done outside the United Kingdom which, if done in the United Kingdom, would constitute such an offence as is mentioned in paragraph (a) above;

'aerodrome' has the same meaning as in the Civil Aviation Act 1982;

'military service' and 'United Kingdom national' have the same meaning as in the Aviation Security Act 1982; and

'unlawfully'—

(a)   in relation to the commission of an act in the United Kingdom, means so as (apart from this section) to constitute an offence under the law of the part of the United Kingdom in which the act is committed, and

(b)   in relation to the commission of an act outside the United Kingdom, means so that the commission of the act would (apart from this section) have been an offence under the law of England and Wales if it had been committed in England and Wales . . .

(b) EMPLOYMENT

HEALTH AND SAFETY AT WORK ETC. ACT 1974

2.   General duties of employers to their employees

(1)   It shall be the duty of every employer to ensure, so far as is reasonably practicable, the health, safety and welfare at work of all his employees.

(2)   Without prejudice to the generality of an employer's duty under the preceding subsection, the matters to which that duty extends include in particular—

(a)   the provision and maintenance of plant and systems of work that are, so far as is reasonably practicable, safe and without risks to health;

(b)   arrangements for ensuring, so far as is reasonably practicable, safety and absence of risks to health in connection with the use, handling, storage and transport of articles and substances;

(c)   the provision of such information, instruction, training and supervision as is necessary to ensure, so far as is reasonably practicable, the health and safety at work of his employees;

(d)   so far as is reasonably practicable as regards any place of work under the employer's control, the maintenance of it in a condition that is safe and without risks to health and the provision and maintenance of means of access to and egress from it that are safe and without such risks;

(e)   the provision and maintenance of a working environment for his employees that is, so far as is reasonably practicable, safe, without risks to health, and adequate as regards facilities and arrangements for their welfare at work.

(3)   Except in such cases as may be prescribed, it shall be the duty of every employer to prepare and as often as may be appropriate revise a written statement of his general policy with respect to the health and safety at work of his employees and the organisation and arrangements for the time being in force for carrying out that policy, and to bring the statement and any revision of it to the notice of all of his employees.

3.   General duties of employers and self-employed to persons other than their employees

(1)   It shall be the duty of every employer to conduct his undertaking in such a way as to ensure, so far is reasonably practicable, that persons not in his employment who may be affected thereby are not thereby exposed to risks to their health or safety.

(3)   In such cases as may be prescribed, it shall be the duty of every employer and every self-employed person, in the prescribed circumstances and in the prescribed manner, to give to persons (not being his employees) who may be affected by the way in which he conducts his undertaking the prescribed information about such aspects of the way in which he conducts his undertaking as might affect their health or safety.

4.   General duties of persons concerned with premises to persons other than their employees

(1)   This section has effect for imposing on persons duties in relation to those who—

(a)   are not their employees; but

(b)   use non-domestic premises made available to them as a place of work or as a place where they may use plant or substances provided for their use there,

and applies to premises so made available and other non-domestic premises used in connection with them.

(2)   It shall be the duty of each person who has, to any extent, control of premises to which this section applies or of the means of access thereto or egress therefrom or of any plant or substance in such premises to take such measures as it is reasonable for a person in his position to take to ensure, so far as is reasonably practicable, that

the premises, all means of access thereto or egress therefrom available for use by persons using the premises, and any plant or substance in the premises or, as the case may be, provided for use there, is or are safe and without risks to health.

(3)   Where a person has, by virtue of any contract or tenancy, an obligation of any extent in relation to—

(a)   the maintenance or repair of any premises to which this section applies or any means of access thereto or egress therefrom; or

(b)   the safety of or the absence of risks to health arising from plant or substances in any such premises;

that person shall be treated, for the purposes of subsection (2) above, as being a person who has control of the matters to which his obligation extends.

(4)   Any reference in this section to a person having control of any premises or matter is a reference to a person having control of the premises or matter in connection with the carrying on by him of a trade, business or other undertaking (whether for profit or not).

5.   General duty of persons in control of certain premises in relation to harmful emissions into atmosphere

(1)   It shall be the duty of the person having control of any premises of a class prescribed for the purposes of section 1(1)(d) to use the best practicable means for preventing the emission into the atmosphere from the premises of noxious or offensive substances and for rendering harmless and inoffensive such substances as may be so emitted.

(2)   The reference in subsection (1) above to the means to be used for the purposes there mentioned includes a reference to the manner in which the plant provided for those purposes is used and to the supervision of any operation involving the emission of the substances to which that subsection applies.

(3)   Any substance or a substance of any description prescribed for the purposes of subsection (1) above as noxious or offensive shall be a noxious or, as the case may be, an offensive substance for those purposes whether or not it would be so apart from this subsection.

(4)   Any reference in this section to a person having control of any premises is a reference to a person having control of the premises in connection with the carrying on by him of a trade, business or other undertaking (whether for profit or not) and any duty imposed on any such person by this section shall extend only to matters within his control.

6.   General duties of manufacturers etc., as regards articles and substances for use at work

(1)   It shall be the duty of any person who designs, manufactures, imports or supplies any article for use at work—

(a)   to ensure, so far as is reasonably practicable, that the article is so designed and constructed as to be safe and without risks to health when properly used;

(b)   to carry out or arrange for the carrying out of such testing and examination as may be necessary for the performance of the duty imposed on him by the preceding paragraph;

(c)   to take such steps as are necessary to secure that there will be available in connection with the use of the article at work adequate information about the use for which it is designed and has been tested, and about any conditions necessary to ensure that, when put to that use, it will be safe and without risks to health.

(2)   It shall be the duty of any person who undertakes the design or manufacture of any article for use at work or of any article of fairground equipment to carry out or arrange for the carrying out of any necessary research with a view to the discovery and, so far as is reasonably practicable, the elimination or minimisation of any risks to health or safety to which the design or article may give rise.

(3) It shall be the duty of any person who erects or installs any article for use at work in any premises where that article is to be used by persons at work or who erects or installs any article of fairground equipment to ensure, so far as is reasonably practicable, that nothing about the way in which it is erected or installed makes it unsafe or a risk to health when properly used.

(4) It shall be the duty of any person who manufactures, imports or supplies any substance for use at work—

    (a) to ensure, so far as is reasonably practicable, that the substance is safe and without risks to health when properly used;

    (b) to carry out or arrange for the carrying out of such testing and examination as may be necessary for the performance of the duty imposed on him by the preceding paragraph;

    (c) to take such steps as are necessary to secure that there will be available in connection with the use of the substance at work adequate information about the results of any relevant tests which have been carried out on or in connection with the substance and about any conditions necessary to ensure that it will be safe and without risks to health when properly used.

(5) It shall be the duty of any person who undertakes the manufacture of any substance for use at work to carry out or arrange for the carrying out of any necessary research with a view to the discovery and, so far as is reasonably practicable, the elimination or minimisation of any risks to health or safety to which the substance may give rise.

(6) Nothing in the preceding provisions of this section shall be taken to require a person to repeat any testing, examination or research which has been carried out otherwise than by him or at his instance, in so far as it is reasonable for him to rely on the results thereof for the purposes of those provisions.

(7) Any duty imposed on any person by any of the preceding provisions of this section shall extend only to things done in the course of a trade, business or other undertaking carried on by him (whether for profit or not) and to matters within his control.

(8) Where a person designs, manufactures, imports or supplies an article for or to another on the basis of a written undertaking by that other to take specified steps sufficient to ensure, so far as is reasonably practicable, that the article will be safe and without risks to health when properly used, the undertaking shall have the effect of relieving the first-mentioned person from the duty imposed by subsection (1) (a) above to such an extent as is reasonable having regard to the terms of the undertaking.

(9) Where a person ('the ostensible supplier') supplies any article for use at work or substance for use at work to another ('the customer') under a hire-purchase agreement, conditional sale agreement or credit-sale agreement, and the ostensible supplier—

    (a) carries on the business of financing the acquisition of goods by others by means of such agreements; and

    (b) in the course of that business acquired his interest in the article or substance supplied to the customer as a means of financing its acquisition by the customer from a third person ('the effective supplier'),

the effective supplier and not the ostensible supplier shall be treated for the purposes of this section as supplying the article or substance to the customer, and any duty imposed by the preceding provisions of this section on suppliers shall accordingly fall on the effective supplier and not on the ostensible supplier.

(10) For the purposes of this section an article or substance is not to be regarded as properly used where it is used without regard to any relevant information or advice relating to its use which has been made available by a person by whom it was designed, manufactured, imported or supplied.

7. General duties of employees at work

It shall be the duty of every employee while at work—

(a) to take reasonable care for the health and safety of himself and of other persons who may be affected by his acts or omissions at work; and

(b) as regards any duty or requirement imposed on his employer or any other person by or under any of the relevant statutory provisions, to co-operate with him so far as is necessary to enable that duty or requirement to be performed or complied with.

8. Duty not to interfere with or misuse things provided pursuant to certain provisions

No person shall intentionally or recklessly interfere with or misuse anything provided in the interests of health, safety or welfare in pursuance of any of the relevant statutory provisions.

33. Offences

(1) It is an offence for a person—

(a) to fail to discharge a duty to which he is subject by virtue of section 2 to 7;

(b) to contravene section 8 or 9;

(c) to contravene any health and safety regulations or agricultural health and safety regulations or any requirement or prohibition imposed under any such regulations (including any requirement or prohibition to which he is subject by virtue of the terms of or any condition or restriction attached to any licence, approval, exemption or other authority issued, given or granted under the regulations);

(k) to make a statement which he knows to be false or recklessly to make a statement which is false where the statement is made—

(i) in purported compliance with a requirement to furnish any information imposed by or under any of the relevant statutory provisions; or

(ii) for the purpose of obtaining the issue of a document under any of the relevant statutory provisions to himself or another person;

(l) intentionally to make a false entry in any register, book, notice or other document required by or under any of the relevant statutory provisions to be kept, served or given or, with intent to deceive, to make use of any such entry which he knows to be false;

(m) with intent to deceive, to forge or use a document issued or authorised to be issued under any of the relevant statutory provisions or required for any purpose thereunder or to make or have in his possession a document so closely resembling any such document as to be calculated to deceive;

(n) falsely to pretend to be an inspector.

36. Offences due to fault of other person

(1) Where the commission by any person of an offence under any of the relevant statutory provisions is due to the act or default of some other person, that other person shall be guilty of the offence, and a person may be charged with and convicted of the offence by virtue of this subsection whether or not proceedings are taken against the first-mentioned person.

(2) Where there would be or have been the commission of an offence under section 33 by the Crown but for the circumstance that that section does not bind the Crown, and that fact is due to the act or default of a person other than the Crown, that person shall be guilty of the offence which, but for that circumstance, the Crown would be committing or would have committed, and may be charged with and convicted of that offence accordingly.

40. Onus of proving limits of what is practicable etc.

In any proceedings for an offence under any of the relevant statutory provisions consisting of a failure to comply with a duty or requirement to do something so far as

is practicable or so far as is reasonably practicable, or to use the best means to do
something, it shall be for the accused to prove (as the case may be) that it was not
practicable or not reasonably practicable to do more than was in fact done to satisfy
the duty or requirement, or that there was no better practicable means than was in
fact used to satisfy the duty or requirement.

(c) EXPLOSIVES AND FIREARMS

OFFENCES AGAINST THE PERSON ACT 1861

31. Setting or allowing to remain spring guns, etc., with intent to inflict grievous bodily harm

Whosoever shall set or place, or cause to be set or placed, any spring gun, man trap, or
other engine calculated to destroy human life or inflict grievous bodily harm, with the
intent that the same or whereby the same may destroy or inflict grievous bodily harm
upon a trespasser or other person coming in contact therewith, shall be guilty of an
offence, and being convicted thereof shall be liable . . . to imprisonment for a term not
exceeding five years; and whosoever shall knowingly and wilfully permit any such
spring gun, man trap, or other engine which may have been set or placed in any place
then being in or afterwards coming into his possession or occupation by some other
person to continue so set or placed, shall be deemed to have set and placed such gun,
trap, or engine with such intent as aforesaid: Provided, that nothing in this section
contained shall extend to make it illegal to set or place any gun or trap such as may
have been or may be usually set or placed with the intent of destroying vermin:
Provided also, that nothing in this section shall be deemed to make it unlawful to set or
place, or cause to be set or placed, or to be continued set or placed, from sunset to
sunrise, any spring gun, man trap, or other engine which shall be set or placed, or
caused or continued to be set or placed, in a dwelling-house, for the protection thereof.

EXPLOSIVE SUBSTANCES ACT 1883

2. Causing explosion likely to endanger life or property

A person who in the United Kingdom or (being a citizen of the United Kingdom and
Colonies) in the Republic of Ireland unlawfully and maliciously causes by any
explosive substance an explosion of a nature likely to endanger life or to cause serious
injury to person or property shall, whether any injury to person or property has been
actually caused or not, be guilty of an offence and on conviction on indictment shall
be liable to imprisonment for life.

FIREARMS ACT 1968

1. Requirement of firearm certificate

(1) Subject to any exemption under this Act, it is an offence for a person—

(a) to have in his possession, or to purchase or acquire, a firearm to which this
section applies without holding a firearm certificate in force at the time, or otherwise
than as authorised by such a certificate;

(b) to have in his possession, or to purchase or acquire, any ammunition to which
this section applies without holding a firearm certificate in force at the time, or otherwise
than as authorised by such a certificate, or in quantities in excess of those so authorised.

(2) It is an offence for a person to fail to comply with a condition subject to which
a firearm certificate is held by him.

(3) This section applies to every firearm except—

(a) a shot gun within the meaning of this Act, that is to say a smooth-bore gun
(not being an air gun) which—

(i)   has a barrel not less than 24 inches in length and does not have any barrel with a bore exceeding 2 inches in diameter;

(ii)   either has no magazine or has a non-detachable magazine incapable of holding more than two cartridges; and

(iii)   is not a revolver gun; and

(b)   an air weapon (that is to say, an air rifle, air gun or air pistol not of a type declared by rules made by the Secretary of State under section 53 of this Act to be specially dangerous).

(3A)   A gun which has been adapted to have such a magazine as is mentioned in subsection (3)(a)(ii) above shall not be regarded as falling within that provision unless the magazine bears a mark approved by the Secretary of State for denoting that fact and that mark has been made, and the adaptation has been certified in writing as having been carried out in a manner approved by him, either by one of the two companies mentioned in section 58(1) of this Act or by such other person as may be approved by him for that purpose.

(4)   This section applies to any ammunition for a firearm, except the following articles, namely:—

(a)   cartridges containing five or more shot, none of which exceeds 0.36 inch in diameter;

(b)   ammunition for an air gun, air rifle or air pistol; and

(c)   blank cartridges not more than one inch in diameter measured immediately in front of the rim or cannelure of the base of the cartridge.

2.   Requirement of certificate for possession of shot guns

(1)   Subject to any exemption under this Act, it is an offence for a person to have in his possession, or to purchase or acquire, a shot gun without holding a certificate under this Act authorising him to possess shot guns.

(2)   It is an offence for a person to fail to comply with a condition subject to which a shot gun certificate is held by him.

3.   Business and other transactions with firearms and ammunition

(1)   A person commits an offence if, by way of trade or business, he—

(a)   manufactures, sells, transfers, repairs, tests or proves any firearm or ammunition to which section 1 of this Act applies, or a shot gun; or

(b)   exposes for sale or transfer, or has in his possession for sale, transfer, repair, test or proof any such firearm or ammunition, or a shot gun,

without being registered under this Act as a firearms dealer.

(2)   It is an offence for a person to sell or transfer to any other person in the United Kingdom, other than a registered firearms dealer, any firearm or ammunition to which section 1 of this Act applies, or a shot gun, unless that other produces a firearm certificate authorising him to purchase or acquire it or as the case may be, his shot gun certificate, or shows that he is by virtue of this Act entitled to purchase or acquire it without holding a certificate.

(3)   It is an offence for a person to undertake the repair, tests or proof of a firearm or ammunition to which section 1 of this Act applies, or of a shot gun, for any other person in the United Kingdom other than a registered firearms dealer as such, unless that other produces or causes to be produced a firearm certificate authorising him to have possession of the firearm or ammunition or, as the case may be, his shot gun certificate, or shows that he is by virtue of this Act entitled to have possession of it without holding a certificate.

(4)   Subsections (1) and (3) above have effect subject to any exemption under subsequent provisions of this Part of this Act.

(5)   A person commits an offence if, with a view to purchasing or acquiring, or procuring the repair, test or proof of, any firearm or ammunition to which section 1 of this Act applies, or a shot gun, he produces a false certificate or a certificate in

which any false entry has been made, or personates a person to whom a certificate has been granted, or makes any false statement.

(6) It is an offence for a pawnbroker to take in pawn any firearm or ammunition to which section 1 of this Act applies, or a shot gun.

4. Conversion of weapons

(1) Subject to this section, it is an offence to shorten the barrel of a shot gun to a length less than 24 inches.

(2) It is not an offence under subsection (1) above for a registered firearms dealer to shorten the barrel of a shot gun for the sole purpose of replacing a defective part of the barrel so as to produce a barrel not less than 24 inches in length.

(3) It is an offence for a person other than a registered firearms dealer to convert into a firearm anything which, though having the appearance of being a firearm, is so constructed as to be incapable of discharging any missile through its barrel.

(4) A person who commits an offence under section 1 of this Act by having in his possession, or purchasing or acquiring, a shotgun which has been shortened contrary to subsection (1) above or a firearm which has been converted contrary to subsection (3) above (whether by a registered firearms dealer or not), without holding a firearm certificate authorising him to have it in his possession, or to purchase or acquire it, shall be treated for the purposes of provisions of this Act relating to the punishment of offences as committing that offence in an aggravated form.

5. Weapons subject to general prohibition

(1) A person commits an offence if, without the authority of the Defence Council, he has in his possession, or purchases or acquires, or manufactures, sells or transfers—

(a) any firearm which is so designed or adapted that two or more missiles can be successively discharged without repeated pressure on the trigger;

(ab) any self-loading or pump-action rifled gun other than one which is chambered for .22 rim-fire cartridges;

(aba) any firearm which either has a barrel less than 30 centimetres in length or is less than 60 centimetres in length overall, other than an air weapon, a muzzle-loading gun or a firearm designed as signalling apparatus;

(ac) any self-loading or pump-action smooth-bore gun which is not an air weapon or chambered for .22 rim-fire cartridges and either has a barrel less than 24 inches in length or (excluding any detachable folding, retractable or other movable butt-stock) is less than 40 inches in length overall;

(ad) any smooth-bore revolver gun other than one which is chambered for 9mm rim-fire cartridges or a muzzle-loading gun;

(ae) any rocket launcher, or any mortar, for projecting a stabilised missile, other than a launcher or mortar designed for line-throwing or pyrotechnic purposes or as signalling apparatus;

(b) any weapon of whatever description designed or adapted for the discharge of any noxious liquid, gas or other thing; and

(c) any cartridge with a bullet designed to explode on or immediately before impact, any ammunition containing or designed or adapted to contain any such noxious thing as is mentioned in paragraph (b) above and, if capable of being used with a firearm of any description, any grenade, bomb (or other like missile), or rocket or shell designed to explode as aforesaid.

(1A) Subject to section 5A of this Act, a person commits an offence if, without the authority of the Secretary of State, he has in his possession, or purchases or acquires, or sells or transfers—

(a) any firearm which is disguised as another object;

(b)   any rocket or ammunition not falling within paragraph (c) of subsection (1) of this section which consists in or incorporates a missile designed to explode on or immediately before impact and is for military use;

(c)   any launcher or other projecting apparatus not falling within paragraph (ae) of that subsection which is designed to be used with any rocket or ammunition falling within paragraph (b) above or with ammunition which would fall within that paragraph but for its being ammunition falling within paragraph (c) of this subsection;

(d)   any ammunition for military use which consists in or incorporates a missile designed so that a substance contained in the missile will ignite on or immediately before impact;

(e)   any ammunition for military use which consists in or incorporates a missile designed, on account of its having a jacket and hard-core, to penetrate armour plating, armour screening or body armour;

(f)   any ammunition which incorporates a missile designed or adapted to expand on impact;

(g)   anything which is designed to be projected as a missile from any weapon and is designed to be, or has been, incorporated in—

(i)   any ammunition falling within any of the preceding paragraphs; or

(ii)   any ammunition which would fall within any of those paragraphs but for its being specified in subsection (1) of this section.

(2)   The weapons and ammunition specified in subsections (1) and (1A) of this section (including, in the case of ammunition, any missiles falling within subsection (1A)(g) of this section) are referred to in this Act as 'prohibited weapons' and 'prohibited ammunition' respectively.

(3)   An authority given to a person by the Defence Council under this section shall be in writing and be subject to conditions specified therein.

(5)   It is an offence for a person to whom an authority is given under this section to fail to comply with any condition of the authority.

(7)   For the purposes of this section and section 5A of this Act—

(a)   any rocket or ammunition which is designed to be capable of being used with a military weapon shall be taken to be for military use;

(b)   references to a missile designed so that a substance contained in the missile will ignite on or immediately before impact include references to any missile containing a substance that ignites on exposure to air; and

(c)   references to a missile's expanding on impact include references to its deforming in any predictable manner on or immediately after impact.

(8)   For the purposes of subsection (1)(aba) and (ac) above, any detachable, folding, retractable or other movable butt-stock shall be disregarded in measuring the length of any firearm.

(9)   Any reference in this section to a muzzle-loading gun is a reference to a gun which is designed to be loaded at the muzzle end of the barrel or chamber with a loose charge and a separate ball (or other missile).

5A.   Exemptions from requirement of authority under section 5

(1)   Subject to subsection (2) below, the authority of the Secretary of State shall not be required by virtue of subsection (1A) of section 5 of this Act for any person to have in his possession, or to purchase, acquire, sell or transfer, any prohibited weapon or ammunition if he is authorised by a certificate under this Act to possess, purchase or acquire that weapon or ammunition subject to a condition that he does so only for the purpose of its being kept or exhibited as part of a collection.

(2)   No sale or transfer may be made under subsection (1) above except to a person who—

(a)   produces the authority of the Secretary of State under section 5 of this Act for his purchase or acquisition; or

(b)   shows that he is, under this section or a licence under the Schedule to the Firearms (Amendment) Act 1988 (museums etc.), entitled to make the purchase or acquisition without the authority of the Secretary of State.

(3)   The authority of the Secretary of State shall not be required by virtue of subsection (1A) of section 5 of this Act for any person to have in his possession, or to purchase or acquire, any prohibited weapon or ammunition if his possession, purchase or acquisition is exclusively in connection with the carrying on of activities in respect of which—

(a)   that person; or

(b)   the person on whose behalf he has possession, or makes the purchase or acquisition,

is recognised, for the purposes of the law of another member State relating to firearms, as a collector of firearms or a body concerned in the cultural or historical aspects of weapons.

(4)   The authority of the Secretary of State shall not be required by virtue of subsection (1A) of section 5 of this Act for any person to have in his possession, or to purchase or acquire or to sell or transfer, any expanding ammunition or the missile for any such ammunition if—

(a)   he is authorised by a firearm certificate or visitor's firearm permit to possess, or purchase or acquire, any expanding ammunition; and

(b)   the certificate or permit is subject to a condition restricting the use of any expanding ammunition to use in connection with any one or more of the following, namely—

(i)   the lawful shooting of deer;

(ii)   the shooting of vermin or, in the course of carrying on activities in connection with the management of any estate other wildlife;

(iii) the humane killing of animals;

(iv)   the shooting of animals for the protection of other animals or humans.

(5)   The authority of the Secretary of State shall not be required by virtue of subsection (1A) of section 5 of this Act for any person to have in his possession any expanding ammunition or the missile for any such ammunition if—

(a)   he is entitled, under section 10 of this Act, to have a slaughtering instrument and the ammunition for it in his possession; and

(b)   the ammunition or missile in question is designed to be capable of being used with a slaughtering instrument.

(6)   The authority of the Secretary of State shall not be required by virtue of subsection (1A) of section 5 of this Act for the sale or transfer of any expanding ammunition or the missile for any such ammunition to any person who produces a certificate by virtue of which he is authorised under subsection (4) above to purchase or acquire it without the authority of the Secretary of State.

(7)   The authority of the Secretary of State shall not be required by virtue of subsection (1A) of section 5 of this Act for a person carrying on the business of a firearms dealer, or any servant of his, to have in his possession, or to purchase, acquire, sell or transfer, any expanding ammunition or the missile for any such ammunition in the ordinary course of that business.

(8)   In this section—

(a)   references to expanding ammunition are references to any ammunition which is designed to be used with a pistol and incorporates a missile which is designed to expand on impact; and

(b)   references to the missile for any such ammunition are references to anything which, in relation to any such ammunition, falls within section 5(1A)(g) of this Act.

7. Police permit

(1) A person who has obtained from the chief officer of police for the area in which he resides a permit for the purpose in the prescribed form may, without holding a certificate under this Act, have in his possession a firearm and ammunition in accordance with the terms of the permit.

(2) It is an offence for a person to make any statement which he knows to be false for the purpose of procuring, whether for himself or for another person, the grant of a permit under this section.

16. Possession of firearm with intent to injure

It is an offence for a person to have in his possession any firearm or ammunition with intent by means thereof to endanger life . . . or to enable another person by means thereof to endanger life . . . whether any injury has been caused or not.

16A. Possession of firearm with intent to cause fear of violence

It is an offence for a person to have in his possession any firearm or imitation firearm with intent—

    (a) by means thereof to cause, or

    (b) to enable another person by means thereof to cause,

any person to believe that unlawful violence will be used against him or another person.

17. Use of firearm to resist arrest

(1) It is an offence for a person to make or attempt to make any use whatsoever of a firearm or imitation firearm with intent to resist or prevent the lawful arrest or detention of himself or another person.

(2) If a person, at the time of his committing or being arrested for an offence specified in Schedule 1 to this Act, has in his possession a firearm or imitation firearm, he shall be guilty of an offence under this subsection unless he shows that he had it in his possession for a lawful object.

(4) For purposes of this section, the definition of 'firearm' in section 57(1) of this Act shall apply without paragraphs (b) and (c) of that subsection, and 'imitation firearm' shall be construed accordingly.

18. Carrying firearm with criminal intent

(1) It is an offence for a person to have with him a firearm or imitation firearm with intent to commit an indictable offence, or to resist arrest or prevent the arrest of another, in either case while he has the firearm or imitation firearm with him.

(2) In proceedings for an offence under this section proof that the accused had a firearm or imitation firearm with him and intended to commit an offence, or to resist or prevent arrest, is evidence that he intended to have it with him while doing so.

19. Carrying firearm in a public place

A person commits an offence if, without lawful authority or reasonable excuse (the proof whereof lies on him) he has with him in a public place a loaded shot gun or loaded air weapon, or any other firearm (whether loaded or not) together with ammunition suitable for use in that firearm.

19A. Having small-calibre pistol outside premises of licensed pistol club

(1) It is an offence for any person to have a small-calibre pistol with him outside licensed premises of a licensed pistol club.

(2) It is not an offence for a person to have with him a small-calibre pistol if—

    (a) he is permitted by virtue of any provision of this Act to have the pistol in his possession without holding a firearm certificate or a visitor's firearm permit;

    (b) he is authorised to have the pistol with him by virtue of a permit granted under section 13 of the Firearms (Amendment) Act 1997; or

(c)   he is authorised to have the pistol in his possession by virtue of a firearm certificate or visitor's firearm permit which is not subject to a condition requiring it to be kept at a licensed pistol club.

(3)   In this section 'licensed pistol club' means a pistol club which is licensed under Part II of the Firearms (Amendment) Act 1997 and 'licensed premises' has the meaning given in section 19 of that Act.

20.   Trespassing with firearm

(1)   A person commits an offence if, while he has a firearm or imitation firearm with him, he enters or is in any building or part of a building as a trespasser and without reasonable excuse (the proof whereof lies on him).

(2)   A person commits an offence if, while he has a firearm or imitation firearm with him, he enters or is on any land as a trespasser and without reasonable excuse (the proof whereof lies on him).

(3)   In subsection (2) of this section the expression 'land' includes land covered with water.

22.   Acquisition and possession of firearms by minors

(1)   It is an offence for a person under the age of seventeen to purchase or hire any firearm or ammunition.

(2)   It is an offence for a person under the age of fourteen to have in his possession any firearm or ammunition to which section 1 of this Act applies, except in circumstances where under section 11 (1), (3) or (4) of this Act or section 15 of the Firearms (Amendment) Act 1988 he is entitled to have possession of it without holding a firearm certificate.

(3)   It is an offence for a person under the age of fifteen to have with him an assembled shot gun except while under the supervision of a person of or over the age of twenty-one, or while the shot gun is so covered with a securely fastened gun cover that it cannot be fired.

(4)   Subject to section 23 below, it is an offence for a person under the age of fourteen to have with him an air weapon or ammunition for an air weapon.

(5)   Subject to section 23 below, it is an offence for a person under the age of seventeen to have an air weapon with him in a public place, except an air gun or air rifle which is so covered with a securely fastened gun cover that it cannot be fired.

23.   Exceptions from s. 22(4) and (5)

(1)   It is not an offence under section 22 (4) of this Act for a person to have with him an air weapon or ammunition while he is under the supervision of a person of or over the age of twenty-one; but where a person has with him an air weapon on any premises in circumstances where he would be prohibited from having it with him but for this subsection, it is an offence—

(a)   for him to use it for firing any missile beyond those premises; or

(b)   for the person under whose supervision he is to allow him so to use it.

(2)   It is not an offence under section 22(4) and (5) of this Act for a person to have with him an air weapon or ammunition at a time when—

(a)   being a member of a rifle club or miniature rifle club for the time being approved by the Secretary of State for the purposes of this section or section 15 of the Firearms (Amendment) Act 1988, he is engaged as such a member in or in connection with target practice; or

(b)   he is using the weapon or ammunition at a shooting gallery where the only firearms used are either air weapons or miniature rifles not exceeding 0.23 inch calibre.

24.   Supplying firearms to minors

(1)   It is an offence to sell or let on hire any firearm or ammunition to a person under the age of seventeen.

(2)   It is an offence—

(a)   to make a gift of or lend any firearm or ammunition to which section 1 of this Act applies to a person under the age of fourteen; or

(b)   to part with the possession of any such firearm or ammunition to a person under that age, except in circumstances where that person is entitled under section 11 (1), (3) or (4) of this Act to have possession thereof without holding a firearm certificate.

(3)   It is an offence to make a gift of a shot gun or ammunition for a shot gun to a person under the age of fifteen.

(4)   It is an offence—

(a)   to make a gift of an air weapon or ammunition for an air weapon to a person under the age of fourteen; or

(b)   to part with the possession of an air weapon or ammunition for an air weapon to a person under that age except where by virtue of section 23 of this Act the person is not prohibited from having it with him.

(5)   In proceedings for an offence under any provision of this section it is a defence to prove that the person charged with the offence believed the other person to be of or over the age mentioned in that provision and had reasonable ground for the belief.

25.   Supplying firearm to person drunk or insane

It is an offence for a person to sell or transfer any firearm or ammunition to, or to repair, prove or test any firearm or ammunition for, another person whom he knows or has reasonable cause for believing to be drunk or of unsound mind.

57.   Interpretation

(1)   In this Act, the expression 'firearm' means a lethal barrelled weapon of any description from which any shot, bullet or other missile can be discharged and includes—

(a)   any prohibited weapon, whether it is such a lethal weapon as aforesaid or not; and

(b)   any component part of such a lethal or prohibited weapon; and

(c)   any accessory to any such weapon designed or adapted to diminish the noise or flash caused by firing the weapon;

and so much of section 1 of this Act as excludes any description of firearm from the category of firearms to which that section applies shall be construed as also excluding component parts of, and accessories to, firearms of that description.

(1A)   In this Act 'small-calibre pistol' means—

(a)   a pistol chambered for .22 or smaller rim-fire cartridges; or

(b)   an air pistol to which section 1 of this Act applies and which is designed to fire .22 or smaller diameter ammunition.

(2)   In this Act, the expression 'ammunition' means ammunition for any firearm and includes grenades, bombs and other like missiles, whether capable of use with a firearm or not, and also includes prohibited ammunition.

(4)   In this Act—

'acquire' means hire, accept as a gift or borrow and 'acquisition' shall be construed accordingly;

'air weapon' has the meaning assigned to it by section 1 (3)(b) of this Act;

'area' means a police area;

'certificate' (except in a context relating to the registration of firearms dealers) and 'certificate under this Act' means a firearm certificate or a shot gun certificate and—

(a)   'firearm certificate' means a certificate granted by a chief officer of police under this Act in respect of any firearm or ammunition to which section 1 of this Act applies and includes a certificate granted in Northern Ireland under section 1 of the Firearms Act 1920 or under an enactment of the Parliament of Northern Ireland amending or substituted for that section; and

(b) 'shot gun certificate' means a certificate granted by a chief officer of police under this Act and authorising a person to possess shot guns;

'firearms dealer' means a person who, by way of trade or business, manufactures, sells, transfers, repairs, tests or proves firearms or ammunition to which section 1 of this Act applies, or shot guns;

'imitation firearm' means any thing which has the appearance of being a firearm (other than such a weapon as is mentioned in section 5 (1) (b) of this Act) whether or not it is capable of discharging any shot, bullet or other missile;

'premises' includes any land;

'prescribed' means prescribed by rules made by the Secretary of State under section 53 of this Act;

'prohibited weapon' and 'prohibited ammunition' have the meanings assigned to them by section 5(2) of this Act;

'public place' includes any highway and any other premises or place to which at the material time the public have or are permitted to have access, whether on payment or otherwise;

'registered', in relation to a firearms dealer, means registered either—

(a) in Great Britain, under section 33 of this Act, or

(b) in Northern Ireland, under section 8 of the Firearms Act 1920 or any enactment of the Parliament of Northern Ireland amending or substituted for that section; and references to 'the register', 'registration' and a 'certificate of registration' shall be construed accordingly, except in section 40;

'shot gun' has the meaning assigned to it by section 1(3)(a) of this Act and, in sections 3(1) and 45(2) of this Act and in the definition of 'firearms dealer', includes any component part of a shot gun and any accessory to a shot gun designed or adapted to diminish the noise or flash caused by firing the gun;

'slaughtering instrument' means a firearm which is specially designed or adapted for the instantaneous slaughter of animals or for the instantaneous stunning of animals with a view to slaughtering them; and

'transfer' includes let on hire, give, lend and part with possession, and 'transferee' and 'transferor' shall be construed accordingly.

(5) The definitions in subsections (1) to (3) above apply to the provisions of this Act except where the context otherwise requires.

(6) For the purposes of this Act—

(a) the length of the barrel of a firearm shall be measured from the muzzle to the point at which the charge is exploded on firing; and

(b) a shot gun or an air weapon shall be deemed to be loaded if there is ammunition in the chamber or barrel or in any magazine or other device which is in such a position that the ammunition can be fed into the chamber or barrel by the manual or automatic operation of some part of the gun or weapon.

58. Particular savings

(2) Nothing in this Act relating to firearms shall apply to an antique firearm which is sold, transferred, purchased, acquired or possessed as a curiosity or ornament.

(3) The provisions of this Act relating to ammunition shall be in addition to and not in derogation of any enactment relating to the keeping and sale of explosives.

SCHEDULE I

OFFENCES TO WHICH SECTION 17(2) APPLIES

1. Offences under section 1 of the Criminal Damage Act 1971

2. Offences under any of the following provisions of the Offences against the Person Act 1861—

section 20 to 22 (inflicting bodily injury; garrotting; criminal use of stupefying drugs);

section 30 (laying explosive to building etc.);

section 32 (endangering railway passengers by tampering with track);

section 38 (assault with intent to commit felony or resist arrest);

section 47 (criminal assaults);

section 56 (child-stealing and abduction).

2A. Offences under Part 1 of the Child Abduction Act 1984 (abduction of children).

4. Theft, robbery, burglary, blackmail and any offence under section 12(1) (taking of motor vehicle or other conveyance without owner's consent) of the Theft Act 1968.

5. Offences under section 51(1) of the Police Act 1964 or section 41 of the Police (Scotland) Act 1967 (assaulting constable in execution of his duty).

5A. An offence under section 90(1) of the Criminal Justice Act 1991 (assaulting prisoner custody officer).

5B An offence under section 13(1) of the Criminal Justice and Public Order Act 1994 (assaulting secure training centre custody officer).

6. Offences under any of the following provisions of the Sexual Offences Act 1956—

section 1 (rape);

sections 17, 18 and 20 (abduction of women).

8. Aiding or abetting the commission of any offence specified in paragraphs 1 to 6 of this Schedule.

9. Attempting to commit any offence so specified.

FIREARMS (AMENDMENT) ACT 1988

5. Restriction on sale of ammunition for smooth-bore guns

(1) This section applies to ammunition to which section 1 of the Firearms Act 1968 does not apply and which is capable of being used in a shot gun or in a smooth-bore gun to which that section applies.

(2) It is an offence for a person to sell any such ammunition to another person in the United Kingdom who is neither a registered firearms dealer nor a person who sells such ammunition by way of trade or business unless that other person—

(a) produces a certificate authorising him to possess a gun of a kind mentioned in subsection (1) above; or

(b) shows that he is by virtue of that Act or this Act entitled to have possession of such a gun without holding a certificate; or

(c) produces a certificate authorising another person to possess such a gun, together with that person's written authority to purchase the ammunition on his behalf.

6. Shortening of barrels

(1) Subject to subsection (2) below, it is an offence to shorten to a length less than 24 inches the barrel of any smooth-bore gun to which section 1 of the Firearms Act 1968 applies other than one which has a barrel with a bore exceeding 2 inches in diameter; and that offence shall be punishable—

(a) on summary conviction, with imprisonment for a term not exceeding six months or a fine not exceeding the statutory maximum or both;

(b) on indictment, with imprisonment for a term not exceeding five years or a fine or both.

(2) It is not an offence under this section for a registered firearms dealer to shorten the barrel of a gun for the sole purpose of replacing a defective part of the barrel so as to produce a barrel not less than 24 inches in length.

14. Auctioneers, carriers and warehousemen

(1) It is an offence for an auctioneer, carrier or warehouseman—

(a) to fail to take reasonable precautions for the safe custody of any firearm or ammunition which, by virtue of section 9(1) of the Firearms Act 1968 he or any servant of his has in his posession without holding a certificate; or

(b) to fail to report forthwith to the police the loss or theft of any such firearm or ammunition.

15. Rifle and pistol clubs

(1) A member of a rifle club, miniature rifle club or pistol club approved by the Secretary of State may, without holding a firearm certificate, have in his possession a firearm and ammunition when engaged as a member of the club in, or in connection with, target practice.

(2) Any approval under this section may be limited so as to apply to target practice with only such types of rifles or pistols as are specified in the approval.

FIREARMS (AMENDMENT) ACT 1997

2. Slaughtering instruments

The authority of the Secretary of State is not required by virtue of subsection (1)(aba) of section 5 of the 1968 Act—

(a) for a person to have in his possession, or to purchase or acquire, or to sell or transfer, a slaughtering instrument if he is authorised by a firearm certificate to have the instrument in his possession, or to purchase or acquire it;

(b) for a person to have a slaughtering instrument in his possession if he is entitled, under section 10 of the 1968 Act, to have it in his possession without a firearm certificate.

3. Firearms used for humane killing of animals

The authority of the Secretary of State is not required by virtue of subsection (1)(aba) of section 5 of the 1968 Act for a person to have in his possession, or to purchase or acquire, or to sell or transfer, a firearm if he is authorised by a firearm certificate to have the firearm in his possession, or to purchase or acquire it, subject to a condition that it is only for use in connection with the humane killing of animals.

4. Shot pistols used for shooting vermin

(1) The authority of the Secretary of State is not required by virtue of subsection (1)(aba) of section 5 of the 1968 Act for a person to have in his possession, or to purchase or acquire, or to sell or transfer, a shot pistol if he is authorised by a firearm certificate to have the shot pistol in his possession, or to purchase or acquire it, subject to a condition that it is only for use in connection with the shooting of vermin.

(2) For the purposes of this section, 'shot pistol' means a smooth-bored gun which is chambered for .410 cartridges or 9mm rim-fire cartridges.

5. Races at athletic meetings

The authority of the Secretary of State is not required by virtue of subsection (1)(aba) of section 5 of the 1968 Act—

(a) for a person to have a firearm in his possession at an athletic meeting for the purpose of starting races at that meeting; or

(b) for a person to have in his possession, or to purchase or acquire, or to sell or transfer, a firearm if he is authorised by a firearm certificate to have the firearm in his possession, or to purchase or acquire it, subject to a condition that it is only for use in connection with starting races at athletic meetings.

6. Trophies of war

The authority of the Secretary of State is not required by virtue of subsection (1)(aba) of section 5 of the 1968 Act for a person to have in his possession a firearm which was acquired as a trophy of war before 1st January 1946 if he is authorised by a firearm certificate to have it in his possession.

7. Firearms of historic interest
(1)   The authority of the Secretary of State is not required by virtue of subsection (1)(aba) of section 5 of the 1968 Act for a person to have in his possession, or to purchase or acquire, or to sell or transfer, a firearm which—

    (a)   was manufactured before 1st January 1919; and

    (b)   is of a description specified under subsection (2) below,

if he is authorised by a firearm certificate to have the firearm in his possession, or to purchase or acquire it, subject to a condition that he does so only for the purpose of its being kept or exhibited as part of a collection.

(2)   The Secretary of State may by order made by statutory instrument specify a description of firearm for the purposes of subsection (1) above if it appears to him that—

    (a)   firearms of that description were manufactured before 1st January 1919, and

    (b)   ammunition for firearms of that type is not readily available.

(3)   The authority of the Secretary of State is not required by virtue of subsection (1)(aba) of section 5 of the 1968 Act for a person to have in his possession, or to purchase or acquire, or to sell or transfer, a firearm which—

    (a)   is of particular rarity, aesthetic quality or technical interest, or

    (b)   is of historical importance,

if he is authorised by a firearm certificate to have the firearm in his possession subject to a condition requiring it to be kept and used only at a place designated for the purposes of this subsection by the Secretary of State.

(4)   This section has effect without prejudice to section 58(2) of the 1968 Act (antique firearms).

8. Weapons and ammunition used for treating animals
The authority of the Secretary of State is not required by virtue of subsection (1)(aba), (b) or (c) of section 5 of the 1968 Act for a person to have in his possession, or to purchase or acquire, or to sell or transfer, any firearm, weapon or ammunition designed or adapted for the purpose of tranquillising or otherwise treating any animal, if he is authorised by a firearm certificate to possess, or to purchase or acquire, the firearm, weapon or ammunition subject to a condition restricting its use to use in connection with the treatment of animals.

48. Firearms powered by compressed carbon dioxide
Any reference to an air rifle, air pistol or air gun—

    (a)   in the Firearms Acts 1968 to 1997; or

    (b)   in the Firearms (Dangerous Air Weapons) Rules 1969 or the Firearms (Dangerous Air Weapons) (Scotland) Rules 1969,

shall include a reference to a rifle, pistol or gun powered by compressed carbon dioxide.

(d) DOGS

DANGEROUS DOGS ACT 1991

1. Dogs bred for fighting
(1)   This section applies to—

    (a)   any dog of the type known as the pit bull terrier;

    (b)   any dog of the type known as the Japanese tosa; and

    (c)   any dog of any type designated for the purposes of this section by an order of the Secretary of State, being a type appearing to him to be bred for fighting or to have the characteristics of a type bred for that purpose.

(2)   No person shall—
(a)   breed, or breed from, a dog to which this section applies;
(b)   sell or exchange such a dog or offer, advertise or expose such a dog for sale or exchange;
(c)   make or offer to make a gift of such a dog or advertise or expose such a dog as a gift;
(d)   allow such a dog of which he is the owner or of which he is for the time being in charge to be in a public place without being muzzled and kept on a lead; or
(e)   abandon such a dog of which he is the owner or, being the owner or for the time being in charge of such a dog, allow it to stray.

(7)   Any person who contravenes this section is guilty of an offence and liable on summary conviction to imprisonment for a term not exceeding six months or a fine not exceeding level 5 on the standard scale or both except that a person who publishes an advertisement in contravention of subsection (2)(b) or (c)—
(a)   shall not on being convicted be liable to imprisonment if he shows that he published the advertisement to the order of someone else and did not himself devise it; and
(b)   shall not be convicted if, in addition, he shows that he did not know and had no reasonable cause to suspect that it related to a dog to which this section applies.

3.   Keeping dogs under proper control

(1)   If a dog is dangerously out of control in a public place—
(a)   the owner; and
(b)   if different, the person for the time being in charge of the dog,
is guilty of an offence, or, if the dog while so out of control injures any person, an aggravated offence, under this subsection.

(2)   In proceedings for an offence under subsection (1) above against a person who is the owner of a dog but was not at the material time in charge of it, it shall be a defence for the accused to prove that the dog was at the material time in the charge of a person whom he reasonably believed to be a fit and proper person to be in charge of it.

(3)   If the owner or, if different, the person for the time being in charge of a dog allows it to enter a place which is not a public place but where it is not permitted to be and while it is there—
(a)   it injures any person; or
(b)   there are grounds for reasonable apprehension that it will do so,
he is guilty of an offence, or, if the dog injures any person, an aggravated offence, under this subsection.

(4)   A person guilty of an offence under subsection (1) or (3) above other than an aggravated offence is liable on summary conviction to imprisonment for a term not exceeding six months or a fine not exceeding level 5 on the standard scale or both; and a person guilty of an aggravated offence under either of those subsections is liable—
(a)   on summary conviction, to imprisonment for a term not exceeding six months or a fine not exceeding the statutory maximum or both;
(b)   on conviction on indictment, to imprisonment for a term not exceeding two years or a fine or both.

6.   Dogs owned by young persons

Where a dog is owned by a person who is less than sixteen years old any reference to its owner in section 1(2)(d) or (e) or 3 above shall include a reference to the head of the household, if any, of which that person is a member . . .

7.   Muzzling and leads

(1)   In this Act—

(a)   references to a dog being muzzled are to its being securely fitted with a muzzle sufficient to prevent it biting any person; and

(b)   references to its being kept on a lead are to its being securely held on a lead by a person who is not less than sixteen years old.

10.   Interpretation

(2)   In this Act—

'advertisement' includes any means of bringing a matter to the attention of the public and 'advertise' shall be construed accordingly;

'public place' means any street, road or other place (whether or not enclosed) to which the public have or are permitted to have access whether for payment or otherwise and includes the common parts of a building containing two or more separate dwellings.

(3)   For the purposes of this Act a dog shall be regarded as dangerously out of control on any occasion on which there are grounds for reasonable apprehension that it will injure any person whether or not it actually does so, but references to a dog injuring a person or there being grounds for reasonable apprehension that it will do so do not include references to any case in which the dog is being used for a lawful purpose by a constable or a person in the service of the Crown.

(e)   ALCOHOL AND OTHER DRUGS

LICENSING ACT 1964

59.   Prohibition of sale, etc., of intoxicating liquor outside permitted hours

(1)   Subject to the provision of this Act, no person shall, except during the permitted hours—

(a)   himself or by his servant or agent sell or supply to any person in licensed premises in respect of which a club is registered any intoxicating liquor, whether to be consumed on or off the premises; or

(b)   consume in or take from such premises any intoxicating liquor.

(3)   This section does not apply in relation to intoxicating liquor sold under an occasional licence.

160.   Selling liquor without licence

(1)   Subject to the provisions of this Act, if any person—

(a)   sells or exposes for sale by retail any intoxicating liquor without holding a justices' licence or occasional permission or

(b)   holding a justices' licence, an occasional licence, or a canteen licence or occasional permission, sells or exposes for sale by retail any intoxicating liquor expect at the place for which that licence or permission authorises . . . the sale of that liquor, he shall be guilty of an offence under this section.

(2)   Where intoxicating liquor is sold in contravention of this section on any premises, every occupier of the premises who is proved to have been privy or consenting to the sale shall be guilty of an offence under this section.

(4)   The holder of a justices' licence or a canteen licence shall, on his second or subsequent conviction of an offence under this section, forfeit the licence.

(5)   The court by or before which a person is convicted of an offence under this section committed after a previous conviction of such an offence may order him to be disqualified for holding a justices' licence—

(a)   on a second conviction, for a period not exceeding five years;

(b)   on a third or subsequent conviction, for any term of years or for life.

(6)   The court by or before which the holder of a justices' licence, an occasional licence or a canteen licence is convicted of an offence under this section may declare

all intoxicating liquor found in his possession, and the vessels containing it, to be forefeited.

161. Selling liquor in breach of conditions of licence

(1) If the holder of a justices' on-licence knowingly sells or supplies intoxicating liquor to persons to whom he is not permitted by the conditions of the licence to sell or supply it he shall be guilty of an offence under this section.

(2) If the holder of a Part IV licence knowingly permits intoxicating liquor sold in pursuance of the licence to be consumed on the licensed premises by persons for whose consumption there he is not permitted by the conditions of the licence to sell it, he shall be guilty of an offence under this section.

162. Keeping on premises of liquor of kind not authorised by licence

If without reasonable excuse the holder of a justices' licence, an occasional licence or a canteen licence has in his possession on the premises in respect of which the licence is in force any kind of intoxicating liquor which he is not authorised to sell, he shall be liable—

(a) on a first conviction, to a fine not exceeding ten pounds,

(b) on a subsequent conviction, to a fine not exceeding twenty pounds, and shall forfeit the liquor and the vessels containing it.

168. Children prohibited from bars

(1) The holder of a justices' licence shall not allow a person under fourteen to be in the bar of the licensed premises during the permitted hours.

(2) No person shall cause or procure, or attempt to cause or procure, any person under fourteen to be in the bar of licensed premises during the permitted hours.

(3) Where it is shown that a person under fourteen was in the bar of any licensed premises during the permitted hours, the holder of the justices' licence shall be guilty of an offence under this section unless he proves either—

(a) that he exercised all due diligence to prevent the person under fourteen from being admitted to the bar, or

(b) that the person under fourteen had apparently attained that age.

(4) No offence shall be committed under this section if the person under fourteen—

(a) is the licence-holder's child, or

(b) resides in the premises, but is not employed there, or

(c) is in the bar solely for the purpose of passing to or from some part of the premises which is not a bar and to or from which there is no other convenient means of access or egress.

(5) No offence shall be committed under this section if the bar is in any railway refreshment-rooms or other premises constructed, fitted and intended to be used bona fide for any purpose to which the holding of a justices' licence is merely ancillary.

(8) Where in any proceedings under this section it is alleged that a person was at any time under fourteen, and he appears to the court to have then been under that age, he shall be deemed for the purposes of the proceedings to have then been under that age, unless the contrary is shown.

169. Serving or delivering intoxicating liquor to or for consumption by persons under 18

(1) Subject to subsection (4) of this section, in licensed premises the holder of the licence or his servant shall not knowingly sell intoxicating liquor to a person under eighteen or knowingly allow a person under eighteen to consume intoxicating liquor in a bar nor shall the holder of the licence knowingly allow any person to sell intoxicating liquor to a person under eighteen.

(2) Subject to subsection (4) of this section, a person under eighteen shall not in licensed premises buy or attempt to buy intoxicating liquor, nor consume intoxicating liquor in a bar.

(3) No person shall buy or attempt to buy intoxicating liquor for consumption in a bar in licensed premises by a person under eighteen.

(4) Subsections (1) and (2) of this section do not prohibit the sale to or purchase by a person who has attained the age of sixteen of beer, porter, cider or perry for consumption at a meal in a part of the premises usually set apart for the service of meals which is not a bar.

(4A) Where a person is charged under subsection (1) of this section with the offence of selling intoxicating liquor to a person under eighteen and he is charged by reason of his own act, it shall be a defence for him to prove—

    (a) that he exercised all due diligence to avoid the commission of such an offence; or

    (b) that he had no reason to suspect that the person was under eighteen.

(4B) Where the person charged with an offence under subsection (1) of this section is the licence holder and he is charged by reason of the act or default of some other person, it shall be a defence for him to prove that he exercised all due diligence to avoid the commission of an offence under that subsection.

(5) Subject to subsection (7) of this section, the holder of the licence or his servant shall not knowingly deliver, nor shall the holder of the licence knowingly allow any person to deliver, to a person under eighteen intoxicating liquor sold in licensed premises for consumption off the premises, except where the delivery is made at the residence or working place of the purchaser.

(6) Subject to subsection (7) of this section, a person shall not knowingly send a person under eighteen for the purpose of obtaining intoxicating liquor sold or to be sold in licensed premises for consumption off the premises, whether the liquor is to be obtained from the licensed premises or other premises from which it is delivered in pursuance of the sale.

(7) Subsection (5) and (6) of this section do not apply where the person under eighteen is a member of the licence holder's family or his servant or apprentice and is employed as a messenger to deliver intoxicating liquor.

(8) A person guilty of an offence under this section shall be liable to a fine not exceeding level 3 on the standard scale; and on a person's second or subsequent conviction of such an offence the court may, if the offence was committed by him or the holder of a justices' licence, order that he shall forfeit the licence.

172. Licence holder not to permit drunkenness, etc.

(1) The holder of a justices' licence shall not permit drunkenness or any violent, quarrelsome or riotous conduct to take place in the licensed premises.

(2) If the holder of a justices' licence is charged under subsection (1) of this section with permitting drunkenness, and it is proved that any person was drunk in the licensed premises, the burden of proving that the licence holder and the person employed by him took all reasonable steps for preventing drunkenness in the premises shall lie upon him.

(3) The holder of a justices' licence shall not sell intoxicating liquor to a drunken person.

173. Procuring drink for drunken person

(1) If any person in licensed premises procures or attempts to procure any intoxicating liquor for consumption by a drunken person he shall be guilty of an offence under this section.

(2) If any person aids a drunken person in obtaining or consuming intoxicating liquor in licensed premises he shall be guilty of an offence under this section.

175. Prostitutes not to be allowed to assemble on licensed premises

(1) The holder of a justices' licence shall not knowingly allow the licensed premises to be the habitual resort or place of meeting of reputed prostitutes, whether the object of their so resorting or meeting is or is not prostitution; but this section does not prohibit his allowing any such persons to remain in the premises for the purpose of obtaining reasonable refreshment for such time as is necessary for that purpose.

176. Permitting licensed premises to be a brothel

(1) If the holder of a justices' licence permits the licensed premises to be a brothel, he shall be liable to a fine not exceeding level 2 on the standard scale.

(2) If the holder of a justices' licence is convicted, whether under this section or under any other enactment, of permitting his premises to be a brothel, he shall forfeit the licence.

177. Gaming on licensed premises

(1) If the holder of a justices' licence suffers any game to be played in the premises in such circumstances that an offence under the Gaming Act 1968 is committed or a requirement or restriction for the time being in force under section 6 of that Act is contravened, he shall be liable, on a first conviction to a fine not exceeding ten pounds, and on a subsequent conviction to a fine not exceeding twenty pounds.

178. Offences in relation to constables

If the holder of a justices' licence—

(a) knowingly suffers to remain on the licensed premises any constable during any part of the time appointed for the constable's being on duty, except for the purpose for the execution of the constable's duty, or

(b) supplies any liquor or refreshment, whether by way of gift or sale, to any constable on duty except by authority of a superior officer of the constable, or

(c) bribes or attempts to bribe any constable,

he shall be liable, on a first conviction to a fine not exceeding ten pounds, and on a subsequent conviction to a fine not exceeding twenty pounds.

196. Proof of sale or consumption of intoxicating liquor

(1) Evidence that a transaction in the nature of a sale of intoxicating liquor took place shall, in any proceedings relating to an offence under this Act, be evidence of the sale of the liquor without proof that money passed.

(2) Evidence that consumption of intoxicating liquor was about to take place shall in any such proceedings be evidence of the consumption of intoxicating liquor without proof of actual consumption.

(3) Evidence that any person, other than the occupier of licensed premises or a servant employed in licensed premises, or, as the case may be, other than the occupier of a licensed canteen or a servant employed in such a canteen, consumed or intended to consume intoxicating liquor in the premises or, as the case may be, canteen, shall be evidence that the liquor was sold by or on behalf of the holder of the justices' licence, occasional licence or canteen licence, as the case may be, to that person.

MISUSE OF DRUGS ACT 1971

2. Controlled drugs and their classification for purposes of this Act

(1) In this Act—

(a) the expression 'controlled drug' means any substance or product for the time being specified in Part I, II or III of Schedule 2 to this Act; and

(b) the expressions 'Class A drug', 'Class B drug', and 'Class C drug' mean any of the substances and products for the time being specified respectively in Part I, Part II and Part III of that Schedule;

and the provisions of Part IV of that Schedule shall have effect with respect to the meanings of expressions used in that Schedule.

3. Restriction of importation and exportation of controlled drugs

(1) Subject to subsection (2) below—

(a) the importation of a controlled drug; and

(b) the exportation of a controlled drug,

are hereby prohibited.

(2) Subsection (1) above does not apply—

(a) to the importation or exportation of a controlled drug which is for the time being excepted from paragraph (a) or, as the case may be, paragraph (b) of subsection (1) above by regulations under section 7 of this Act; or

(b) to the importation or exportation of a controlled drug under and in accordance with the terms of a licence issued by the Secretary of State and in compliance with any conditions attached thereto.

4. Restriction of production and supply of controlled drugs

(1) Subject to any regulations under section 7 of this Act for the time being in force, it shall not be lawful for a person—

(a) to produce a controlled drug; or

(b) to supply or offer to supply a controlled drug to another.

(2) Subject to section 28 of this Act, it is an offence for a person—

(a) to produce a controlled drug in contravention of subsection (1) above; or

(b) to be concerned in the production of such a drug in contravention of that subsection by another.

(3) Subject to section 28 of this Act, it is an offence for a person—

(a) to supply or offer to supply a controlled drug to another in contravention of subsection (1) above; or

(b) to be concerned in the supplying of such a drug to another in contravention of that subsection; or

(c) to be concerned in the making to another in contravention of that subsection of an offer to supply such a drug.

5. Restriction of possession of controlled drugs

(1) Subject to any regulations under section 7 of this Act for the time being in force, it shall not be lawful for a person to have a controlled drug in his possession.

(2) Subject to section 28 of this Act and to subsection (4) below, it is an offence for a person to have a controlled drug in his possession in contravention of subsection (1) above.

(3) Subject to section 28 of this Act, it is an offence for a person to have a controlled drug in his possession, whether lawfully or not, with intent to supply it to another in contravention of section 4(1) of this Act.

(4) In any proceedings for an offence under subsection (2) above in which it is proved that the accused had a controlled drug in his possession, it shall be a defence for him to prove—

(a) that, knowing or suspecting it to be a controlled drug, he took possession of it for the purpose of preventing another from committing or continuing to commit an offence in connection with that drug and that as soon as possible after taking possession of it he took all such steps as were reasonably open to him to destroy the drug or to deliver it into the custody of a person lawfully entitled to take custody of it; or

(b) that, knowing or suspecting it to be a controlled drug, he took possession of it for the purpose of delivering it into the custody of a person lawfully entitled to take custody of it and that as soon as possible after taking possession of it he took all such steps as were reasonably open to him to deliver it into the custody of such a person.

(6)   Nothing in subsection (4) above shall prejudice any defence which is open to a person charged with an offence under this section to raise apart from that subsection.

6.   Restriction of cultivation of cannabis plants

(1)   Subject to any regulations under section 7 of this Act for the time being in force, it shall not be lawful for a person to cultivate any plant of the genus Cannabis.

(2)   Subject to section 28 of this Act, it is an offence to cultivate any such plant in contravention of subsection (1) above.

7.   Authorisation of activities otherwise unlawful under foregoing provisions

(1)   The Secretary of State may by regulations—

(a)   except from section 3(1)(a) or (b), 4(1)(a) or (b) or 5(1) of this Act such controlled drugs as may be specified in the regulations; and

(b)   make such other provision as he thinks fit for the purpose of making it lawful for persons to do things which under any of the following provisions of this Act, that is to say sections 4(1), 5(1) and 6(1), it would otherwise be unlawful for them to do.

(2)   Without prejudice to the generality of paragraph (b) of subsection (1) above, regulations under that subsection authorising the doing of any such thing as is mentioned in that paragraph may in particular provide for the doing of that thing to be lawful—

(a)   if it is done under and in accordance with the terms of a licence or other authority issued by the Secretary of State and in compliance with any conditions attached thereto; or

(b)   if it is done in compliance with such conditions as may be prescribed.

(3)   Subject to subsection (4) below, the Secretary of State shall so exercise his power to make regulations under subsection (1) above as to secure—

(a)   that it is not unlawful under section 4(1) of this Act for a doctor, dentist, veterinary practitioner or veterinary surgeon, acting in his capacity as such, to prescribe, administer, manufacture, compound or supply a controlled drug, or for a pharmacist or a person lawfully conducting a retail pharmacy business, acting in either case in his capacity as such, to manufacture, compound or supply a controlled drug; and

(b)   that it is not unlawful under section 5(1) of this Act for a doctor, dentist, veterinary practitioner, veterinary surgeon, pharmacist or person lawfully conducting a retail pharmacy business to have a controlled drug in his possession for the purpose of acting in his capacity as such.

(4)   If in the case of any controlled drug the Secretary of State is of the opinion that it is in the public interest—

(a)   for production, supply and possession of that drug to be either wholly unlawful or unlawful except for purposes of research or other special purposes; or

(b)   for it to be unlawful for practitioners, pharmacists and persons lawfully conducting retail pharmacy business to do in relation to that drug any of the things mentioned in subsection (3) above except under a licence or other authority issued by the Secretary of State,

he may by order designate that drug as a drug to which this subsection applies; and while there is in force an order under this subsection designating a controlled drug as one to which this subsection applies subsection (3) above shall not apply as regards that drug.

(8)   References in this section to a person's 'doing' things include references to his having things in his possession.

8.   Occupiers etc., of premises to be punishable for permitting certain activities to take place there

A person commits an offence if, being the occupier or concerned in the management of any premises, he knowingly permits or suffers any of the following activities to take place on those premises, that is to say—

(a)   producing or attempting to produce a controlled drug in contravention of section 4(1) of this Act;

(b)   supplying or attempting to supply a controlled drug to another in contravention of section 4(1) of this Act, or offering to supply a controlled drug to another in contravention of section 4(1);

(c)   preparing opium for smoking;

(d)   smoking cannabis, cannabis resin or prepared opium.

9.   Prohibition of certain activities etc., relating to opium

Subject to section 28 of this Act, it is an offence for a person—

(a)   to smoke or otherwise use prepared opium; or

(b)   to frequent a place used for the purpose of opium smoking; or

(c)   to have in his possession

(i)   any pipes or other utensils made or adapted for use in connection with the smoking of opium, being pipes or utensils which have been used by him or with his knowledge and permission in that connection or which he intends to use or permit others to use in that connection; or

(ii)   any utensils which have been used by him or with his knowledge and permission in connection with the preparation of opium for smoking.

9A.   Prohibition of supply etc., of articles for administering or preparing controlled drugs

(1)   A person who supplies or offers to supply any article which may be used or adapted to be used (whether by itself or in combination with another article or other articles) in the administration by any person of a controlled drug to himself or another, believing that the article (or the article as adapted) is to be so used in circumstances where the administration is unlawful, is guilty of an offence.

(2)   It is not an offence under subsection (1) above to supply or offer to supply a hypodermic syringe, or any part of one.

(3)   A person who supplies or offers to supply any article which may be used to prepare a controlled drug for administration by any person to himself or another believing that the article is to be so used in circumstances where the administration is unlawful is guilty of an offence.

(4)   For the purposes of this section, any administration of a controlled drug is unlawful except—

(a)   the administration by any person of a controlled drug to another in circumstances where the administration of the drug is not unlawful under section 4(1) of this Act, or

(b)   the administration by any person of a controlled drug to himself in circumstances where having the controlled drug in his possession is not unlawful under section 5(1) of this Act.

(5)   In this section, references to administration by any person of a controlled drug to himself include a reference to his administering it to himself with the assistance of another.

19.   Attempts etc., to commit offences

It is an offence for a person to attempt to commit an offence under any other provision of this Act or to incite another to commit such an offence.

20.   Assisting in or inducing commission outside United Kingdom of offence punishable under a corresponding law

A person commits an offence if in the United Kingdom he assists in or induces the commission in any place outside the United Kingdom of an offence punishable under the provisions of a corresponding law in force in that place.

28. Proof of lack of knowledge etc., to be a defence in proceedings for certain offences

(1) This section applies to offences under any of the following provisions of this Act; that is to say section 4(2) and (3), section 5(2) and (3), section 6(2) and section 9.

(2) Subject to subsection (3) below, in any proceedings for an offence to which this section applies it shall be a defence for the accused to prove that he neither knew of nor suspected nor had reason to suspect the existence of some fact alleged by the prosecution which is necessary for the prosecution to prove if he is to be convicted of the offence charged.

(3) Where in any proceedings for an offence to which this section applies it is necessary, if the accused is to be convicted of the offence charged, for the prosecution to prove that some substance or product involved in the alleged offence was the controlled drug which the prosecution alleges it to have been, and it is proved that the substance or product in question was that controlled drug, the accused—

(a) shall not be acquitted of the offence charged by reason only of proving that he neither knew or suspected nor had reason to suspect that the substance or product in question was the particular controlled drug alleged; but

(b) shall be acquitted thereof—

(i) if he proves that he neither believed nor suspected nor had reason to suspect that the substance or product in question was a controlled drug; or

(ii) if he proves that he believed the substance or product in question to be a controlled drug, or a controlled drug of a description, such that, if it had in fact been that controlled drug or a controlled drug of that description, he would not at the material time have been committing any offence to which this section applies.

(4) Nothing in this section shall prejudice any defence which it is open to a person charged with an offence to which this section applies to raise apart from this section.

36. Meaning of 'corresponding law', and evidence of certain matters by certificate

(1) In this Act the expression 'corresponding law' means a law stated in a certificate purporting to be issued by or on behalf of the government of a country outside the United Kingdom to be a law providing for the control and regulation in that country of the production, supply, use, export and import of drugs and other substances in accordance with the provisions of the Single Convention on Narcotic Drugs signed at New York on 30th March 1961 or a law providing for the control and regulation in that country of the production, supply, use, export and import of dangerous or otherwise harmful drugs in pursuance of any treaty, convention or other agreement or arrangement to which the government of that country and Her Majesty's Government in the United Kingdom are for the time being parties.

37. Interpretation

(1) In this Act, except in so far as the context otherwise requires, the following expressions have the meanings hereby assigned to them respectively, that is to say:—

'produce', where the reference is to producing a controlled drug, means producing it by manufacture, cultivation or any other method and 'production' has a corresponding meaning;

'supplying' includes distributing;

(2) References in this Act to misusing a drug are references to misusing it by taking it; and the reference in the foregoing provision to the taking of a drug is a reference to the taking of it by a human being by way of any form of self administration, whether or not involving assistance by another.

(3) For the purposes of this Act the things which a person has in his possession shall be taken to include any thing subject to his control which is in the custody of another.

INTOXICATING SUBSTANCES (SUPPLY) ACT 1985

1. Offence of supplying intoxicating substance

(1)   It is an offence for a person to supply or offer to supply a substance other than a controlled drug—

(a)   to a person under the age of eighteen whom he knows, or has reasonable cause to believe, to be under that age; or

(b)   to a person—

(i)   who is acting on behalf of a person under that age; and

(ii)   whom he knows, or has reasonable cause to believe, to be so acting,

if he knows or has reasonable cause to believe that the substance is, or its fumes are, likely to be inhaled by the person under the age of eighteen for the purpose of causing intoxication.

(2)   In proceedings against any person for an offence under subsection (1) above it is a defence for him to show that at the time he made the supply or offer he was under the age of eighteen and was acting otherwise than in the course of furtherance of a business.

(4)   In this section 'controlled drug' has the same meaning as in the Misuse of Drugs Act 1971.

DRUG TRAFFICKING ACT 1994

1. Meaning of 'drug trafficking' and 'drug trafficking offence'

(1)   In this Act 'drug trafficking' means, subject to subsection (2) below, doing or being concerned in any of the following, whether in England and Wales or elsewhere—

(a)   producing or supplying a controlled drug where the production or supply contravenes section 4(1) of the Misuse of Drugs Act 1971 or a corresponding law;

(b)   transporting or storing a controlled drug where possession of the drug contravenes section 5(1) of that Act or a corresponding law;

(c)   importing or exporting a controlled drug where the importation or exportation is prohibited by section 3(1) of that Act or a corresponding law;

(d)   manufacturing or supplying a scheduled substance within the meaning of section 12 of the Criminal Justice (International Co-operation) Act 1990 where the manufacture or supply is an offence under that section or would be such an offence if it took place in England and Wales;

(e)   using any ship for illicit traffic in controlled drugs in circumstances which amount to the commission of an offence under section 19 of that Act;

(f)   conduct which is an offence under section 49 of this Act or which would be such an offence if it took place in England and Wales;

(g)   acquiring, having possession of or using property in circumstances which amount to the commission of an offence under section 51 of this Act or which would amount to such an offence if it took place in England and Wales.

(2)   'Drug trafficking' also includes a person doing the following, whether in England and Wales or elsewhere, that is to say, entering into or being otherwise concerned in an arrangement whereby—

(a)   the retention or control by or on behalf of another person of the other person's proceeds of drug trafficking is facilitated; or

(b)   the proceeds of drug trafficking by another person are used to secure that funds are placed at the other person's disposal or are used for the other person's benefit to acquire property by way of investment.

(3)   In this Act 'drug trafficking offence' means any of the following—

(a)   an offence under section 4(2) or (3) or 5(3) of the Misuse of Drugs Act 1971 (production, supply and possession for supply of controlled drugs);

(b)   an offence under section 20 of that Act (assisting in or inducing commission outside United Kingdom of offence punishable under a corresponding law);

(c)   an offence under—
    (i)   section 50(2) or (3) of the Customs and Excise Management Act 1979 (improper importation),
    (ii)   section 68(2) of that Act (exportation), or
    (iii) section 170 of that Act (fraudulent evasion),
in connection with a prohibition or restriction on importation or exportation having effect by virtue of section 3 of the Misuse of Drugs Act 1971;
    (d)   an offence under section 12 of the Criminal Justice (International Co-operation) Act 1990 (manufacture or supply of substance specified in Schedule 2 to that Act);
    (e)   an offence under section 19 of that Act (using ship for illicit traffic in controlled drugs);
    (f)   an offence under section 49, 50 or 51 of this Act or section 14 of the Criminal Justice (International Co-operation) Act 1990 (which makes, in relation to Scotland and Northern Ireland, provision corresponding to section 49 of this Act);
    (g)   an offence under section 1 of the Criminal Law Act 1977 of conspiracy to commit any of the offences in paragraphs (a) to (f) above;
    (h)   an offence under section 1 of the Criminal Attempts Act 1981 of attempting to commit any of those offences; and
    (i)   an offence of inciting another person to commit any of those offences, whether under section 19 of the Misuse of Drugs Act 1971 or at common law;
and includes aiding, abetting, counselling or procuring the commission of any of the offences in paragraphs (a) to (f) above.
    (4)   In this section 'corresponding law' has the same meaning as in the Misuse of Drugs Act 1971.

49.   Concealing or transferring proceeds of drug trafficking

    (1)   A person is guilty of an offence if he—
    (a)   conceals or disguises any property which is, or in whole or in part directly or indirectly represents, his proceeds of drug trafficking, or
    (b)   converts or transfers that property or removes it from the jurisdiction,
for the purpose of avoiding prosecution for a drug trafficking offence or the making or enforcement in his case of a confiscation order.
    (2)   A person is guilty of an offence if, knowing or having reasonable grounds to suspect that any property is, or in whole or in part directly or indirectly represents, another person's proceeds of drug trafficking, he—
    (a)   conceals or disguises that property, or
    (b)   converts or transfers that property or removes it from the jurisdiction,
for the purpose of assisting any person to avoid prosecution for a drug trafficking offence or the making or enforcement of a confiscation order.
    (3)   In subsections (1)(a) and (2)(a) above the references to concealing or disguising any property include references to concealing or disguising its nature, source, location, disposition, movement or ownership or any rights with respect to it.

50.   Assisting another person to retain the benefit of drug trafficking

    (1)   Subject to subsection (3) below, a person is guilty of an offence if he enters into or is otherwise concerned in an arrangement whereby—
    (a)   the retention or control by or on behalf of another person (call him 'A') of A's proceeds of drug trafficking is facilitated (whether by concealment, removal from the jurisdiction, transfer to nominees or otherwise), or
    (b)   A's proceeds of drug trafficking—
        (i)   are used to secure that funds are placed at A's disposal, or
        (ii)   are used for A's benefit to acquire property by way of investment,
and he knows or suspects that A is a person who carries on or has carried on drug trafficking or has benefited from drug trafficking.

(2) In this section, references to any person's proceeds of drug trafficking include a reference to any property which in whole or in part directly or indirectly represented in his hands his proceeds of drug trafficking.

(3) Where a person discloses to a constable a suspicion or belief that any funds or investments are derived from or used in connection with drug trafficking, or discloses to a constable any matter on which such a suspicion or belief is based—

(a) the disclosure shall not be treated as a breach of any restriction upon the disclosure of information imposed by statute or otherwise; and

(b) if he does any act in contravention of subsection (1) above and the disclosure relates to the arrangement concerned, he does not commit an offence under this section if—

(i) the disclosure is made before he does the act concerned and the act is done with the consent of the constable; or

(ii) the disclosure is made after he does the act, but is made on his initiative and as soon as it is reasonable for him to make it.

(4) In proceedings against a person for an offence under this section, it is a defence to prove—

(a) that he did not know or suspect that the arrangement related to any person's proceeds of drug trafficking;

(b) that he did not know or suspect that by the arrangement the retention or control by or on behalf of A of any property was facilitated or, as the case may be, that by the arrangement any property was used as mentioned in subsection (1)(b) above; or

(c) that—

(i) he intended to disclose to a constable such a suspicion, belief or matter as is mentioned in subsection (3) above in relation to the arrangement, but

(ii) there is reasonable excuse for his failure to make any such disclosure in the manner mentioned in paragraph (b)(i) or (ii) of that subsection.

(5) In the case of a person who was in employment at the time in question, subsections (3) and (4) above shall have effect in relation to disclosures, and intended disclosures, to the appropriate person in accordance with the procedure established by his employer for the making of such disclosures as they have effect in relation to disclosures, and intended disclosures, to a constable.

51. Acquisition, possession or use of proceeds of drug trafficking

(1) A person is guilty of an offence if, knowing that any property is, or in whole or in part directly or indirectly represents, another person's proceeds of drug trafficking, he acquires or uses that property or has possession of it.

(2) It is a defence to a charge of committing an offence under this section that the person charged acquired or used the property or had possession of it for adequate consideration.

(3) For the purposes of subsection (2) above—

(a) a person acquires property for inadequate consideration if the value of the consideration is significantly less than the value of the property; and

(b) a person uses or has possession of property for inadequate consideration if the value of the consideration is significantly less than the value of his use or possession of the property.

(4) The provision for any person of services or goods which are of assistance to him in drug trafficking shall not be treated as consideration for the purposes of subsection (2) above.

(5) Where a person discloses to a constable a suspicion or belief that any property is, or in whole or in part directly or indirectly represents, another person's proceeds of drug trafficking, or discloses to a constable any matter on which such a suspicion or belief is based—

(a)   the disclosure shall not be treated as a breach of any restriction upon the disclosure of information imposed by statute or otherwise; and

(b)   if he does any act in relation to the property in contravention of subsection (1) above, he does not commit an offence under this section if—

(i)   the disclosure is made before he does the act concerned and the act is done with the consent of the constable; or

(ii)   the disclosure is made after he does the act, but is made on his initiative and as soon as it is reasonable for him to make it.

(6)   For the purposes of this section, having possession of any property shall be taken to be doing an act in relation to it.

(7)   In proceedings against a person for an offence under this section, it is a defence to prove that—

(a)   he intended to disclose to a constable such a suspicion, belief or matter as is mentioned in subsection (5) above, but

(b)   there is reasonable excuse for his failure to make any such disclosure in the manner mentioned in paragraph (b)(i) or (ii) of that subsection.

(8)   In the case of a person who was in employment at the time in question, subsections (5) and (7) above shall have effect in relation to disclosures, and intended disclosures, to the appropriate person in accordance with the procedure established by his employer for the making of such disclosures as they have effect in relation to disclosures, and intended disclosures, to a constable.

(9)   No constable or other person shall be guilty of an offence under this section in respect of anything done by him in the course of acting in connection with the enforcement, or intended enforcement, of any provision of this Act or of any other enactment relating to drug trafficking or the proceeds of drug trafficking.

52.   Failure to disclose knowledge or suspicion of money laundering

(1)   A person is guilty of an offence if—

(a)   he knows or suspects that another person is engaged in drug money laundering.

(b)   the information, or other matter, on which that knowledge or suspicion is based came to his attention in the course of his trade, profession, business or employment, and

(c)   he does not disclose the information or other matter to a constable as soon as is reasonably practicable after it comes to his attention.

(2)   Subsection (1) above does not make it an offence for a professional legal adviser to fail to disclose any information or other matter which has come to him in privileged circumstances.

(3)   It is a defence to a charge of committing an offence under this section that the person charged had a reasonable excuse for not disclosing the information or other matter in question.

(4)   Where a person discloses to a constable—

(a)   his suspicion or belief that another person is engaged in drug money laundering, or

(b)   any information or other matter on which that suspicion or belief is based, the disclosure shall not be treated as a breach of any restriction imposed by statute or otherwise.

(5)   Without prejudice to subsection (3) or (4) above, in the case of a person who was in employment at the time in question, it is a defence to a charge of committing an offence under this section that he disclosed the information or other matter in question to the appropriate person in accordance with the procedure established by his employer for the making of such disclosures.

(6)   A disclosure to which subsection (5) above applies shall not be treated as a breach of any restriction imposed by statute or otherwise.

(7)   In this section 'drug money laundering' means doing any act—

(a)   which constitutes an offence under section 49, 50 or 51 of this Act; or

(b)   in the case of an act done otherwise than in England and Wales, which would constitute such an offence if done in England and Wales;

and for the purposes of this subsection, having possession of any property shall be taken to be doing an act in relation to it.

(8)   For the purposes of this section, any information or other matter comes to a professional legal adviser in privileged circumstances if it is communicated, or given, to him—

(a)   by, or by a representative of, a client of his in connection with the giving by the adviser of legal advice to the client;

(b)   by, or by a representative of, a person seeking legal advice from the adviser; or

(c)   by any person—

(i)   in contemplation of, or in connection with, legal proceedings; and

(ii)   for the purpose of those proceedings.

(9)   No information or other matter shall be treated as coming to a professional legal adviser in privileged circumstances if it is communicated or given with a view to furthering any criminal purpose.

53.   Tipping-off

(1)   A person is guilty of an offence if—

(a)   he knows or suspects that a constable is acting, or is proposing to act, in connection with an investigation which is being, or is about to be, conducted into drug money laundering, and

(b)   he discloses to any other person information or any other matter which is likely to prejudice that investigation or proposed investigation.

(2)   A person is guilty of an offence if—

(a)   he knows or suspects that a disclosure has been made to a constable under section 50, 51 or 52 of this Act ('the disclosure'), and

(b)   he discloses to any other person information or any other matter which is likely to prejudice any investigation which might be conducted following the disclosure.

(3)   A person is guilty of an offence if—

(a)   he knows or suspects that a disclosure of a kind mentioned in section 50(5), 51(8) or 52(5) of this Act ('the disclosure') has been made, and

(b)   he discloses to any person information or any other matter which is likely to prejudice any investigation which might be conducted following the disclosure.

(4)   Nothing in subsections (1) to (3) above makes it an offence for a professional legal adviser to disclose any information or other matter—

(a)   to, or to a representative of, a client of his in connection with the giving by the adviser of legal advice to the client; or

(b)   to any person—

(i)   in contemplation of, or in connection with, legal proceedings; and

(ii)   for the purpose of those proceedings.

(5)   Subsection (4) above does not apply in relation to any information or other matter which is disclosed with a view to furthering any criminal purpose.

(6)   In proceedings against a person for an offence under subsection (1), (2) or (3) above, it is a defence to prove that he did not know or suspect that the disclosure was likely to be prejudicial in the way mentioned in that subsection.

(7)   No constable or other person shall be guilty of an offence under this section in respect of anything done by him in the course of acting in connection with the enforcement, or intended enforcement, of any provision of this Act or of any other enactment relating to drug trafficking or the proceeds of drug trafficking.

(8)   In this section 'drug money laundering' has the same meaning as in section 52 of this Act.

58.   Offence of prejudicing investigation

(1)   Where, in relation to an investigation into drug trafficking—

(a)   an order under section 55 of this Act has been made or has been applied for and has not been refused, or

(b)   a warrant under section 56 of this Act has been issued,

a person is guilty of an offence if, knowing or suspecting that the investigation is taking place he makes any disclosure which is likely to prejudice the investigation.

(2)   In proceedings against a person for an offence under this section, it is a defence to prove—

(a)   that he did not know or suspect that the disclosure was likely to prejudice the investigation; or

(b)   that he had lawful authority or reasonable excuse for making the disclosure.

(3)   Nothing in subsection (1) above makes it an offence for a professional legal adviser to disclose any information or other matter—

(a)   to, or to a representative of, a client of his in connection with the giving by the adviser of legal advice to the client; or

(b)   to any person—

(i)   in contemplation of, or in connection with, legal proceedings; and

(ii)   for the purpose of those proceedings.

(4)   Subsection (3) above does not apply in relation to any information or other matter which is disclosed with a view to furthering any criminal purpose.

(f)   SUPPLY OF GOODS AND SERVICES

FOOD SAFETY ACT 1990

1.   Meaning of 'food' and other basic expressions

(1)   In this Act 'food' includes—

(a)   drink;

(b)   articles and substances of no nutritional value which are used for human consumption;

(c)   chewing gum and other products of a like nature and use; and

(d)   articles and substances used as ingredients in the preparation of food or anything falling within this subsection.

(2)   In this Act 'food' does not include—

(a)   live animals or birds, or live fish which are not used for human consumption while they are alive;

(b)   fodder or feeding stuffs for animals, birds or fish;

(c)   controlled drugs within the meaning of the Misuse of Drugs Act 1971; or

(d)   subject to such exceptions as may be specified in an order made by the Ministers—

(i)   medicinal products within the meaning of the Medicines Act 1968 in respect of which product licences within the meaning of that Act are for the time being in force; or

(ii)   other articles or substances in respect of which such licences are for the time being in force in pursuance of orders under section 104 or 105 of that Act (application of Act to other articles and substances).

(3)   In this Act, unless the context otherwise requires—

'business' includes the undertaking of a canteen, club, school, hospital or institution, whether carried on for profit or not, and any undertaking or activity carried on by a public or local authority;

'commercial operation', in relation to any food or contact material, means any of the following, namely—

    (a)   selling, possessing for sale and offering, exposing or advertising for sale;

    (b)   consigning, delivering or serving by way of sale;

    (c)   preparing for sale or presenting, labelling or wrapping for the purpose of sale;

    (d)   storing or transporting for the purpose of sale;

    (e)   importing and exporting;

and, in relation to any food source, means deriving food from it for the purpose of sale or for purposes connected with sale;

'contact material' means any article or substance which is intended to come into contact with food;

'food business' means any business in the course of which commercial operations with respect to food or food sources are carried out;

'food premises' means any premises used for the purposes of a food business;

'food source' means any growing crop or live animal, bird or fish from which food is intended to be derived (whether by harvesting, slaughtering, milking, collecting eggs or otherwise);

'premises' includes any place, any vehicle, stall or moveable structure and, for such purposes as may be specified in an order made by the Ministers, any ship or aircraft of a description so specified.

    (4)   The reference in subsection (3) above to preparing for sale shall be construed, in relation to any contact material, as a reference to manufacturing or producing for the purpose of sale.

2. Extended meaning of 'sale' etc.

    (1)   For the purposes of this Act—

    (a)   the supply of food, otherwise than on sale, in the course of a business; and

    (b)   any other thing which is done with respect to food and is specified in an order made by the Ministers,

shall be deemed to be a sale of the food, and references to purchasers and purchasing shall be construed accordingly.

    (2)   This Act shall apply—

    (a)   in relation to any food which is offered as a prize or reward or given away in connection with any entertainment to which the public are admitted, whether on payment of money or not, as if the food were, or had been, exposed for sale by each person concerned in the organisation of the entertainment;

    (b)   in relation to any food which, for the purpose of advertisement or in furtherance of any trade or business, is offered as a prize or reward or given away, as if the food were, or had been, exposed for sale by the person offering or giving away the food; and

    (c)   in relation to any food which is exposed or deposited in any premises for the purpose of being so offered or given away as mentioned in paragraph (a) or (b) above, as if the food were, or had been, exposed for sale by the occupier of the premises;

and in this subsection 'entertainment' includes any social gathering, amusement, exhibition, performance, game, sport or trial of skill.

3. Presumptions that food intended for human consumption

    (1)   The following provisions shall apply for the purposes of this Act.

    (2)   Any food commonly used for human consumption shall, if sold or offered, exposed or kept for sale, be presumed, until the contrary is proved, to have been sold or, as the case may be, to have been or to be intended for sale for human consumption.

    (3)   The following, namely—

    (a)   any food commonly used for human consumption which is found on premises used for the preparation, storage, or sale of that food; and

(b)   any article or substance commonly used in the manufacture of food for human consumption which is found on premises used for the preparation, storage or sale of that food,

shall be presumed, until the contrary is proved, to be intended for sale, or for manufacturing food for sale, for human consumption.

(4)   Any article or substance capable of being used in the composition or preparation of any food commonly used for human consumption which is found on premises on which that food is prepared shall, until the contrary is proved, be presumed to be intended for such use.

7.   Rendering food injurious to health

(1)   Any person who renders any food injurious to health by means of any of the following operations, namely—

(a)   adding any article or substance to the food;
(b)   using any article or substance as an ingredient in the preparation of the food;
(c)   abstracting any constituent from the food; and
(d)   subjecting the food to any other process or treatment,

with intent that it shall be sold for human consumption, shall be guilty of an offence.

(2)   In determining for the purposes of this section and section 8(2) below whether any food is injurious to health, regard shall be had—

(a)   not only to the probable effect of that food on the health of a person consuming it; but
(b)   also to the probable cumulative effect of food of substantially the same composition on the health of a person consuming it in ordinary quantities.

(3)   In this Part 'injury', in relation to health, includes any impairment, whether permanent or temporary, and 'injurious to health' shall be construed accordingly.

8.   Selling food not complying with food safety requirements

(1)   Any person who—

(a)   sells for human consumption, or offers, exposes or advertises for sale for such consumption, or has in his possession for the purpose of such sale or of preparation for such sale; or
(b)   deposits with, or consigns to, any other person for the purpose of such sale or of preparation for such sale,

any food which fails to comply with food safety requirements shall be guilty of an offence.

(2)   For the purposes of this Part food fails to comply with food safety requirements if—

(a)   it has been rendered injurious to health by means of any of the operations mentioned in section 7(1) above;
(b)   it is unfit for human consumption; or
(c)   it is so contaminated (whether by extraneous matter or otherwise) that it would not be reasonable to expect it to be used for human consumption in that state; and references to such requirements or to food complying with such requirements shall be construed accordingly.

(3)   Where any food which fails to comply with food safety requirements is part of a batch, lot or consignment of food of the same class or description, it shall be presumed for the purposes of this section and section 9 below, until the contrary is proved, that all of the food in that batch, lot or consignment fails to comply with those requirements.

(4)   For the purposes of this Part, any part of, or product derived wholly or partly from, an animal—

(a)   which has been slaughtered in a knacker's yard, or of which the carcase has been brought into a knacker's yard; . . .

shall be deemed to be unfit for human consumption.

14. Selling food not of the nature or substance or quality demanded

(1) Any person who sells to the purchaser's prejudice any food which is not of the nature or substance or quality demanded by the purchaser shall be guilty of an offence.

(2) In subsection (1) above the reference to sale shall be construed as a reference to sale for human consumption; and in proceedings under that subsection it shall not be a defence that the purchaser was not prejudiced because he bought for analysis or examination.

15. Falsely describing or presenting food

(1) Any person who gives with any food sold by him, or displays with any food offered or exposed by him for sale or in his possession for the purpose of sale, a label, whether or not attached to or printed on the wrapper or container, which—

(a) falsely described the food; or

(b) is likely to mislead as to the nature or substance or quality of the food,

shall be guilty of an offence.

(2) Any person who publishes, or is a party to the publication of, an advertisement (not being such a label given or displayed by him as mentioned in subsection (1) above) which—

(a) falsely describes any food; or

(b) is likely to mislead as to the nature or substance or quality of any food,

shall be guilty of an offence.

(3) Any person who sells, or offers or exposes for sale, or has in his possession for the purpose of sale, any food the presentation of which is likely to mislead as to the nature or substance or quality of the food shall be guilty of an offence.

(4) In proceedings for an offence under subsection (1) or (2) above, the fact that a label or advertisement in respect of which the offence is alleged to have been committed contained an accurate statement of the composition of the food shall not preclude the court from finding that the offence was committed.

(5) In this section references to sale shall be construed as references to sale for human consumption.

20. Offences due to fault of another person

Where the commission by any person of an offence under any of the preceding provisions of this Part is due to an act or default of some other person, that other person shall be guilty of the offence; and a person may be charged with and convicted of the offence by virtue of this section whether or not proceedings are taken against the first-mentioned person.

21. Defence of due diligence

(1) In any proceedings for an offence under any of the preceding provisions of this Part (in this section referred to as 'the relevant provision'), it shall, subject to subsection (5) below, be a defence for the person charged to prove that he took all reasonable precautions and exercised all due diligence to avoid the commission of the offence by himself or by a person under his control.

(2) Without prejudice to the generality of subsection (1) above, a person charged with an offence under section 8, 14 or 15 above who neither—

(a) prepared the food in respect of which the offence is alleged to have been committed; nor

(b) imported it into Great Britain,

shall be taken to have established the defence provided by that subsection if he satisfies the requirements of subsection (3) or (4) below.

(3) A person satisfies the requirements of this subsection if he proves—

(a) that the commission of the offence was due to an act or default of another person who was not under his control, or to reliance on information supplied by such a person;

(b) that he carried out all such checks of the food in question as were reasonable in all the circumstances, or that it was reasonable in all the circumstances for him to rely on checks carried out by the person who supplied the food to him; and

(c) that he did not know and had no reason to suspect at the time of the commission of the alleged offence that his act or omission would amount to an offence under the relevant provision.

(4) A person satisfies the requirements of this subsection if he proves—

(a) that the commission of the offence was due to an act or default of another person who was not under his control, or to reliance on information supplied by such a person;

(b) that the sale or intended sale of which the alleged offence consisted was not a sale or intended sale under his name or mark; and

(c) that he did not know, and could not reasonably have been expected to know, at the time of the commission of the alleged offence that his act or omission would amount to an offence under the relevant provision.

(5) If in any case the defence provided by subsection (1) above involves the allegation that the commission of the offence was due to an act or default of another person, or to reliance on information supplied by another person, the person charged shall not, without leave of the court, be entitled to rely on that defence unless—

(a) at least seven clear days before the hearing; and

(b) where he has previously appeared before a court in connection with the alleged offence, within one month of his first such appearance,

he has served on the prosecutor a notice in writing giving such information identifying or assisting in the identification of that other person as was then in his possession.

(6) In subsection (5) above any reference to appearing before a court shall be construed as including a reference to being brought before a court.

22. Defence of publication in the course of business

In proceedings for an offence under any of the preceding provisions of this Part consisting of the advertisement for sale of any food, it shall be a defence for the person charged to prove—

(a) that he is a person whose business it is to publish or arrange for the publication of advertisements; and

(b) that he received the advertisement in the ordinary course of business and did not know and had no reason to suspect that its publication would amount to an offence under that provision.

33. Obstruction etc., of officers

(1) Any person who—

(a) intentionally obstructs any person acting in the execution of this Act; or

(b) without reasonable cause, fails to give to any person acting in the execution of this Act any assistance or information which that person may reasonably require of him for the performance of his functions under this Act,

shall be guilty of an offence.

(2) Any person who, in purported compliance with any such requirement as is mentioned in subsection (1)(b) above—

(a) furnishes information which he knows to be false or misleading in a material particular; or

(b) recklessly furnishes information which is false or misleading in a material particular,

shall be guilty of an offence.

(3) Nothing in subsection (1)(b) above shall be construed as requiring any person to answer any question or give information if to do so might incriminate him.

36. Offences by bodies corporate

(1) Where an offence under this Act which has been committed by a body corporate is proved to have been committed with the consent or connivance of, or to be attributable to any neglect on the part of—

(a) any director, manager, secretary or other similar officer of the body corporate; or

(b) any person who was purporting to act in any such capacity,

he as well as the body corporate shall be deemed to be guilty of that offence and shall be liable to be proceeded against and punished accordingly.

(2) In subsection (1) above 'director', in relation to any body corporate established by or under any enactment for the purpose of carrying on under national ownership any industry or part of an industry or undertaking, being a body corporate whose affairs are managed by its members, means a member of that body corporate.

CONSUMER PROTECTION ACT 1987

10. The general safety requirement

(1) A person shall be guilty of an offence if he—

(a) supplies any consumer goods which fail to comply with the general safety requirement;

(b) offers or agrees to supply any such goods; or

(c) exposes or possesses any such goods for supply.

(2) For the purposes of this section consumer goods fail to comply with the general safety requirement if they are not reasonably safe having regard to all the circumstances, including—

(a) the manner in which, and purposes for which, the goods are being or would be marketed, the get-up of the goods, the use of any mark in relation to the goods and any instructions or warnings which are given or would be given with respect to the keeping, use or consumption of the goods;

(b) any standards of safety published by any person either for goods of a description which applies to the goods in question or for matters relating to goods of that description; and

(c) the existence of any means by which it would have been reasonable (taking into account the cost, likelihood and extent of any improvement) for the goods to have been made safer.

(3) For the purposes of this section consumer goods shall not be regarded as failing to comply with the general safety requirement in respect of—

(a) anything which is shown to be attributable to compliance with any requirement imposed by or under any enactment or with any Community obligation;

(b) any failure to do more in relation to any matter than is required by—

(i) any safety regulations imposing requirements with respect to that matter;

(ii) any standards of safety approved for the purposes of this subsection by or under any such regulations and imposing requirements with respect to that matter;

(iii) any provision of any enactment or subordinate legislation imposing such requirements with respect to that matter as are designated for the purposes of this subsection by any such regulations.

(4) In any proceedings against any person for an offence under this section in respect of any goods it shall be a defence for that person to show—

(a) that he reasonably believed that the goods would not be used or consumed in the United Kingdom; or

(b) that the following conditions are satisfied, that is to say—

(i) that he supplied the goods, offered or agreed to supply them, or as the case may be, exposed or possessed them for supply in the course of carrying on a retail business; and

(ii)   that, at the time he supplied the goods or offered or agreed to supply them or exposed or possessed them for supply, he neither knew nor had reasonable grounds for believing that the goods failed to comply with the general safety requirement; or

(c)   that the terms on which he supplied the goods or agreed or offered to supply them or, in the case of goods which he exposed or possessed for supply, the terms on which he intended to supply them—

(i)   indicated that the goods were not supplied or to be supplied as new goods; and

(ii)   provided for, or contemplated, the acquisition of an interest in the goods by the person supplied or to be supplied.

(5)   For the purposes of subsection (4)(b) above goods are supplied in the course of carrying on a retail business if—

(a)   whether or not they are themselves acquired for a person's private use or consumption, they are supplied in the course of carrying on a business of making a supply of consumer goods available to persons who generally acquire them for private use or consumption; and

(b)   the descriptions of goods the supply of which is made available in the course of that business do not, to a significant extent, include manufactured or imported goods which have not previously been supplied in the United Kingdom.

(6)   A person guilty of an offence under this section shall be liable on summary conviction to imprisonment for a term not exceeding six months or to a fine not exceeding level 5 on the standard scale or to both.

(7)   In this section 'consumer goods' means any goods which are ordinarily intended for private use or consumption, not being—

(a)   growing crops or things comprised in land by virtue of being attached to it;

(b)   water, food, feeding stuff or fertiliser;

(c)   gas which is, is to be or has been supplied by a person authorised to supply it by or under section 6, 7 or 8 of the Gas Act 1986 (authorisation of supply of gas through pipes);

(d)   aircraft (other than hang-gliders) or motor vehicles;

(e)   controlled drugs or licensed medicinal products;

(f)   tobacco.

11.   Safety regulations

(1)   The Secretary of State may by regulations under this section ('safety regulations') make such provision as he considers appropriate for the purposes of section 10(3) above and for the purpose of securing—

(a)   that goods to which this section applies are safe;

(b)   that goods to which this section applies which are unsafe, or would be unsafe in the hands of persons of a particular description, are not made available to persons generally or, as the case may be, to persons of that description; and

(c)   that appropriate information is, and inappropriate information is not, provided in relation to goods to which this section applies.

12.   Offences against the safety regulations

(1)   Where safety regulations prohibit a person from supplying or offering or agreeing to supply any goods or from exposing or possessing any goods for supply, that person shall be guilty of an offence if he contravenes the prohibition.

(2)   Where safety regulations require a person who makes or processes any goods in the course of carrying on a business—

(a)   to carry out a particular test or use a particular procedure in connection with the making or processing of the goods with a view to ascertaining whether the goods satisfy any requirements of such regulations; or

(b)   to deal or not to deal in a particular way with a quantity of the goods of which the whole or part does not satisfy such a test or does not satisfy standards connected with such a procedure,

that person shall be guilty of an offence if he does not comply with the requirement.

(3)   If a person contravenes a provision of safety regulations which prohibits or requires the provision, by means of a mark or otherwise, of information of a particular kind in relation to goods, he shall be guilty of an offence.

(4)   Where safety regulations require any person to give information to another for the purpose of enabling that other to exercise any function, that person shall be guilty of an offence if—

(a)   he fails without reasonable cause to comply with the requirement; or

(b)   in giving the information which is required of him—

(i)   he makes any statement which he knows is false in a material particular; or

(ii)   he recklessly makes any statement which is false in a material particular.

(5)   A person guilty of an offence under this section shall be liable on summary conviction to imprisonment for a term not exceeding six months or to a fine not exceeding level 5 on the standard scale or to both.

39.   Defence of due diligence

(1)   Subject to the following provisions of this section, in proceedings against any person for an offence to which this section applies it shall be a defence for that person to show that he took all reasonable steps and exercised all due diligence to avoid committing the offence.

(2)   Where in any proceedings against any person for such an offence the defence provided by subsection (1) above involves an allegation that the commission of the offence was due—

(a)   to the act or default of another; or

(b)   to reliance on information given by another,

that person shall not, without the leave of the court, be entitled to rely on the defence unless, not less than seven clear days before the hearing of the proceedings, he has served a notice under subsection (3) below on the person bringing the proceedings.

(3)   A notice under this subsection shall give such information identifying or assisting in the identification of the person who committed the act or default or gave the information as is in the possession of the person serving the notice at the time he serves it.

(4)   It is hereby declared that a person shall not be entitled to rely on the defence provided by subsection (1) above by reason of his reliance on information supplied by another, unless he shows that it was reasonable in all the circumstances for him to have relied on the information, having regard in particular—

(a)   to the steps which he took, and those which might reasonably have been taken, for the purpose of verifying the information; and

(b)   to whether he had any reason to disbelieve the information.

(5)   This section shall apply to an offence under section 10, 12(1), (2) or (3), 13(4), 14(6) or 20(1) above.

40.   Liability of persons other than principal offender

(1)   Where the commission by any person of an offence to which section 39 above applies is due to an act or default committed by some other person in the course of any business of his, the other person shall be guilty of the offence and may be proceeded against and punished by virtue of this subsection whether or not proceedings are taken against the first-mentioned person.

(2)   Where a body corporate is guilty of an offence under this Act (including where it is so guilty by virtue of subsection (1) above) in respect of any act or default which is shown to have been committed with the consent or connivance of, or to be

attributable to any neglect on the part of, any director, manager, secretary or other similar officer of the body corporate or any person who was purporting to act in any such capacity he, as well as the body corporate, shall be guilty of that offence and shall be liable to be proceeded against and punished accordingly.

(3)   Where the affairs of a body corporate are managed by its members, subsection (2) above shall apply in relation to the acts and defaults of a member in connection with his functions of management as if he were a director of the body corporate.

5 HARM TO ANIMALS AND THE ENVIRONMENT

PROTECTION OF ANIMALS ACT 1911

1. Offences of cruelty

(1) If any person—

(a) shall cruelly beat, kick, ill-treat, over-ride, over-drive, over-load, torture, infuriate, or terrify any animal, or shall cause or procure, or, being the owner, permit any animal to be so used, or shall, by wantonly or unreasonably doing or omitting to do any act, or cause or procuring the commission or omission of any act, cause any unnecessary suffering to be so caused to any animal or

(b) shall convey or carry, or cause or procure, or, being the owner, permit to be conveyed or carried, any animal in such manner or position as to cause that animal any unnecessary suffering; or

(c) shall cause, procure, or assist at the fighting or baiting of any animal; or shall keep, use, manage, or act or assist in the management of, any premises or place for the purpose, or partly for the purpose of fighting or baiting any animal, or shall permit any premises or place to be kept, managed, or used, or shall receive, or cause or procure any person to receive, money for the admission of any person to such premises or place; or

(d) shall wilfully, without any reasonable cause or excuse, administer, or cause or procure, or being the owner permit, such administration of, any poisonous or injurious drug or substance to any animal, or shall wilfully, without any reasonable cause or excuse, cause any such substance to be taken by any animal; or

(e) shall subject, or cause or procure, or being the owner permit, to be subjected, any animal to any operation which is performed without due care and humanity; or

(f) shall tether any horse, ass or mule under such conditions or in such manner as to cause that animal unnecessary suffering;

such person shall be guilty of an offence of cruelty within the meaning of this Act, and shall be liable upon summary conviction to imprisonment for a term not exceeding six months or to a fine not exceeding level 5 on the standard scale, or both.

(2) For the purposes of this section, an owner shall be deemed to have permitted cruelty within the meaning of this Act if he shall have failed to exercise reasonable care and supervision in respect of the protection of the animal therefrom:

Provided that, where an owner is convicted of permitting cruelty within the meaning of this Act by reason only of his having failed to exercise such care and supervision, he shall not be liable to imprisonment without the option of a fine.

(3) Nothing in this section shall render illegal any act lawfully done under the Animals (Scientific Procedures) Act 1986 or shall apply—

(a) to the commission or omission of any act in the course of the destruction, or the preparation for destruction, of any animal as food for mankind, unless such destruction or such preparation was accompanied by the infliction of unnecessary suffering; or

(b)   to the coursing or hunting of any captive animal, unless such animal is liberated in an injured, mutilated, or exhausted conditon; but a captive animal shall not, for the purposes of this section, be deemed to be coursed or hunted before it is liberated for the purpose of being coursed or hunted, or after it has been recaptured, or if it is under control, and a captive animal shall not be deemed to be coursed or hunted within the meaning of this subsection if it is coursed or hunted in an enclosed space from which it has no reasonable chance of escape.

5A.   Attendance at animal fights

A person who, without reasonable excuse, is present when animals are placed together for the purpose of their fighting each other shall be liable on summary conviction to a fine not exceeding level 4 on the standard scale.

5B.   Advertising of animal fights

If a person who publishes or causes to be published an advertisement for a fight between animals knows that it is such an advertisement he shall be liable on summary conviction to a fine not exceeding level 4 on the standard scale.

ABANDONMENT OF ANIMALS ACT 1960

1.   Penalties for abandonment of animals

If any person being the owner or having charge or control of any animal shall without reasonable cause or excuse abandon it, whether permanently or not, in circumstances likely to cause the animal any unnecessary suffering, or cause or procure or, being the owner, permit it to be so abandoned, he shall be guilty of an offence of cruelty within the meaning of the principal Act and liable to the penalties prescribed by subsection (1) of section one of that Act, and the provisions of the Protection of Animals Acts shall apply to an offence under this section as they apply to an offence against the said subsection (1).

2.   Interpretation

In this Act 'the principal Act' and 'the Protection of Animals Acts' mean respectively,—

(a)   in relation to England and Wales, the Protection of Animals Act 1911, as amended by or under any other enactment, and the Protection of Animals Acts 1911 to 1954;

and 'animal' has the same meaning as in the principal Act.

WILD MAMMALS (PROTECTION) ACT 1996

1.   Offences

If, save as permitted by this Act, any person mutilates, kicks, beats, nails or otherwise impales, stabs, burns, stones, crushes, drowns, drags or asphyxiates any wild mammal with intent to inflict unnecessary suffering he shall be guilty of an offence.

2.   Exceptions from offences under the Act

A person shall not be guilty of an offence under this Act by reason of—

(a)   the attempted killing of any such wild mammal as an act of mercy if he shows that the mammal had been so seriously disabled otherwise than by his unlawful act that there was no reasonable chance of its recovering;

(b)   the killing in a reasonably swift and humane manner of any such wild mammal if he shows that the wild mammal had been injured or taken in the course of either lawful shooting, hunting, coursing or pest control activity;

(c)   doing anything which is authorised by or under any enactment;

(d)   any act made unlawful by section 1 if the act was done by means of any snare, trap, dog, or bird lawfully used for the purpose of killing or taking any wild mammal; or

(e)   the lawful use of any poisonous or noxious substance on any wild mammal.

3.   Interpretation

In this Act 'wild mammal' means any mammal which is not a domestic or captive animal within the meaning of the Protection of Animals Act 1911 or the Protection of Animals (Scotland) Act 1912.

LITTER ACT 1983

1.   Penalty for leaving litter

(1)   If any person throws down, drops or otherwise deposits in, into or from any place in the open air to which the public are entitled or permitted to have access without payment, and leaves anything whatsoever in such circumstances as to cause, or contribute to, or tend to lead to, the defacement by litter of any place in the open air, he shall be guilty of an offence, unless that depositing and leaving was authorised by law or was done with the consent of the owner, occupier or other person or authority having control of the place in or into which that thing was deposited.

(2)   For the purposes of subsection (1) above, any covered place open to the air on at least one side and available for public use shall be treated as being a place in the open air.

(3)   A person guilty of an offence under this section shall be liable on summary conviction to a fine not exceeding level 3 on the standard scale.

(4)   In sentencing a person convicted of an offence under this section, the court shall have regard not only to the purpose of this section in preventing the defacement by litter of places in the open air, but also to the nature of the litter and any resulting risk (in the circumstances of the offence) of injury to the persons or animals or of damage to property.

WATER RESOURCES ACT 1991

85.   Offences of polluting controlled waters

(1)   A person contravenes this section if he causes or knowingly permits any poisonous, noxious or polluting matter or any solid waste matter to enter any controlled waters.

(3)   A person contravenes this section if he causes or knowingly permits any trade effluent or sewage effluent to be discharged—

(a)   into any controlled waters; or

(b)   from land in England and Wales, through a pipe, into the sea outside the seaward limits of controlled waters.

(5)   A person contravenes this section if he causes or knowingly permits any matter whatever to enter any inland freshwaters so as to tend (either directly or in combination with other matter which he or another person causes or permits to enter those waters) to impede the proper flow of the waters in a manner leading, or likely to lead, to a substantial aggravation of—

(a)   pollution due to other causes; or

(b)   the consequences of such pollution.

(6)   Subject to the following provisions of this Chapter, a person who contravenes this section or the conditions of any consent given under this Chapter for the purposes of this section shall be guilty of an offence and liable—

(a)   on summary conviction, to imprisonment for a term not exceeding three months or to a fine not exceeding £20,000 or to both;

(b)   on conviction on indictment, to imprisonment for a term not exceeding two years or to a fine or to both.

89.   Other defences to principal offences

(1)   A person shall not be guilty of an offence under section 85 above in respect of the entry of any matter into any waters or any discharge if—

(a)   the entry is caused or permitted, or the discharge is made, in an emergency in order to avoid danger to life or health;

(b)   that person takes all such steps as are reasonably practicable in the circumstances for minimising the extent of the entry or discharge and of its polluting effects; and

(c)   particulars of the entry or discharge are furnished to the Authority as soon as reasonably practicable after the entry occurs.

(2)   A person shall not be guilty of an offence under section 85 above by reason of his causing or permitting any discharge of trade or sewage effluent from a vessel.

(3)   A person shall not be guilty of an offence under section 85 above by reason only of his permitting water from an abandoned mine to enter controlled waters.

(4)   A person shall not, otherwise than in respect of the entry of any poisonous, noxious or polluting matter into any controlled waters, be guilty of an offence under section 85 above by reason of his depositing the solid refuse of a mine or quarry on any land so that it falls or is carried into inland freshwaters if—

(a)   he deposits the refuse on the land with the consent of the Authority;

(b)   no other site for the deposit is reasonably practicable; and

(c)   he takes all reasonably practicable steps to prevent the refuse from entering those inland freshwaters.

6 PROPERTY DAMAGE

CRIMINAL DAMAGE ACT 1971

1. Destroying or damaging property

(1) A person who without lawful excuse destroys or damages any property belonging to another intending to destroy or damage any such property or being reckless as to whether any such property would be destroyed or damaged shall be guilty of an offence.

(2) A person who without lawful excuse destroys or damages any property, whether belonging to himself or another—

(a) intending to destroy or damage any property or being reckless as to whether any property would be destroyed or damaged; and

(b) intending by the destruction or damage to endanger the life of another or being reckless as to whether the life of another would be thereby endangered;

shall be guilty of an offence.

(3) An offence committed under this section by destroying or damaging property by fire shall be charged as arson.

2. Threats to destroy or damage property

A person who without lawful excuse makes to another a threat, intending that that other would fear it would be carried out,—

(a) to destroy or damage any property belonging to that other or a third person; or

(b) to destroy or damage his own property in a way which he knows is likely to endanger the life of that other or a third person;

shall be guilty of an offence.

3. Possessing anything with intent to destroy or damage property

A person who has anything in his custody or under his control intending without lawful excuse to use it or cause or permit another to use it—

(a) to destroy or damage any property belonging to some other person; or

(b) to destroy or damage his own or the user's property in a way which he knows is likely to endanger the life of some other person;

shall be guilty of an offence.

4. Punishment of offences

(1) A person guilty of arson under section 1 above or of an offence under section 1 (2) above (whether arson or not) shall on conviction on indictment be liable to imprisonment for life.

(2) A person guilty of any other offence under this Act shall on conviction on indictment be liable to imprisonment for a term not exceeding ten years.

5. 'Without lawful excuse'

(1)   This section applies to any offence under section 1(1) above and any offence under section 2 or 3 above other than one involving a threat by the person charged to destroy or damage property in a way which he knows is likely to endanger the life of another or involving an intent by the person charged to use or cause or permit the use of something in his custody or under his control so to destroy or damage property.

(2)   A person charged with an offence to which this section applies shall whether or not he would be treated for the purposes of this Act as having a lawful excuse apart from this subsection, be treated for those purposes as having a lawful excuse—

(a)   if at the time of the act or acts alleged to constitute the offence he believed that the person or persons whom he believed to be entitled to consent to the destruction of or damage to the property in question had so consented, or would have so consented to it if he or they had known of the destruction or damage and its circumstances; or

(b)   if he destroyed or damaged or threatened to destroy or damage the property in question or, in the case of a charge of an offence under section 3 above, intended to use or cause or permit the use of something to destroy or damage it, in order to protect property belonging to himself or another or a right or interest in property which was or which he believed to be vested in himself or another, and at the time of the act or acts alleged to constitute the offence he believed—

(i)   that the property, right or interest was in immediate need of protection; and

(ii)   that the means of protection adopted or proposed to be adopted were or would be reasonable having regard to all the circumstances.

(3)   For the purposes of this section it is immaterial whether a belief is justified or not if it is honestly held.

(4)   For the purposes of subsection (2) above a right or interest in property includes any right or privilege in or over land, whether created by grant, licence or otherwise.

(5)   This section shall not be construed as casting doubt on any defence recognised by law as a defence to criminal charges.

10. Interpretation

(1)   In this Act 'property' means property of a tangible nature, whether real or personal, including money and—

(a)   including wild creatures which have been tamed or are ordinarily kept in captivity, and any other wild creatures or their carcasses if, but only if, they have been reduced into possession which has not been lost or abandoned or are in the course of being reduced into possession; but

(b)   not including mushrooms growing wild on any land or flowers, fruit or foliage of a plant growing wild on any land.

For the purposes of this subsection 'mushroom' includes any fungus and 'plant' includes any shrub or tree.

(2)   Property shall be treated for the purposes of this Act as belonging to any person—

(a)   having the custody or control of it;

(b)   having in it any proprietary right or interest (not being an equitable interest arising only from an agreement to transfer or grant an interest); or

(c)   having a charge on it.

(3)   Where property is subject to a trust, the persons to whom it belongs shall be so treated as including any person having a right to enforce the trust.

(4)   Property of a corporation sole shall be so treated as belonging to the corporation notwithstanding a vacancy in the corporation.

CRIME AND DISORDER ACT 1998

30. Racially-aggravated criminal damage
[See page 36]

FIRE SERVICES ACT 1947

30. Powers of firemen and police in extinguishing fires
(1) Any member of a fire brigade maintained in pursuance of this Act who is on duty, any member of any other fire brigade who is acting in pursuance of any arrangements made under this Act, or any constable, may enter and if necessary break into any premises or place in which a fire has or is reasonably believed to have broken out, or any premises or place which it is necessary to enter for the purposes of extinguishing a fire or of protecting the premises or place from acts done for fire-fighting purposes, without the consent of the owner or occupier thereof, and may do all such things as he may deem necessary for extinguishing the fire or for protecting from fire, or from acts done as aforesaid, any such premises or place or for rescuing any person or property therein.

(2) [See page 249]

POST OFFICE ACT 1953

60. Prohibition of placing injurious substances in or against post office letter boxes or telephone kiosks
(1) A person shall not place or attempt to place in or against any post office letter box . . . any fire, match, light, explosive substance, dangerous substance, filth, noxious or deleterious substance, or fluid, and shall not commit a nuisance in or against any post office letter box . . . , and shall not do or attempt to do anything likely to injure the box, . . . or its appurtenances or contents.

(2) If any person acts in contravention of this section, he shall be liable on summary conviction to a fine not exceeding the prescribed sum, or on conviction on indictment to imprisonment for a term not exceeding twelve months.

61. Prohibition of affixing placards, notices, etc on post office letter boxes, etc.
(1) A person shall not without due authority affix or attempt to affix any placard, advertisement, notice, list, document, board or thing in or on, or paint or tar, any post office, post office letter box, . . . or other property belonging to or used by or on behalf of the Post Office, and shall not in any way disfigure any such office, box, . . . or property.

(2) If any person acts in contravention of this section, he shall be liable on summary conviction to a fine not exceeding level 1 on the standard scale.

COMPUTER MISUSE ACT 1990

1. Unauthorised access to computer material
(1) A person is guilty of an offence if—

(a) he causes a computer to perform any function with intent to secure access to any program or data held in any computer;

(b) the access he intends to secure is unauthorised; and

(c) he knows at the time when he causes the computer to perform the function that that is the case.

(2) The intent a person has to have to commit an offence under this section need not be directed at—

(a) any particular program or data;

(b)   a program or data of any particular kind; or

(c)   a program or data held in any particular computer.

(3)   A person guilty of an offence under this section shall be liable on summary conviction to imprisonment for a term not exceeding six months or to a fine not exceeding level 5 on the standard scale or to both.

2.   Unauthorised access with intent to commit or facilitate commission of further offences

(1)   A person is guilty of an offence under this section if he commits an offence under section 1 above ('the unauthorised access offence') with intent—

(a)   to commit an offence to which this section applies; or

(b)   to facilitate the commission of such an offence (whether by himself or by any other person);

and the offence he intends to commit or facilitate is referred to below in this section as the further offence.

(2)   This section applies to offences—

(a)   for which the sentence is fixed by law; or

(b)   for which a person of twenty-one years of age or over (not previously convicted) may be sentenced to imprisonment for a term of five years (or, in England and Wales, might be so sentenced but for the restrictions imposed by section 33 of the Magistrates' Courts Act 1980).

(3)   It is immaterial for the purposes of this section whether the further offence is to be committed on the same occasion as the unauthorised access offence or on any future occasion.

(4)   A person may be guilty of an offence under this section even though the facts are such that the commission of the further offence is impossible.

(5)   A person guilty of an offence under this section shall be liable—

(a)   on summary conviction, to imprisonment for a term not exceeding six months or to a fine not exceeding the statutory maximum or to both; and

(b)   on conviction on indictment, to imprisonment for a term not exceeding five years or to a fine or to both.

3.   Unauthorised modification of computer material

(1)   A person is guilty of an offence if—

(a)   he does any act which causes an unauthorised modification of the contents of any computer; and

(b)   at the time when he does the act he has the requisite intent and the requisite knowledge.

(2)   For the purposes of subsection (1)(b) above the requisite intent is an intent to cause a modification of the contents of any computer and by so doing—

(a)   to impair the operation of any computer;

(b)   to prevent or hinder access to any program or data held in any computer; or

(c)   to impair the operation of any such program or the reliability of any such data.

(3)   The intent need not be directed at—

(a)   any particular computer;

(b)   any particular program or data or a program or data of any particular kind; or

(c)   any particular modification or a modification of any particular kind.

(4)   For the purposes of subsection (1)(b) above the requisite knowledge is knowledge that any modification he intends to cause is unauthorised.

(5)   It is immaterial for the purposes of this section whether an unauthorised modification or any intended effect of it of a kind mentioned in subsection (2) above is, or is intended to be, permanent or merely temporary.

(6)   For the purposes of the Criminal Damage Act 1971 a modification of the contents of a computer shall not be regarded as damaging any computer or computer

storage medium unless its effect on that computer or computer storage medium impairs its physical condition.

(7)   A person guilty of an offence under this section shall be liable—

(a)   on summary conviction, to imprisonment for a term not exceeding six months or to a fine not exceeding the statutory maximum or to both; and

(b)   on conviction on indictment, to imprisonment for a term not exceeding five years or to a fine or to both.

4.   Territorial scope of offences under this Act

(1)   Except as provided below in this section, it is immaterial for the purposes of any offence under section 1 or 3 above—

(a)   whether any act or other event proof of which is required for conviction of the offence occured in the home country concerned; or

(b)   whether the accused was in the home country concerned at the time of any such act or event.

(2)   Subject to subsection (3) below, in the case of such an offence at least one significant link with domestic jurisdiction must exist in the circumstances of the case for the offence to be committed.

(3)   There is no need for any such link to exist for the commission of an offence under section 1 above to be established in proof of an allegation to that effect in proceedings for an offence under section 2 above.

(4)   Subject to section 8 below, where—

(a)   any such link does in fact exist in the case of an offence under section 1 above; and

(b)   commission of that offence is alleged in proceedings for an offence under section 2 above;

section 2 above shall apply as if anything the accused intended to do or facilitate in any place outside the home country concerned which would be an offence to which section 2 applies if it took place in the home country concerned were the offence in question.

(6)   References in this Act to the home country concerned are references—

(a)   in application of this Act to England and Wales, to England and Wales;

(b)   in the application of this Act to Scotland, to Scotland; and

(c)   in the application of this Act to Northern Ireland, to Northern Ireland.

5.   Significant links with domestic jurisdiction

(1)   The following provisions of this section apply for the interpretation of section 4 above.

(2)   In relation to an offence under section 1, either of the following is a significant link with domestic jurisdiction—

(a)   that the accused was in the home country concerned at the time when he did the act which caused the computer to perform the function; or

(b)   that any computer containing any program or data to which the accused secured or intended to secure unauthorised access by doing that act was in the home country concerned at that time.

(3)   In relation to an offence under section 3, either of the following is a significant link with domestic jurisdiction—

(a)   that the accused was in the home country concerned at the time when he did the act which caused the unauthorised modification; or

(b)   that the unauthorised modification took place in the home country concerned.

6.   Territorial scope of inchoate offences related to offences under this Act

(1)   On a charge of conspiracy to commit an offence under this Act the following questions are immaterial to the accused's guilt—

(a)   the question where any person became a party to the conspiracy; and

(b)   the question whether any act, omission or other event occured in the home country concerned.

(2)   On a charge of attempting to commit an offence under section 3 above the following questions are immaterial to the accused's guilt—

(a)   the question where the attempt was made; and

(b)   the question whether it had an effect in the home country concerned.

(3)   On a charge of incitement to commit an offence under this Act the question where the incitement took place is immaterial to the accused's guilt.

7. Territorial scope of inchoate offences related to offences under external law corresponding to offences under this Act

(1)   [See Criminal Law Act 1977 s. 1(1A) [pages 254–255]]

(2)   [See Criminal Law Act 1977, s. 1(5), (6) [page 256]]

(3)   [See Criminal Attempts Act 1981, s. 1(1A) [page 254–255]]

(4)   Subject to section 8 below, if any act done by a person in England and Wales would amount to the offence of incitement to commit an offence under this Act but for the fact that what he had in view would not be an offence triable in England and Wales—

(a)   what he had in view shall be treated as an offence under this Act for the purposes of any charge of incitement brought in respect of that act; and

(b)   any such charge shall accordingly be triable in England and Wales.

8. Relevance of external law

(1)   A person is guilty of an offence triable by virtue of section 4(4) above only if what he intended to do or facilitate would involve the commission of an offence under the law in force where the whole or any part of it was intended to take place.

(2)   A person is guilty of an offence triable by virtue of section 1(1A) of the Criminal Law Act 1977 only if the pursuit of the agreed course of conduct would at some stage involve—

(a)   an act or omission by one or more of the parties; or

(b)   the happening of some other event;

constituting an offence under the law in force where the act, omission or other event was intended to take place.

(3)   A person is guilty of an offence triable by virtue of section 1(1A) of the Criminal Attempts Act 1981 or by virtue of section 7(4) above only if what he had in view would involve the commission of an offence under the law in force where the whole or any part of it was intended to take place.

(4)   Conduct punishable under the law in force in any place is an offence under that law for the purposes of this section, however it is described in that law.

(5)   Subject to subsection (7) below, a condition specified in any of subsections (1) to (3) above shall be taken to be satisfied unless not later than rules of course may provide the defence serve on the prosecution a notice—

(a)   stating that, on the facts as alleged with respect to the relevant conduct, the condition is not in their opinion satisfied;

(b)   showing their grounds for that opinion; and

(c)   requiring the prosecution to show that it is satisfied.

(6)   In subsection (5) above 'the relevant conduct' means—

(a)   where the condition in subsection (1) above is in question, what the accused intended to do or facilitate;

(b)   where the condition in subsection (2) above is in question, the agreed course of conduct; and

(c)   where the condition in subsection (3) above is in question, what the accused had in view.

(7) The court, if it thinks fit, may permit the defence to require the prosecution to show that the condition is satisfied without the prior service of a notice under subsection (5) above.

(9) In the Crown Court the question whether the condition is satisfied shall be decided by the judge alone.

9. British citizenship immaterial

(1) In any proceedings brought in England and Wales in respect of any offence to which this section applies it is immaterial to guilt whether or not the accused was a British citizen at the time of any act, omission or other event proof of which is required for conviction of the offence.

(2) This section applies to the following offences—
    (a) any offence under this Act;
    (b) conspiracy to commit an offence under this Act;
    (c) any attempt to commit an offence under section 3 above; and
    (d) incitement to commit an offence under this Act.

17. Interpretation

(1) The following provisions of this section apply for the interpretation of this Act.

(2) A person secures access to any program or data held in a computer if by causing a computer to perform any function he—
    (a) alters or erases the program or data;
    (b) copies or moves it to any storage medium other than that in which it is held or to a different location in the storage medium in which it is held;
    (c) uses it; or
    (d) has it output from the computer in which it is held (whether by having it displayed or in any other manner);
and references to access to a program or data (and to an intent to secure such access) shall be read accordingly.

(3) For the purposes of subsection (2)(c) above a person uses a program if the function he causes the computer to perform—
    (a) causes the program to be executed; or
    (b) is itself a function of the program.

(4) For the purposes of subsection (2)(d) above—
    (a) a program is output if the instructions of which it consists are output; and
    (b) the form in which any such instructions or any other data is output (and in particular whether or not it represents a form in which, in the case of instructions, they are capable of being executed or, in the case of data, it is capable of being processed by a computer) is immaterial.

(5) Access of any kind by any person to any program or data held in a computer is unauthorised if—
    (a) he is not himself entitled to control access of the kind in question to the program or data; and
    (b) he does not have consent to access by him of the kind in question to the program or data from any person who is so entitled.

(6) References to any program or data held in a computer include references to any program or data held in any removable storage medium which is for the time being in the computer; and a computer is to be regarded as containing any program or data held in any such medium.

(7) A modification of the contents of any computer takes place if, by the operation of any function of the computer concerned or any other computer—
    (a) any program or data held in the computer concerned is altered or erased; or

(b)   any program or data is added to its contents;
and any act which contributes towards causing such a modification shall be regarded as causing it.

(8)   Such a modification is unauthorised if—

(a)   the person whose act causes it is not himself entitled to determine whether the modification should be made; and

(b)   he does not have consent to the modification from any person who is so entitled.

(9)   References to the home country concerned shall be read in accordance with section 4(6) above.

(10)   References to a program include references to part of a program.

7 THEFT, FRAUD AND COMMERCIAL MALPRACTICE

THEFT ACT 1968

1. Basic definition of theft

(1) A person is guilty of theft if he dishonestly appropriates property belonging to another with the intention of permanently depriving the other of it; and 'theft' and 'steal' shall be construed accordingly.

(2) It is immaterial whether the appropriation is made with a view to gain, or is made for the thief's own benefit.

(3) The five following sections of this Act shall have effect as regards the interpretation and operation of this section (and, except as otherwise provided by this Act, shall apply only for purposes of this section).

2. 'Dishonestly'

(1) A person's appropriation of property belonging to another is not to be regarded as dishonest—

  (a) if he appropriates the property in the belief that he has in law the right to deprive the other of it, on behalf of himself or of a third person; or

  (b) if he appropriates the property in the belief that he would have the other's consent if the other knew of the appropriation and the circumstances of it; or

  (c) (except where the property came to him as trustee or personal representative) if he appropriates the property in the belief that the person to whom the property belongs cannot be discovered by taking reasonable steps.

(2) A person's appropriation of property belonging to another may be dishonest notwithstanding that he is willing to pay for the property.

3. 'Appropriates'

(1) Any assumption by a person of the rights of an owner amounts to an appropriation, and this includes, where he has come by the property (innocently or not) without stealing it, any later assumption of a right to it by keeping or dealing with it as owner.

(2) Where property or a right or interest in property is or purports to be transferred for value to a person acting in good faith, no later assumption by him of rights which he believed himself to be acquiring shall, by reason of any defect in the transferor's title, amount to theft of the property.

4. 'Property'

(1) 'Property' includes money and all other property, real or personal, including things in action and other intangible property.

(2) A person cannot steal land, or things forming part of land and severed from it by him or by his directions, except in the following cases, that is to say—

(a)   when he is a trustee or personal representative, or is authorised by power of attorney, or as liquidator of a company, or otherwise, to sell or dispose of land belonging to another, and he appropriates the land or anything forming part of it by dealing with it in breach of the confidence reposed in him; or

(b)   when he is not in possession of the land and appropriates anything forming part of the land by severing it or causing it to be severed, or after it has been severed; or

(c)   when, being in possession of the land under a tenancy, he appropriates the whole or part of any fixture or structure let to be used with the land.

For purposes of this subsection 'land' does not include incorporeal hereditaments; 'tenancy' means a tenancy for years or less period and includes an agreement for such a tenancy, but a person who after the end of a tenancy remains in possession as statutory tenant or otherwise is to be treated as having possession under the tenancy, and 'let' shall be construed accordingly.

(3)   A person who picks mushrooms growing wild on any land, or who picks flowers, fruit or foliage from a plant growing wild on any land, does not (although not in possession of the land) steal what he picks, unless he does it for reward or for sale or other commercial purpose.

For purposes of this subsection 'mushroom' includes any fungus, and 'plant' includes any shrub or tree.

(4)   Wild creatures, tamed or untamed, shall be regarded as property; but a person cannot steal a wild creature not tamed nor ordinarily kept in captivity, or the carcase of any such creature, unless either it has been reduced into possession by or on behalf of another person and possession of it has not since been lost or abandoned, or another person is in course of reducing it into possession.

5.   'Belonging to another'

(1)   Property shall be regarded as belonging to any person having possession or control of it, or having in it any proprietary right or interest (not being an equitable interest arising only from an agreement to transfer or grant an interest).

(2)   Where property is subject to a trust, the persons to whom it belongs shall be regarded as including any person having a right to enforce the trust, and an intention to defeat the trust shall be regarded accordingly as an intention to deprive of the property any person having that right.

(3)   Where a person receives property from or on account of another, and is under an obligation to the other to retain and deal with that property or its proceeds in a particular way, the property or proceeds shall be regarded (as against him) as belonging to the other.

(4)   Where a person gets property by another's mistake, and is under an obligation to make restoration (in whole or in part) of the property or its proceeds or of the value thereof, then to the extent of that obligation the property or proceeds shall be regarded (as against him) as belonging to the person entitled to restoration, and an intention not to make restoration shall be regarded accordingly as an intention to deprive that person of the property or proceeds.

(5)   Property of a corporation sole shall be regarded as belonging to the corporation notwithstanding a vacancy in the corporation.

6.   'With the intention of permanently depriving the other of it'

(1)   A person appropriating property belonging to another without meaning the other permanently to lose the thing itself is nevertheless to be regarded as having the intention of permanently depriving the other of it if his intention is to treat the thing as his own to dispose of regardless of the other's rights; and a borrowing or lending of it may amount to so treating it if, but only if, the borrowing or lending is for a period and in circumstances making it equivalent to an outright taking or disposal.

(2)   Without prejudice to the generality of subsection (1) above, where a person, having possession or control (lawfully or not) of property belonging to another, parts with the property under a condition as to its return which he may not be able to perform, this (if done for purposes of his own and without the other's authority) amounts to treating the property as his own to dispose of regardless of the other's rights.

7.   Theft
A person guilty of theft shall on conviction on indictment be liable to imprisonment for a term not exceeding seven years.

8.   Robbery
(1)   A person is guilty of robbery if he steals, and immediately before or at the time of doing so, and in order to do so, he uses force on any person or puts or seeks to put any person in fear of being then and there subjected to force.

(2)   A person guilty of robbery, or of an assault with intent to rob, shall on conviction on indictment be liable to imprisonment for life.

9.   Burglary
[See page 192]

10.   Aggravated burglary
[See page 192]

11.   Removal of articles from places open to the public
(1)   Subject to subsections (2) and (3) below, where the public have access to a building in order to view the building or part of it, or a collection or part of a collection housed in it, any person who without lawful authority removes from the building or its grounds the whole or part of any article displayed or kept for display to the public in the building or that part of it or in its grounds shall be guilty of an offence.
For this purpose 'collection' includes a collection got together for a temporary purpose, but references in this section to a collection do not apply to a collection made or exhibited for the purpose of effecting sales or other commercial dealings.

(2)   It is immaterial for purposes of subsection (1) above, that the public's access to a building is limited to a particular period or particular occasion; but where anything removed from a building or its grounds is there otherwise than as forming part of, or being on loan for exhibition with, a collection intended for permanent exhibition to the public, the person removing it does not thereby commit an offence under this section unless he removes it on a day when the public have access to the building as mentioned in subsection (1) above.

(3)   A person does not commit an offence under this section if he believes that he has lawful authority for the removal of the thing in question or that he would have it if the person entitled to give it knew of the removal and the circumstances of it.

(4)   A person guilty of an offence under this section shall, on conviction on indictment, be liable to imprisonment for a term not exceeding five years.

12.   Taking motor vehicle or other conveyance without authority
(1)   Subject to subsections (5) and (6) below, a person shall be guilty of an offence if, without having the consent of the owner or other lawful authority, he takes any conveyance for his own or another's use or, knowing that any conveyance has been taken without such authority, drives it or allows himself to be carried in or on it.

(2)   A person guilty of an offence under subsection (1) above shall be liable on summary conviction to a fine not exceeding level 5 on the standard scale, to imprisonment for a term not exceeding six months, or both.

(4)   If on the trial of an indictment for theft the jury are not satisfied that the accused committed theft, but it is proved that the accused committed an offence

under subsection (1) above, the jury may find him guilty of the offence under subsection (1), and if he is found guilty of it, he shall be liable as he would have been liable under subsection (2) above on summary conviction.

(5) Subsection (1) above shall not apply in relation to pedal cycles; but, subject to subsection (6) below, a person who, without having the consent of the owner or other lawful authority, takes a pedal cycle for his own or another's use, or rides a pedal cycle knowing it to have been taken without such authority, shall on summary conviction be liable to a fine not exceeding fifty pounds.

(6) A person does not commit an offence under this section by anything done in the belief that he has lawful authority to do it or that he would have the owner's consent if the owner knew of his doing it and the circumstances of it.

(7) For purposes of this section—

(a) 'conveyance' means any conveyance constructed or adapted for the carriage of a person or persons whether by land, water, or air, except that it does not include a conveyance constructed or adapted for use only under the control of a person not carried in or on it, and 'drive' shall be construed accordingly; and

(b) 'owner', in relation to conveyance which is the subject of a hiring agreement or hire-purchase agreement, means the person in possession of the conveyance under that agreement.

12A. Aggravated vehicle-taking

(1) Subject to subsection (3) below, a person is guilty of aggravated taking of a vehicle if—

(a) he commits an offence under section 12(1) above (in this section referred to as a 'basic offence') in relation to a mechanically propelled vehicle; and

(b) it is proved that, at any time after the vehicle was unlawfully taken (whether by him or another) and before it was recovered, the vehicle was driven, or injury or damage was caused, in one or more of the circumstances set out in paragraphs (a) to (d) of subsection (2) below.

(2) The circumstances referred to in subsection (1)(b) above are—

(a) that the vehicle was driven dangerously on a road or other public place;

(b) that, owing to the driving of the vehicle, an accident occurred by which injury was caused to any person;

(c) that, owing to the driving of the vehicle, an accident occurred by which damage was caused to any property, other than the vehicle;

(d) that damage was caused to the vehicle.

(3) A person is not guilty of an offence under this section if he proves that, as regards any such proven driving, injury or damage as is referred to in subsection (1)(b) above, either—

(a) the driving, accident or damage referred to in subsection (2) above occurred before he committed the basic offence; or

(b) he was neither in nor on nor in the immediate vicinity of the vehicle when that driving, accident or damage occurred.

(4) A person guilty of an offence under this section shall be liable on conviction on indictment to imprisonment for a term not exceeding two years or, if it is proved that, in circumstances falling within subsection (2)(b) above, the accident caused the death of the person concerned, ten years.

(5) If a person who is charged with an offence under this section is found not guilty of that offence but it is proved that he committed a basic offence, he may be convicted of the basic offence.

(7) For the purposes of this section a vehicle is driven dangerously if—

(a) it is driven in a way which falls far below what would be expected of a competent and careful driver; and

(b) it would be obvious to a competent and careful driver that driving the vehicle in that way would be dangerous.

(8) For the purposes of this section a vehicle is recovered when it is restored to its owner or to other lawful possession or custody; and in this subsection 'owner' has the same meaning as in section 12 above.

13. Abstracting of electricity

A person who dishonestly uses without due authority, or dishonestly causes to be wasted or diverted, any electricity shall on conviction on indictment be liable to imprisonment for a term not exceeding five years.

15. Obtaining property by deception

(1) A person who by any deception dishonestly obtains property belonging to another, with the intention of permanently depriving the other of it, shall on conviction on indictment be liable to imprisonment for a term not exceeding ten years.

(2) For purposes of this section a person is to be treated as obtaining property if he obtains ownership, possession or control of it, and 'obtain' includes obtaining for another or enabling another to obtain or to retain.

(3) Section 6 above shall apply for purposes of this section, with the necessary adaptation of the reference to appropriating, as it applies for purposes of section 1.

(4) For purposes of this section 'deception' means any deception (whether deliberate or reckless) by words or conduct as to fact or as to law, including a deception as to the present intentions of the person using the deception or any other person.

15A. Obtaining a money transfer by deception

(1) A person is guilty of an offence if by any deception he dishonestly obtains a money transfer for himself or another.

(2) A money transfer occurs when—
   (a) a debit is made to one account,
   (b) a credit is made to another, and
   (c) the credit results from the debit or the debit results from the credit.

(3) References to a credit and to a debit are to a credit of an amount of money and to a debit of an amount of money.

(4) It is immaterial (in particular)—
   (a) whether the amount credited is the same as the amount debited;
   (b) whether the money transfer is effected on presentment of a cheque or by another method;
   (c) whether any delay occurs in the process by which the money transfer is effected;
   (d) whether any intermediate credits or debits are made in the course of the money transfer;
   (e) whether either of the accounts is overdrawn before or after the money transfer is effected.

(5) A person guilty of an offence under this section shall be liable on conviction on indictment to imprisonment for a term not exceeding ten years.

15B. Section 15A: supplementary

(1) The following provisions have effect for the interpretation of section 15A of this Act.

(2) 'Deception' has the same meaning as in section 15 of this Act.

(3) 'Account' means an account kept with—
   (a) a bank; or
   (b) a person carrying on a business which falls within subsection (4) below.

(4) A business falls within this subsection if—

(a) in the course of the business money received by way of deposit is lent to others; or

(b) any other activity of the business is financed, wholly or to any material extent, out of the capital of or the interest on money received by way of deposit;
and 'deposit' here has the same meaning as in section 35 of the Banking Act 1987 (fraudulent inducement to make a deposit).

(5) For the purposes of subsection (4) above—

(a) all the activities which a person carries on by way of business shall be regarded as a single business carried on by him; and

(b) 'money' includes money expressed in a currency other than sterling or in the European currency unit (as defined in Council Regulation No. 3320/94/EC or any Community instrument replacing it).

16. Obtaining pecuniary advantage by deception

(1) A person who by any deception dishonestly obtains for himself or another any pecuniary advantage shall on conviction on indictment be liable to imprisonment for a term not exceeding five years.

(2) The cases in which a pecuniary advantage within the meaning of this section is to be regarded as obtained for a person are cases where—

. . .

(b) he is allowed to borrow by way of overdraft, or to take out any policy of insurance or annuity contract, or obtains an improvement of the terms on which he is allowed to do so; or

(c) he is given the opportunity to earn remuneration or greater remuneration in an office or employment, or to win money by betting.

(3) For purposes of this section 'deception' has the same meaning as in section 15 of this Act.

17. False accounting

(1) Where a person dishonestly, with a view to gain for himself or another or with intent to cause loss to another,—

(a) destroys, defaces, conceals or falsifies any account or any record or document made or required for any accounting purpose; or

(b) in furnishing information for any purpose produces or makes use of any account, or any such record or document as aforesaid, which to his knowledge is or may be misleading, false or deceptive in a material particular;
he shall, on conviction on indictment, be liable to imprisonment for a term not exceeding seven years.

(2) For purposes of this section a person who makes or concurs in making in an account or other document an entry which is or may be misleading, false or deceptive in a material particular, or who omits or concurs in omitting a material particular from an account or other document, is to be treated as falsifying the account or document.

18. Liability of company officers for certain offences by company

(1) Where an offence committed by a body corporate under section 15, 16 or 17 of this Act is proved to have been committed with the consent or connivance of any director, manager, secretary or other similar officer of the body corporate or any person who was purporting to act in any such capacity, he as well as the body corporate shall be guilty of that offence, and shall be liable to be proceeded against and punished accordingly.

(2) Where the affairs of a body corporate are managed by its members, this section shall apply in relation to the acts and defaults of a member in connection with his functions of management as if he were a director of the body corporate.

19. False statements by company directors, etc.

(1) Where an officer of a body corporate or unincorporated association (or person purporting to act as such), with intent to deceive members or creditors of the body corporate or association about its affairs, publishes or concurs in publishing a written statement or account which to his knowledge is or may be misleading, false or deceptive in a material particular, he shall on conviction on indictment be liable to imprisonment for a term not exceeding seven years.

(2) For the purposes of this section a person who has entered into a security for the benefit of a body corporate or association is to be treated as a creditor of it.

(3) Where the affairs of a body corporate or association are managed by its members, this section shall apply to any statement which a member publishes or concurs in publishing in connection with his functions or management as if he were an officer of the body corporate or association.

20. Suppression, etc., of documents

(1) A person who dishonestly, with a view to gain for himself or another or with intent to cause loss to another, destroys, defaces or conceals any valuable security, any will or other testamentary document or any original document of or belonging to, or filed or deposited in, any court of justice or any government department shall on conviction on indictment be liable to imprisonment for a term not exceeding seven years.

(2) A person who dishonestly, with a view to gain for himself or another or with intent to cause loss to another, by any deception procures the execution of a valuable security shall on conviction on indictment be liable to imprisonment for a term not exceeding seven years; and this subsection shall apply in relation to the making, acceptance, indorsement, alteration, cancellation or destruction in whole or in part of a valuable security, and in relation to the signing or sealing of any paper or other material in order that it may be made or converted into, or used or dealt with as, a valuable security, as if that were the execution of a valuable security.

(3) For the purposes of this section 'deception' has the same meaning as in section 15 of this Act, and 'valuable security' means any document creating, transferring, surrendering or releasing any right to, in or over property, or authorising the payment of money or delivery of any property, or evidencing the creation, transfer, surrender or release of any such right, or the payment of money or delivery of any property, or the satisfaction of any obligation.

21. Blackmail

(1) A person is guilty of blackmail if, with a view to gain for himself or another or with intent to cause loss to another, he makes any unwarranted demand with menaces; and for this purpose a demand with menaces is unwarranted unless the person making it does so in the belief—

(a)   that he has reasonable grounds for making the demand; and

(b)   that the use of the menaces is a proper means of reinforcing the demand.

(2) The nature of the act or omission demanded is immaterial, and it is also immaterial whether the menaces relate to action to be taken by the person making the demand.

(3) A person guilty of blackmail shall on conviction on indictment be liable to imprisonment for a term not exceeding fourteen years.

22. Handling stolen goods

(1) A person handles stolen goods if (otherwise than in the course of the stealing) knowing or believing them to be stolen goods he dishonestly receives the goods, or dishonestly undertakes or assists in their retention, removal, disposal or realisation by or for the benefit of another person, or if he arranges to do so.

(2)   A person guilty of handling stolen goods shall on conviction on indictment be liable to imprisonment for a term not exceeding fourteen years.

23.   Advertising rewards for return of goods stolen or lost

Where any public advertisement of a reward for the return of any goods which have been stolen or lost uses any words to the effect that no questions will be asked, or that the person producing the goods will be safe from apprehension or inquiry, or that any money paid for the purchase of the goods or advances by way of a loan on them will be repaid, the person advertising the reward and any person who prints or publishes the advertisement shall on summary conviction be liable to a fine not exceeding one hundred pounds.

24.   Scope of offences relating to stolen goods

(1)   The provisions of this Act relating to goods which have been stolen shall apply whether the stealing occurred in England or Wales or elsewhere, and whether it occurred before or after the commencement of this Act, provided that the stealing (if not an offence under this Act) amounted to an offence where and at the time when the goods were stolen; and references to stolen goods shall be construed accordingly.

(2)   For purposes of those provisions references to stolen goods shall include, in addition to the goods originally stolen and parts of them (whether in their original state or not),—

(a)   any other goods which directly or indirectly represent or have at any time represented the stolen goods in the hands of the thief as being the proceeds of any disposal or realisation of the whole or part of the goods stolen or of goods so representing the stolen goods; and

(b)   any other goods which directly or indirectly represent or have at any time represented the stolen goods in the hands of a handler of the stolen goods or any part of them as being the proceeds of any disposal or realisation of the whole or part of the stolen goods handled by him or of goods so representing them.

(3)   But no goods shall be regarded as having continued to be stolen goods after they have been restored to the person from whom they were stolen or to other lawful possession or custody, or after that person and any other person claiming through him have otherwise ceased as regards those goods to have any right to restituton in respect of the theft.

(4)   For purposes of the provisions of this Act relating to goods which have been stolen (including subsections (1) to (3) above) goods obtained in England or Wales or elsewhere either by blackmail or in the circumstances described in section 15 (1) of this Act shall be regarded as stolen; and 'steal', 'theft' and 'thief' shall be construed accordingly.

24A.   Dishonestly retaining a wrongful credit

(1)   A person is guilty of an offence if—

(a)   a wrongful credit has been made to an account kept by him or in respect of which he has any right or interest;

(b)   he knows or believes that the credit is wrongful; and

(c)   he dishonestly fails to take such steps as are reasonable in the circumstances to secure that the credit is cancelled.

(2)   References to a credit are to a credit of an amount of money.

(3)   A credit to an account is wrongful if it is the credit side of a money transfer obtained contrary to section 15A of this Act.

(4)   A credit to an account is also wrongful to the extent that it derives from—

(a)   theft;

(b)   an offence under section 15A of this Act;

(c)   blackmail; or

(d)   stolen goods.

(5) In determining whether a credit to an account is wrongful, it is immaterial (in particular) whether the account is overdrawn before or after the credit is made.

(6) A person guilty of an offence under this section shall be liable on conviction on indictment to imprisonment for a term not exceeding ten years.

(7) Subsection (8) below applies for purposes of provisions of this Act relating to stolen goods (including subsection (4) above).

(8) References to stolen goods include money which is dishonestly withdrawn from an account to which a wrongful credit has been made, but only to the extent that the money derives from the credit.

(9) In this section 'account' and 'money' shall be construed in accordance with section 15B of this Act.

25. Going equipped for stealing, etc.

(1) A person shall be guilty of an offence if, when not at his place of abode, he has with him any article for use in the course of or in connection with any burglary, theft or cheat.

(2) A person guilty of an offence under this section shall on conviction on indictment be liable to imprisonment for a term not exceeding three years.

(3) Where a person is charged with an offence under this section, proof that he had with him any article made or adapted for use in committing a burglary, theft or cheat shall be evidence that he had it with him for such use.

(4) Any person may arrest without warrant anyone who is, or whom he, with reasonable cause, suspects to be, committing an offence under this section.

(5) For purposes of this section an offence under section 12 (1) of this Act of taking a conveyance shall be treated as theft, and 'cheat' means an offence under section 15 of this Act.

27. Evidence and procedure on charge of theft or handling stolen goods

(3) Where a person is being proceeded against for handling stolen goods (but not for any offence other than handling stolen goods), then at any stage of the proceedings, if evidence has been given of his having or arranging to have in his possession the goods the subject of the charge, or of his undertaking or assisting in, or arranging to undertake or assist in, their retention, removal, disposal or realisation, the following evidence shall be admissible for the purpose of proving that he knew or believed the goods to be stolen goods:—

(a) evidence that he has had in his possession, or has undertaken or assisted in the retention, removal, disposal or realisation of, stolen goods from any theft taking place not earlier than twelve months before the offence charged; and

(b) (provided that seven days' notice in writing has been given to him of the intention to prove the conviction) evidence that he has within the five years preceding the date of the offence charged been convicted of theft or of handling stolen goods.

30. Husband and wife
[See page 3]

32. Effect on existing law and construction of references to offences

(1) The following offences are hereby abolished for all purposes not relating to offences committed before the commencement of this Act, that is to say—

(a) any offence at common law of larceny, robbery, burglary, receiving stolen property, obtaining property by threats, extortion by colour of office or franchise, false accounting by public officers, concealment of treasure trove and, except as regards offences relating to the public revenue, cheating; . . .

34. Interpretation

(1) Sections 4 (1) and 5 (1) of this Act shall apply generally for purposes of this Act as they apply for purposes of section 1.

(2)   For purposes of this Act—

(a)   'gain' and 'loss' are to be construed as extending only to gain or loss in money or other property, but as extending to any such gain or loss whether temporary or permanent; and—

(i)   'gain' includes a gain by keeping what one has, as well as a gain by getting what one has not; and

(ii)   'loss' includes a loss by not getting what one might get, as well as a loss by parting with what one has;

(b)   'goods' except in so far as the context otherwise requires, includes money and every other description of property except land, and includes things severed from the land by stealing.

SCHEDULE 1

OFFENCES OF TAKING, ETC. FISH

2.   Taking or destroying fish

(1)   Subject to subparagraph (2) below, a person who unlawfully takes or destroys, or attempts to take or destroy, any fish in water which is private property or in which there is any private right of fishery shall on summary conviction be liable to a fine not exceeding fifty pounds or, for an offence committed after a previous conviction of an offence under this subparagraph, to imprisonment for a term not exceeding three months or to a fine not exceeding one hundred pounds or to both.

(2)   Subparagraph (1) above shall not apply to taking or destroying fish by angling in the daytime (that is to say, in the period beginning one hour before sunrise and ending one hour after sunset); but a person who by angling in the daytime unlawfully takes or destroys, or attempts to take or destroy, any fish in water which is private property or in which there is any private right of fishery shall on summary conviction be liable to a fine not exceeding twenty pounds.

NIGHT POACHING ACT 1828

1.   Taking or destroying game or rabbits by night
[See page 196]

DEER ACT 1991

1.   Poaching of deer
[See pages 196–197]

THEFT ACT 1978

1.   Obtaining services by deception

(1)   A person who by any deception dishonestly obtains services from another shall be guilty of an offence.

(2)   It is an obtaining of services where the other is induced to confer a benefit by doing some act, or causing or permitting some act to be done, on the understanding that the benefit has been or will be paid for.

(3)   Without prejudice to the generality of subsection (2) above, it is an obtaining of services where the other is induced to make a loan, or to cause or permit a loan to be made, on the understanding that any payment (whether by way of interest or otherwise) will be or has been made in respect of the loan.

2.   Evasion of liability by deception

(1)   Subject to subsection (2) below, where a person by any deception—

(a)   dishonestly secures the remission of the whole or part of any existing liability to make a payment, whether his own liability or another's; or

(b)   with intent to make permanent default in whole or in part on any existing liability to make a payment, or with intent to let another do so, dishonestly induces the creditor or any person claiming payment on behalf of the creditor to wait for payment (whether or not the due date for payment is deferred) or to forgo payment; or

(c)   dishonestly obtains any exemption from or abatement of liability to make a payment;

he shall be guilty of an offence.

(2)   For purposes of this section 'liability' means legally enforceable liability; and subsection (1) shall not apply in relation to a liability that has not been accepted or established to pay compensation for a wrongful act or omission.

(3)   For purposes of subsection (1) (b) a person induced to take in payment a cheque or other security for money by way of conditional satisfaction of a pre-existing liability is to be treated not as being paid but as being induced to wait for payment.

(4)   For purposes of subsection (1) (c) 'obtains' includes obtaining for another or enabling another to obtain.

3. Making off without payment

(1)   Subject to subsection (3) below, a person who, knowing that payment on the spot for any goods supplied or service done is required or expected from him, dishonestly makes off without having paid as required or expected and with intent to avoid payment of the amount due shall be guilty of an offence.

(2)   For purposes of this section 'payment on the spot' includes payment at the time of collecting goods on which work has been done or in respect of which service has been provided.

(3)   Subsection (1) above shall not apply where the supply of the goods or the doing of the service is contrary to law, or where the service done is such that payment is not legally enforceable.

(4)   Any person may arrest without warrant anyone who is, or whom he, with reasonable cause, suspects to be, committing or attempting to commit an offence under this section.

4. Punishments

(1)   Offences under this Act shall be punishable either on conviction on indictment or on summary conviction.

(2)   A person convicted on indictment shall be liable—

(a)   for an offence under section 1 or section 2 of this Act, to imprisonment for a term not exceeding five years; and

(b)   for an offence under section 3 of this Act, to imprisonment for a term not exceeding two years.

(3)   A person convicted summarily of any offence under this Act shall be liable—

(a)   to imprisonment for a term not exceeding six months; or

(b)   to a fine not exceeding the prescribed sum for the purposes of section 32 of the Magistrates' Courts Act 1980 (punishment on summary conviction of offences triable either way: £1,000 or other sum substituted by order under that Act),

or to both.

5. Supplementary

(1)   For purposes of section 1 and 2 above 'deception' has the same meaning as in section 15 of the Theft Act 1968, that is to say, it means any deception (whether deliberate or reckless) by words or conduct as to fact or as to law, including a deception as to the present intentions of the person using the deception or any other person; and section 18 of that Act (liability of company officers for offences by the

company) shall apply in relation to sections 1 and 2 above as it applies in relation to
section 15 of that Act.

(2) Sections 30(1) (husband and wife), 31(1) (effect on civil proceedings) and 34
(interpretation) of the Theft Act 1968, so far as they are applicable in relation to this
Act, shall apply as they apply in relation to that Act.

POST OFFICE ACT 1953

53. Unlawfully taking away or opening mail bag

If any person unlawfully takes away or opens a mail bag sent by any ship, vehicle or
aircraft employed by or under the Post Office for the transmission of postal packets
under contract, or unlawfully takes a postal packet in course of transmission by post
out of a mail bag so sent, he shall be guilty of an offence and be liable to imprisonment
for a term not exceeding five years.

55. Fraudulent retention of mail bag or postal packet

Any person who fraudulently retains, or wilfully secretes or keeps, or detains, or who,
when required by a person engaged in the business of the Post Office, neglects or
refuses to deliver up—

(a) any postal packet which is in course of transmission by post and which ought
to have been delivered to any other person; or

(b) any postal packet in course of transmission by post or any mail bag which
has been found by him or by any other person,

shall be guilty of an offence and be liable to a fine and to imprisonment for a term not
exceeding two years.

56. Criminal diversion of letters from addressee

(1) If any person not engaged in the business of the Post Office wilfully and
maliciously, with intent to injure any other person, either opens or causes to be
opened any postal packet which ought to have been delivered to that other person, or
does any act or thing whereby the due delivery of the packet to that other person is
prevented or impeded, he shall be liable on summary conviction to a fine not
exceeding level 4 on the standard scale or to imprisonment for a term not exceeding
six months or to both.

(2) Nothing in this section shall apply to a person who does any act to which this
section applies where he is parent, or in the position of parent or guardian, of the
person to whom the postal packet is addressed.

(4) In this section the expression 'postal packet' means a postal packet which is
in course of transmission by post or which has been delivered by post.

57. Stealing, embezzlement, destruction etc. by officer of Post Office of postal packet

If any person engaged in the business of the Post Office . . . secretes . . . , a postal
packet in course of transmission by post, he shall be guilty of an offence and be liable
to imprisonment for a term not exceeding seven years . . .

58. Opening or delaying of postal packets by officers of the Post Office

(1) If any person engaged in the business of the Post Office, contrary to his duty,
opens, or procures or suffers to be opened, any postal packet in course of transmission
by post, or wilfully detains or delays, or procures or suffers to be detained or delayed,
any such postal packet, he shall be guilty of an offence and be liable to imprisonment
for a term not exceeding two years or to a fine, or to both:

Provided that nothing in this section shall extend to the opening, detaining or delaying
of a postal packet returned for want of a true direction, or returned by reason that the
person to whom it is directed has refused it, or has refused or neglected to pay the

postage thereof, or that the packet cannot for any other reason be delivered, or to the opening, detaining or delaying of a postal packet under the authority of this Act or in obedience to a warrant issued by the Secretary of State under section 2 of the Interception of Communications Act 1985.

TREASURE ACT 1996

8. Duty of finder of treasure to notify coroner

(1) A person who finds an object which he believes or has reasonable grounds for believing is treasure must notify the coroner for the district in which the object was found before the end of the notice period.

(2) The notice period is fourteen days beginning with—

(a) the day after the find; or

(b) if later, the day on which the finder first believes or has reason to believe the object is treasure.

(3) Any person who fails to comply with subsection (1) is guilty of an offence and liable on summary conviction to—

(a) imprisonment for a term not exceeding three months;

(b) a fine of an amount not exceeding level 5 on the standard scale; or

(c) both.

(4) In proceedings for an offence under this section, it is a defence for the defendant to show that he had, and has continued to have, a reasonable excuse for failing to notify the coroner.

ROAD TRAFFIC REGULATION ACT 1984

47. Interfering with parking meters

(3) A person who, with intent to defraud, interferes with a parking meter, or operates or attempts to operate a parking meter by the insertion of objects other than current coins or bank notes of the appropriate denomination, or the appropriate credit or debit cards, shall be guilty of an offence.

TELECOMMUNICATIONS ACT 1984

42. Fraudulent use of telecommunication system

(1) A person who dishonestly obtains a service to which this subsection applies with intent to avoid payment of any charge applicable to the provision of that service shall be guilty of an offence and liable—

(a) on summary conviction, to imprisonment for a term not exceeding six months or to a fine not exceeding the statutory maximum or to both;

(b) on conviction on indictment, to imprisonment for a term not exceeding five years or to a fine or to both.

(2) Subsection (1) above applies to any service (other than a service to which section 53 of the Cable and Broadcasting Act 1984 applies) which is provided by means of a telecommunication system the running of which is authorised by a licence granted under section 7 of this Act.

42A. Possession or supply of anything for fraudulent purpose in connection with use of telecommunication system

(1) Subsection (2) below applies if a person has in his custody or under his control anything which may be used for the purpose of obtaining, or for a purpose connected with the obtaining of, a service to which section 42(1) above applies.

(2) If the person intends—

(a) to use the thing—

    (i)   to obtain such a service dishonestly, or

    (ii)   for a purpose connected with the dishonest obtaining of such a service,

(b) dishonestly to allow the thing to be used to obtain such a service, or

(c) to allow the thing to be used for a purpose connected with the dishonest obtaining of such a service,

he shall be guilty of an offence.

(3) Subsection (4) below applies if a person supplies or offers to supply anything which may be used for the purpose of obtaining, or for a purpose connected with the obtaining of, a service to which section 42(1) above applies.

(4) If the person supplying or offering to supply the thing knows or believes that the person to whom it is supplied or offered intends or intends if it is supplied to him—

(a) to use it—

    (i)   to obtain such a service dishonestly, or

    (ii)   for a purpose connected with the dishonest obtaining of such a service,

(b) dishonestly to allow it to be used to obtain such a service, or

(c) to allow it to be used for a purpose connected with the dishonest obtaining of such a service,

he shall be guilty of an offence.

(5) A person guilty of an offence under this section shall be liable—

(a) on summary conviction, to imprisonment for a term not exceeding six months or to a fine not exceeding the statutory maximum or to both, and

(b) on conviction on indictment, to imprisonment for a term not exceeding five years or to a fine or to both.

(6) In this section, references to use of a thing include, in the case of a thing which is used to record any data, use of any of the data.

GAS ACT 1995

SCHEDULE 2

10. Injury to gas fittings and interference with meters

(1) If any person intentionally or by culpable negligence—

(a) injures or allows to be injured any gas fitting belonging to a public gas transporter or gas supplier or any service pipe by which any premises are connected to such transporter's mains;

(b) alters the index to any meter used for measuring the quantity of gas supplied by such a transporter or supplier; or

(c) prevents any such meter from duly registering the quantity of gas conveyed or supplied,

he shall be guilty of an offence and liable on summary conviction to a fine not exceeding level 3 on the standard scale.

(2) In the case of any offence under sub-paragraph (1) above, the transporter or supplier may disconnect the premises or cut off the supply of gas to the person so offending.

(3) Where any person is prosecuted for an offence under sub-paragraph (1)(b) or (c) above, the possession by him of artificial means for causing an alteration of the index of the meter or, as the case may be, the prevention of the meter from duly registering shall, if the meter was in his custody or under his control, be prima facie evidence that the alteration or prevention was intentionally caused by him.

11. Restoration of supply without consent

(1) Where a consumer's premises has been disconnected by a public gas transporter or a supply of gas to a consumer's premises has been cut off by a gas supplier

otherwise than in the exercise of certain powers, no person shall, without the relevant consent, reconnect the premises or restore the supply.

(2)   If any person acts in contravention of sub-paragraph (1) above, (a) he shall be guilty of an offence and liable on summary conviction to a fine not exceeding level 3 on the standard scale and (b) the transporter or supplier may again disconnect the premises or, as the case may be, cut off the supply.

COMPANIES ACT 1985

458.   Punishment for fraudulent trading

If any business of a company is carried on with intent to defraud creditors of the company or creditors of any other person, or for any fraudulent purpose, every person who was knowingly a party to the carrying on of the business in that manner is liable to imprisonment or a fine, or both.

This applies whether or not the company has been, or is in the course of being, wound up.

INSOLVENCY ACT 1986

CHAPTER VI
BANKRUPTCY OFFENCES

Preliminary

350.   Scheme of this Chapter

(1)   Subject to section 360(3) below, this Chapter applies where the court has made a bankruptcy order on a bankruptcy petition.

(2)   This Chapter applies whether or not the bankruptcy order is annulled, but proceedings for an offence under this Chapter shall not be instituted after the annulment.

(3)   Without prejudice to his liability in respect of a subsequent bankruptcy, the bankrupt is not guilty of an offence under this Chapter in respect of anything done after his discharge; but nothing in this Group of Parts prevents the institution of proceedings against a discharged bankrupt for an offence committed before his discharge.

(4)   It is not a defence in proceedings for an offence under this Chapter that anything relied on, in whole or in part, as constituting that offence was done outside England and Wales.

. . .

(6)   A person guilty of any offence under this Chapter is liable to imprisonment or a fine, or both.

351.   Definitions

In the following provisions of this Chapter—

(a)   references to property comprised in the bankrupt's estate or to property possession of which is required to be delivered up to the official receiver or the trustee of the bankrupt's estate include any property which would be such property if a notice in respect of it were given under section 307 (after-acquired property) or 308 (personal property and effects of bankrupt having more than replacement value);

(b)   "the initial period" means the period between the presentation of the bankruptcy petition and the commencement of the bankruptcy; and

(c)   a reference to a number of months or years before petition is to that period ending with the presentation of the bankruptcy petition.

352.   Defence of innocent intention

Where in the case of an offence under any provision of this Chapter it is stated that this section applies, a person is not guilty of the offence if he proves that, at the time of the conduct constituting the offence, he had no intent to defraud or to conceal the state of his affairs.

Wrongdoing by the bankrupt before and after bankruptcy

353. Non-disclosure

(1)   The bankrupt is guilty of an offence if—

(a)   he does not to the best of his knowledge and belief disclose all the property comprised in his estate to the official receiver or the trustee, or

(b)   he does not inform the official receiver or the trustee of any disposal of any property which but for the disposal would be so comprised, stating how, when, to whom and for what consideration the property was disposed of.

(2)   Subsection (1)(b) does not apply to any disposal in the ordinary course of a business carried on by the bankrupt or to any payment of the ordinary expenses of the bankrupt or his family.

(3)   Section 352 applies to this offence.

354. Concealment of property

(1)   The bankrupt is guilty of an offence if—

(a)   he does not deliver up possession to the official receiver or trustee, or as the official receiver or trustee may direct, of such part of the property comprised in his estate as is in his possession or under his control and possession of which he is required by law so to deliver up,

(b)   . . . he conceals any property the value of which is not less than the prescribed amount and possession of which he is required to deliver up to the official receiver or trustee, or

(c)   in the 12 months before petition, or in the initial period, he did anything which would have been an offence under paragraph (b) above if the bankruptcy order had been made immediately before he did it.

Section 352 applies to this offence.

(2)   The bankrupt is guilty of an offence if he removes, or in the initial period removed, any property the value of which was not less than the prescribed amount and possession of which he has or would have been required to deliver up to the official receiver or the trustee.

Section 352 applies to this offence.

(3)   The bankrupt is guilty of an offence if he without reasonable excuse fails, on being required to do so by the official receiver or the court—

(a)   to account for the loss of any substantial part of his property incurred in the 12 months before petition or in the initial period, or

(b)   to give a satisfactory explanation of the manner in which such a loss was incurred.

355. Concealment of books and papers; falsification

(1)   The bankrupt is guilty of an offence if he does not deliver up possession to the official receiver or the trustee, or as the official receiver or trustee may direct, of all books, papers and other records of which he has possession or control and which relate to his estate or his affairs.

Section 352 applies to this offence.

(2)   The bankrupt is guilty of an offence if—

(a)   he prevents, or in the initial period prevented, the production of any books, papers or records relating to his estate or affairs;

(b)   he conceals, destroys, mutilates or falsifies, or causes or permits the concealment, destruction, mutilation or falsification of, any books, papers or other records relating to his estate or affairs;

(c)   he makes, or causes or permits the making of, any false entries in any book, document or record relating to his estate or affairs; or

(d) in the 12 months before petition, or in the initial period, he did anything which would have been an offence under paragraph (b) or (c) above if the bankruptcy order had been made before he did it.

Section 352 applies to this offence.

(3) The bankrupt is guilty of an offence if—

(a) he disposes of, or alters or makes any omission in, or causes or permits the disposal, altering or making of any omission in, any book, document or record relating to his estate or affairs, or

(b) in the 12 months before petition, or in the initial period he did anything which would have been an offence under paragraph (a) if the bankruptcy order had been made before he did it.

Section 352 applies to this offence.

356. False statements

(1) The bankrupt is guilty of an offence if he makes or has made any material omission in any statement made under any provision in this Group of Parts and relating to his affairs.

Section 352 applies to this offence.

(2) The bankrupt is guilty of an offence if—

(a) knowing or believing that a false debt has been proved by any person under the bankruptcy, he fails to inform the trustee as soon as practicable; or

(b) he attempts to account for any part of his property by fictitious losses or expenses; or

(c) at any meeting of his creditors in the 12 months before petition or (whether or not at such a meeting) at any time in the initial period, he did anything which would have been an offence under paragraph (b) if the bankruptcy order had been made before he did it; or

(d) he is, or at any time has been, guilty of any false representation or other fraud for the purpose of obtaining the consent of his creditors, or any of them, to an agreement with reference to his affairs or to his bankruptcy.

357. Fraudulent disposal of property

(1) The bankrupt is guilty of an offence if he makes or causes to be made, or has in the period of 5 years ending with the commencement of the bankruptcy made or caused to be made, any gift or transfer of, or any charge on, his property.

Section 352 applies to this offence.

(2) The reference to making a transfer of or charge on any property includes causing or conniving at the levying of any execution against that property.

(3) The bankrupt is guilty of an offence if he conceals or removes, or has at any time before the commencement of the bankruptcy concealed or removed, any part of his property after, or within 2 months before, the date on which a judgment or order for the payment of money has been obtained against him, being a judgment or order which was not satisfied before the commencement of the bankruptcy.

Section 352 applies to this offence.

358. Absconding

The bankrupt is guilty of an offence if—

(a) he leaves, or attempts or makes preparations to leave, England and Wales with any property the value of which is not less than the prescribed amount and possession of which he is required to deliver up to the official receiver or the trustee, or

(b) in the 6 months before petition, or in the initial period, he did anything which would have been an offence under paragraph (a) if the bankruptcy order had been made immediately before he did it.

Section 352 applies to this offence.

359. Fraudulent dealing with property obtained on credit

(1) The bankrupt is guilty of an offence if, in the 12 months before petition, or in the initial period, he disposed of any property which he had obtained on credit and, at the time he disposed of it, had not paid for.

Section 352 applies to this offence.

(2) A person is guilty of an offence if, in the 12 months before petition or in the initial period, he acquired or received property from the bankrupt knowing or believing—

(a) that the bankrupt owed money in respect of the property, and

(b) that the bankrupt did not intend, or was unlikely to be able, to pay the money he so owed.

(3) A person is not guilty of an offence under subsection (1) or (2) if the disposal, acquisition or receipt of the property was in the ordinary course of a business carried on by the bankrupt at the time of the disposal, acquisition or receipt.

(4) In determining for the purposes of this section whether any property is disposed of, acquired or received in the ordinary course of a business carried on by the bankrupt, regard may be had, in particular, to the price paid for the property.

(5) In this section references to disposing of property include pawning or pledging it; and references to acquiring or receiving property shall be read accordingly.

360. Obtaining credit; engaging in business

(1) The bankrupt is guilty of an offence if—

(a) either alone or jointly with any other person, he obtains credit to the extent of the prescribed amount or more without giving the person from whom he obtains it the relevant information about his status; or

(b) he engages (whether directly or indirectly) in any business under a name other than that in which he was adjudged bankrupt without disclosing to all persons with whom he enters into any business transaction the name in which he was so adjudged.

(2) The reference to the bankrupt obtaining credit includes the following cases—

(a) where goods are bailed to him under a hire-purchase agreement, or agreed to be sold to him under a conditional sale agreement, and

(b) where he is paid in advance (whether in money or otherwise) for the supply of goods or services.

(3) A person whose estate has been sequestrated in Scotland, or who has been adjudged bankrupt in Northern Ireland, is guilty of an offence if, before his discharge, he does anything in England and Wales which would be an offence under subsection (1) if he were an undischarged bankrupt and the sequestration of his estate or the adjudication in Northern Ireland were an adjudication under this Part.

(4) For the purposes of subsection (1)(a), the relevant information about the status of the person in question is the information that he is an undischarged bankrupt or, as the case may be, that his estate has been sequestrated in Scotland and that he has not been discharged.

361. Failure to keep proper accounts of business

(1) Where the bankrupt has been engaged in any business for any of the period of 2 years before petition, he is guilty of an offence if he—

(a) has not kept proper accounting records throughout that period and through-out any part of the initial period in which he was so engaged, or

(b) has not preserved all the accounting records which he has kept.

(2) The bankrupt is not guilty of an offence under subsection (1)—

(a) if his unsecured liabilities at the commencement of the bankruptcy did not exceed the prescribed amount, or

(b) if he proves that in the circumstances in which he carried on business the omission was honest and excusable.

(3)   For the purposes of this section a person is deemed not to have kept proper accounting records if he has not kept such records as are necessary to show or explain his transactions and financial position in his business, including—

(a)   records containing entries from day to day, in sufficient detail, of all cash paid and received.

(b)   where the business involved dealings in goods, statements of annual stock-takings, and

(c)   except in the case of goods sold by way of retail trade to the actual customer, records of all goods, sold and purchased showing the buyers and sellers in sufficient detail to enable the goods and the buyers and sellers to be identified.

(4)   In relation to any such records as are mentioned in subsection (3), subsections (2)(d) and (3)(b) of section 355 apply with the substitution of 2 years for 12 months.

362.   Gambling

(1)   The bankrupt is guilty of an offence if he has—

(a)   in the 2 years before petition, materially contributed to, or increased the extent of, his insolvency by gambling or by rash and hazardous speculations, or

(b)   in the initial period, lost any part of his property by gambling or by rash and hazardous speculations.

(2)   In determining for the purposes of this section whether any speculations were rash and hazardous, the financial position of the bankrupt at the time when he entered into them shall be taken into consideration.

FINANCIAL SERVICES ACT 1986

47.   Misleading statements and practices

(1)   Any person who—

(a)   makes a statement, promise or forecast which he knows to be misleading, false or deceptive or dishonestly conceals any material facts; or

(b)   recklessly makes (dishonestly or otherwise) a statement, promise or forecast which is misleading, false or deceptive,

is guilty of an offence if he makes the statement, promise or forecast or conceals the facts for the purpose of inducing, or is reckless as to whether it may induce, another person (whether or not the person to whom the statement, promise or forecast is made or from whom the facts are concealed) to enter or offer to enter into, or to refrain from entering or offering to enter into, an investment agreement or to exercise, or refrain from exercising, any rights conferred by an investment.

(2)   Any person who does any act or engages in any course of conduct which creates a false or misleading impression as to the market in or the price or value of any investments is guilty of an offence if he does so for the purpose of creating that impression and of thereby inducing another person to acquire, dispose of, subscribe for or underwrite those investments or to refrain from doing so or to exercise, or refrain from exercising, any rights conferred by those investments.

(3)   In proceedings brought against any person for an offence under subsection (2) above it shall be a defence for him to prove that he reasonably believed that his act or conduct would not create an impression that was false or misleading as to the matters mentioned in that subsection.

(4)   Subsection (1) above does not apply unless—

(a)   the statement, promise or forecast is made in or from, or the facts are concealed in or from, the United Kingdom;

(b)   the person on whom the inducement is intended to or may have effect is in the United Kingdom; or

(c)   the agreement is or would be entered into or the rights are or would be exercised in the United Kingdom.

(5)   Subsection (2) above does not apply unless—

(a)   the act is done or the course of conduct is engaged in in the United Kingdom; or

(b)   the false or misleading impression is created there.

(6)   A person guilty of an offence under this section shall be liable—

(a)   on conviction on indictment, to imprisonment for a term not exceeding seven years or to a fine or to both;

(b)   on summary conviction, to imprisonment for a term not exceeding six months or to a fine not exceeding the statutory maximum or to both.

BANKING ACT 1987

35.   Fraudulent inducement to make a deposit

(1)   Any person who—

(a)   makes a statement, promise or forecast which he knows to be misleading, false or deceptive, or dishonestly conceals any material facts; or

(b)   recklessly makes (dishonestly or otherwise) a statement, promise or forecast which is misleading, false or deceptive,

is guilty of an offence if he makes the statement, promise or forecast or conceals the facts for the purpose of inducing, or is reckless as to whether it may induce, another person (whether or not the person to whom the statement, promise or forecast is made or from whom the facts are concealed)—

(i)   to make, or refrain from making, a deposit with him or any other person; or

(ii)   to enter, or refrain from entering, into an agreement for the purpose of making such a deposit.

(2)   This section does not apply unless—

(a)   the statement, promise or forecast is made in or from, or the facts are concealed in or from, the United Kingdom or arrangements are made in or from the United Kingdom for the statement, promise or forecast to be made or the facts to be concealed;

(b)   the person on whom the inducement is intended to or may have effect is in the United Kingdom; or

(c)   the deposit is or would be made, or the agreement is or would be entered into, in the United Kingdom.

(3)   A person guilty of an offence under this section shall be liable—

(a)   on conviction on indictment, to imprisonment for a term not exceeding seven years or to a fine or to both;

(b)   on summary conviction, to imprisonment for a term not exceeding six months or to a fine not exceeding the statutory maximum or to both.

CRIMINAL JUSTICE ACT 1993

PART V   INSIDER DEALING

52.   The offence of insider dealing

(1)   An individual who has information as an insider is guilty of insider dealing if, in the circumstances mentioned in subsection (3), he deals in securities that are price-affected securities in relation to the information.

(2)   An individual who has information as an insider is also guilty of insider dealing if—

(a)   he encourages another person to deal in securities that are (whether or not that other knows it) price-affected securities in relation to the information, knowing or having reasonable cause to believe that the dealing would take place in the circumstances mentioned in subsection (3); or

(b)   he discloses the information, otherwise than in the proper performance of the functions of his employment, office or profession, to another person.

(3)   The circumstances referred to above are that the acquisition or disposal in question occurs on a regulated market, or that the person dealing relies on a professional intermediary or is himself acting as a professional intermediary.

(4)   This section has effect subject to section 53.

53.   Defences

(1)   An individual is not guilty of insider dealing by virtue of dealing in securities if he shows—

(a)   that he did not at the time expect the dealing to result in a profit attributable to the fact that the information in question was price-sensitive information in relation to the securities, or

(b)   that at the time he believed on reasonable grounds that the information had been disclosed widely enough to ensure that none of those taking part in the dealing would be prejudiced by not having the information, or

(c)   that he would have done what he did even if he had not had the information.

(2)   An individual is not guilty of insider dealing by virtue of encouraging another person to deal in securities if he shows—

(a)   that he did not at the time expect the dealing to result in a profit attributable to the fact that the information in question was price-sensitive information in relation to the securities, or

(b)   that at the time he believed on reasonable grounds that the information had been or would be disclosed widely enough to ensure that none of those taking part in the dealing would be prejudiced by not having the information, or

(c)   that he would have done what he did even if he had not had the information.

(3)   An individual is not guilty of insider dealing by virtue of a disclosure of information if he shows—

(a)   that he did not at the time expect any person, because of the disclosure, to deal in securities in the circumstances mentioned in subsection (3) of section 52; or

(b)   that, although he had such an expectation at the time, he did not expect the dealing to result in a profit attributable to the fact that the information was price-sensitive information in relation to the securities.

(4)   Schedule 1 (special defences) shall have effect.

(5)   The Treasury may by order amend Schedule 1.

(6)   In this section references to a profit include references to the avoidance of a loss.

54.   Securities to which Part V applies

(1)   This Part applies to any security which—

(a)   falls within any paragraph of Schedule 2; and

(b)   satisfies any conditions applying to it under an order made by the Treasury for the purposes of this subsection;

and in the provisions of this Part (other than that Schedule) any reference to a security is a reference to a security to which this Part applies.

55.   Meaning of 'dealing'

(1)   For the purposes of this Part, a person deals in securities if—

(a)   he acquires or disposes of the securities (whether as principal or agent); or

(b)   he procures, directly or indirectly, an acquisition or disposal of the securities by any other person.

(2)   For the purposes of this Part, 'acquire', in relation to a security, includes—

   (a) agreeing to acquire the security; and

   (b) entering into a contract which creates the security.

  (3) For the purposes of this Part, 'dispose', in relation to a security, includes—

   (a) agreeing to dispose of the security; and

   (b) bringing to an end a contract which created the security.

  (4) For the purposes of subsection (1), a person procures an acquisition or disposal of a security if the security is acquired or disposed of by a person who is—

   (a) his agent,

   (b) his nominee, or

   (c) a person who is acting at his direction,

in relation to the acquisition or disposal.

  (5) Subsection (4) is not exhaustive as to the circumstances in which one person may be regarded as procuring an acquisition or disposal of securities by another.

56. Meaning of 'inside information'

  (1) For the purposes of this section and section 57, 'inside information' means information which—

   (a) relates to particular securities or to a particular issuer of securities or to particular issuers of securities and not to securities generally or to the issuers of securities generally;

   (b) is specific or precise;

   (c) has not been made public; and

   (d) if it were made public would be likely to have a significant effect on the price of any securities.

  (2) For the purposes of this Part, securities are 'price-affected securities' in relation to inside information, and inside information is 'price-sensitive information' in relation to securities, if and only if the information would, if made public, be likely to have a significant effect on the price of the securities.

  (3) For the purpose of this section 'price' includes value.

57. 'Insiders'

  (1) For the purposes of this Part, a person has information as an insider if and only if—

   (a) it is, and he knows that it is, inside information, and

   (b) he has it, and knows that he has it, from an inside source.

  (2) For the purposes of subsection (1), a person has information from an inside source if and only if—

   (a) he has it through—

     (i) being a director, employee or shareholder of an issuer of securities; or

     (ii) having access to the information by virtue of his employment, office or profession; or

   (b) the direct or indirect source of his information is a person within paragraph (a).

58. Information 'made public'

  (1) For the purposes of section 56, 'made public', in relation to information, shall be construed in accordance with the following provisions of this section; but those provisions are not exhaustive as to the meaning of that expression.

  (2) Information is made public if—

   (a) it is published in accordance with the rules of a regulated market for the purpose of informing investors and their professional advisers;

   (b) it is contained in records which by virtue of any enactment are open to inspection by the public;

   (c) it can be readily acquired by those likely to deal in any securities—

    (i)   to which the information relates, or

    (ii) of an issuer to which the information relates; or

  (d) it is derived from information which has been made public.

  (3) Information may be treated as made public even though—

    (a) it can be acquired only by persons exercising diligence or expertise;

    (b) it is communicated to a section of the public and not to the public at large;

    (c) it can be acquired only by observation;

    (d) it is communicated only on payment of a fee; or

    (e) it is published only outside the United Kingdom.

59. 'Professional intermediary'

  (1) For the purposes of this Part, a 'professional intermediary' is a person—

    (a) who carries on a business consisting of an activity mentioned in subsection (2) and who holds himself out to the public or any section of the public (including a section of the public constituted by persons such as himself) as willing to engage in any such business; or

    (b) who is employed by a person falling within paragraph (a) to carry out any such activity.

  (2) The activities referred to in subsection (1) are—

    (a) acquiring or disposing of securities (whether as principal or agent); or

    (b) acting as an intermediary between persons taking part in any dealing in securities.

  (3) A person is not to be treated as carrying on a business consisting of an activity mentioned in subsection (2)—

    (a) if the activity in question is merely incidental to some other activity not falling within subsection (2); or

    (b) merely because he occasionally conducts one of those activities.

  (4) For the purposes of section 52, a person dealing in securities relies on a professional intermediary if and only if a person who is acting as a professional intermediary carries out an activity mentioned in subsection (2) in relation to that dealing.

60. Other interpretation provisions

  (1) For the purposes of this Part, 'regulated market' means any market, however operated, which, by an order made by the Treasury, is identified (whether by name or by reference to criteria prescribed by the order) as a regulated market for the purposes of this Part.

  (2) For the purposes of this Part an 'issuer', in relation to any securities, means any company, public sector body or individual by which or by whom the securities have been or are to be issued.

  (3) For the purposes of this Part—

    (a) 'company' means any body (whether or not incorporated and wherever incorporated or constituted) which is not a public sector body; and

    (b) 'public sector body' means—

      (i)   the government of the United Kingdom, of Northern Ireland or of any country or territory outside the United Kingdom;

      (ii)   a local authority in the United Kingdom or elsewhere;

      (iii) any international organisation the members of which include the United Kingdom or another member state;

      (iv) the Bank of England; or

      (v)   the central bank of any sovereign State.

  (4) For the purposes of this Part, information shall be treated as relating to an issuer of securities which is a company not only where it is about the company but also where it may affect the company's business prospects.

61. Penalties and prosecution

(1) An individual guilty of insider dealing shall be liable—

(a) on summary conviction, to a fine not exceeding the statutory maximum or imprisonment for a term not exceeding six months or to both; or

(b) on conviction on indictment, to a fine or imprisonment for a term not exceeding seven years or to both.

62. Territorial scope of offence of insider dealing

(1) An individual is not guilty of an offence falling within subsection (1) of section 52 unless—

(a) he was within the United Kingdom at the time when he is alleged to have done any act constituting or forming part of the alleged dealing;

(b) the regulated market on which the dealing is alleged to have occurred is one which is declared by an order made by the Treasury to be a market which for the purposes of this Part is to be treated as regulated in the United Kingdom; or

(c) the professional intermediary was within the United Kingdom at the time when he is alleged to have done anything by means of which the offence is alleged to have been committed.

(2) An individual is not guilty of an offence falling within subsection (2) of section 52 unless—

(a) he was within the United Kingdom at the time when he is alleged to have disclosed the information or encouraged the dealing; or

(b) the alleged recipient of the information or encouragement was within the United Kingdom at the time when he is alleged to have received the information or encouragement.

63. Limits on section 52

(1) Section 52 does not apply to anything done by an individual acting on behalf of a public sector body in pursuit of monetary policies or policies with respect to exchange rates or the management of public debt or foreign exchange reserves.

SCHEDULE 1

SPECIAL DEFENCES

Market makers

1. (1) An individual is not guilty of insider dealing by virtue of dealing in securities or encouraging another person to deal if he shows that he acted in good faith in the course of—

(a) his business as a market maker, or

(b) his employment in the business of a market maker.

(2) A market maker is a person who—

(a) holds himself out at all normal times in compliance with the rules of a regulated market or an approved organisation as willing to acquire or dispose of securities; and

(b) is recognised as doing so under those rules.

(3) In this paragraph 'approved organisation' means an international securities self-regulating organisation approved under paragraph 25B of Schedule 1 to the Financial Services Act 1986.

Market information

2. (1) An individual is not guilty of insider dealing by virtue of dealing in securities or encouraging another person to deal if he shows that—

(a) the information which he had as an insider was market information; and

(b) is was reasonable for an individual in his position to have acted as he did despite having that information as an insider at the time.

(2) In determining whether it is reasonable for an individual to do any act despite having market information at the time, there shall, in particular, be taken into account—

(a) the content of the information;

(b) the circumstances in which he first had the information and in what capacity; and

(c) the capacity in which he now acts.

3. An individual is not guilty of insider dealing by virtue of dealing in securities or encouraging another person to deal if he shows—

(a) that he acted—

(i) in connection with an acquisition or disposal which was under consideration or the subject of negotiation, or in the course of a series of such acquisitions or disposals; and

(ii) with a view to facilitating the accomplishment of the acquisition or disposal or the series of acquisitions or disposals; and

(b) that the information which he had as an insider was market information arising directly out of his involvement in the acquisition or disposal or series of acquisitions or disposals.

4. For the purposes of paragraphs 2 and 3 market information is information consisting of one or more of the following facts—

(a) that securities of a particular kind have been or are to be acquired or disposed of, or that their acquisition or disposal is under consideration or the subject of negotiation;

(b) that securities of a particular kind have not been or are not to be acquired or disposed of;

(c) the number of securities acquired or disposed of or to be acquired or disposed of or whose acquisition or disposal is under consideration or the subject of negotiation;

(d) the price (or range of prices) at which securities have been or are to be acquired or disposed of or the price (or range of prices) at which securities whose acquisition or disposal is under consideration or the subject of negotiation may be acquired or disposed of;

(e) the identity of the persons involved or likely to be involved in any capacity in an acquisition or disposal.

Price stabilisation

5. — (1) An individual is not guilty of insider dealing by virtue of dealing in securities or encouraging another person to deal if he shows that he acted in conformity with the price stabilisation rules.

(2) In this paragraph 'the price stabilisation rules' means rules which—

(a) are made under section 48 of the Financial Services Act 1986 (conduct of business rules); and

(b) make provision of a description mentioned in paragraph (i) of subsection (2) of that section (price stabilisation rules).

SCHEDULE 2

SECURITIES

Shares

1. Shares and stock in the share capital of a company ('shares').

Debt securities

2.   Any instrument creating or acknowledging indebtedness which is issued by a company or public sector body, including, in particular, debentures, debenture stock, loan stock, bonds and certificates of deposit ('debt securities').

Warrants

3.   Any right (whether conferred by warrant or otherwise) to subscribe for shares or debt securities ('warrants').

Depositary receipts

4.   (1)   The rights under any depositary receipt.
   (2)   For the purposes of sub-paragraph (1) a 'depositary receipt' means a certificate or other record (whether or not in the form of a document)—
      (a)   which is issued by or on behalf of a person who holds any relevant securities of a particular issuer; and
      (b)   which acknowledges that another person is entitled to rights in relation to the relevant securities or relevant securities of the same kind.
   (3)   In sub-paragraph (2) 'relevant securities' means shares, debt securities and warrants.

Options

5.   Any option to acquire or dispose of any thing falling within any other paragraph of this Schedule.

Futures

6.   (1)   Rights under a contract for the acquisition or disposal at a future date of any relevant securities at a price agreed when the contract is made.
   (2)   In sub-paragraph (1)—
      (a)   the references to a future date and to a price agreed when the contract is made include references to a date and a price determined in accordance with terms of the contract; and
      (b)   'relevant securities' means any security falling within any other paragraph of this Schedule.

Contracts, for differences

7.   (1)   Rights under a contract which does not provide for the delivery of securities but whose purpose or pretended purpose is to secure a profit or avoid a loss by reference to fluctuations in—
      (a)   a share index or other similar factor connected with relevant securities;
      (b)   the price of particular relevant securities; or
      (c)   the interest rate offered on money placed on deposit.
   (2)   In sub-paragraph (1) 'relevant securities' means any thing falling within any other paragraph of this Schedule.

PREVENTION OF CORRUPTION ACT 1906

1.   Corrupt transactions by agents

   (1)   If any agent corruptly accepts or obtains, or agrees to accept or attempts to obtain, from any person, for himself or for any other person, any gift or consideration as an inducement or reward for doing or forbearing to do, or for having after the passing of this Act done or forborne to do, any act in relation to his principal's affairs

or business, or for showing or forbearing to show favour or disfavour to any person in relation to his principal's affairs or business; or

If any person corruptly gives or agrees to give or offers any gift or consideration to any agent as an inducement or reward for doing or forbearing to do, or for having after the passing of this Act done or forborne to do, any act in relation to his principal's affairs or business, or for showing or forbearing to show favour or disfavour to any person in relation to his principal's affairs or business; or

If any person knowingly gives to any agent, or if any agent knowingly uses with intent to deceive his principal, any receipt, account, or other document in respect of which the principal is interested, and which contains any statement which is false or erroneous or defective in any material particular, and which to his knowledge is intended to mislead the principal;

he shall be guilty of a misdemeanour, and shall be liable

(a) on summary conviction to imprisonment for a term not exceeding six months, or to a fine, or to both; and

(b) on conviction on indictment to imprisonment for a term not exceeding seven years, or to a fine, or to both.

(2) For the purposes of this Act the expression 'consideration' includes valuable consideration of any kind; the expression 'agent' includes any person employed by or acting for another; and the expression 'principal' includes an employer.

(3) A person serving under the Crown or under any corporation or any municipal, borough, county, or district council, or any board of guardians, is an agent within the meaning of this Act.

PREVENTION OF CORRUPTION ACT 1916

2. Presumption of corruption in certain cases
[See page 241]

AUCTIONS (BIDDING AGREEMENTS) ACT 1927

1. Certain bidding agreements to be illegal

(1) If any dealer agrees to give, or gives, or offers any gift or consideration to any other person as an inducement or reward for abstaining, or for having abstained, from bidding at a sale by auction either generally or for any particular lot, or if any person agrees to accept, or accepts, or attempts to obtain from any dealer any such gift or consideration as aforesaid, he shall be guilty of an offence under this Act, and shall be liable on summary conviction to a fine not exceeding one hundred pounds, or to a term of imprisonment for any period not exceeding six months, or to both such fine and such imprisonment; Provided that, where it is proved that a dealer has previously to an auction entered into an agreement in writing with one or more persons to purchase goods at the auction bona fide on a joint account and has before the goods were purchased at the auction deposited a copy of the agreement with the auctioneer, such an agreement shall not be treated as an agreement made in contravention of this section.

(2) For the purposes of this section the expression 'dealer' means a person who in the normal course of his business attends sales by auction for the purpose of purchasing goods with a view to reselling them.

MOCK AUCTIONS ACT 1961

1. Penalties for promoting or conducting mock auctions

(1) It shall be an offence to promote or conduct, or to assist in the conduct of, a mock auction at which one or more lots to which this Act applies are offered for sale.

(2)   Any person guilty of an offence under this Act shall be liable—

(a)   on summary conviction to a fine not exceeding one hundred pounds, or to imprisonment for a term not exceeding three months, or to both such a fine and such imprisonment;

(b)   on conviction on indictment, to a fine not exceeding one thousand pounds or to imprisonment for a term not exceeding two years, or to both such a fine and such imprisonment.

(3)   Subject to the following provisions of this section, for the purposes of this Act a sale of goods by way of competitive bidding shall be taken to be a mock auction if, but only if, during the course of the sale—

(a)   any lot to which this Act applies is sold to a person bidding for it, and either it is sold to him at a price lower than the amount of his highest bid for that lot, or part of the price at which it is sold to him is repaid or credited to him or is stated to be so repaid or credited, or

(b)   the right to bid for any lot to which this Act applies is restricted, or is stated to be restricted, to persons who have bought or agreed to buy one or more articles, or

(c)   any articles are given away or offered as gifts.

(4)   A sale of goods shall not be taken to be a mock auction by virtue of paragraph (a) of the last preceding subsection, if it is proved that the reduction in price, or the repayment or credit as the case may be—

(a)   was on account of a defect discovered after the highest bid in question had been made, being a defect of which the person conducting the sale was unaware when that bid was made, or

(b)   was on account of damage sustained after that bid was made.

3.   Interpretation

(1)   In this Act 'sale of goods by way of competitive bidding' means any sale of goods at which the persons present, or some of them, are invited to buy articles by way of competitive bidding, and 'competitive bidding' includes any mode of sale whereby prospective purchasers may be enabled to compete for the purchase of articles, whether by way of increasing bids or by the offer of articles to be bid for at successively decreasing prices or otherwise.

(2)   In this Act 'lot to which this Act applies' means a lot consisting of or including one or more prescribed articles; and 'prescribed articles' means any plate, plated articles, linen, china, glass, books, pictures, prints, furniture, jewellery, articles of household or personal use or ornament or any musical or scientific instrument or apparatus.

(3)   In this Act 'stated', in relation to a sale of goods by way of competitive bidding, means stated by or on behalf of the person conducting the sale, by an announcement made to the persons for the time being present at the sale.

(4)   For the purposes of this Act any bid stated to have been made at a sale of goods by way of competitive bidding shall be conclusively presumed to have been made, and to have been a bid of the amount stated; and any reference in this Act to the sale of a lot to a person who has made a bid for it includes a reference to a purported sale thereof to a person stated to have bid for it, whether that person exists or not.

(5)   For the purposes of this Act anything done in or about the place where a sale of goods by way of competitive bidding is held, if done in connection with the sale, shall be taken to be done during the course of the sale, whether it is done at the time when the articles are being sold or offered for sale by way of competitive bidding or before or after any such time.

FORGERY AND COUNTERFEITING ACT 1981

PART I   FORGERY AND KINDRED OFFENCES

1.   The offence of forgery

A person is guilty of forgery if he makes a false instrument, with the intention that he or another shall use it to induce somebody to accept it as genuine, and by reason of so accepting it to do or not to do some act to his own or any other person's prejudice.

2.   The offence of copying a false instrument

It is an offence for a person to make a copy of an instrument which is, and which he knows or believes to be, a false instrument, with the intention that he or another shall use it to induce somebody to accept it as a copy of a genuine instrument, and by reason of so accepting it to do or not to do some act to his own or any other person's prejudice.

3.   The offence of using a false instrument

It is an offence for a person to use an instrument which is, and which he knows or believes to be, false, with the intention of inducing somebody to accept it as genuine, and by reason of so accepting it to do or not to do some act to his own or any other person's prejudice.

4.   The offence of using a copy of a false instrument

It is an offence for a person to use a copy of an instrument which is, and which he knows or believes to be, a false instrument, with the intention of inducing somebody to accept it as a copy of a genuine instrument, and by reason of so accepting it to do or not to do some act to his own or any other person's prejudice.

5.   Offences relating to money orders, share certificates, passports, etc.

(1)   It is an offence for a person to have in his custody or under his control an instrument to which this section applies which is, and which he knows or believes to be, false, with the intention that he or another shall use it to induce somebody to accept it as genuine, and by reason of so accepting it to do or not to do some act to his own or any other person's prejudice.

(2)   It is an offence for a person to have in his custody or under his control, without lawful authority or excuse, an instrument to which this section applies which is, and which he knows or believes to be, false.

(3)   It is an offence for a person to make or to have in his custody or under his control a machine or implement, or paper or any other material, which to his knowledge is or has been specially designed or adapted for the making of an instrument to which this section applies, with the intention that he or another shall make an instrument to which this section applies which is false and that he or another shall use the instrument to induce somebody to accept it as genuine, and by reason of so accepting it to do or not to do some act to his own or any other person's prejudice.

(4)   It is an offence for a person to make or to have in his custody or under his control any such machine, implement, paper or material, without lawful authority or excuse.

(5)   The instruments to which this section applies are—
   (a)   money orders;
   (b)   postal orders;
   (c)   United Kingdom postage stamps;
   (d)   Inland Revenue stamps;
   (e)   share certificates;
   (f)   passports and documents which can be used instead of passports;

    (g)   cheques;

    (h)   travellers' cheques;

    (i)   cheque cards;

    (j)   credit cards;

    (k)   certified copies relating to an entry in a register of births, adoptions, marriages or deaths and issued by the Registrar General, the Registrar General for Northern Ireland, a registration officer or person lawfully authorised to register marriages; and

    (l)   certificates relating to entries in such registers.

    (6)   In subsection (5) (e) above 'share certificate' means an instrument entitling or evidencing the title of a person to a share or interest—

    (a)   in any public stock, annuity, fund or debt of any government or state, including a state which forms part of another state; or

    (b)   in any stock, fund or debt of a body (whether corporate or unincorporated) established in the United Kingdom or elsewhere.

8. Meaning of 'instrument'

    (1)   Subject to subsection (2) below, in this Part of this Act 'instrument' means—

    (a)   any document, whether of a formal or informal character;

    (b)   any stamp issued or sold by the Post Office;

    (c)   any Inland Revenue stamp; and

    (d)   any disc, tape, sound track or other device on or in which information is recorded or stored by mechanical, electronic or other means.

    (2)   A currency note within the meaning of Part II of this Act is not an instrument for the purposes of this Part of this Act.

    (3)   A mark denoting payment of postage which the Post Office authorise to be used instead of an adhesive stamp is to be treated for the purposes of this Part of this Act as if it were a stamp issued by the Post Office.

9. Meaning of 'false' and 'making'

    (1)   An instrument is false for the purposes of this Part of this Act—

    (a)   if it purports to have been made in the form in which it is made by a person who did not in fact make it in that form; or

    (b)   if it purports to have been made in the form in which it is made on the authority of a person who did not in fact authorise its making in that form; or

    (c)   if it purports to have been made in the terms in which it is made by a person who did not in fact make it in those terms; or

    (d)   if it purports to have been made in the terms in which it is made on the authority of a person who did not in fact authorise its making in those terms; or

    (e)   if it purports to have been altered in any respect by a person who did not in fact alter it in that respect; or

    (f)   if it purports to have been altered in any respect on the authority of a person who did not in fact authorise the alteration in that respect; or

    (g)   if it purports to have been made or altered on a date on which, or at a place at which, or otherwise in circumstances in which, it was not in fact made or altered; or

    (h)   if it purports to have been made or altered by an existing person but he did not in fact exist.

    (2)   A person is to be treated for the purposes of this Part of this Act as making a false instrument if he alters an instrument so as to make it false in any respect (whether or not it is false in some other respect apart from that alteration).

10. Meaning of 'prejudice' and 'induce'

    (1)   Subject to subsections (2) and (4) below, for the purposes of this Part of this Act an act or omission intended to be induced is to a person's prejudice if, and only if, it is one which if it occurs—

    (a)   will result—

(i)   in his temporary or permanent loss of property; or

(ii)   in his being deprived of an opportunity to earn remuneration or greater remuneration; or

(iii) in his being deprived of an opportunity to gain a financial advantage otherwise than by way of remuneration; or

(b)   will result in somebody being given an opportunity—

(i)   to earn remuneration or greater remuneration from him; or

(ii)   to gain a financial advantage from him otherwise than by way of remuneration; or

(c)   will be the result of his having accepted a false instrument as genuine, or a copy of a false instrument as a copy of a genuine one, in connection with his performance of any duty.

(2)   An act which a person has an enforceable duty to do and an omission to do an act which a person is not entitled to do shall be disregarded for the purposes of this Part of this Act.

(3)   In this Part of this Act references to inducing somebody to accept a false instrument as genuine, or a copy of a false instrument as a copy of a genuine one, include references to inducing a machine to respond to the instrument or copy as if it were a genuine instrument or, as the case may be, a copy of a genuine one.

(4)   Where subsection (3) above applies, the act or omission intended to be induced by the machine responding to the instrument or copy shall be treated as an act or omission to a person's prejudice.

(5)   In this section 'loss' includes not getting what one might get as well as parting with what one has.

PART II   COUNTERFEITING AND KINDRED OFFENCES

14.   Offences of counterfeiting notes and coins

(1)   It is an offence for a person to make a counterfeit of a currency note or of a protected coin, intending that he or another shall pass or tender it as genuine.

(2)   It is an offence for a person to make a counterfeit of a currency note or of a protected coin without lawful authority or excuse.

15.   Offences of passing, etc., counterfeit notes and coins

(1)   It is an offence for a person—

(a)   to pass or tender as genuine any thing which is, and which he knows or believes to be, a counterfeit of a currency note or of a protected coin; or

(b)   to deliver to another any thing which is, and which he knows or believes to be, such a counterfeit, intending that the person to whom it is delivered or another shall pass or tender it as genuine.

(2)   It is an offence for a person to deliver to another, without lawful authority or excuse, any thing which is, and which he knows or believes to be, a counterfeit of a currency note or of a protected coin.

16.   Offences involving the custody or control of counterfeit notes and coins

(1)   It is an offence for a person to have in his custody or under his control any thing which is, and which he knows or believes to be, a counterfeit of a currency note or of a protected coin, intending either to pass or tender it as genuine or to deliver it to another with the intention that he or another shall pass or tender it as genuine.

(2)   It is an offence for a person to have in his custody or under his control, without lawful authority or excuse, anything which is, and which he knows or believes to be, a counterfeit of a currency note or of a protected coin.

(3)   It is immaterial for the purposes of subsections (1) and (2) above that a coin or note is not in a fit state to be passed or tendered or that the making or counterfeiting of a coin or note has not been finished or perfected.

17. Offences involving the making or custody or control of counterfeiting materials and implements

(1)   It is an offence for a person to make, or to have in his custody or under his control, anything which he intends to use, or to permit any other person to use, for the purpose of making a counterfeit of a currency note or of a protected coin with the intention that it be passed or tendered as genuine.

(2)   It is an offence for a person without lawful authority or excuse—

(a)   to make; or

(b)   to have in his custody or under his control,

anything which, to his knowledge, is or has been specially designed or adapted for the making of a counterfeit of a currency note.

(3)   Subject to subsection (4) below, it is an offence for a person to make, or to have in his custody or under his control, any implement which, to his knowledge, is capable of imparting to anything a resemblance—

(a)   to the whole or part of either side of a protected coin; or

(b)   to the whole or part of the reverse of the image on either side of a protected coin.

(4)   It shall be a defence for a person charged with an offence under subsection (3) above to show—

(a)   that he made the implement or, as the case may be, had it in his custody or under his control, with the written consent of the Treasury; or

(b)   that he had lawful authority otherwise than by virtue of paragraph (4) above, or a lawful excuse, for making it or having it in his custody or under his control.

18. The offence of reproducing British currency notes

(1)   It is an offence for any person, unless the relevant authority has previously consented in writing, to reproduce on any substance whatsoever, and whether or not on the correct scale, any British currency note or any part of a British currency note.

(2)   In this section—

'British currency note' means any note which—

(a)   has been lawfully issued in England and Wales, Scotland or Northern Ireland; and

(b)   is or has been customarily used as money in the country where it was issued; and

(c)   is payable on demand; and

'the relevant authority', in relation to a British currency note of any particular description, means the authority empowered by law to issue notes of that description.

19. Offences in making, etc., imitation British coins

(1)   It is an offence for a person—

(a)   to make an imitation British coin in connection with a scheme intended to promote the sale of any product or the making of contracts for the supply of any service; or

(b)   to sell or distribute imitation British coins in connection with any such scheme, or to have imitation British coins in his custody or under his control with a view to such sale or distribution,

unless the Treasury have previously consented in writing to the sale or distribution of such imitation British coins in connection with that scheme.

(2)   In this section—

'British coin' means any coin which is legal tender in any part of the United Kingdom; and

'imitation British coin' means any thing which resembles a British coin in shape, size and the substance of which it is made.

20. Prohibition of importation of counterfeit notes and coins

The importation, landing or unloading of a counterfeit of a currency note or of a protected coin without the consent of the Treasury is hereby prohibited.

21. Prohibition of exportation of counterfeit notes and coins

(1) The exportation of a counterfeit of a currency note or of a protected coin without the consent of the Treasury is hereby prohibited.

27. Meaning of 'currency note' and 'protected coin'

(1) In this Part of this Act—

'currency note' means—

(a) any note which—

(i) has been lawfully issued in England and Wales, Scotland, Northern Ireland, any of the Channel Islands, the Isle of Man or the Republic of Ireland; and

(ii) is or has been customarily used as money in the country where it was issued; and

(iii) is payable on demand; or

(b) any note which—

(i) has been lawfully issued in some country other than those mentioned in paragraph (a) (i) above; and

(ii) is customarily used as money in that country; and

'protected coin' means any coin which—

(a) is customarily used as money in any country; or

(b) is specified in an order made by the Treasury for the purposes of this Part of this Act.

28. Meaning of 'counterfeit'

(1) For the purposes of this Part of this Act a thing is a counterfeit of a currency note or of a protected coin—

(a) if it is not a currency note or a protected coin but resembles a currency note or protected coin (whether on one side only or on both) to such an extent that it is reasonably capable of passing for a currency note or protected coin of that description; or

(b) if it is a currency note or protected coin which has been so altered that it is reasonably capable of passing for a currency note or protected coin of some other description.

(2) For the purposes of this Part of this Act—

(a) a thing consisting of one side only of a currency note, with or without the addition of other material, is a counterfeit of such a note;

(b) a thing consisting—

(i) of parts of two or more currency notes; or

(ii) of parts of a currency note, or of parts of two or more currency notes, with the addition of other material,

is capable of being a counterfeit of a currency note.

(3) References in this Part of this Act to passing or tendering a counterfeit of a currency note or a protected coin are not to be construed as confined to passing or tendering it as legal tender.

COPYRIGHT, DESIGNS AND PATENTS ACT 1988

107. Criminal liability for making or dealing with infringing articles, etc.

(1) A person commits an offence who, without the licence of the copyright owner—

(a) makes for sale or hire, or

(b)   imports into the United Kingdom otherwise than for his private and domestic use, or

(c)   possesses in the course of a business with a view to committing any act infringing the copyright, or

(d)   in the course of a business—

(i)   sells or lets for hire, or

(ii)   offers or exposes for sale or hire, or

(iii)   exhibits in public, or

(iv)   distributes, or

(e)   distributes otherwise than in the course of a business to such an extent as to affect prejudicially the owner of the copyright,

an article which is, and which he knows or has reason to believe is, an infringing copy of a copyright work.

(2)   A person commits an offence who—

(a)   makes an article specifically designed or adapted for making copies of a particular copyright work, or

(b)   has such an article in his possession,

knowing or having reason to believe that it is to be used to make infringing copies for sale or hire or for use in the course of a business.

(3)   Where copyright is infringed (otherwise than by reception of a broadcast or cable programme)—

(a)   by the public performance of a literary, dramatic or musicial work, or

(b)   by the playing or showing in public of a sound recording or film,

any person who caused the work to be so performed, played or shown is guilty of an offence if he knew or had reason to believe that copyright would be infringed.

(4)   A person guilty of an offence under subsection (1)(a), (b), (d)(iv) or (e) is liable—

(a)   on summary conviction to imprisonment for a term not exceeding six months or a fine not exceeding the statutory maximum, or both;

(b)   on conviction on indictment to a fine or imprisonment for a term not exceeding two years, or both.

(5)   A person guilty of any other offence under this section is liable on summary conviction to imprisonment for a term not exceeding six months or a fine not exceeding level 5 on the standard scale, or both.

TRADE MARKS ACT 1994

92.   Unauthorised use of trade mark, etc., in relation to goods

(1)   A person commits an offence who with a view to gain for himself or another, or with intent to cause loss to another, and without the consent of the proprietor—

(a)   applies to goods or their packaging a sign identical to or likely to be mistaken for, a registered trade mark, or

(b)   sells or lets for hire, offers or exposes for sale or hire or distributes goods which bear, or the packaging of which bears, such a sign, or

(c)   has in his possession, custody or control in the course of a business any such goods with a view to the doing of anything, by himself or another, which would be an offence under paragraph (b).

(2)   A person commits an offence who with a view to gain for himself or another, or with intent to cause loss to another, and without the consent of the proprietor—

(a)   applies a sign identical to, or likely to be mistaken for, a registered trade mark to material intended to be used—

(i)   for labelling or packaging goods,

(ii)   as a business paper in relation to goods, or

      (iii) for advertising goods, or

    (b) uses in the course of a business material bearing such a sign for labelling or packaging goods, as a business paper in relation to goods, or for advertising goods, or

    (c) has in his possession, custody or control in the course of a business any such material with a view to the doing of anything, by himself or another, which would be an offence under paragraph (b).

    (3) A person commits an offence who with a view to gain for himself or another, or with intent to cause loss to another, and without the consent of the proprietor—

    (a) makes an article specifically designed or adapted for making copies of a sign identical to, or likely to be mistaken for, a registered trade mark, or

    (b) has such an article in his possession, custody or control in the course of a business,

knowing or having reason to believe that it has been, or is to be, used to produce goods, or material for labelling or packaging goods, as a business paper in relation to goods, or for advertising goods.

    (4) A person does not commit an offence under this section unless—

    (a) the goods are goods in respect of which the trade mark is registered, or

    (b) the trade mark has a reputation in the United Kingdom and the use of the sign takes or would take unfair advantage of, or is or would be detrimental to, the distinctive character or the repute of the trade mark.

    (5) It is a defence for a person charged with an offence under this section to show that he believed on reasonable grounds that the use of the sign in the manner in which it was used, or was to be used, was not an infringement of the registered trade mark.

TRADE DESCRIPTIONS ACT 1968

1. Prohibition of false trade descriptions

    (1) Any person who, in the course of a trade or business,—

    (a) applies a false trade description to any goods; or

    (b) supplies or offers to supply any goods to which a false trade description is applied;

shall, subject to the provisions of this Act, be guilty of an offence.

    (2) Sections 2 to 6 of this Act shall have effect for the purposes of this section and for the interpretation of expressions used in this section, wherever they occur in this Act.

2. Trade description

    (1) A trade description is an indication, direct or indirect, and by whatever means given, of any of the following matters with respect to any goods or parts of goods, that is to say—

    (a) quantity, size or gauge;

    (b) method of manufacture, production, processing or reconditioning;

    (c) composition;

    (d) fitness for purpose, strength, performance, behaviour or accuracy;

    (e) any physical characteristics not included in the preceding paragraphs;

    (f) testing by any person and results thereof;

    (g) approval by any person or conformity with a type approved by any person;

    (h) place or date of manufacture, production, processing or reconditioning;

    (i) person by whom manufactured, produced, processed or reconditioned;

    (j) other history, including previous ownership or use.

    (2) The matters specified in subsection (1) of this section shall be taken—

    (a) in relation to any animal, to include sex, breed or cross, fertility and soundness;

(b)   in relation to any semen, to include the identity and characteristics of the animal from which it was taken and measure of dilution.

(3)   In this section 'quantity' includes length, width, height, area, volume, capacity, weight and number.

3. False trade description

(1)   A false trade description is a trade description which is false to a material degree.

(2)   A trade description which though not false, is misleading, that is to say, likely to be taken for such an indication of any of the matters specified in section 2 of this Act as would be false to a material degree, shall be deemed to be a false trade description.

(3)   Anything which, though not a trade description, is likely to be taken for an indication of any of those matters and, as such an indication, would be false to a material degree, shall be deemed to be a false trade description.

(4)   A false indication, or anything likely to be taken as an indication which would be false, that any goods comply with a standard specified or recognised by any person or implied by the approval of any person shall be deemed to be a false trade description, if there is no such person or no standard so specified, recognised or implied.

4. Applying a trade description to goods

(1)   A person applies a trade description to goods if he—

(a)   affixes or annexes it to or in any manner marks it on or incorporates it with—
(i)   the goods themselves, or
(ii)   anything in, on or with which the goods are supplied; or

(b)   places the goods in, on or with anything which the trade description has been affixed or annexed to, marked on or incorporated with, or places any such thing with the goods; or

(c)   uses the trade description in any manner likely to be taken as referring to the goods.

(2)   An oral statement may amount to the use of a trade description.

(3)   Where goods are supplied in pursuance of a request in which a trade description is used and the circumstances are such as to make it reasonable to infer that the goods are supplied as goods corresponding to that trade description, the person supplying the goods shall be deemed to have applied that trade description to the goods.

5. Trade descriptions used in advertisements

(1)   The following provisions of this section shall have effect where in an advertisement a trade description is used in relation to any class of goods.

(2)   The trade description shall be taken as referring to all goods of the class, whether or not in existence at the time the advertisement is published—

(a)   for the purpose of determining whether an offence has been committed under paragraph (a) of section 1(1) of this Act; and

(b)   where goods of the class are supplied or offered to be supplied by a person publishing or displaying the advertisement, also for the purpose of determining whether an offence has been committed under paragraph (b) of the said section 1(1).

(3)   In determining for the purposes of this section whether any goods are of a class to which a trade description used in an advertisement relates regard shall be had not only to the form and content of the advertisement but also to the time, place, manner and frequency of its publication and all other matters making it likely or unlikely that a person to whom the goods are supplied would think of the goods as belonging to the class in relation to which the trade description is used in the advertisement.

6. Offer to supply

A person exposing goods for supply or having goods in his possession for supply shall be deemed to offer to supply them.

13. False representations as to supply of goods or services

If any person, in the course of any trade or business, gives, by whatever means, any false indication, direct or indirect, that any goods or services supplied by him are of a kind supplied to any person he shall, subject to the provisions of this Act, be guilty of an offence.

14. False or misleading statements as to services, etc.

(1) It shall be an offence for any person in the course of any trade or business—

(a) to make a statement which he knows to be false; or

(b) recklessly to make a statement which is false;

as to any of the following matters, that is to say,—

(i) the provision in the course of any trade or business of any services, accommodation or facilities;

(ii) the nature of any services, accommodation or facilities provided in the course of any trade or business;

(iii) the time at which, manner in which or persons by whom any services, accommodation or facilities are so provided;

(iv) the examination, approval or evaluation by any person of any services, accommodation or facilities so provided; or

(v) the location or amenities of any accommodation so provided.

(2) For the purposes of this section—

(a) anything (whether or not a statement as to any of the matters specified in the preceding subsection) likely to be taken for such a statement as to any of those matters as would be false shall be deemed to be a false statement as to that matter; and

(b) a statement made regardless of whether it is true or false shall be deemed to be made recklessly, whether or not the person making it had reasons for believing that it might be false.

(3) In relation to any services consisting of or including the application of any treatment or process or the carrying out of any repair, the matters specified in subsection (1) of this section shall be taken to include the effect of the treatment, process or repair.

(4) In this section 'false' means false to a material degree and 'services' does not include anything done under a contract of service.

23. Offences due to fault of other person

Where the commission by any person of an offence under this Act is due to the act or default of some other person that other person shall be guilty of the offence, and a person may be charged with and convicted of the offence by virtue of this section whether or not proceedings are taken against the first-mentioned person.

24. Defence of mistake, accident, etc.

(1) In any proceedings for an offence under this Act it shall, subject to subsection (2) of this section, be a defence for the person charged to prove—

(a) that the commission of the offence was due to a mistake or to reliance on information supplied to him or to the act or default of another person, an accident or some other cause beyond his control; and

(b) that he took all reasonable precautions and exercised all due diligence to avoid the commission of such an offence by himself or any person under his control.

(2) If in any case the defence provided by the last foregoing subsection involves the allegation that the commission of the offence was due to the act or default of another person or to reliance on information supplied by another person, the person

charged shall not, without leave of the court, be entitled to rely on that defence unless, within a period ending seven clear days before the hearing, he has served on the prosecutor a notice in writing giving such information identifying or assisting in the identification of that other person as was then in his possession.

(3)   In any proceedings for an offence under this Act of supplying or offering to supply goods to which a false trade description is applied it shall be a defence for the person charged to prove that he did not know, and could not with reasonable diligence have ascertained, that the goods did not conform to the description or that the description had been applied to the goods.

25.   Innocent publication of advertisement

In proceedings for an offence under this Act committed by the publication of an advertisement it shall be a defence for the person charged to prove that he is a person whose business it is to publish or arrange for the publication of advertisements and that he received the advertisement for publication in the ordinary course of business and did not know and had no reason to suspect that its publication would amount to an offence under this Act.

WEIGHTS AND MEASURES ACT 1985

28.   Short weight, etc.

(1)   Subject to sections 33 to 37 below, any person who, in selling or purporting to sell any goods by weight or other measurement or by number, delivers or causes to be delivered to the buyer—

(a)   a lesser quantity than that purported to be sold, or

(b)   a lesser quantity than corresponds with the price charged,

shall be guilty of an offence.

(2)   For the purposes of this section—

(a)   the quantity of the goods in a regulated package (as defined by section 68(1) below) shall be deemed to be the nominal quantity (as so defined) on the package, and

(b)   any statement, whether oral or in writing, as to the weight of any goods shall be taken, unless otherwise expressed, to be a statement as to the net weight of the goods.

29.   Misrepresentation

(1)   Subject to sections 33 to 37 below, any person who—

(a)   on or in connection with the sale or purchase of any goods,

(b)   in exposing or offering any goods for sale,

(c)   in purporting to make known to the buyer the quantity of any goods sold, or

(d)   in offering to purchase any goods,

makes any misrepresentation whether oral or otherwise as to the quantity of the goods, or does any other act calculated to mislead a person buying or selling the goods as to the quantity of the goods, shall be guilty of an offence.

(2)   Subsection (2) of section 28 above shall have effect for the purposes of this section as it has effect for the purposes of that section.

30.   Quantity less than stated

(1)   If, in the case of any goods pre-packed in or on a container marked with a statement in writing with respect to the quantity of the goods, the quantity of the goods is at any time found to be less than that stated, then, subject to sections 33 to 37 below—

(a)   any person who has those goods in his possession for sale shall be guilty of an offence, and

(b)   if it is shown that the deficiency cannot be accounted for by anything occurring after the goods had been sold by retail and delivered to, or to a person nominated in that behalf by, the buyer, any person by whom or on whose behalf those goods have been sold or agreed to be sold at any time while they were pre-packed in or on the container in question, shall be guilty of an offence.

(2) If—

(a) in the case of a sale of or agreement to sell any goods which, not being pre-packed, are made up for sale or for delivery after sale in or on a container marked with a statement in writing with respect to the quantity of the goods, or

(b) in the case of any goods which, in connection with their sale or an agreement for their sale, have associated with them a document containing such a statement,

the quantity of the goods is at any time found to be less than that stated, then, if it is shown that the deficiency cannot be accounted for by anything occurring after the goods had been delivered to, or to a person nominated in that behalf by, the buyer, and subject to sections 33 to 37 below and paragraph 10 of Schedule 4 to this Act, the person by whom, and any other person on whose behalf, the goods were sold or agreed to be sold shall be guilty of an offence.

(3) Subsections (1) and (2) above shall have effect notwithstanding that the quantity stated is expressed to be the quantity of the goods at a specified time falling before the time in question, or is expressed with some other qualification of whatever description, except where

(a) that quantity is so expressed in pursuance of an express requirement of this Part of this Act or any instrument made under this Part, or

(b) the goods, although falling within subsection (1) or subsection (2)(a) above—

(i) are not required by or under this Part of this Act to be pre-packed as mentioned in subsection (1) or, as the case may be, to be made up for sale or for delivery after sale in or on a container only if the container is marked as mentioned in subsection (2)(a), and

(ii) are not goods on a sale of which (whether any sale or a sale of any particular description) the quantity sold is required by or under any provision of this Part of this Act other than section 26, to be made known to the buyer at or before a particular time, or

(c) the goods, although falling within subsection (2)(b) above, are not required by or under this Part of this Act to have associated with them such a document as is mentioned in that provision.

(4) In any case to which, by virtue of paragraph (a), (b) or (c) of subsection (3) above, the provisions of subsection (1) or (2) above do not apply, if it is found at any time that the quantity of the goods in question is less than that stated and it is shown that the deficiency is greater than can be reasonably justified on the ground justifying the qualification in question, then, subject to sections 33 to 37 below—

(a) in the case of goods such as are mentioned in subsection (1) above, if it is further shown as mentioned in that subsection, then—

(i) where the container in question was marked in great Britain, the person by whom, and any other person on whose behalf, the container was marked, or

(ii) where the container in question was marked outside Great Britain, the person by whom, and any other person on whose behalf, the goods were first sold in Great Britain,

shall be guilty of an offence;

(b) in the case of goods such as are mentioned in subsection (2) above, the person by whom, and any other person on whose behalf, the goods were sold or agreed to be sold shall be guilty of an offence if, but only if, he would, but for paragraph (a), (b) or (c) of subsection (3) above have been guilty of an offence under subsection (2).

(5) Subsection (2) of section 28 above shall have effect for the purposes of this section as it has effect for the purposes of that section.

31. Incorrect statements

(1) Without prejudice to section 30(2) to (4) above, if in the case of any goods required by or under this Part of this Act to have associated with them a document containing particular statements, that document is found to contain any such statement which is materially incorrect, any person who, knowing or having reasonable cause to suspect that statement to be materially incorrect, inserted it or caused it to be inserted in the document, or used the document for the purposes of this Part of this Act while that statement was contained in the document, shall be guilty of an offence.

(2) Subsection (2) of section 28 above shall have effect for the purposes of this section as it has effect for the purposes of that section.

32. Offences due to default of third person

Where the commission by any person of an offence under this Part of this Act or an instrument made under this Part is due to the act or default of some other person, the other person shall be guilty of an offence and may be charged with and convicted of the offence whether or not proceedings are taken against the first-mentioned person.

33. Warranty

(1) Subject to the following provisions of this section, in any proceedings for an offence under this Part of this Act or any instrument made under this Part, being an offence relating to the quantity or pre-packing of any goods, it shall be a defence for the person charged to prove—

(a) that he bought the goods from some other person—

(i) as being of the quantity which the person charged purported to sell or represented, or which was marked on any container or stated in any document to which the proceedings relate, or

(ii) as conforming with the statement marked on any container to which the proceedings relate, or with the requirements with respect to the pre-packing of goods of this Part of this Act or any instrument made under this Part,
as the case may require, and

(b) that he so bought the goods with a written warranty from that other person that they were of that quantity or, as the case may be, did so conform, and

(c) that at the time of the commission of the offence he did in fact believe the statement contained in the warranty to be accurate and had no reason to believe it to be inaccurate, and

(d) if the warranty was given by a person who at the time he gave it was resident outside Great Britain and any designated country, that the person charged had taken reasonable steps to check the accuracy of the statement contained in the warranty, and

(e) in the case of proceedings relating to the quantity of any goods, that he took all reasonable steps to ensure that, while in his possession, the quantity of the goods remained unchanged and, in the case of such or any other proceedings, that apart from any change in their quantity the goods were at the time of the commission of the offence in the same state as when he bought them.

(2) A warranty shall not be a defence in any such proceedings as are mentioned in subsection (1) above unless, not later than three days before the date of the hearing, the person charged has sent to the prosecutor a copy of the warranty with a notice stating that he intends to rely on it and specifying the name and address of the person from whom the warranty was received, and has also sent a like notice to that person.

(3) Where the person charged is the employee of a person who, if he had been charged, would have been entitled to plead a warranty as a defence under this section, subsection (1) above shall have effect—

(a) with the substitution, for any reference (however expressed) in paragraphs (a), (b), (d) and (e) to the person charged, of a reference to his employer, and

(b)   with the substitution for paragraph (c) of the following—

'(c)   that at the time of the commission of the offence his employer did in fact believe the statement contained in the warranty to be accurate and the person charged had no reason to believe it to be inaccurate'.

(4)   The person by whom the warranty is alleged to have been given shall be entitled to appear at the hearing and to give evidence.

(5)   If the person charged in any such proceedings as are mentioned in subsection (1) above wilfully attributes to any goods a warranty given in relation to any other goods, he shall be guilty of an offence.

(6)   A person who, in respect of any goods sold by him in respect of which a warranty might be pleaded under this section, gives to the buyer a false warranty in writing shall be guilty of an offence unless he proves that when he gave the warranty he took all reasonable steps to ensure that the statements contained in it were, and would continue at all relevent times to be, accurate.

(7)   Where in any such proceedings as are mentioned in subsection (1) above ('the original proceedings') the person charged relies successfully on a warranty given to him or to his employer, any proceedings under subsection (6) above in respect of the warranty may, at the option of the prosecutor, be taken either before a court having jurisdiction in the place where the original proceedings were taken or before a court having jurisdiction in the place where the warranty was given.

(8)   For the purposes of this section, any statement with respect to any goods which is contained in any document required by or under this Part of this Act to be associated with the goods or in any invoice, and, in the case of goods made up in or on a container for sale or for delivery after sale, any statement with respect to those goods with which that container is marked, shall be taken to be a written warranty of the accuracy of that statement.

34.   Reasonable precautions and due diligence

(1)   In any proceedings for an offence under this Part of this Act or any instrument made under this Part, it shall be a defence for the person charged to prove that he took all reasonable precautions and exercised all due diligence to avoid the commission of the offence.

(2)   If in any case the defence provided by subsection (1) above involves an allegation that the commission of the offence in question was due to the act or default of another person or due to reliance on information supplied by another person, the person charged shall not, without the leave of the court, be entitled to rely on the defence unless, before the beginning of the period of seven days ending with the date when the hearing of the charge began, he served on the prosecutor a notice giving such information identifying or assisting in the identification of the other person as was then in his possession.

35.   Subsequent deficiency

(1)   This subsection applies to any proceedings for an offence under this Part of this Act, or any instrument made under this Part, by reason of the quantity—

(a)   of any goods made up for sale or for delivery after sale (whether by way of pre-packing or otherwise) in or on a container marked with an indication of quantity,

(b)   of any goods which, in connection with their sale or an agreement for their sale, have associated with them a document purporting to state the quantity of the goods, or

(c)   of any goods required by or under this Part of this Act to be pre-packed, or to be otherwise made up in or on a container for sale or for delivery after sale, or to be made for sale, only in particular quantities,

being less than that marked on the container or stated in the document in question or than the relevant particular quantity, as the case may be.

(2)   In any proceedings to which subsection (1) above applies, it shall be a defence for the person charged to proved that the deficiency arose—

(a)   in a case falling within paragraph (a) of subsection (1) above, after the making up of the goods and the marking of the container,

(b)   in a case falling within paragraph (b) of that subsection, after the preparation of the goods for delivery in pursuance of the sale or agreement and after the completion of the document,

(c)   in a case falling within paragraph (c) of that subsection, after the making up or making, as the case may be, of the goods for sale,

and was attributable wholly to factors for which reasonable allowance was made in stating the quantity of the goods in the marking or document or in making up or making the goods for sale, as the case may be.

(3)   In the case of a sale by retail of food, other than food pre-packed in a container which is, or is required by or under this Part of this Act to be, marked with an indication of quantity, in any proceedings for an offence under this Part of this Act or any instrument made under this Part, by reason of the quantity delivered to the buyer being less than that purported to be sold, it shall be a defence for the person charged to prove that the deficiency was due wholly to unavoidable evaporation or drainage since the sale and that due care and precaution were taken to minimise any such evaporation or drainage.

(4)   If in any proceedings for an offence under this Part of this Act or any instrument made under this Part, being an offence in respect of any deficiency in the quantity of any goods sold, it is shown that between the sale and the discovery of the deficiency the goods were with the consent of the buyer subjected to treatment which could result in a reduction in the quantity of those goods for delivery to, or to any person nominated in that behalf by, the buyer, the person charged shall not be found guilty of that offence unless it is shown that the deficiency cannot be accounted for by the subjecting of the goods to that treatment.

36.   Excess due to precautions

In any proceedings for an offence under this Part of this Act or any instrument made under this Part, being an offence in respect of any excess in the quantity of any goods, it shall be a defence for the person charged to prove that the excess was attributable to the taking of measures reasonably necessary in order to avoid the commission of an offence in respect of a deficiency in those or other goods.

37.   Provisions as to testing

(1)   If proceedings for an offence under this Part of this Act, or any instrument made under this Part, in respect of any deficiency or excess in the quantity—

(a)   of any goods made up for sale (whether by way of pre-packing or otherwise) in or on a container marked with an indication of quantity, or

(b)   of any goods which have been pre-packed or otherwise made up in or on a container for sale or for delivery after sale, or which have been made for sale, and which are required by or under this Part of this Act to be pre-packed, or to be otherwise so made up, or to be so made, as the case may be, only in particular quantities,

are brought with respect to any article, and it is proved that, at the time and place at which that article was tested, other articles of the same kind, being articles which, or articles containing goods which, had been sold by the person charged or were in that person's possession for sale or for delivery after sale, were available for testing, the person charged shall not be convicted of such an offence with respect to that article unless a reasonable number of those other articles was also tested.

(2)   In any proceedings for such an offence as is mentioned in subsection (1) above, the court—

(a) if the proceedings are with respect to one or more of a number of articles tested on the same occasion, shall have regard to the average quantity in the articles tested,

(b) if the proceedings are with respect to a single article, shall disregard any inconsiderable deficiency or excess, and

(c) shall have regard generally to all the circumstances of the case.

(3) Subsections (1) and (2) above shall apply with the necessary modifications to proceedings for an offence in respect of the size, capacity or contents of a container as they apply to proceedings for an offence in respect of the excess or deficiency in the quantity of certain goods.

(4) Where by virtue of section 32 above a person is charged with an offence with which some other person might have been charged, the reference in subsection (1) above to articles or goods sold by or in the possession of the person charged shall be construed as a reference to articles or goods sold by or in the possession of that other person.

82. Offences by corporations

(1) Where an offence under, or under any instrument made under, this Act which has been committed by a body corporate is proved to have been committed with the consent or connivance of, or to be attributable to any neglect on the part of, any director, manager, secretary or other similar officer of the body corporate, or any person who was purporting to act in any such capacity, he as well as the body corporate shall be guilty of that offence and shall be liable to be proceeded against and punished accordingly.

(2) In subsection (1) above 'director' in relation to any body corporate established by or under any enactment for the purpose of carrying on under national ownership any industry or part of an industry or undertaking, being a body corporate whose affairs are managed by its members, means a member of that body corporate.

CONSUMER PROTECTION ACT 1987

20. Offence of giving misleading indication of price

(1) Subject to the following provisions of this Part, a person shall be guilty of an offence if, in the course of any business of his, he gives (by any means whatever) to any consumers an indication which is misleading as to the price at which any goods, services, accommodation or facilities are available (whether generally or from particular persons).

(2) Subject as aforesaid, a person shall be guilty of an offence if—

(a) in the course of any businss of his, he has given an indication to any consumers which, after it was given, has become misleading as mentioned in subsection (1) above; and

(b) some or all of those consumers might reasonably be expected to rely on the indication at a time after it has become misleading; and

(c) he fails to take all such steps as are reasonable to prevent those consumers from relying on the indication.

(3) For the purposes of this section it shall be immaterial—

(a) whether the person who gives or gave the indication is or was acting on his own behalf or on behalf of another;

(b) whether or not that person is the person, or included among the persons, from whom the goods, services, accommodation or facilities are available; and

(c) whether the indication is or has become misleading in relation to all the consumers to whom it is or was given or only in relation to some of them.

(6) In this Part—
'Consumer'—

(a)   in relation to any goods, means any person who might wish to be supplied with the goods for his own private use or consumption;

(b)   in relation to any services or facilities, means any person who might wish to be provided with the services or facilities otherwise than for the purposes of any business of his; and

(c)   in relation to any accommodation, means any person who might wish to occupy the accommodation otherwise than for the purposes of any business of his;

'price', in relation to any goods, services, accommodation or facilities, means—

(a)   the aggregate of the sums required to be paid by a consumer for or otherwise in respect of the supply of the goods or the provision of the services, accommodation or facilities; or

(b)   except in section 21 below, any method which will be or has been applied for the purpose of determining that aggregate.

21.   Meaning of 'misleading'

(1)   For the purposes of section 20 above an indication given to any consumers is misleading as to a price if what is conveyed by the indication, or what those consumers might reasonably be expected to infer from the indication or any omission from it, includes any of the following, that is to say—

(a)   that the price is less than in fact it is;

(b)   that the applicability of the price does not depend on facts or circumstances on which its applicability does in fact depend;

(c)   that the price covers matters in respect of which an additional charge is in fact made;

(d)   that a person who in fact has no such expectation—

(i)   expects the price to be increased or reduced (whether or not at a particular time or by a particular amount); or

(ii)   expects the price, or the price as increased or reduced, to be maintained (whether or not for a particular period); or

(e)   that the facts or circumstances by reference to which the consumers might reasonably be expected to judge the validity of any relevant comparison made or implied by the indication are not what in fact they are.

(2)   For the purposes of section 20 above, an indication given to any consumers is misleading as to a method of determining a price if what is conveyed by the indication, or what those consumers might reasonably be expected to infer from the indication or any omission from it, includes any of the following, that is to say—

(a)   that the method is not what in fact it is;

(b)   that the applicability of the method does not depend on facts or circumstances on which its applicability does in fact depend;

(c)   that the method takes into account matters in respect of which an additional charge will in fact be made;

(d)   that a person who in fact has no such expectation—

(i)   expects the method to be altered (whether or not at a particular time or in a particular respect); or

(ii)   expects the method, or that method as altered, to remain unaltered (whether or not for a particular period); or

(e)   that the facts or circumstances by reference to which the consumers might reasonably be expected to judge the validity of any relevant comparison made or implied by the indication are not what in fact they are.

(3)   For the purposes of subsection (1)(e) and (2)(e) above a comparison is a relevant comparison in relation to a price or method of determining a price if it is made between that price or that method, or any price which has been or may be determined by that method, and—

(a)   any price or value which is stated or implied to be, to have been or to be likely to be attributed or attributable to the goods, services, accommodation or facilities in question or to any other goods, services, accommodation, or facilities; or

(b)   any method, or other method, which is stated or implied to be, to have been or to be likely to be applied or applicable for the determination of the price or value of the goods, services, accommodation or facilities in question or of the price or value of any other goods, services, accommodation or facilities.

22.   Application to provision of services and facilities

(1)   Subject to the following provisions of this section, references in this Part to services or facilities are references to any services or facilities whatever including, in particular—

(a)   the provision of credit or of banking or insurance services and the provision of facilities incidental to the provision of such services;

(b)   the purchase or sale of foreign currency;

(c)   the supply of electricity;

(d)   the provision of a place, other than on a highway, for the parking of a motor vehicle;

(e)   the making of arrangements for a person to put or keep a caravan on any land other than arrangements by virtue of which that person may occupy the caravan as his only or main residence.

(2)   References in this Part to services shall not include references to services provided to an employer under a contract of employment.

(3)   References in this Part to services or facilities shall not include references to services or facilities which are provided by an authorised person or appointed representative in the course of the carrying on of an investment business.

(4)   In relation to a service consisting in the purchase or sale of foreign currency, references in this Part to the method by which the price of the service is determined shall include references to the rate of exchange.

(5)   In this section—

'appointed representative', 'authorised person' and 'investment business' have the same meanings as in the Financial Services Act 1986;

'caravan' has the same meaning as in the Caravan Sites and Control of Development Act 1960;

'contract of employment' and 'employer' have the same meanings as in the Employment Protection (Consolidation) Act 1978;

'credit' has the same meaning as in the Consumer Credit Act 1974.

23.   Application to provision of accommodation etc.

(1)   Subject to subsection (2) below, references in this Part to accommodation or facilities being available shall not include references to accommodation or facilities being available to be provided by means of the creation or disposal of an interest in land except where—

(a)   the person who is to create or dispose of the interest will do so in the course of any business of his; and

(b)   the interest to be created or disposed of is a relevant interest in a new dwelling and is to be created or disposed of for the purpose of enabling that dwelling to be occupied as a residence, or one of the residences, of the person acquiring the interest.

(2)   Subsection (1) above shall not prevent the application of any provision of this Part in relation to—

(a)   the supply of any goods as part of the same transaction as any creation or disposal of an interest in land; or

(b)   the provision of any services or facilities for the purposes of, or in connection with, any transaction for the creation or disposal of such an interest.

(3)   In this section—

'new dwelling' means any building or part of a building in Great Britain which—

(a)   has been constructed or adapted to be occupied as a residence; and

(b)   has not previously been so occupied or has been so occupied only with other premises or as more than one residence,

and includes any yard, garden, out-house or appurtenances which belong to that building or part or are to be enjoyed with it;

'relevant interest'—

(a)   in relation to a new dwelling in England and Wales, means the freehold estate in the dwelling or a leasehold interest in the dwelling for a term of years absolute of more than twenty-one years, not being a term of which twenty-one years or less remains unexpired; . . .

24.   Defences

(1)   In any proceedings against a person for an offence under subsection (1) or (2) of section 20 above in respect of any indication it shall be a defence for the person to show that his acts or omissions were authorised for the purposes of this subsection by regulations made under section 26 below.

(2)   In proceedings against a person for an offence under subsection (1) or (2) of section 20 above in respect of an indication published in a book, newspaper, magazine, or film or in a programme included in a programme service (within the meaning of the Broadcasting Act 1990) it shall be a defence for that person to show that the indication was not contained in an advertisement.

(3)   In proceedings against a person for an offence under subsection (1) or (2) of section 20 above in respect of an indication published in an advertisement it shall be a defence for that person to show that—

(a)   he is a person who carries on a business of publishing or arranging for the publication of advertisements;

(b)   he received the advertisement for publication in the ordinary course of that business; and

(c)   at the time of publication he did not know and had no grounds for suspecting that the publication would involve the commission of the offence.

(4)   In any proceedings against a person for an offence under subsection (1) of section 20 above in respect of any indication, it shall be a defence for that person to show that—

(a)   the indication did not relate to the availability from him of any goods, services, accommodation or facilities;

(b)   a price had been recommended to every person from whom the goods, services, accommodation or facilities were indicated as being available;

(c)   the indication related to that price and was misleading as to that price only by reason of a failure by any person to follow the recommendation; and

(d)   it was reasonable for the person who gave the indication to assume that the recommendation was for the most part being followed.

(5)   The provisions of this section are without prejudice to the provisions of section 39 below.

(6)   In this section—

'advertisement' includes a catalogue, a circular and a price list.

39.   Defence of due diligence

[See page 129]

40.   Liability of persons other than the principal offender

[See pages 129–130]

CRIMINAL JUSTICE ACT 1993

PART I   JURISDICTION

1.   Offences to which this Part applies

(1)   This Part applies to two groups of offences—

(a)   any offence mentioned in subsection (2) (a 'Group A offence'); and

(b)   any offence mentioned in subsection (3) (a 'Group B offence').

(2)   The Group A offences are—

(a)   an offence under any of the following provisions of the Theft Act 1968—

section 1 (theft);

section 15 (obtaining property by deception);

section 15A (obtaining a money transfer by deception);

section 16 (obtaining pecuniary advantage by deception);

section 17 (false accounting);

section 19 (false statements by company directors etc.);

section 20(2) (procuring execution of valuable security by deception);

section 21 (blackmail);

section 22 (handling stolen goods);

section 24A (retaining credits from dishonest sources, etc.);

(b)   an offence under either of the following provisions of the Theft Act 1978—

section 1 (obtaining services by deception);

section 2 (avoiding liability by deception);

(c)   an offence under any of the following provisions of the Forgery and Counterfeiting Act 1981—

section 1 (forgery);

section 2 (copying a false instrument);

section 3 (using a false instrument);

section 4 (using a copy of a false instrument);

section 5 (offences which relate to money orders, share certificates, passports, etc.);

(d)   the common law offence of cheating in relation to the public revenue.

(3)   The Group B offences are—

(a)   conspiracy to commit a Group A offence;

(b)   conspiracy to defraud;

(c)   attempting to commit a Group A offence;

(d)   incitement to commit a Group A offence.

2.   Jurisdiction in respect of Group A offences

(1)   For the purposes of this Part, 'relevant event', in relation to any Group A offence, means any act or omission or other event (including any result of one or more acts or omissions) proof of which is required for conviction of the offence.

(2)   For the purpose of determining whether an event is a relevant event, any question as to where it occurred is to be disregarded.

(3)   A person may be guilty of a Group A offence if any of the events which are relevant events in relation to the offence occurred in England and Wales.

3.   Questions immaterial to jurisdiction in the case of certain offences

(1)   A person may be guilty of a Group A or Group B offence whether or not—

(a)   he was a British citizen at any material time;

(b)   he was in England and Wales at any such time.

(2)   On a charge of conspiracy to commit a Group A offence, or on a charge of conspiracy to defraud in England and Wales, the defendant may be guilty of the offence whether or not—

(a)   he became a party to the conspiracy in England and Wales;

(b)   any act or omission or other event in relation to the conspiracy occurred in England and Wales.

(3)   On a charge of attempting to commit a Group A offence, the defendant may be guilty of the offence whether or not—

(a)   the attempt was made in England and Wales;

(b)   it had an effect in England and Wales.

(4)   Subsection (1)(a) does not apply where jurisdiction is given to try the offence in question by an enactment which makes provision by reference to the nationality of the person charged.

(5)   Subsection (2) does not apply in relation to any charge under the Criminal Law Act 1977 brought by virtue of section 1A of that Act.

(6)   Subsection (3) does not apply in relation to any charge under the Criminal Attempts Act 1981 brought by virtue of section 1A of that Act.

4.   Rules for determining certain jurisdictional questions relating to the location of events

In relation to a Group A or Group B offence—

(a)   there is an obtaining of property in England and Wales if the property is either despatched from or received at a place in England and Wales; and

(b)   there is a communication in England and Wales of any information, instruction, request, demand or other matter if it is sent by any means—

(i)   from a place in England and Wales to a place elsewhere; or

(ii)   from a place elsewhere to a place in England and Wales.

5.   Extended jurisdiction over conspiracies to defraud and incitement

(3)   A person may be guilty of conspiracy to defraud if—

(a)   a party to the agreement constituting the conspiracy, or a party's agent, did anything in England and Wales in relation to the agreement before its formation, or

(b)   a party to it became a party in England and Wales (by joining it either in person or through an agent), or

(c)   a party to it, or a party's agent, did or omitted anything in England and Wales in pursuance of it,

and the conspiracy would be triable in England and Wales but for the fraud which the parties to it had in view not being intended to take place in England and Wales.

(4)   A person may be guilty of incitement to commit a Group A offence if—

(a)   the incitement takes place in England and Wales; and

(b)   a charge in respect of incitement would be triable in England and Wales but for what the person charged had in view not being an offence triable in England and Wales.

(5)   Subsections (3) and (4) are subject to section 6.

6.   Relevance of external law

(1)   A person is guilty of an offence triable by virtue of section 1A of the Criminal Law Act 1977, or by virtue of section 5(3), only if the pursuit of the agreed course of conduct would at some stage involve—

(a)   an act or omission by one or more of the parties, or

(b)   the happening of some other event,

constituting an offence under the law in force where the act, omission or other event was intended to take place.

(2)   A person is guilty of an offence triable by virtue of section 1A of the Criminal Attempts Act 1981, or by virtue of section 5(4), only if what he had in view would involve the commission of an offence under the law in force where the whole or any part of it was intended to take place.

(3)   Conduct punishable under the law in force in any place is an offence under that law for the purposes of this section, however it is described in that law.

(4)   Subject to subsection (6), a condition specified in subsection (1) or (2) shall be taken to be satisfied unless, not later than rules of court may provide, the defence serve on the prosecution a notice—

(a)   stating that, on the facts as alleged with respect to the relevant conduct, the condition is not in their opinion satisfied;

(b)   showing their grounds for that opinion; and

(c)   requiring the prosecution to show that it is satisfied.

(5)   In subsection (4) 'the relevant conduct' means—

(a)   where the condition in subsection (1) is in question, the agreed course of conduct; and

(b)   where the condition in subsection (2) is in question, what the defendant had in view.

(6)   The court, if it thinks fit, may permit the defence to require the prosecution to show that the condition is satisfied without the prior service of a notice under subsection (4).

(7)   In the Crown Court, the question whether the condition is satisfied shall be decided by the judge alone.

8   TRESPASS AND INVASION OF PRIVACY

THEFT ACT 1968

9.   Burglary

(1)   A person is guilty of burglary if—

(a)   he enters any building or part of a building as a trespasser and with intent to commit any such offence as is mentioned in subsection (2) below; or

(b)   having entered into any building or part of a building as a trespasser he steals or attempts to steal anything in the building or that part of it or inflicts or attempts to inflict on any person therein any grievous bodily harm.

(2)   The offences referred to in subsection (1)(a) above are offences of stealing anything in the building or part of a building in question, of inflicting on any person therein any grievous bodily harm or raping any person therein, and of doing unlawful damage to the building or anything therein.

(3)   A person guilty of burglary shall on conviction on indictment be liable to imprisonment for a term not exceeding—

(a)   where the offence was committed in respect of a building or part of a building which is a dwelling, fourteen years;

(b)   in any other case, ten years.

(4)   References in subsection (1) and (2) above to a building, and the reference in subsection (3) above to a building which is a dwelling, shall apply also to an inhabited vehicle or vessel, and shall apply to any such vehicle or vessel at times when the person having a habitation in it is not there as well as at times when he is.

10.   Aggravated burglary

(1)   A person is guilty of aggravated burglary if he commits any burglary and at the time has with him any firearm or imitation firearm, any weapon of offence, or any explosive; and for this purpose—

(a)   'firearm' includes an airgun or air pistol, and 'imitation firearm' means anything which has the appearance of being a firearm, whether capable of being discharged or not; and

(b)   'weapon of offence' means any article made or adapted for use for causing injury to or incapacitating a person, or intended by the person having it with him for such use; and

(c)   'explosive' means any article manufactured for the purpose of producing a practical effect by explosion, or intended by the person having it with him for that purpose.

(2)   A person guilty of aggravated burglary shall on conviction on indictment be liable to imprisonment for life.

FIREARMS ACT 1968

20. Trespassing with firearm
[See page 102]

CRIMINAL LAW ACT 1977

6. Violence for securing entry

(1) Subject to the following provisions of this section, any person who, without lawful authority, uses or threatens violence for the purpose of securing entry into any premises for himself or for any other person is guilty of an offence, provided that—

(a) there is someone present on those premises at the time who is opposed to the entry which the violence is intended to secure; and

(b) the person using or threatening the violence knows that that is the case.

(1A) Subsection (1) above does not apply to a person who is a displaced residential occupier or a protected intending occupier of the premises in question or who is acting on behalf of such an occupier; and if the accused adduces sufficient evidence that he was, or was acting on behalf of, such an occupier he shall be presumed to be, or to be acting on behalf of, such an occupier unless the contrary is proved by the prosecution.

(2) Subject to subsection (1A) above, the fact that a person has any interest in or right to possession or occupation of any premises shall not for the purposes of subsection (1) above constitute lawful authority for the use or threat of violence by him or anyone else for the purpose of securing his entry into those premises.

(4) It is immaterial for the purposes of this section—

(a) whether the violence in question is directed against the person or against the property; and

(b) whether the entry which the violence is intended to secure is for the purpose of acquiring possession of the premises in question or for any other purpose.

7. Adverse occupation of residential premises

(1) Subject to the following provisions of this section and to section 12A(9) below, any person who is on any premises as a trespasser after having entered as such is guilty of an offence if he fails to leave those premises on being required to do so by or on behalf of—

(a) a displaced residential occupier of the premises; or

(b) an individual who is a protected intending occupier of the premises.

(2) In any proceedings for an offence under this section it shall be a defence for the accused to prove that he believed that the person requiring him to leave the premises was not a displaced residential occupier or protected intending occupier of the premises or a person acting on behalf of a displaced residential occupier or protected intending occupier.

(3) In any proceedings for an offence under this section it shall be a defence for the accused to prove—

(a) that the premises in question are or form part of premises used mainly for non-residential purposes; and

(b) that he was not on any part of the premises used wholly or mainly for residential purposes.

(4) Any reference in the preceding provisions of this section to any premises includes a reference to any access to them, whether or not any such access itself constitutes premises, within the meaning of this Part of this Act.

(7) Section 12 below contains provisions which apply for determining when any person is to be regarded for the purposes of this Part of this Act as a displaced

residential occupier of any premises or of any access to any premises and section 12A below contains provisions which apply for determining when any person is to be regarded for the purposes of this Part of this Act as a protected intending occupier of any premises or of any access to any premises.

8. Trespassing with a weapon of offence

(1) A person who is on any premises as a trespasser, after having entered as such, is guilty of an offence if, without lawful authority or reasonable excuse, he has with him on the premises any weapon of offence.

(2) In subsection (1) above 'weapon of offence' means any article made or adapted for use for causing injury to or incapacitating a person, or intended by the person having it with him for such use.

9. Trespassing on premises of foreign missions, etc.

(1) Subject to subsection (3) below, a person who enters or is on any premises to which this section applies as a trespasser is guilty of an offence.

(2) This section applies to any premises which are or form part of—

(a) the premises of a diplomatic mission within the meaning of the definition in Article 1(i) of the Vienna Convention on Diplomatic Relations signed in 1961 as that Article has effect in the United Kingdom by virtue of section 2 of and Schedule 1 to the Diplomatic Privileges Act 1964;

(aa) the premises of a closed diplomatic mission;

(b) consular premises within the meaning of the definition in paragraph 1(j) of Article 1 of the Vienna Convention on Consular Relations signed in 1963 as that Article has effect in the United Kingdom by virtue of section 1 of and Schedule 1 to the Consular Relations Act 1968;

(bb) the premises of a closed consular post;

(c) any other premises in respect of which any organisation or body is entitled to inviolability by or under any enactment; and

(d) any premises which are the private residence of a diplomatic agent (within the meaning of Article 1(e) of the Convention mentioned in paragraph (a) above) or of any other person who is entitled to inviolability of residence by or under any enactment.

(3) In any proceedings for an offence under this section it shall be a defence for the accused to prove that he believed that the premises in question were not premises to which this section applies.

12. Supplementary provisions

(1) In this Part of this Act—

(a) 'premises' means any building, any part of a building under separate occupation, any land ancillary to a building, the site comprising any building or buildings together with any land ancillary thereto, and (for the purposes only of sections 10 and 11 above) any other place; and

(b) 'access' means, in relation to any premises, any part of any site or building within which those premises are situated which constitutes an ordinary means of access to those premises (whether or not that is its sole or primary use).

(2) References in this section to a building shall apply also to any structure other than a movable one, and to any movable structure, vehicle or vessel designed or adapted for use for residential purposes; and for the purposes of subsection (1) above—

(a) part of a building is under separate occupation if anyone is in occupation or entitled to occupation of that part as distinct from the whole; and

(b) land is ancillary to a building if it is adjacent to it and used (or intended for use) in connection with the occupation of that building or any part of it.

(3)   Subject to subsection (4) below, any person who was occupying any premises as a residence immdiately before being excluded from occupation by anyone who entered those premises, or any access to those premises, as a trespasser is a displaced residential occupier of the premises for the purposes of this Part of this Act so long as he continues to be excluded from occupation of the premises by the original trespasser or by any subsequent trespasser.

(4)   A person who was himself occupying the premises in question as a trespasser immediately before being excluded from occupation shall not by virtue of subsection (3) above be a displaced residential occupier of the premises for the purposes of this Part of this Act.

(5)   A person who by virtue of subsection (3) above is a displaced residential occupier of any premises shall be regarded for the purposes of this Part of this Act as a displaced residential occupier also of any access to those premises.

12A. Protected intending occupiers: supplementary provisions

(1)   For the purposes of this Part of this Act an individual is a protected intending occupier of any premises at any time if at that time he falls within subsections (2), (4) or (6) below.

(2)   An individual is a protected occupier of any premises if—

(a)   he has in those premises a freehold interest or a leasehold interest with not less than two years still to run;

(b)   he requires the premises for his own occupation as a residence;

(c)   he is excluded from occupation of the premises by a person who entered them, or any access to them, as a trespasser; and

(d)   he or a person acting on his behalf holds a written statement—

(i)   which specifies his interest in the premises;

(ii)   which states that he requires the premises for occupation as a residence for himself; and

(iii)   with respect to which the requirements in subsection (3) below are fulfilled.

(3)   The requirements referred to in subsection (2)(d)(iii) above are—

(a)   that the statement is signed by the person whose interest is specified in it in the presence of a justice of the peace or commissioner for oaths; and

(b)   that the justice of the peace or commissioner for oaths has subscribed his name as a witness to the signature.

(4)   An individual is also a protected intending occupier of any premises if —

(a)   he has a tenancy of those premises (other than a tenancy falling within subsection (2)(a) above or (6)(a) below) or a licence to occupy those premises granted by a person with a freehold interest or a leasehold interest with not less than two years still to run in the premises;

(b)   he requires the premises for his own occupation as a residence;

(c)   he is excluded from occupation of the premises by a person who entered them, or any access to them, as a trespasser; and

(d)   he or a person acting on his behalf holds a written statement—

(i)   which states that he has been granted a tenancy of those premises or a licence to occupy those premises;

(ii)   which specifies the interest in the premises of the person who granted that tenancy or licence to occupy ('the landlord');

(iii)   which states that he requires the premises for occupation as a residence for himself; and

(iv)   with respect to which the requirements in subsection (5) below are fulfilled.

(5)   The requirements referred to in subsection (4)(d)(iv) above are—

(a)   that the statement is signed by the landlord and by the tenant or licensee in the presence of a justice of the peace or commissioner for oaths;

(b)   that the justice of the peace or commissioner for oaths has subscribed his name as a witness to the signatures.

(6)   An individual is also a protected intending occupier of any premises if —

(a)   he has a tenancy of those premises (other than a tenancy falling within subsection (2)(a) or (4)(a) above) or a licence to occupy those premises granted by an authority to which this subsection applies;

(b)   he requires the premises for his own occupation as a residence;

(c)   he is excluded from occupation of the premises by a person who entered the premises, or any access to them, as a trespasser; and

(d)   there has been issued to him by or on behalf of the authority referred to in paragraph (a) above a certificate stating that—

(i)   he has been granted a tenancy of those premises or a licence to occupy those premises as a residence by the authority; and

(ii)   the authority which granted that tenancy or licence to occupy is one to which this subsection applies, being of a description specified in the certificate.

(7)   Subsection (6) above applies to the following authorities—

(a)   any body mentioned in section 14 of the Rent Act 1977 (landlord's interest belonging to local authority etc);

(b)   the Housing Corporation

(c)   Housing for Wales; and

(d)   a registered housing association within the meaning of the Housing Associations Act 1985.

(8)   A person is guilty of an offence if he makes a statement for the purposes of subsection (2)(d) or (4)(d) above which he knows to be false in a material particular or if he recklessly makes such a statement which is false in a material particular.

(9)   In any proceedings for an offence under section 7 of this Act where the accused was requested to leave the premises by a person claiming to be or to act on behalf of a protected intending occupier of the premises—

(a)   it shall be a defence for the accused to prove that, although asked to do so by the accused at the time the accused was requested to leave, that person failed at that time to produce to the accused such a statement as is referred to in subsection (2)(d) or (4)(d) above or such a certificate as is referred to in subsection (6)(d) above; and

(b)   any document purporting to be a certificate under subsection (6)(d) above shall be received in evidence and, unless the contrary is proved, shall be deemed to have been issued by or on behalf of the authority stated in the certificate.

(11)   A person who is protected intending occupier of any premises shall be regarded for the purposes of this Part of this Act as a protected intending occupier also of any access to those premises.

NIGHT POACHING ACT 1828

1.   Persons taking or destroying game or rabbits by night, or entering any land for that purpose

. . . If any person shall . . . by night, unlawfully take or destroy any game or rabbits in any land, whether open or enclosed, or shall by night unlawfully enter or be in any land, whether open or enclosed, with any gun, net, engine, or other instrument, for the purpose of taking or destroying game, he shall be liable on summary conviction to a fine not exceeding level 3 on the standard scale.

9.   If persons to the number of three, being armed, enter any land for the purpose of taking or destroying game or rabbits, they shall be deemed guilty of a misdemeanour

. . . If any persons, to the number of three or more together, shall by night unlawfully enter or be on any land whether open or enclosed, for the purpose of taking or destroying game or rabbits, any of such persons being armed with any gun, crossbow, fire arms, bludgeon, or any other offensive weapon, each and every of such persons shall be guilty of a misdemeanour, and being convicted thereof . . . shall be liable on summary conviction to imprisonment for a term not exceeding six months or to a fine not exceeding level 4 on the standard scale, or to both.

12. What time shall be considered night
Provided always . . . that for the purposes of this Act the night shall be considered and is hereby declared to commence at the expiration of the first hour of sunset, and to conclude at the beginning of the last hour before sunrise.

13. What shall be deemed game
. . . For the purposes of this Act the word "game" shall be deemed to include hares, pheasants, partridges, grouse, heath or moor game, black game, and bustards.

GAME ACT 1831

30. Penalty on persons trespassing in the daytime upon lands in search of game, or woodcocks, etc. — Leave of occupier not to be a defence where game is reserved to landlord, etc. — Landlords and lords of manors, etc, to be deemed legal occupiers
. . . If any person whatsoever shall commit any trespass by entering or being in the daytime upon any land in search or pursuit of game, or woodcocks, snipes, . . . or conies, such person shall, on conviction thereof before a justice of the peace, forfeit and pay such sum of money, not exceeding level 1 on the standard scale, as to the justice shall seem meet, . . . ; and . . . if any persons to the number of five or more together shall commit any trespass, by entering or being in the daytime upon any land in search or pursuit of game, woodcocks, snipes, . . . or conies, each of such persons shall, on conviction thereof before a justice of the peace, forfeit and pay such sum of money , not exceeding level 3 on the standard scale as to the said justice shall seem meet, . . . : Provided always, that any person charged with any such trespass shall be at liberty to prove, by way of defence, any matter which would have been a defence to an action at law for such trespass; save and except that the leave and licence of the occupier of the land so trespassed upon shall not be a sufficient defence in any case where the landlord, lessor, or other person shall have the right of killing the game upon such land, by virtue of any reservation or otherwise, as herein-before mentioned; but such landlord, lessor, or other person shall, for the purpose of prosecuting for each of the two offences herein last before mentioned, be deemed to be the legal occupier of such land, whenever the actual occupier thereof shall have given such leave or licence; and that the lord or steward of the crown of any manor, lordship, or royalty, or reputed manor, lordship, or royalty, shall be deemed to be the legal occupier of the land of the wastes or commons within such manor, lordship, or royalty, or reputed manor, lordship, or royalty.

32. Penalty in case of five or more persons found armed in daytime in search of game, etc., and using violence, etc.
. . . Where any persons, to the number of five or more together, shall be found on any land, . . . in the daytime, in search or pursuit of game, or woodcocks, snipes, . . . or conies, any of such persons being then and there armed with a gun, and such persons or any of them shall then and there, by violence, intimidation, or menace, prevent or endeavour to prevent any person authorized as herein-before mentioned from approaching such persons so found, or any of them, for the purpose of requiring them or any of them to quit the land whereon they shall be so found, or to tell their or his christian name, surname, or place of abode respectively, as herein-before mentioned,

every person so offending by such violence, intimidation, or menace as aforesaid, and every person then and there aiding or abetting such offender, shall, upon being convicted thereof before two justices of the peace, forfeit and pay for every such offence such penalty, not exceeding level 4 on the standard scale, as to the convicting justices shall seem meet, . . . ; which said penalty shall be in addition to and independent of any other penalty to which any such person may be liable for any other offence against this Act.

34. What to be deemed daytime
. . . For the purposes of this Act the daytime shall be deemed to commence at the beginning of the last hour before sunrise, and to conclude at the expiration of the first hour after sunset.

35. Provisions as to trespassers not to apply to persons hunting, etc
. . . Provided always, that the aforesaid provisions against trespassers and persons found on any land shall not extend to any person hunting or coursing upon any lands with hounds or greyhounds, and being in fresh pursuit of any deer, hare, or fox already started upon any other land, . . . nor to any lord or any steward of the crown of any manor, lordship, or royalty, or reputed manor, lordship or royalty, nor to any gamekeeper lawfully appointed by such lord or steward within the limits of such manor, lordship, or royalty, or reputed manor, lordship, or royalty.

DEER ACT 1991

1. Poaching of deer
(1) Subject to subsection (3) below, if any person enters any land without the consent of the owner or occupier or other lawful authority in search or pursuit of any deer with the intention of taking, killing or injuring it, he shall be guilty of an offence.

(2) Subject to subsection (3) below, if any person while on any land—
   (a) intentionally takes, kills or injures, or attempts to take, kill or injure, any deer,
   (b) searches for or pursues any deer with the intention of taking, killing or injuring it, or
   (c) removes the carcase of any deer,
without the consent of the owner or occupier of the land or other lawful authority, he shall be guilty of an offence.

(3) A person shall not be guilty of an offence under subsection (1) or subsection (2) above by reason of anything done in the belief that—
   (a) he would have the consent of the owner or occupier of the land if the owner or occupier knew of his doing it and the circumstances of it; or
   (b) he has other lawful authority to do it.

CRIMINAL JUSTICE AND PUBLIC ORDER ACT 1994

68. Offence of aggravated trespass
(1) A person commits the offence of aggravated trespass if he trespasses on land in the open air and, in relation to any lawful activity which persons are engaging in or are about to engage in on that or adjoining land in the open air, does there anything which is intended by him to have the effect—
   (a) of intimidating those persons or any of them so as to deter them or any of them from engaging in that activity,
   (b) of obstructing that activity, or
   (c) of disrupting that activity.

(2)   Activity on any occasion on the part of a person or persons on land is 'lawful' for the purposes of this section if he or they may engage in the activity on the land on that occasion without committing an offence or trespassing on the land.

69.   Powers to remove persons committing or participating in aggravated trespass

(1)   If the senior police officer present at the scene reasonably believes—

(a)   that a person is committing, has committed or intends to commit the offence of aggravated trespass on land in the open air; or

(b)   that two or more persons are trespassing on land in the open air and are present there with the common purpose of intimidating persons so as to deter them from engaging in a lawful activity or of obstructing or disrupting a lawful activity,

he may direct that person or (as the case may be) those persons (or any of them) to leave the land.

(2)   A direction under subsection (1) above, if not communicated to the persons referred to in subsection (1) by the police officer giving the direction, may be communicated to them by any constable at the scene.

(3)   If a person knowing that a direction under subsection (1) above has been given which applies to him—

(a)   fails to leave the land as soon as practicable, or

(b)   having left again enters the land as a trespasser within the period of three months beginning with the day on which the direction was given,

he commits an offence and liable on summary conviction to imprisonment for a term not exceeding three months or a fine not exceeding level 4 on the standard scale, or both.

(4)   In proceedings for an offence under subsection (3) it is a defence for the accused to show—

(a)   that he was not trespassing on the land, or

(b)   that he had a reasonable excuse for failing to leave the land as soon as practicable or, as the case may be, for again entering the land as a trespasser.

PUBLIC ORDER ACT 1986

39.   Power to direct trespasser to leave land

(1)   If the senior police officer reasonably believes that two or more persons have entered land as trespassers and are present there with the common purpose of residing there for any period, that reasonable steps have been taken by or on behalf of the occupier to ask them to leave and—

(a)   that any of those persons has caused damage to property on the land or used threatening, abusive or insulting words or behaviour towards the occupier, a member of his family or an employee or agent of his, or

(b)   that those persons have between them brought twelve or more vehicles on to the land,

he may direct those persons, or any of them, to leave the land.

(2)   If a person knowing that such a direction has been given which applies to him—

(a)   fails to leave the land as soon as reasonably practicable, or

(b)   having left again enters the land as a trespasser within the period of three months beginning with the day on which the direction was given,

he commits an offence and is liable on summary conviction to imprisonment for a term not exceeding three months or a fine not exceeding level 4 on the standard scale, or both.

(4)   In proceedings for an offence under this section it is a defence for the accused to show—

(a) that his original entry on the land was not as a trespasser, or

(b) that he had a reasonable excuse for failing to leave the land as soon as reasonably practicable or, as the case may be, for again entering the land as a trespasser.

(5) In this section—

'land' does not include—

(a) buildings other than—

(i) agricultural buildings within the meaning of section 26(4) of the General Rate Act 1967, or

(ii) scheduled monuments within the meaning of the Ancient Monuments and Archaeological Areas Act 1979;

(b) land forming part of a highway;

'occupier' means the person entitled to possession of the land by virtue of an estate or interest held by him;

'property' means property within the meaning of section 10(1) of the Criminal Damage Act 1971;

'senior police officer' means the most senior in rank of the police officers present at the scene;

'trespasser', in relation to land, means a person who is a trespasser as against the occupier of the land;

'vehicle' includes a caravan as defined in section 29(1) of the Caravan Sites and Control of Development Act 1960;

and a person may be regarded for the purposes of this section as having the purpose of residing in a place notwithstanding that he has a home elsewhere.

FOOTBALL (OFFENCES) ACT 1991

4. Going onto the playing area
[See page 37]

INTERCEPTION OF COMMUNICATIONS ACT 1985

1. Prohibition on interception

(1) Subject to the following provisions of this section, a person who intentionally intercepts a communication in the course of its transmission by post or by means of a public telecommunication system shall be guilty of an offence and liable—

(a) on summary conviction, to a fine not exceeding the statutory maximum;

(b) on conviction on indictment, to imprisonment for a term not exceeding two years or to a fine or to both.

(2) A person shall not be guilty of an offence under this section if—

(a) the communication is intercepted in obedience to a warrant issued by the Secretary of State under section 2 below; or

(b) that person has reasonable grounds for believing that the person to whom, or the person by whom, the communication is sent has consented to the interception.

(3) A person shall not be guilty of an offence under this section if—

(a) the communication is intercepted for purposes connected with the provision of postal or public telecommunication services or with the enforcement of any enactment relating to the use of those services; or

(b) the communication is being transmitted by wireless telegraphy and is intercepted, with the authority of the Secretary of State, for purposes connected with the issue of licences under the Wireless Telegraphy Act 1949 or the prevention or detection of interference with wireless telegraphy.

9   OFFENSIVE CONDUCT

(a)   BIGAMY

OFFENCES AGAINST THE PERSON ACT 1861

57.   Bigamy

Whosoever, being married, shall marry any other person during the life of the former husband or wife, whether the second marriage shall have taken place in England or Ireland or elsewhere, shall be guilty of felony, and being convicted thereof shall be liable to be kept in penal servitude for any term not exceeding seven years . . .: Provided, that nothing in this section contained shall extend to any second marriage contracted elsewhere than in England and Ireland by any other than a subject of Her Majesty, or to any person marrying a second time whose husband or wife shall have been continually absent from such person for the space of seven years then last past, and shall not have been known by such person to be living within that time, or shall extend to any person who, at the time of such second marriage, shall have been divorced from the bond of the first marriage, or to any person whose former marriage shall have been declared void by the sentence of any court of competent jurisdiction.

PERJURY ACT 1911

3.   False statements, etc., with reference to marriage

(1)   If any person—

(a)   for the purpose of procuring a marriage, or a certificate or licence for marriage, knowingly and wilfully makes a false oath, or makes or signs a false declaration, notice or certificate required under any Act of Parliament for the time being in force relating to marriage; or

(b)   knowingly and wilfully makes, or knowingly and wilfully causes to be made, for the purpose of being inserted in any register of marriage, a false statement as to any particular required by law to be known and registered relating to any marriage; or

(c)   forbids the issue of any certificate or licence for marriage by falsely representing himself to be a person whose consent to the marriage is required by law knowing such representation to be false,

he shall be guilty of a misdemeanour, and, on conviction thereof on indictment shall be liable to penal servitude for a term not exceeding seven years.

FORGERY ACT 1861

36.   Destroying, injuring, forging, or falsifying registers of births, baptisms, marriages, deaths, or burials, or certified copies

Whosoever shall unlawfully destroy, deface, or injure, or cause or permit to be destroyed, defaced, or injured, any register of births, baptisms, marriages, deaths, or burials which now is or hereafter shall be by law authorised or required to be kept in England or Ireland, or any part of any such register, or any certified copy of any such register, or any part thereof, . . . or shall knowingly and unlawfully insert or cause or permit to be inserted in any such register, or in any certified copy thereof, any false entry of any matter relating to any birth, baptism, marriage, death, or burial, or shall knowingly and unlawfully give any false certificate relating to any birth, baptism, marriage, death, or burial, or shall certify any writing to be a copy or extract from any such register, knowing such writing, or the part of such register whereof such copy or extract shall be so given, to be false in any material particular . . . or shall offer, utter, dispose of, or put off any such register, entry, certified copy, certificate, . . . knowing the same to be false, . . . or shall offer, utter, dispose of, or put off any copy of any entry in any such register, knowing such entry to be false, . . . shall be guilty of felony, and being convicted thereof, shall be liable . . . to be kept in penal servitude for life . . .

37. Making false entries in copies of registers of baptisms, marriages, or burials, directed to be sent to any registrar, or destroying or concealing copies of registers

Whosoever shall knowingly and wilfully insert or cause or permit to be inserted in any copy of any register directed or required by law to be transmitted to any registrar or other officer any false entry of any matter relating to any baptism, marriage, or burial . . . or shall knowingly and wilfully sign or verify any copy of any register so directed or required to be transmitted as aforesaid, which copy shall be false in any part thereof, knowing the same to be false, or shall unlawfully destroy, deface, or injure, or shall for any fraudulent purpose take from its place of deposit, or conceal, any such copy of any register, shall be guilty of felony, and being convicted thereof shall be liable . . . to be kept in penal servitude for life . . .

(b) SURROGACY

SURROGACY ARRANGEMENTS ACT 1985

1. Meaning of 'surrogate mother', 'surrogacy arrangement' and other terms

(1)   The following provisions shall have effect for the interpretation of this Act.

(2)   'Surrogate mother' means a woman who carries a child in pursuance of an arrangement—

(a)   made before she began to carry the child, and

(b)   made with a view to any child carried in pursuance of it being handed over to, and parental responsibility being met (so far as practicable) by, another person or other persons.

(3)   An arrangement is a surrogacy arrangement if, were a woman to whom the arrangement relates to carry a child in pursuance of it, she would be a surrogate mother.

(4)   In determining whether an arrangement is made with such a view as is mentioned in subsection (1) above regard may be had to the circumstances as a whole (and, in particular, where there is a promise or understanding that any payment will or may be made to the woman or for her benefit in respect of the carrying of any child in pursuance of the arrangement, to that promise or understanding).

(5)   An arrangement may be regarded as made with such a view though subject to conditions relating to the handing over of any child.

(6)   A woman who carries a child is to be treated for the purposes of subsection (2)(a) above as beginning to carry it at the time of the insemination or of the placing in her of an embryo, of an egg in the process of fertilisation, or of sperm and eggs, as the case may be, that results in her carrying the child.

(7) 'Body of persons' means a body of persons corporate or unincorporate.

(8) 'Payment' means payment in money or money's worth.

(9) This Act applies to arrangements whether or not they are lawful.

2. Negotiating surrogacy arrangements on a commercial basis, etc.

(1) No person shall on a commercial basis do any of the following acts in the United Kingdom, that is—

(a) initiate or take part in any negotiations with a view to the making of a surrogacy arrangement.

(b) offer or agree to negotiate the making of a surrogacy arrangement, or

(c) compile any information with a view to its use in making, or negotiating the making of, surrogacy arrangements;

and no person shall in the United Kingdom knowingly cause another to do any of those acts on a commercial basis.

(2) A person who contravenes subsection (1) above is guilty of an offence; but it is not a contravention of that subsection—

(a) for a woman, with a view to becoming a surrogate mother herself, to do any act mentioned in that subsection or to cause such an act to be done, or

(b) for any person, with a view to a surrogate mother carrying a child for him, to do such an act or to cause such an act to be done.

(3) For the purpose of this section, a person does an act on a commercial basis (subject to subsection (4) below) if—

(a) any payment is at any time received by himself or another in respect of it, or

(b) he does it with a view to any payment being received by himself or another in respect of making, or negotiating or facilitating the making of, any surrogacy arrangement.

In this subsection 'payment' does not include payment to or for the benefit of a surrogate mother or prospective surrogate mother.

(4) In proceedings against a person for an offence under subsection (1) above, he is not to be treated as doing an act on a commercial basis by reason of any payment received by another in respect of the act if it is proved that—

(a) in a case where the payment was received before he did the act, he did not do the act knowing or having reasonable cause to suspect that any payment had been received in respect of the act; and

(b) in any other case, he did not do the act with a view to any payment being received in respect of it.

(5) Where—

(a) a person acting on behalf of a body of persons takes any part in negotiating or facilitating the making of a surrogacy arrangement in the United Kingdom, and

(b) negotiating or facilitating the making of surrogacy arrrangements is an activity of the body,

then, if the body at any time receives any payment made by or on behalf of—

(i) a woman who carries a child in pursuance of the arrangement,

(ii) the person or persons for whom she carries it, or

(iii) any person connected with the woman or with that person or those persons,

the body is guilty of an offence.

For the purposes of this subsection, a payment received by a person connected with a body is to be treated as received by the body.

(6) In proceeding against a body for an offence under subsection (5) above, it is a defence to prove that the payment concerned was not made in respect of the arrangement mentioned in paragraph (a) of the subsection

(7) A person who in the United Kingdom takes part in the management or control—

(a)   of any body of persons, or

(b)   of any of the activities of any body of persons,

is guilty of an offence if the activity described in subsection (8) below is an activity of the body concerned.

(8)   The activity referred to in subsection (7) above is negotiating or facilitating the making of surrogacy arrangements in the United Kingdom, being—

(a)   arrangements the making of which is negotiated or facilitated on a commercial basis, or

(b)   arrangements in the case of which payments are received (or treated for the purposes of subsection (5) above as received) by the body concerned in contravention of subsection (5) above.

(9)   In proceedings against a person for an offence under subsection (7) above, it is a defence to prove that he neither knew nor had reasonable cause to suspect that the activity described in subsection (8) above was an activity of the body concerned; and for the purposes of such proceedings any arrangement falling within subsection (8)(b) above shall be disregarded if it is proved that the payment concerned was not made in respect of the arrangement.

3.   Advertisement about surrogacy

(1)   This section applies to any advertisement containing an indication (however expressed)—

(a)   that any person is or may be willing to enter into a surrogacy arrangement or to negotiate or facilitate the making of a surrogacy arrangement, or

(b)   that any person is looking for a woman willing to become a surrogate mother or for persons wanting a woman to carry a child as a surrogate mother.

(2)   Where a newspaper or periodical containing an advertisement to which this section applies is published in the United Kingdom, any proprietor, editor or publisher of the newspaper or periodical is guilty of an offence.

(3)   Where an advertisement to which this section applies is conveyed by means of a telecommunication system so as to be seen or heard (or both) in the United Kingdom, any person who in the United Kingdom causes it to be so conveyed knowing it to contain such an indication as is mentioned in subsection (1) above is guilty of an offence.

(4)   A person who publishes or causes to be published in the United Kingdom an advertisement to which this section applies (not being an advertisement contained in a newspaper or periodical or conveyed by means of a telecommunication system) is guilty of an offence.

(5)   A person who distributes or causes to be distributed in the United Kingdom an advertisement to which this section applies (not being an advertisement contained in a newspaper or periodical published outside the United Kingdom or an advertisement conveyed by means of a telecommunication system) knowing it to contain such an indication as is mentioned in subsection (1) above is guilty of an offence.

(6)   In this section 'telecommunication system' has the same meaning as in the Telecommunications Act 1984.

4.   Offences

(3)   Where an offence under this Act committed by a body corporate is proved to have been committed with the consent or connivance of, or to be attributable to any neglect on the part of, any director, manager, secretary or other similar officer of the body corporate or any person who was purporting to act in any such capacity, he as well as the body corporate is guilty of the offence and is liable to be proceeded against and punished accordingly.

(4)   Where the affairs of a body corporate are managed by its members, subsection (3) above shall apply in relation to the acts and defaults of a member in connection with his functions of management as if he were a director of the body corporate.

(5)   If any proceedings for an offence under section 2 of this Act, proof of things done or of words written, spoken or published (whether or not in the presence of any party to the proceedings) by any person taking part in the management or control of a body of persons or of any of the activities of the body, or by any person doing any of the acts mentioned in subsection (1)(a) to (c) of that section on behalf of the body, shall be admissible as evidence of the activities of the body.

(c)   MEDICAL PROCEDURES

HUMAN FERTILISATION AND EMBRYOLOGY ACT 1990

1.   Meaning of 'embryo', 'gamete' and associated expressions
   (1)   In this Act, except where otherwise stated—
      (a)   embryo means a live human embryo where fertilisation is complete, and
      (b)   references to an embryo include an egg in the process of fertilisation,
and, for this purpose, fertilisation is not complete until the appearance of a two cell zygote.
   (2)   This Act, so far as it governs bringing about the creation of an embryo, applies only to bringing about the creation of an embryo outside the human body; and in this Act—
      (a)   references to embryos the creation of which was brought about *in vitro* (in their application to those where fertilisation is complete) are to those where fertilisation began outside the human body whether or not it was completed there, and
      (b)   references to embryos taken from a woman do not include embryos whose creation was brought about *in vitro*.
   (3)   This Act, so far as it governs the keeping or use of an embryo, applies only to keeping or using an embryo outside the human body.
   (4)   References in this Act to gametes, eggs or sperm, except where otherwise stated, are to live human gametes, eggs or sperm but references below in this Act to gametes or eggs do not include eggs in the process of fertilisation.

2.   Other terms
   (1)   In this Act—
. . .
      'licence' means a licence under Schedule 2 to this Act and, in relation to a licence, 'the person responsible' has the meaning given by section 17 of this Act, and 'treatment services' means medical, surgical or obstetric services provided to the public or a section of the public for the purpose of assisting women to carry children.
   (2)   References in this Act to keeping, in relation to embryos or gametes, include keeping while preserved, whether preserved by cryopreservation or in any other way; and embryos or gametes so kept are referred to in this Act as 'stored' (and 'store' and 'storage' are to be interpreted accordingly).
   (3)   For the purposes of this Act, a woman is not to be treated as carrying a child until the embryo has become implanted.

3.   Prohibitions in connection with embryos
   (1)   No person shall—
      (a)   bring about the creation of an embryo, or
      (b)   keep or use an embryo,
except in pursuance of a licence.
   (2)   No person shall place in a woman—
      (a)   a live embryo other than a human embryo, or
      (b)   any live gametes other than human gametes.
   (3)   A licence cannot authorise—

    (a)   keeping or using an embryo after the appearance of the primitive streak,

    (b)   placing an embryo in any animal,

    (c)   keeping or using an embryo in any circumstances in which regulations prohibit its keeping or use, or

    (d)   replacing a nucleus of a cell of an embryo with a nucleus taken from a cell of any person, embryo or subsequent development of an embryo.

    (4)   For the purposes of subsection (3)(a) above, the primitive streak is to be taken to have appeared in an embryo not later than the end of the period of 14 days beginning with the day when the gametes are mixed, not counting any time during which the embryo is stored.

3A. Prohibition in connection with germ cells

    (1)   No person shall, for the purpose of providing fertility services for any woman, use female germ cells taken or derived from an embryo or a foetus or use embryos created by using such cells.

    (2)   In this section—

    'female germ cells' means cells of the female germ line and includes such cells at any stage of maturity and accordingly includes eggs; and

    'fertility services' means medical, surgical or obstetric services provided for the purpose of assisting women to carry children.

4. Prohibitions in connection with gametes

    (1)   No person shall—

    (a)   store any gametes, or

    (b)   in the course of providing treatment services for any woman, use the sperm of any man unless the services are being provided for the woman and the man together or use the eggs of any other woman, or

    (c)   mix gametes with the live gametes of any animal,

except in pursuance of a licence.

    (2)   A licence cannot authorise storing or using gametes in any circumstances in which regulations prohibit their storage or use.

    (3)   No person shall place sperm and eggs in a woman in any circumstances specified in regulations except in pursuance of a licence.

41. Offences

    (1)   A person who—

    (a)   contravenes section 3(2), 3A or 4(1)(c) of this Act, or

    (b)   does anything which, by virtue of section 3(3) of this Act, cannot be authorised by a licence,

is guilty of an offence and liable on conviction on indictment to imprisonment for a term not exceeding ten years or a fine or both.

    (2)   A person who—

    (a)   contravenes section 3(1) of this Act, otherwise than by doing something which, by virtue of section 3(3) of this Act, cannot be authorised by a licence,

    (b)   keeps or uses any gametes in contravention of section 4(1)(a) or (b) of this Act,

    (c)   contravenes section 4(3) of this Act, or

    (d)   fails to comply with any directions given by virtue of section 24(7)(a) of this Act,

is guilty of an offence.

HUMAN ORGAN TRANSPLANTS ACT 1989

1. Prohibition of commercial dealings in human organs

    (1)   A person is guilty of an offence if in Great Britain he—

(a) makes or receives any payment for the supply of, or for an offer to supply, an organ which has been or is to be removed from a dead or living person and is intended to be transplanted into another person whether in Great Britain or elsewhere;

(b) seeks to find a person willing to supply for payment such an organ as is mentioned in paragraph (a) above or offers to supply such an organ for payment;

(c) initiates or negotiates any arrangement involving the making of any payment for the supply of, or for an offer to supply, such an organ; or

(d) takes part in the management or control of a body of persons corporate or unincorporate whose activities consist of or include the initiation or negotiation of such arrangements.

(2) Without prejudice to paragraph (b) of subsection (1) above, a person is guilty of an offence if he causes to be published or distributed, or knowingly publishes or distributes, in Great Britain an advertisement—

(a) inviting persons to supply for payment any such organs as are mentioned in paragraph (a) of that subsection or offering to supply any such organs for payment; or

(b) indicating that the advertiser is willing to initiate or negotiate any such arrangement as is mentioned in paragraph (c) of that subsection.

(3) In this section 'payment' means payment in money or money's worth but does not include any payment for defraying or reimbursing—

(a) the cost of removing, transporting or preserving the organ to be supplied; or

(b) any expenses or loss of earnings incurred by a person so far as reasonably and directly attributable to his supplying an organ from his body.

(4) In this section 'advertisement' includes any form of advertising whether to the public generally, to any section of the public or individually to selected persons.

(5) A person guilty of an offence under subsection (1) above is liable on summary conviction to imprisonment for a term not exceeding three months or a fine not exceeding level 5 on the standard scale or both; and a person guilty of an offence under subsection (2) above is liable on summary conviction to a fine not exceeding level 5 on that scale.

2. Restriction on transplants between persons not genetically related

(1) Subject to subsection (3) below, a person is guilty of an offence if in Great Britain he—

(a) removes from a living person an organ intended to be transplanted into another person; or

(b) transplants an organ removed from a living person into another person, unless the person into whom the organ is to be or, as the case may be, is transplanted is genetically related to the person from whom the organ is removed.

(2) For the purposes of this section a person is genetically related to—

(a) his natural parents and children;

(b) his brothers and sisters of the whole or half blood;

(c) the brothers and sisters of the whole or half blood of either of his natural parents; and

(d) the natural children of his brothers and sisters of the whole or half blood or of the brothers and sisters of the whole or half blood of either of his natural parents; but persons shall not in any particular case be treated as related in any of those ways unless the fact of the relationship has been established by such means as are specified by regulations made by the Secretary of State.

(3) The Secretary of State may by regulations provide that the prohibition in subsection (1) above shall not apply in cases where—

(a) such authority as is specified in or constituted by the regulations is satisfied—

(i)   that no payment has been or is to be made in contravention of section 1 above; and
(ii)   that such other conditions as are specified in the regulations are satisfied; and
(b)   such other requirements as may be specified in the regulations are complied with.

4.   Offences by bodies corporate

(1)   Where an offence under this Act committed by a body corporate is proved to have been committed with the consent or connivance of, or to be attributable to any neglect on the part of, any director, manager, secretary or other similar officer of the body corporate or any person who was purporting to act in any such capacity, he as well as the body corporate is guilty of the offence and is liable to be proceeded against and punished accordingly.

(2)   Where the affairs of a body corporate are managed by its members, subsection (1) above shall apply to the acts and defaults of a member in connection with his functions of management as if he were a director of the body corporate.

7.   Interpretation

(2)   In this Act 'organ' means any part of a human body consisting of a structured arrangement of tissues which, if wholly removed, cannot be replicated by the body.

(d)   SEXUAL ACTS

SEXUAL OFFENCES ACT 1956

10.   Incest by a man

(1)   It is an offence for a man to have sexual intercourse with a woman whom he knows to be his grand-daughter, daughter, sister or mother.

(2)   In the foregoing subsection 'sister' includes half-sister, and for the purposes of that subsection any expression importing a relationship between two people shall be taken to apply notwithstanding that the relationship is not traced through lawful wedlock.

11.   Incest by a woman

(1)   It is an offence for a woman of the age of sixteen or over to permit a man whom she knows to be her grandfather, father, brother or son to have sexual intercourse with her by her consent.

(2)   In the foregoing subsection 'brother' includes half-brother, and for the purposes of the subsection any expression importing a relationship between two people shall be taken to apply notwithstanding that the relationship is not traced through lawful wedlock.

12.   Buggery

(1)   It is felony for a person to commit buggery with another person otherwise than in the circumstances described in subsection 1A below or with an animal.

(1A)   The circumstances referred to in subsection (1) are that the act of buggery takes place in private and both parties have attained the age of eighteen.

(1B)   An act of buggery by one man with another shall not be treated as taking place in private if it takes place—
(a)   when more than two persons take part or are present; or
(b)   in a lavatory to which the public have or are permitted to have access, whether on payment or otherwise.

(1C)   In any proceedings against a person for buggery with another person it shall be for the prosecutor to prove that the act of buggery took place otherwise than in private or that one of the parties to it had not attained the age of eighteen.

13. Indecency between men

It is an offence for a man to commit an act of gross indecency with another man, whether in public or private, or to be a party to the commission by a man of an act of gross indecency with another man, or to procure the commission by a man of an act of gross indecency with another man.

SEXUAL OFFENCES ACT 1993

1. Abolition of presumption of sexual incapacity
[See page 28]

SEXUAL OFFENCES ACT 1967

1. Amendment of law relating to homosexual acts in private

(1)   Notwithstanding any statutory or common law provision, a homosexual act in private shall not be an offence provided that the parties consent thereto and have attained the age of eighteen years.

(2)   An act which would otherwise be treated for the purposes of this Act as being done in private shall not be so treated if done—

(a)   when more than two persons take part or are present; or

(b)   in a lavatory to which the public have or are permitted to have access, whether on payment or otherwise.

(3)   A man who is suffering from severe mental handicap cannot in law give any consent which, by virtue of subsection (1) of this section, would prevent a homosexual act from being an offence, but a person shall not be convicted, on account of the incapacity of such a man to consent, of an offence consisting of such an act if he proves that he did not know and had no reason to suspect that man to be suffering from severe mental handicap.

(4)   Section 128 of the Mental Health Act 1959 (prohibition on men on the staff of a hospital, or otherwise having responsibility for mental patients, having sexual intercourse with women patients) shall have effect as if any reference therein to having unlawful sexual intercourse with a woman included a reference to committing buggery or an act of gross indecency with another man.

(6)   It is hereby declared that where in any proceedings it is charged that a homosexual act is an offence the prosecutor shall have the burden of proving that the act was done otherwise than in private or otherwise than with the consent of the parties or that any of the parties had not attained the age of eighteen years.

(7)   For the purposes of this section a man shall be treated as doing a homosexual act if, and only if, he commits buggery with another man or commits an act of gross indecency with another man or is a party to the commission by a man of such an act.

4. Procuring others to commit homosexual acts

(1)   A man who procures another man to commit with a third man an act of buggery which by reason of section 1 of this Act is not an offence shall be liable on conviction on indictment to imprisonment for a term not exceeding two years.

(3)   It shall not be an offence under section 13 of the Act of 1956 for a man to procure the commission by another man of an act of gross indecency with the first-mentioned man which by reason of section 1 of this Act is not an offence under the said section 13.

5. Living on earnings of male prostitution

(1)   A man or woman who knowingly lives wholly or in part on the earnings of prostitution of another man shall be liable—

(a)   on summary conviction to imprisonment for a term not exceeding six months; or

(b)   on conviction on indictment to imprisonment for a term not exceeding seven years.

6.   Premises resorted to for homosexual practices

Premises shall be treated for purposes of section 33 to 35 of the Act of 1956 as a brothel if people resort to it for the purpose of lewd homosexual practices in circumstances in which resort thereto for lewd heterosexual practices would have led to its being treated as a brothel for the purposes of those sections.

(e)   PROSTITUTION

SEXUAL OFFENCES ACT 1956

22.   Causing prostitution of women

(1)   It is an offence for a person—

(a)   to procure a woman to become, in any part of the world, a common prostitute; or

(b)   to procure a woman to leave the United Kingdom, intending her to become an inmate of or frequent a brothel elsewhere; or

(c)   to procure a woman to leave her usual place of abode in the United Kingdom, intending her to become an inmate of or frequent a brothel in any part of the world for the purposes of prostitution.

23.   Procuration of girl under twenty-one

(1)   It is an offence for a person to procure a girl under the age of twenty-one to have unlawful sexual intercourse in any part of the world with a third person.

29.   Causing or encouraging prostitution of defective

(1)   It is an offence, subject to the exception mentioned in this section, for a person to cause or encourage the prostitution in any part of the world of a woman who is a defective.

(2)   A person is not guilty of an offence under this section because he causes or encourages the prostitution of such a woman, if he does not know and has no reason to suspect her to be a defective.

30.   Man living on earnings of prostitution

(1)   It is an offence for a man knowingly to live wholly or in part on the earnings of prostitution.

(2)   For the purposes of this section a man who lives with or is habitually in the company of a prostitute, or who exercises control, direction or influence over a prostitute's movements in a way which shows he is aiding, abetting or compelling her prostitution with others, shall be presumed to be knowingly living on the earnings of prostitution, unless he proves the contrary.

31.   Woman exercising control over prostitute

It is an offence for a woman for purposes of gain to exercise control, direction or influence over a prostitute's movements in a way which shows she is aiding, abetting or compelling her prostitution.

32.   Solicitation

It is an offence for a man persistently to solicit or importune in a public place for immoral purposes.

33.   Keeping a brothel

It is an offence for a person to keep a brothel, or to manage, or act or assist in the management of, a brothel.

34. Landlord letting premises for use as brothel

It is an offence for the lessor or landlord of any premises or his agent to let the whole or part of the premises with the knowledge that it is to be used, in whole or in part, as a brothel, or where the whole or part of the premises is used as a brothel, to be wilfully a party to that use continuing.

35. Tenant permitting premises to be used as a brothel

(1) It is an offence for the tenant or occupier, or person in charge, of any premises knowingly to permit the whole or part of the premises to be used as a brothel.

(2) Where the tenant or occupier of any premises is convicted (whether under this section or, for an offence committed before the commencement of this Act, under section thirteen of the Criminal Law Amendment Act, 1885) of knowingly permitting the whole or part of the premises to be used as a brothel, the First Schedule to this Act shall apply to enlarge the rights of the lessor or landlord with respect to the assignment or determination of the lease or other contract under which the premises are held by the person convicted.

(3) Where the tenant or occupier of any premises is so convicted, or was so convicted under the said section thirteen before the commencement of this Act, and either—

(a) the lessor or landlord, after having the conviction brought to his notice, fails or failed to exercise his statutory rights in relation to the lease or contract under which the premises are or were held by the person convicted; or

(b) the lessor or landlord, after exercising his statutory rights so as to determine that lease or contract, grants or granted a new lease or enters or entered into a new contract of tenancy of the premises to, with or for the benefit of the same person, without having all reasonable provisions to prevent the recurrence of the offence inserted in the new lease or contract;

then, if subsequently an offence under this section is committed in respect of the premises during the subsistence of the lease or contract referred to in paragraph (a) of this subsection or (where paragraph (b) applies) during the subsistence of the new lease or contract, the lessor or landlord shall be deemed to be a party to that offence unless he shows that he took all reasonable steps to prevent the recurrence of the offence.

36. Tenant permitting premises to be used for prostitution

It is an offence for the tenant or occupier of any premises knowingly to permit the whole or part of the premises to be used for the purposes of habitual prostitution.

44. Meaning of 'sexual intercourse'

[See page 27]

45. Meaning of defective

[See page 28]

46. Use of words 'man', 'boy', 'woman' and 'girl'

[See page 28]

47. Proof of exceptions

[See page 28]

STREET OFFENCES ACT 1959

1. Loitering or soliciting for purposes of prostitution

(1) It shall be an offence for a common prostitute to loiter or solicit in a street or public place for the purpose of prostitution.

(2) A person guilty of an offence under this section shall be liable, on summary conviction, to a fine not exceeding level 2 on the standard scale, as defined in section

75 of the Criminal Justice Act 1982, or, for an offence committed after a previous conviction, to a fine of an amount not exceeding level 3 on that scale.

(4)   For the purposes of this section 'street' includes any bridge, road, lane, footway, subway, square, court, alley or passage, whether a thoroughfare or not, which is for the time being open to the public; and the doorways and entrances of premises adjoining and open to a street, shall be treated as forming part of the street.

SEXUAL OFFENCES ACT 1985

1.   Kerb-crawling

A man commits an offence if he solicits a woman (or different women) for the purpose of prostitution—

(a)   from a motor vehicle while it is in a street or public place; or

(b)   in a street or public place while in the immediate vicinity of a motor vehicle that he has just got out of or off,

persistently or . . . in such manner or in such circumstances as to be likely to cause annoyance to the woman (or any of the women) solicited, or nuisance to other persons in the neighbourhood.

2.   Persistent soliciting of women for the purpose of prostitution

(1)   A man commits an offence if in a street or public place he persistently solicits a woman (or different women) for the purpose of prostitution.

4.   Interpretation

(1)   Reference in this Act to a man soliciting a woman for the purpose of prostitution are references to his soliciting her for the purpose of obtaining her services as a prostitute.

(2)   The use in any provision of this Act of the word 'man' without the addition of the word 'boy' shall not prevent the provision applying to any person to whom it would have applied if both words had been used, and similarly with the words 'woman' and 'girl'.

(3)   Paragraphs (a) and (b) of section 6 of the Interpretation Act 1978 (words importing the masculine gender to include the feminine, and vice versa) do not apply to this Act.

(4)   For the purposes of this Act 'street' includes any bridge, road, lane, footway, subway, square, court, alley or passage, whether a throughfare or not, which is for the time being open to the public; and the doorways and entrances of premises abutting on a street (as hereinbefore defined), and any ground adjoining and open to a street, shall be treated as forming part of the street.

(f)   OBSCENITY AND INDECENCY

OBSCENE PUBLICATIONS ACT 1959

1.   Test of obscenity

(1)   For the purpose of this Act an article shall be deemed to be obscene if its effect or (where the article comprises two or more distinct items) the effect of any one of its items is, if taken as a whole, such as to tend to deprave and corrupt persons who are likely, having regard to all relevant circumstances, to read, see or hear the matter contained or embodied in it.

(2)   In this Act 'article' means any description of article containing or embodying matter to be read or looked at or both, and sound record, and any film or other record of a picture or pictures.

(3)   For the purposes of this Act a person publishes an article who—

(a) distributes, circulates, sells, lets on hire, gives, or lends it, or who offers it for sale or for letting on hire; or

(b) in the case of an article containing or embodying matter to be looked at or a record, shows, plays or projects it, or, where the matter is data stored electronically, transmits that data.

(4) For the purposes of this Act a person also publishes an article to the extent that any matter recorded on it is included by him in a programme included in a programme service.

(5) Where the inclusion of any matter in a programme so included would, if that matter were recorded matter, constitute the publication of an obscene article for the purposes of this Act by virtue of subsection (4) above, this Act shall have effect in relation to the inclusion of that matter in the programme as if it were recorded matter.

(6) In this section 'programme' and 'programme service' have the same meaning as in the Broadcasting Act 1990.

2. Prohibition of publication of obscene matter

(1) Subject as hereinafter provided, any person who, whether for gain or not publishes an obscene article or who has an obscene article for publication for gain (whether gain to himself or gain to another) shall be liable—

(a) on summary conviction to a fine not exceeding the prescribed sum or to imprisonment for a term not exceeding six months;

(b) on conviction on indictment to a fine or to imprisonment for a term not exceeding three years or both.

(3) A prosecution for an offence against this section shall not be commenced more than two years after the commission of the offence.

(3A) Proceedings for an offence under this section shall not be instituted except by or with the consent of the Director of Public Prosecutions in any case where the article in question is a moving picture film of a width of not less than sixteen millimetres and the relevant publication or the only other publication which followed or could reasonably have been expected to follow from the relevant publication took place or (as the case may be) was to take place in the course of a film exhibition; and in this subsection 'the relevant publication' means—

(a) in the case of any proceedings under this section for publishing an obscene article, the publication in respect of which the defendant would be charged if the proceedings were brought; and

(b) in the case of any proceedings under this section for having an obscene article for publication for gain, the publication which, if the proceedings were brought, the defendant would be alleged to have had in contemplation.

(4) A person publishing an article shall not be proceeded against for an offence at common law consisting of the publication of any matter contained or embodied in the article where it is of the essence of the offence that the matter is obscene.

(4A) Without prejudice to subsection (4) above, a person shall not be proceeded against for an offence at common law—

(a) in respect of a film exhibition or anything said or done in the course of a film exhibition, where it is of the essence of the common law offence that the exhibition or, as the case may be, what was said or done was obscene, indecent, offensive, disgusting or injurious to morality; or

(b) in respect of an agreement to give a film exhibition or to cause anything to be said or done in the course of such an exhibition where the common law offence consists of conspiring to corrupt public morals or to do any act contrary to public morals or decency.

(5) A person shall not be convicted of an offence against this section if he proves that he had not examined the article in respect of which he is charged and had no

reasonable cause to suspect that it was such that his publication of it would make him liable to be convicted of an offence against this section.

(6)   In any proceedings against a person under this section the question whether an article is obscene shall be determined without regard to any publication by another person unless it could reasonably have been expected that the publication by the other person would follow from publication by the person charged.

(7)   In this section 'film exhibition' has the same meaning as in the Cinema Act 1985.

3.   Powers of search and seizure

(1)   If a justice of the peace is satisfied by information on oath that there is reasonable ground for suspecting that, in any premises in the petty sessions area for which he acts, or on any stall or vehicle in that area, being premises or a stall or vehicle specified in the information, obscene articles are, or are from time to time kept for publication for gain, the justice may issue a warrant under his hand empowering any constable to enter (if need be by force) and search the premises, or to search the stall or vehicle, and to sieze and remove any articles found therein or thereon which the constable has reason to believe to be obscene articles and to be kept for publication for gain.

(2)   A warrant under the foregoing subsection shall, if any obscene articles are seized under the warrant, also empower the seizure and removal of any documents found in the premises or, as the case may be, on the stall or vehicle which relate to a trade or business carried on at the premises or from the stall or vehicle.

(3)   Subject to subsection (3A) of this section—

Any articles seized under subsection (1) of this section shall be brought before a justice of the peace acting for the same petty sessions area as the justice who issued the warrant, and the justice before whom the articles are brought may thereupon issue a summons to the occupier of the premises or, as the case may be, the user of the stall or vehicle to appear on a day specified in the summons before a magistrates' court for that petty sessions area to show cause why the articles or any of them should not be forfeited; and if the court is satisfied, as respects any of the articles, that at the time when they were seized they were obscene articles kept for publication for gain, the court shall order those articles to be forfeited:

Provided that if the person summoned does not appear, the court shall not make an order unless service of the summons is proved; Provided also that this subsection does not apply in relation to any article seized under subsection (1) of this section which is returned to the occupier of the premises or, as the case may be, to the user of the stall or vehicle in or on which it was found.

(3A)   Without prejudice to the duty of a court to make an order for the forfeiture of an article where section 1(4) of the Obscene Publications Act 1964 applies (order made on conviction), in a case where by virtue of subsection (3A) of section 2 of this Act proceedings under the said section 2 for having an article for publication for gain could not be initiated except by or with the consent of the Director of Public Prosecutions; no order for the forfeiture of the article shall be made under this section unless the warrant under which the article was seized was issued on an information laid by or on behalf of the Director of Public Prosecutions.

(4)   In addition to the person summoned, any other person being the owner, author or maker of any of the articles brought before the court, or any other person through whose hands they had passed before being seized, shall be entitled to appear before the court on the day specified in the summons to show cause why they should not be forfeited.

(7)   For the purposes of this section the question whether an article is obscene shall be determined on the assumption that copies of it would be published in any manner

likely having regard to the circumstances in which it was found, but in no other manner.

4. Defence of public good

(1) Subject to subsection (1A) of this section—

A person shall not be convicted of an offence against section two of this Act, and an order for forfeiture shall not be made under the foregoing section, if it is proved that publication of the article in question is justified as being for the public good on the ground that it is in the interests of science, literature, art or learning, or of other objects of general concern.

(1A) Subsection (1) of this section shall not apply where the article in question is a moving picture film or soundtrack, but—

(a) a person shall not be convicted of an offence against section 2 of this Act in relation to any such film or soundtrack, and

(b) an order for forfeiture of any such film or soundtrack shall not be made under section 3 of this Act,

if it is proved that publication of the film or soundtrack is justified as being for the public good on the grounds that it is in the interests of drama, opera, ballet or any other art, or of literature or learning.

(2) It is hereby declared that the opinion of experts as to the literary, artistic, scientific or other merits of an article may be admitted in any proceedings under this Act either to establish or to negative the said ground.

(3) In this section 'moving picture soundtrack' means any sound record designed for playing with a moving picture film, whether incorporated with the film or not.

TOWN POLICE CLAUSES ACT 1847

28. Penalty on persons committing any of the offences herein named

Every person who in any street, to the obstruction, annoyance, or danger of the residents or passengers, commits any of the following offences, shall be liable to a penalty not exceeding level 3 on the standard scale for each offence, or, in the discretion of the justice before whom he is convicted, may be committed to prison, there to remain for a period not exceeding fourteen days; and any officer appointed by virtue of this or the special Act or any constable shall take into custody, without warrant, and forthwith convey before a justice, any person who within his view commits any such offence; (that is to say,)

Every person who wilfully and indecently exposes his person;

Every person who publicly offers for sale or distribution, or exhibits to public view any profane book, paper, print, drawing, printing or representation, or sings any profane or obscene song or ballad, or uses any profane or obscene language.

INDECENT DISPLAYS (CONTROL) ACT 1981

1. Indecent displays

(1) If any indecent matter is publicly displayed the person making the display and any person causing or permitting the display to be made shall be guilty of an offence.

(2) Any matter which is displayed in or so as to be visible from any public place shall, for the purposes of this section, be deemed to be publicly displayed.

(3) In subsection (2) above, 'public place', in relation to the display of any matter, means any place to which the public have or are permitted to have access (whether on payment or otherwise) while that matter is displayed except—

(a) a place to which the public are permitted to have access only on payment which is or includes payment for that display; or

(b)   a shop or any part of a shop to which the public can only gain access by passing beyond an adequate warning notice;
but the exclusions contained in paragraphs (a) and (b) above shall only apply where persons under the age of 18 years are not permitted to enter while the display in question is continuing.

(4)   Nothing in this section applies in relation to any matter—

(a)   included by any person in a television broadcasting service or other television programme service (within the meaning of Part I of the Broadcasting Act 1990); or

(b)   included in the display of an art gallery or museum and visible only from within the gallery or museum; or

(c)   displayed by or with the authority of, and visible only from within a building occupied by, the Crown or any local authority; or

(d)   included in a performance of a play (within the meaning of the Theatres Act 1968); or

(e)   included in a film exhibition as defined in the Cinema Act 1985—

(i)   given in a place which as regards that exhibition is required to be licensed under section 1 of that Act or by virtue only of section 5, 7 or 8 of that Act, is not required to be so licensed; or

(ii)   which is an exempted exhibition to which section 6 of that Act applies given by an exempted organisation as defined in subsection (6) of that section.

(5)   In this section 'matter' includes anything capable of being displayed, except that it does not include an actual human body or any part thereof; and in determining for the purpose of this section whether any displayed matter is indecent—

(a)   there shall be disregarded any part of that matter which is not exposed to view; and

(b)   account may be taken of the effect of juxtaposing one thing with another.

(6)   A warning notice shall not be adequate for the purposes of this section unless it complies with the following requirements—

(a)   The warning notice must contain the following words, and no others—

'WARNING

Persons passing beyond this notice will find material on display which they may consider indecent. No admittance to persons under 18 years of age.'

(b)   The word 'WARNING' must appear as a heading.

(c)   No pictures or other matter shall appear on the notice.

(d)   The notice must be so situated that no one could reasonably gain access to the shop or part of the shop in question without being aware of the notice and it must be easily legible by any person gaining such access.

POST OFFICE ACT 1953

11.   Prohibition on sending by post of certain articles

(1)   A person shall not send or attempt to send or procure to be sent a postal packet which—

(a)   save as the Post Office may either generally or in any particular case allow, encloses any explosive, dangerous, noxious or deleterious substance, any filth, any sharp instrument not properly protected, any noxious living creature, or any creature, article or thing whatsoever which is likely to injure either other postal packets in course of conveyance or a person engaged in the business of the Post Office; or

(b)   encloses any indecent or obscene print, painting, photograph, lithograph, engraving, cinematograph film, book, card or written communication, or any indecent or obscene article whether similar to the above or not; or

(c) has on the packet, or on the cover thereof, any words, marks or designs which are grossly offensive or of an indecent or obscene character.

(2) If any person acts in contravention of the foregoing subsection, he shall be liable on summary conviction to a fine not exceeding the prescribed sum or on conviction on indictment to imprisonment for a term not exceeding twelve months.

CHILDREN AND YOUNG PERSONS (HARMFUL PUBLICATIONS) ACT 1955

[See pages 52]

UNSOLICITED GOODS AND SERVICES ACT 1971

4. Unsolicited publications

(1) A person shall be guilty of an offence if he sends or causes to be sent to another person any book, magazine or leaflet (or advertising material for any such publication) which he knows or ought reasonably to know is unsolicited and which describes or illustrates human sexual techniques.

(3) A prosecution for an offence under this section shall not in England and Wales be instituted except by, or with the consent of, the Director of Public Prosecutions.

6. Interpretation

(1) In this Act, unless the context or subject matter otherwise requires,—
'send' includes deliver and 'sender' shall be construed accordingly;
'unsolicited' means, in relation to goods sent to any person, that they are sent without any prior request made by him or on his behalf.

THEATRES ACT 1968

2. Prohibition of presentation of obscene performances of plays

(1) For the purposes of this section a performance of a play shall be deemed to be obscene if, taken as a whole, its effect was such as to tend to deprave and corrupt persons who were likely, having regard to all relevant circumstances, to attend it.

(2) Subject to sections 3 and 7 of this Act, if an obscene performance of a play is given, whether in public or private, any person who (whether for gain or not) presented or directed that performance shall be liable—
(a) on summary conviction, to a fine not exceeding the prescribed sum or to imprisonment for a term not exceeding six months;
(b) on conviction on indictment, to a fine or to imprisonment for a term not exceeding three years, or both.

(4) No person shall be proceeded against in respect of a performance of a play or anything said or done in the course of such a performance—
(a) for an offence at common law where it is of the essence of the offence that the performance or, as the case may be, what was said or done was obscene, indecent, offensive, disgusting or injurious to morality; . . .
and no person shall be proceeded against for an offence at common law of conspiring to corrupt, or to do any act contrary to public morals or decency, in respect of an agreement to present or give a performance of a play, or to cause anything to be said or done in the course of such a performance.

3. Defence of public good

(1) A person shall not be convicted of an offence under section 2 of this Act if it is proved that the giving of the performance in question was justified as being for the

public good on the ground that it was in the interests of drama, opera, ballet, or any other art, or of literature or learning.

(2)   It is hereby declared that the opinion of experts as to the artistic, literary or other merits of a performance of a play may be admitted in any proceedings for an offence under section 2 of this Act either to establish or negative the said ground.

6.   Provocation of breach of peace by means of public performance of a play

(1)   Subject to section 7 of this Act, if there is given a public performance of a play involving the use of threatening, abusive or insulting words or behaviour, any person who (whether for gain or not) presented or directed that performance shall be guilty of an offence under this section if—

(a)   he did so with intent to provoke a breach of the peace; or

(b)   the performance, taken as a whole, was likely to occasion a breach of the peace.

7.   Exceptions for performances given in certain circumstances

(1)   Nothing in sections 2 to 4 of this Act shall apply in relation to a performance of a play given on a domestic occasion in a private dwelling.

(2)   Nothing in sections 2 to 6 of this Act shall apply in relation to a performance of play given solely or primarily for one or more of the following purposes, that is to say—

(a)   rehearsal; or

(b)   to enable—

(i)   a record or cinematograph film to be made from or by means of the performance; or

(ii)   the performance to be broadcast; or

(iii)   the performance to be included in a programme service (within the meaning of the Broadcasting Act 1990) other than a sound or television broadcasting service;

but in any proceedings for an offence under section 2, 5 or 6 of this Act alleged to have been committed in respect of a performance of a play or an offence at common law alleged to have been committed in England and Wales by the publication of defamatory matter in the course of a performance of a play, if it is proved that the performance was attended by persons other than persons directly connected with the giving of the performance or the doing in relation thereto of any of the things mentioned in paragraph (b) above, the performance shall be taken not to have been given solely or primarily for one or more of the said purposes unless the contrary is shown.

18.   Interpretation

(1)   In this Act—

'Play' means—

(a)   any dramatic piece, whether involving improvisation or not, which is given wholly or in part by one or more persons actually present and performing and in which the whole or a major proportion of what is done by the person or persons performing, whether by way of speech, singing or acting, involves the playing of a role; and

(b)   any ballet given wholly or in part by one or more persons actually present and performing, whether or not it falls within paragraph (a) of this definition;

'premises' includes any place;

'public performance' includes any performance in a public place within the meaning of the Public Order Act 1936, any performance which is not open for the public but which is promoted for private gain; and any performance which the public or any section thereof are permitted to attend, whether on payment or otherwise; . . .

(2)   For the purposes of this Act—

(a)   a person shall not be treated as presenting a performance of a play by reason only of his taking part therein as a performer;

(b)   a person taking part as a performer in a performance of a play directed by another person shall be treated as a person who directed the performance if without reasonable excuse he performs otherwise than in accordance with that person's direction; and

(c)   a person shall be taken to have directed a performance of a play given under his direction notwithstanding that he was not present during the performance;

and a person shall not be treated as aiding or abetting the commission of an offence under section 2 or 6 of this Act in respect of a performance of a play by reason only of his taking part in that performance as a performer.

VIDEO RECORDINGS ACT 1984

1.   Interpretation of terms

(1)   The provisions of this section shall have effect for the interpretation of terms used in this Act.

(2)   'Video work' means any series of visual images (with or without sound)—

(a)   produced electronically by the use of information contained on any disc, magnetic tape or any other device capable of storing data electronically, and

(b)   shown as a moving picture.

(3)   'Video recording' means any disc, magnetic tape or any other device capable of storing data electronically containing information by the use of which the whole or a part of a video work may be produced.

(4)   'Supply' means supply in any manner, whether or not for reward, and, therefore, includes supply by way of sale, letting on hire, exchange or loan; and references to a supply are to be interpreted accordingly.

2.   Exempted works

(1)   Subject to subsection (2) below, a video work is for the purposes of this Act an exempted work if, taken as a whole—

(a)   it is designed to inform, educate or instruct;

(b)   it is concerned with sport, religion or music; or

(c)   it is a video game.

(2)   A video work is not an exempted work for those purposes if, to any significant extent, it depicts—

(a)   a human sexual activity or acts of force or restraint associated with such activity;

(b)   mutilation or torture of, or other acts of gross violence towards, humans or animals;

(c)   human genital organs or human urinary or excretory functions;

or is designed to any significant extent to stimulate or encourage anything falling within paragraph (a) or, in the case of anything falling within paragraph (b), is designed to any extent to do so.

3.   Exempted supplies

(1)   The provisions of this section apply to determine whether or not a supply of a video recording is an exempted supply for the purposes of this Act.

(2)   The supply of a video recording by any person is an exempted supply if it is neither—

(a)   a supply for reward, nor

(b)   a supply in the course of furtherance of a business.

(3)   Where on any premises facilities are provided in the course or furtherance of a business for supplying video recordings, the supply by any person of a video

recording on those premises is to be treated for the purposes of subsection (2) above as a supply in the course or furtherance of a business.

(4) Where a person (in this subsection referred to as the 'original supplier') supplies a video recording to a person who, in the course of a business, makes video works or supplies video recordings, the supply is an exempted supply—

(a) if it is not made with a view to any further supply of that recording, or

(b) if it is so made, but is not made with a view to the eventual supply of that recording to the public or is made with a view to the eventual supply of that recording to the original supplier.

For the purposes of this subsection, any supply is a supply to the public unless it is—

(i) a supply to a person who, in the course of a business, makes video works or supplies video recordings,

(ii) an exempted supply by virtue of subsection (2) above or subsections (5) to (10) below, or

(iii) a supply outside the United Kingdom.

(5) Where a video work—

(a) is designed to provide a record of an event or occasion for those who took part in the event or occasion or are connected with those who did so,

(b) does not, to any significant extent, depict anything falling within paragraph (a), (b) or (c) of section 2(2) of this Act, and

(c) is not designed to any significant extent to stimulate or encourage anything falling within paragraph (a) of that subsection or, in the case of anything falling within paragraph (b) of that subsection, is not designed to any extent to do so,

the supply of a video recording containing only that work to a person who took part in the event or occasion or is connected with someone who did so is an exempted supply.

(6) The supply of a video recording for the purpose only of the exhibition of any video work contained in the recording in premises other than a dwelling-house—

(a) being premises mentioned in subsection (7) below, or

(b) being an exhibition which in England and Wales or Scotland would be a film exhibition to which section 6 of the Cinemas Act 1985 applies (film exhibition to which public not admitted or are admitted without payment), or in Northern Ireland would be an exempted exhibition within the meaning of section 5 of the Cinematograph Act (Northern Ireland) 1959 (similar provision for Northern Ireland),

is an exempted supply.

(7) The premises referred to in subsection (6) above are—

(a) premises in respect of which a licence under Article 3 of the Cinemas (Northern Ireland) Order 1991 is in force,

(b) premises falling within Article 9 of that Order (premises used only occasionally and exceptionally for film exhibitions), or

(c) premises falling within Article 10 of that Order (building or structure of a movable character) in respect of which such a licence as is mentioned in paragraph (1)(a) of that Article has been granted.

(8) The supply of a video recording with a view only to its use for or in connection with—

(a) a programme service (within the meaning of the Broadcasting Act 1990)

is an exempted supply.

(9) The supply of a video recording for the purpose only of submitting a video work contained in the recording for the issue of a classification certificate or otherwise only for purposes of arrangements made by the designated authority is an exempted supply.

(10) The supply of a video recording with a view only to its use—

(a) in training for or carrying on any medical or related occupation,

(b)   for the purpose of—
(i)   services provided in pursuance of the National Health Service Act 1977 or the National Health Service (Scotland) Act 1978, or
(ii)   such of the services provided in pursuance of the Health and Personal Social Services (Northern Ireland) Order 1972 as are health services (within the meaning of that Order), or
(c)   in training persons employed in the course of services falling within paragraph (b) above,
is an exempted supply.

(11)   For the purposes of subsection (10) above, an occupation is a medical or related occupation if, to carry on the occupation, a person is required to be registered under the Professions Supplementary to Medicine Act 1960, the Nurses, Midwives and Health Visitors Act 1979 or the Medical Act 1983.

(12)   The supply of a video recording otherwise than for reward, being a supply made for the purpose only of supplying it to a person who previously made an exempted supply of the recording, is also an exempted supply.

7.   Classification certificates

(1)   In this Act 'classification certificate' means a certificate—
(a)   issued in respect of a video work in pursuance of arrangements made by the designated authority; and
(b)   satisfying the requirements of subsection (2) below.

(2)   Those requirements are that the certificate must contain the title assigned to the video work in accordance with section 4(1)(ia) of this Act and—
(a)   a statement that the video work concerned is suitable for general viewing and unrestricted supply (with or without any advice as to the desirability of parental guidance with regard to the viewing of the work by young children or as to the particular suitability of the work for viewing by children); or
(b)   a statement that the video work concerned is suitable for viewing only by persons who have attained the age (not being more than eighteen years) specified in the certificate and that no video recording containing that work is to be supplied to any person who has not attained the age so specified; or
(c)   the statement mentioned in paragraph (b) above together with a statement that no video recording containing that work is to be supplied other than in a licensed sex shop.

9.   Supplying video recording of unclassified work

(1)   A person who supplies or offers to supply a video recording containing a video work in respect of which no classification certificate has been issued is guilty of an offence unless—
(a)   the supply is, or would if it took place be, an exempted supply, or
(b)   the video work is an exempted work.

(2)   It is a defence to a charge of committing an offence under this section to prove that the accused believed on reasonable grounds—
(a)   that the video work concerned or, if the video recording contained more than one work to which the charge relates, each of those works was either an exempted work or a work in respect of which a classification certificate had been issued, or
(b)   that the supply was, or would if it took place be, an exempted supply by virtue of section 3(4) or (5) of this Act.

10.   Possession of video recording of unclassified work for the purposes of supply

(1)   Where a video recording contains a video work in respect of which no classification certificate has been issued, a person who has the recording in his possession for the purpose of supplying it is guilty of an offence unless—

(a) he has it in his possession for the purpose only of a supply which, if it took place, would be an exempted supply, or

(b) the video work is an exempted work.

(2) It is a defence to a charge of committing an offence under this section to prove—

(a) that the accused believed on reasonable grounds that the video work concerned or, if the video recording contained more than one work to which the charge relates, each of those works was either an exempted work or a work in respect of which a classification certificate had been issued,

(b) that the accused had the video recording in his possession for the purpose only of a supply which he believed on reasonable grounds would, if it took place, be an exempted supply by virtue of section 3(4) or (5) of this Act, or

(c) that the accused did not intend to supply the video recording until a classification certificate had been issued in respect of the video work concerned.

11. Supplying video recording of classified work in breach of classification

(1) Where a classification certificate issued in respect of a video work states that no video recording containing that work is to be supplied to any person who has not attained the age specified in the certificate, a person who supplies or offers to supply a video recording containing that work to a person who has not attained the age so specified is guilty of an offence unless the supply is, or would if it took place be, an exempted supply.

(2) It is a defence to a charge of committing an offence under this section to prove—

(a) that the accused neither knew nor had reasonable grounds to believe that the classification certificate contained the statement concerned,

(b) that the accused neither knew nor had reasonable grounds to believe that the person concerned had not attained that age, or

(c) that the accused believed on reasonable grounds that the supply was, or would if it took place be, an exempted supply by virtue of section 3(4) or (5) of this Act.

12. Certain video recordings only to be supplied in licensed sex shops

(1) Where a classification certificate issued in respect of a video work states that no video recording containing that work is to be supplied other than in a licensed sex shop, a person who at any place other than in a sex shop for which a licence is in force under the relevant enactment—

(a) supplies a video recording containing the work, or

(b) offers to do so,

is guilty of an offence unless the supply is, or would if it took place be, an exempted supply.

(2) It is a defence to a charge of committing an offence under subsection (1) above to prove—

(a) that the accused neither knew nor had reasonable grounds to believe that the classification certificate contained the statement concerned,

(b) that the accused believed on reasonable grounds that the place concerned was a sex shop for which a licence was in force under the relevant enactment, or

(c) that the accused believed on reasonable grounds that the supply was, or would if it took place be, an exempted supply by virtue of section 3(4) of this Act or subsection (6) below.

(3) Where a classification certificate issued in respect of a video work states that no video recording containing that work is to be supplied other than in a licensed sex shop, a person who has a video recording containing the work in his possession for the purpose of supplying it at any place other than in such a sex shop is guilty of an offence, unless he has it in his possession for the purpose only of a supply which, if it took place, would be an exempted supply.

(4)   It is a defence to a charge of committing an offence under subsection (3) above to prove—

(a)   that the accused neither knew nor had reasonable grounds to believe that the classification certificate contained the statement concerned,

(b)   that the accused believed on reasonable grounds that the place concerned was a sex shop for which a licence was in force under the relevant enactment, or

(c)   that the accused had the video recording in his possession for the purpose only of a supply which he believed on reasonable grounds would, if it took place, be an exempted supply by virtue of section 3(4) of this Act or subsection (6) below.

(5)   In this section 'relevant enactment' means Schedule 3 to the Local Government (Miscellaneous Provisions) Act 1982 . . . and 'sex shop' has the same meaning as in the relevant enactment.

(6)   For the purposes of this section, where a classification certificate issued in respect of a video work states that no video recording containing that work is to be supplied other than in a licensed sex shop, the supply of a video recording containing that work—

(a)   to a person who, in the course of a business, makes video works or supplies video recordings, and

(b)   with a view to its eventual supply in sex shops, being sex shops for which licences are in force under the relevant enactment,

is an exempted supply.

14A.   General defence to offences under this Act

Without prejudice to any defence specified in the preceding provisions of this Act in relation to a particular offence, it is a defence to a charge of committing any offence under this Act to prove—

(a)   that the commission of the offence was due to the act or default of a person other than the accused, and

(b)   that the accused took all reasonable precautions and exercised all due diligence to avoid the commission of the offence by any person under his control.

16.   Offences by bodies corporate

(1)   Where an offence under this Act committed by a body corporate is proved to have been committed with the consent or connivance of, or to be attributable to any neglect on the part of, any director, manager, secretary or other similar officer of the body corporate, or any person who was purporting to act in any such capacity, he as well as the body corporate shall be guilty of the offence and shall be liable to be proceeded against and punished accordingly.

(2)   Where the affairs of a body corporate are managed by its members, subsection (1) above shall apply in relation to the acts and defaults of a member in connection with his functions of management as if he were a director of the body corporate.

22.   Other interpretation

(1)   In this Act—
'business', except in section 3(4), includes any activity carried on by a club; and 'premises' includes any vehicle, vessel or stall.

(2)   For the purposes of this Act, a video recording contains a video work if it contains information by the use of which the whole or a part of the work may be produced; but where a video work includes any extract from another video work, that extract is not to be regarded for the purposes of this subsection as a part of that other work.

(3)   Where any alteration is made to a video work in respect of which a classification certificate has been issued, the classification certificate is not to be treated for the purposes of this Act as issued in respect of the altered work.

In this subsection, 'alteration' includes addition.

(g) DRUNKENNESS

METROPOLITAN POLICE ACT 1839

44. Penalty on keepers of refreshment houses permitting drunkenness, disorderly conduct, or gaming, etc., therein

. . . Every person who shall have or keep any house, shop, room, or place of public resort within the metropolitan police district, wherein provisions, liquors, or refreshments of any kind shall be sold or consumed, (whether the same shall be kept or retailed therein or procured elsewhere,) and who shall wilfully or knowingly permit drunkenness or other disorderly conduct in such house, shop, room, or place, or knowingly suffer any unlawful games or any gaming whatsoever therein, or knowingly permit or suffer prostitutes or persons of notoriously bad character to meet together and remain therein, shall for every such offence be liable to a penalty of not more than level 1 on the standard scale.

LICENSING ACT 1872

12. Penalty on persons found drunk

Every person found drunk in any highway or other public place, whether a building or not, or on any licensed premises, shall be liable to a penalty not exceeding level 1 on the standard scale.

Every person who is drunk while in charge on any highway or other public place of any carriage, horse, cattle, or steam engine, or who is drunk when in possession of any loaded firearms, may be apprehended, and shall be liable to a penalty not exceeding level 1 on the standard scale or in the discretion of the court to imprisonment . . . for any term not exceeding one month.

LICENSING ACT 1902

8. Interpretation of 'public place'

[See page 43]

CRIMINAL JUSTICE ACT 1967

91. Drunkenness in a public place

(1) Any person who in any public place is guilty, while drunk, of disorderly behaviour may be arrested without warrant by any person and shall be liable on summary conviction to a fine not exceeding level 3 on the standard scale.

(4) In this section 'public place' includes any highway and any other premises or place to which at the material time the public have or are permitted to have access, whether on payment or otherwise.

SPORTING EVENTS (CONTROL OF ALCOHOL ETC.) ACT 1985

1. Offences in connection with alcohol on coaches and trains

(1) This section applies to a vehicle which—

(a) is a public service vehicle or railway passenger vehicle, and

(b) is being used for the principal purpose of carrying passengers for the whole or part of a journey to or from a designated sporting event.

(2) A person who knowingly causes or permits intoxicating liquor to be carried on a vehicle to which this section applies is guilty of an offence—

(a) if the vehicle is a public service vehicle and he is the operator of the vehicle or the servant or agent of the operator, or

(b) if the vehicle is a hired vehicle and he is the person to whom it is hired or the servant or agent of that person.

(3) A person who has intoxicating liquor in his possession while on a vehicle to which this section applies is guilty of an offence.

(4) A person who is drunk on a vehicle to which this section applies is guilty of an offence.

(5) In this section 'public service vehicle' and 'operator' have the same meaning as in the Public Passenger Vehicles Act 1981.

2. Offences in connection with alcohol, containers etc., at sports grounds

(1) A person who has intoxicating liquor or an article to which this section applies in his possession—

(a) at any time during the period of a designated sporting event when he is in any area of a designated sports ground from which the event may be directly viewed, or

(b) while entering or trying to enter a designated sports ground at any time during the period of a designated sporting event at that ground,

is guilty of an offence.

(2) A person who is drunk in a designated sports ground at any time during the period of a designated sporting event at that ground or is drunk while entering or trying to enter such a ground at any time during the period of a designated sporting event at that ground is guilty of an offence.

(3) This section applies to any article capable of causing injury to a person struck by it, being—

(a) a bottle, can or other portable container (including such an article when crushed or broken) which—

(i) is for holding any drink, and

(ii) is of a kind which, when empty, is normally discarded or returned to, or left to be recovered by, the supplier, or

(b) part of an article falling within paragraph (a) above;

but does not apply to anything that is for holding any medicinal product (within the meaning of the Medicines Act 1968).

9. Interpretation

(1) The following provisions shall have effect for the interpretation of this Act.

(2) 'Designated sports ground' means any place—

(a) used (wholly or partly) for sporting events where accommodation is provided for spectators, and

(b) for the time being designated, or of a class designated, by order made by the Secretary of State;

and an order under this subsection may include provision for determining for the purposes of this Act the outer limit of any designated sports ground.

(3) 'Designated sporting event'—

(a) means a sporting event or proposed sporting event for the time being designated, or of a class designated, by order made by the Secretary of State, and

(b) includes a designated sporting event within the meaning of Part V of the Criminal Justice (Scotland) Act 1980;

and an order under this subsection may apply to events or proposed events outside Great Britain as well as those in England and Wales.

(4) The period of a designated sporting event is the period beginning two hours before the start of the event or (if earlier) two hours before the time at which it is advertised to start and ending one hour after the end of the event, but—

(a) where an event advertised to start at a particular time on a particular day is postponed to a later day, the period includes the period in the day on which it is advertised to take place beginning two hours before and ending one hour after that time, and

(b)   where an event advertised to start at a particular time on a particular day does not take place, the period is the period referred to in paragraph (a) above.

(6)   This Act does not apply to any sporting event or proposed sporting event—

(a)   where all competitors are to take part otherwise than for reward, and

(b)   to which all spectators are to be admitted free of charge.

(h) NOISE

CRIMINAL JUSTICE AND PUBLIC ORDER ACT 1994

63. Raves

(1)   This section applies to a gathering on land in the open air of 100 or more persons (whether or not trespassers) at which amplified music is played during the night (with or without intermissions) and is such as, by reason of its loudness and duration and the time at which it is played, is likely to cause serious distress to the inhabitants of the locality; and for this purpose—

(a)   such a gathering continues during intermissions in the music and, where the gathering extends over several days, throughout the period during which amplified music is played at night (with or without intermissions); and

(b)   "music" includes sounds wholly or predominantly characterised by the emission of a succession of repetitive beats.

(2)   If, as respects any land in the open air, a police officer of at least the rank of superintendent reasonably believes that—

(a)   two or more persons are making preparations for the holding there of a gathering to which this section applies,

(b)   ten or more persons are waiting for such a gathering to begin there, or

(c)   ten or more persons are attending such a gathering which is in progress,
he may give a direction that those persons and any other persons who come to prepare or wait for or to attend the gathering are to leave the land and remove any vehicles or other property which they have with them on the land.

(3)   A direction under subsection (2) above, if not communicated to the persons referred to in subsection (2) by the police officer giving the direction, may be communicated to them by any constable at the scene.

(4)   Persons shall be treated as having had a direction under subsection (2) above communicated to them if reasonable steps have been taken to bring it to their attention.

(5)   A direction under subsection (2) above does not apply to an exempt person.

(6)   If a person knowing that a direction has been given which applies to him—

(a)   fails to leave the land as soon as reasonably practicable, or

(b)   having left again enters the land within the period of 7 days beginning with the day on which the direction was given,
he commits an offence and is liable on summary conviction to imprisonment for a term not exceeding three months or a fine not exceeding level 4 on the standard scale, or both.

(7)   In proceedings for an offence under this section it is a defence for the accused to show that he had a reasonable excuse for failing to leave the land as soon as reasonably practicable or, as the case may be, for again entering the land.

(10)   In this section—
"exempt peson", in relation to land (or any gathering on land), means the occupier, any member of his family and any employee or agent of his and any person whose home is situated on the land;
"land in the open air" includes a place partly open to the air;
"occupier", "trespasser" and "vehicle" have the same meaning as in section 61.

10 INTERFERENCE WITH THE ADMINISTRATION OF JUSTICE OR THE POLICE

OFFENCES AGAINST THE PERSON ACT 1861

18. Wounding or causing grievous bodily harm with intent to resist apprehension
[See page 18]

38. Assault with intent to resist arrest
[See page 24]

PERJURY ACT 1911

1. Perjury

(1) If any person lawfully sworn as a witness or as an interpreter in a judicial proceeding wilfully makes a statement material in that proceeding, which he knows to be false or does not believe to be true, he shall be guilty of perjury, and shall, on conviction thereof on indictment, be liable to penal servitude for a term not exceeding seven years, or to imprisonment for a term not exceeding two years, or to a fine or to both such penal servitude or imprisonment and fine.

(2) The expression 'judicial proceeding' includes a proceeding before any court, tribunal, or person having by law power to hear, receive, and examine evidence on oath.

(3) Where a statement made for the purposes of a judicial proceeding is not made before the tribunal itself, but is made on oath before a person authorised by law to administer an oath to the person who makes the statement, and to record or authenticate the statement, it shall, for the purposes of this section, be treated as having been made in a judicial proceeding.

(4) A statement made by a person lawfully sworn in England for the purposes of a judical proceeding—

    (a) in another part of Her Majesty's dominions; or

    (b) in a British tribunal lawfully constituted in any place by sea or land outside Her Majesty's dominions; or

    (c) in a tribunal of any foreign state,

shall, for the purposes of this section, be treated as a statement made in a judicial proceeding in England.

(5) Where for the purposes of a judicial proceeding in England, a person is lawfully sworn under the authority of an Act of Parliament—

    (a) in any other part of Her Majesty's dominions; or

(b)   before a British tribunal or a British officer in a foreign country, or within the jurisdiction of the Admiralty of England;

a statement made by such person so sworn as aforesaid (unless the Act of Parliament under which it was made otherwise specifically provides) shall be treated for the purposes of this section as having been made in the judicial proceeding in England for the purposes whereof it was made.

(6)   The question whether a statement on which perjury is assigned was material is a question of law to be determined by the court of trial.

1A.   False unsworn statement under Evidence (Proceedings in other Jurisdictions) Act 1975

If any person in giving any testimony (either orally or in writing) otherwise than on oath, where required to do so by an order under section 2 of the Evidence (Proceedings in other Jurisdictions) Act 1975, makes a statement—

(a)   which he knows to be false in a material particular, or

(b)   which is false in a material particular and which he does not believe to be true,

he shall be guilty of an offence and shall be liable on conviction on indictment to imprisonment for a term not exceeding two years or a fine or both.

2.   False statements on oath made otherwise than in a judicial proceeding

If any person—

(1)   being required or authorised by law to make any statement or oath for any purpose, and being lawfully sworn (otherwise than in a judicial proceeding) wilfully makes a statement which is material for that purpose and which he knows to be false or does not believe to be true; or

(2)   wilfully uses any false affidavit for the purposes of the Bills of Sale Act, 1878, as amended by any subsequent enactment, he shall be guilty of a misdemeanour, and, on conviction thereof on indictment, shall be liable to penal servitude for a term not exceeding seven years or to imprisonment for a term not exceeding two years, or to a fine or to both such penal servitude or imprisonment and fine.

4.   False statements, etc., as to births or deaths

(1)   If any person—

(a)   wilfully makes any false answer to any question put to him by any registrar of births or deaths relating to the particulars required to be registered concerning any birth or death, or, wilfully gives to any such registrar any false information concerning any birth or death or the cause of any death; or

(b)   wilfully makes any false certificate or declaration under or for the purposes of any Act relating to the registration of births or deaths, or, knowing any such certificate or declaration to be false, uses the same as true or gives or sends the same as true to any person; or

(c)   wilfully makes, gives or uses any false statement or declaration as to a child born alive as having been still-born, or as to the body of a deceased person or a still-born child in any coffin, or falsely pretends that any child born alive was still-born; or

(d)   makes any false statement with intent to have the same inserted in any register of births or deaths,

he shall be guilty of a misdemeanour and shall be liable—

(i)   on conviction thereof on indictment, to penal servitude for a term not exceeding seven years, or to imprisonment for a term not exceeding two years, or to a fine instead of either of the said punishments; and

(ii)   on summary conviction thereof, to a penalty not exceeding the prescribed sum.

5. False statutory declarations and other false statements without oath

If any person knowingly and wilfully makes (otherwise than on oath) a statement false in a material particular, and the statement is made—

(a)   in a statutory declaration; or

(b)   in an abstract, account, balance sheet, book, certificate, declaration, entry, estimate, inventory, notice, report, return, or other document which he is authorised or required to make, attest, or verify, by any public general Act of Parliament for the time being in force; or

(c)   in any oral declaration or oral answer which he is required to make by, under, or in pursuance of any public general Act of Parliament for the time being in force, he shall be guilty of a misdemeanour and shall be liable on conviction thereof on indictment to imprisonment for any term not exceeding two years, or to a fine or to both such imprisonment and fine.

6. False declarations, etc., to obtain registration, etc., for carrying on a vocation

If any person—

(a)   procures or attempts to procure himself to be registered on any register or roll kept under or in pursuance of any public general Act of Parliament for the time being in force of persons qualified by law to practise any vocation or calling; or

(b)   procures or attempts to procure a certificate of the registration of any person on any such register or roll as aforesaid,

by wilfully making or producing or causing to be made or produced either verbally or in writing, any declaration, certificate, or representation which he knows to be false or fraudulent, he shall be guilty of misdemeanour and shall be liable on conviction thereof on indictment to imprisonment for any term not exceeding twelve months, or to a fine, or to both such imprisonment and fine.

7. Aiders, abettors, suborners, etc.

(1)   Every person who aids, abets, counsels, procures, or suborns another person to commit an offence against this Act shall be liable to be proceeded against, indicted, tried and punished as if he were a principal offender.

(2)   Every person who incites another person to commit an offence against this Act shall be guilty of a misdemeanour, and on conviction thereof on indictment, shall be liable to imprisonment, or to a fine, or to both such imprisonment and fine.

15. Interpretation, etc.

(1)   For the purposes of this Act, the forms and ceremonies used in administering an oath are immaterial, if the court or person before whom the oath is taken has power to administer an oath for the purpose of verifying the statement in question, and if the oath has been administered in a form and with ceremonies which the person taking the oath has accepted without objection, or has declared to be binding on him.

(a)   In this Act—

The expression 'oath' includes 'affirmation' and 'declaration', and the expression 'swear' includes 'affirm' and 'declare'; and

The expression 'statutory declaration' means a declaration made by virtue of the Statutory Declarations Act, 1835, or of any Act, Order in Council, rule or regulation applying or extending the provisions thereof.

CRIMINAL JUSTICE ACT 1967

89. False written statements tendered in evidence

(1)   If any person in a written statement tendered in evidence in criminal proceedings by virtue of section 9 of this Act or in proceedings before a court-martial by virtue

of the said section 9 or extended by section 12 above or by section 99A of the Army Act 1955 or section 99A of the Air Force Act 1955 wilfully makes a statement material in those proceedings which he knows to be false or does not believe to be true, he shall be liable on conviction on indictment to imprisonment for a term not exceeding two years or a fine or both.

(2)   The Perjury Act 1911 shall have effect as if this section were contained in that Act.

CRIMINAL JUSTICE AND PUBLIC ORDER ACT 1994

51.   Intimidation, etc, of witnesses, jurors and others

(1)   A person who does to another person—

(a)   an act which intimidates, and is intended to intimidate, that other person;

(b)   knowing or believing that the other person is assisting in the investigation of an offence or is a witness or potential witness or juror or potential juror in proceedings for an offence; and

(c)   intending thereby to cause the investigation or the course of justice to be obstructed, perverted or interfered with,

commits an offence.

(2)   A person who does or threatens to do to another person—

(a)   an act which harms or would harm, and is intended to harm, that other person;

(b)   knowing or believing that the other person, or some other person, has assisted in an investigation into an offence or has given evidence or particular evidence in proceedings for an offence, or has acted as a juror or concurred in a particular verdict in proceedings for an offence; and

(c)   does or threatens to do the act because of what (within paragraph (b)) he knows or believes,

commits an offence.

(3)   A person does an act 'to' another person with the intention of intimidating, or (as the case may be) harming, that other person not only where the act is done in the presence of that other and directed at him directly but also where the act is done to a third person and is intended, in the circumstances, to intimidate or (as the case may be) harm the person at whom the act is directed.

(4)   The harm that may be done or threatened may be financial as well as physical (whether to the person or a person's property) and similarly as respects an intimidatory act which consists of threats.

(5)   The intention required by subsection (1)(c) and the motive required by subsection (2)(c) above need not be the only or the predominating intention or motive with which the act is done or, in the case of subsection (2), threatened.

(7)   If, in proceedings against a person for an offence under subsection (1) above, it is proved that he did an act falling within paragraph (a) with the knowledge or belief required by paragraph (b), he shall be presumed, unless the contrary is proved, to have done the act with the intention required by paragraph (c) of that subsection.

(8)   If, in proceedings against a person for an offence under subsection (2) above, it is proved that he did or threatened to do an act falling within paragraph (a) within the relevant period with the knowledge or belief required by paragraph (b), he shall be presumed, unless the contrary is proved, to have done the act with the motive required by paragraph (c) of that subsection.

(9)   In this section—

'investigation into an offence' means such an investigation by the police or other person charged with the duty of investigating offences or charging offenders;

'offence' includes an alleged or suspected offence;

'potential', in relation to a juror, means a person who has been summoned for jury service at the court at which proceedings for the offence are pending; and 'the relevant period'—

(a)   in relation to a witness or juror in any proceedings for an offence, means the period beginning with the institution of the proceedings and ending with the first anniversary of the conclusion of the trial or, if there is an appeal or reference under section 17 of the Criminal Appeal Act 1968, of the conclusion of the appeal;

(b)   in relation to a person who has, or is believed by the accused to have assisted in an investigation into an offence, but was not also a witness in proceedings for an offence, means the period of one year beginning with any act of his, or any act believed by the accused to be an act of his, assisting in the investigation; and

(c)   in relation to a person who both has, or is believed by the accused to have, assisted in the investigation into an offence and was a witness in proceedings for the offence, means the period beginning with any act of his, or any act believed by the accused to be an act of his, assisting in the investigation and ending with the anniversary mentioned in paragraph (a) above.

(10)   For the proposes of the definition of the relevant period in subsection (9) above—

(a)   proceedings for an offence are instituted at the earliest of the following times—

(i)   when a justice of the peace issues a summons or warrant under section 1 of the Magistrates' Courts Act 1980 in respect of the offence;

(ii)   when a person is charged with the offence after being taken into custody without a warrant;

(iii)   when a bill of indictment is preferred by virtue of section 2(2)(b) of the Administration of Justice (Miscellaneous Provisions) Act 1933;

(b)   proceedings at a trial of an offence are concluded with the occurrence of any of the following, the discontinuance of the prosecution, the discharge of the jury without a finding, the acquittal of the accused or the sentencing of or other dealing with the accused for the offence of which he was convicted; and

(c)   proceedings on an appeal are concluded on the determination of the appeal or the abandonment of the appeal.

(11)   This section is in addition to, and not in derogation of, any offence subsisting at common law.

CRIMINAL LAW ACT 1967

4.   Penalties for assisting offenders

(1)   Where a person has committed an arrestable offence, any other person who, knowing or believing him to be guilty of the offence or of some other arrestable offence, does without lawful authority or reasonable excuse any act with intent to impede his apprehension or prosecution shall be guilty of an offence.

(2)   If on the trial of an indictment for an arrestable offence the jury are satisfied that the offence charged (or some other offence of which the accused might on that charge be found guilty) was committed, but find the accused not guilty of it, they may find him guilty of any offence under subsection (1) above of which they are satisfied that he is guilty in relation to the offence charged (or that other offence).

(3)   A person committing an offence under subsection (1) above with intent to impede another person's apprehension or prosecution shall on conviction on indictment be liable to imprisonment according to the gravity of the other person's offence, as follows:—

(a)   if that offence is one for which the sentence is fixed by law, he shall be liable to imprisonment for not more than ten years;

(b)   if it is one for which a person (not previously convicted) may be sentenced to imprisonment for a term of fourteen years, he shall be liable to imprisonment for not more than seven years;

(c)   if it is not one included above but is one for which a person (not previously convicted) may be sentenced to imprisonment for a term of ten years, he shall be liable to imprisonment for not more than five years;

(d)   in any other case, he shall be liable to imprisonment for not more than three years.

(4)   No proceedings shall be instituted for an offence under subsection (1) above except by or with the consent of the Director of Public Prosecutions.

5.   Penalties for concealing offences or giving false information

(1)   Where a person has committed an arrestable offence, any other person who, knowing or believing that the offence or some other arrestable offence has been committed, and that he has information which might be of material assistance in securing the prosecution or conviction of an offender for it, accepts or agrees to accept for not disclosing that information any consideration other than the making good of loss or injury caused by the offence, or the making of reasonable compensation for that loss or injury, shall be liable on conviction on indictment to imprisonment for not more than two years.

(2)   Where a person causes any wasteful employment of the police by knowingly making to any person a false report tending to show that an offence has been committed, or to give rise to apprehension for the safety of any persons or property, or tending to show that he has information material to any police inquiry, he shall be liable on summary conviction to imprisonment for not more than six months or to a fine of not more than two hundred pounds or to both.

(3)   No proceedings shall be instituted for an offence under this section except by or with the consent of the Director of Public Prosecutions.

(5)   The compounding of an offence other than treason shall not be an offence otherwise than under this section.

CRIMINAL JUSTICE ACT 1988

PART VI

71.   [Interpretation]

(9)   In this Part of this Act—

(b)   'drug trafficking offence' has the same meaning as in the Drug Trafficking Act 1994;

(c)   references to an offence to which this Part of this Act applies are references to any offence which—

(i)   is listed in Schedule 4 to this Act;

[Sch. 4: the summary offences under—

Local Government (Miscellaneous Provisions) Act 1982, sch. 3, paras. 20, 21;

Video Recordings Act 1984, ss. 9,10;

Cinemas Act 1985, s. 10(1)(a).] or

(ii)   if not so listed, is an indictable offence, other than a drug trafficking offence.

93A.   Assisting another to retain the benefit of criminal conduct

(1)   Subject to subsection (3) below, if a person enters into or is otherwise concerned in an arrangement whereby—

(a)   the retention or control by or on behalf of another ('A') of A's proceeds of criminal conduct is facilitated (whether by concealment, removal from the jurisdiction, transfer to nominees or otherwise); or

(b)   A's proceeds of criminal conduct—

(i)   are used to secure that funds are placed at A's disposal; or

(ii)   are used for A's benefit to acquire property by way of investment,

knowing or suspecting that A is a person who is or has been engaged in criminal conduct or has benefited from criminal conduct, he is guilty of an offence.

(2)   In this section, references to any person's proceeds of criminal conduct include a reference to any property which in whole or in part directly or indirectly represented in his hands his proceeds of criminal conduct.

(3)   Where a person discloses to a constable a suspicion or belief that any funds or investments are derived from or used in connection with criminal conduct or discloses to a constable any matter on which such a suspicion or belief is based—

(a)   the disclosure shall not be treated as a breach of any restriction upon the disclosure of information imposed by statute or otherwise; and

(b)   if he does any act in contravention of subsection (1) above and the disclosure relates to the arrangement concerned, he does not commit an offence under this section if—

(i)   the disclosure is made before he does the act concerned and the act is done with the consent of the constable; or

(ii)   the disclosure is made after he does the act, but is made on his initiative and as soon as it is reasonable for him to make it.

(4)   In proceedings against a person for an offence under this section, it is a defence to prove—

(a)   that he did not know or suspect that the arrangement related to any person's proceeds of criminal conduct; or

(b)   that he did not know or suspect that by the arrangement the retention or control by or on behalf of A of any property was facilitated or, as the case may be, that by the arrangement any property was used, as mentioned in subsection (1) above; or

(c)   that—

(i)   he intended to disclose to a constable such a suspicion, belief or matter as is mentioned in subsection (3) above in relation to the arrangement; but

(ii)   there is reasonable excuse for his failure to make disclosure in accordance with subsection (3)(b) above.

(5)   In the case of a person who was in employment at the relevant time, subsections (3) and (4) above shall have effect in relation to disclosures, and intended disclosures, to the appropriate person in accordance with the procedure established by his employer for the making of such disclosures as they have effect in relation to disclosures, and intended disclosures, to a constable.

(6)   A person guilty of an offence under this section shall be liable—

(a)   on summary conviction, to imprisonment for a term not exceeding six months or a fine not exceeding the statutory maximum or to both; or

(b)   on conviction on indictment, to imprisonment for a term not exceeding fourteen years or a fine or to both.

(7)   In this Part of this Act 'criminal conduct' means conduct which constitutes an offence to which this Part of this Act applies or would constitute such an offence if it had occurred in England and Wales or (as the case may be) Scotland.

93B.   Acquisition, possession or use of proceeds of criminal conduct

(1)   A person is guilty of an offence if, knowing that any property is, or in whole or in part directly or indirectly represents, another person's proceeds of criminal conduct, he acquires or uses that property or has possession of it.

(2)   It is a defence to a charge of committing an offence under this section that the person charged acquired or used the property or had possession of it for adequate consideration.

(3)   For the purposes of subsection (2) above—

(a)   a person acquires property for inadequate consideration if the value of the consideration is significantly less than the value of the property; and

(b)   a person uses or has possession of property for inadequate consideration if the value of the consideration is significantly less than the value of his use or possession of the property.

(4)   The provision for any person of services or goods which are of assistance to him in criminal conduct shall not be treated as consideration for the purposes of subsection (2) above.

(5)   Where a person discloses to a constable a suspicion or belief that any property is, or in whole or in part directly or indirectly represents, another person's proceeds of criminal conduct or discloses to a constable any matter on which such a suspicion or belief is based—

(a)   the disclosure shall not be treated as a breach of any restriction upon the disclosure of information imposed by statute or otherwise;

(b)   if he does any act in relation to that property in contravention of subsection (1) above, he does not commit an offence under this section if—

(i)   the disclosure is made before he does the act concerned and the act is done with the consent of the constable; or

(ii)   the disclosure is made after he does the act, but on his initiative and as soon as it is reasonable for him to make it.

(6)   For the purposes of subsection (5) above, having possession of any property shall be taken to be doing an act in relation to it.

(7)   In proceedings against a person for an offence under this section, it is a defence to prove that—

(a)   he intended to disclose to a constable such a suspicion, belief or matter as is mentioned in subsection (5) above; but

(b)   there is reasonable excuse for his failure to make the disclosure in accordance with paragraph (b) of that subsection.

(8)   In the case of a person who was in employment at the relevant time, subsections (5) and (7) above shall have effect in relation to disclosures, and intended disclosures, to the appropriate person in accordance with the procedure established by his employer for the making of such disclosures as they have effect in relation to disclosures, and intended disclosures, to a constable.

(9)   A person guilty of an offence under this section is liable—

(a)   on summary conviction, to imprisonment for a term not exceeding six months or a fine not exceeding the statutory maximum or to both; or

(b)   on conviction on indictment, to imprisonment for a term not exceeding fourteen years or a fine or to both.

(10)   No constable or other person shall be guilty of an offence under this section in respect of anything done by him in the course of acting in connection with the enforcement, or intended enforcement, of any provision of this Act or of any other enactment relating to criminal conduct or the proceeds of such conduct.

93C.   Concealing or transferring proceeds of criminal conduct

(1)   A person is guilty of an offence if he—

(a)   conceals or disguises any property which is, or in whole or in part directly or indirectly represents, his proceeds of criminal conduct; or

(b)   converts or transfers that property or removes it from the jurisdiction, for the purposes of avoiding prosecution for an offence to which this Part of this Act applies or the making or enforcement in his case of a confiscation order.

(2)   A person is guilty of an offence if, knowing or having reasonable grounds to suspect that any property is, or in whole or in part directly or indirectly represents, another person's proceeds of criminal conduct, he—

(a)   conceals or disguises that property; or
(b)   converts or transfers that property or removes it from the jurisdiction,
for the purpose of assisting any person to avoid prosecution for an offence to which this Part of this Act applies or the making or enforcement in his case of a confiscation order.

(3)   In subsections (1) and (2) above, the references to concealing or disguising any property include references to concealing or disguising its nature, source, location, disposition, movement or ownership or any rights with respect to it.

(4)   A person guilty of an offence under this section is liable—
(a)   on summary conviction, to imprisonment for a term not exceeding six months or a fine not exceeding the statutory maximum or to both; or
(b)   on conviction on indictment, to imprisonment for a term not exceeding fourteen years or a fine or to both.

93D.   Tipping-off

(1)   A person is guilty of an offence if—
(a)   he knows or suspected that a constable is acting, or is proposing to act, in connection with an investigation which is being, or is about to be, conducted into money laundering;
(b)   and he discloses to any other person information or any other matter which is likely to prejudice the investigation, or proposed investigation.

(2)   A person is guilty of an offence if—
(a)   he knows or suspects that a disclosure ('the disclosure') has been made to a constable under section 93A or 93B above; and
(b)   he discloses to any other person information or any other matter which is likely to prejudice any investigation which might be conducted following the disclosure.

(3)   A person is guilty of an offence if—
(a)   he knows or suspects that a disclosure of a kind mentioned in section 93A(5) or 93B(8) above ('the disclosure') has been made; and
(b)   he discloses to any person information or any other matter which is likely to prejudice any investigation which might be conducted following the disclosure.

(4)   Nothing in subsections (1) to (3) above makes it an offence for a professional legal adviser to disclose any information or other matter—
(a)   to, or to a representative of, a client of his in connection with the giving by the adviser of legal advice to the client; or
(b)   to any person—
(i)   in contemplation of, or in connection with, legal proceedings; and
(ii)   for the purpose of those proceedings.

(5)   Subsection (4) above does not apply in relation to any information or other matter which is disclosed with a view to furthering any criminal purpose.

(6)   In proceedings against a person for an offence under subsection (1), (2) or (3) above, it is a defence to prove that he did not know or suspect that the disclosure was likely to be prejudicial in the way mentioned in that subsection.

(7)   In this section—
'money laundering' means doing any act which constitutes an offence under section 93A, 93B or 93C above or, in the case of an act done otherwise than in England and Wales or Scotland, would constitute such an offence if done in England and Wales or (as the case may be) Scotland.

(8)   For the purposes of subsection (7) above, having possession of any property shall be taken to be doing an act in relation to it.

(9)   A person guilty of an offence under this section shall be liable—
(a)   on summary conviction, to imprisonment for a term not exceeding six months or a fine not exceeding the statutory maximum or to both; or

(b) on conviction on indictment, to imprisonment for a term not exceeding five years or a fine or to both.

(10) No constable or other person shall be guilty of an offence under this section in respect of anything done by him in the course of acting in connection with the enforcement, or intended enforcement, of any provision of this Act or of any other enactment relating to an offence to which this Part of this Act applies.

102. Interpretation

(2) In this Part of this Act—

'proceeds of criminal conduct', in relation to any person who has benefited from criminal conduct, means that benefit.

PRISON ACT 1952

39. Assisting prisoner to escape

Any person who aids any prisoner in escaping or attempting to escape from a prison or who, with intent to facilitate the escape of any prisoner, conveys any thing into a prison or to a prisoner or sends anything (by post or otherwise) into a prison or to a prisoner or places any thing anywhere outside a prison with a view to its coming into the possession of a prisoner, shall be guilty of felony and liable to imprisonment for a term not exceeding ten years.

41. Unlawful introduction of other articles

Any person who contrary to the regulations of a prison conveys or attempts to convey any letter of any other thing into or out of the prison or to a prisoner or places it anywhere outside the prison with intent that it shall come into the possession of a prisoner shall, where he is not thereby guilty of an offence under either of the two last preceding sections, be liable on summary conviction to a fine not exceeding level 3 on the standard scale.

PRISON SECURITY ACT 1992

1. Offence of prison mutiny

(1) Any prisoner who takes part in a prison mutiny shall be guilty of an offence and liable, on conviction on indictment, to imprisonment for a term not exceeding ten years or to a fine or to both.

(2) For the purposes of this section there is a prison mutiny where two or more prisoners, while on the premises of any prison, engage in conduct which is intended to further a common purpose of overthrowing lawful authority in that prison.

(3) For the purposes of this section the intentions and common purpose of prisoners may be inferred from the form and circumstances of their conduct and it shall be immaterial that conduct falling within subsection (2) above takes a different form in the case of different prisoners.

(4) Where there is a prison mutiny, a prisoner who has or is given a reasonable opportunity of submitting to lawful authority and fails, without reasonable excuse, to do so shall be regarded for the purposes of this section as taking part in the mutiny.

(6) In this section—

'conduct' includes acts and omissions;

'prison' means any prison, young offender institution or remand centre which is under the general superintendence of, or is provided by, the Secretary of State under the Prison Act 1952, including a contracted out prison within the meaning of Part IV of the Criminal Justice Act 1991;

'prisoner' means any person for the time being in a prison as a result of any requirement imposed by a court or otherwise that he be detained in legal custody.

PREVENTION OF TERRORISM (TEMPORARY PROVISIONS) ACT 1989

18. Information about acts of terrorism

(1)   A person is guilty of an offence if he has information which he knows or believes might be of material assistance—

(a)   in preventing the commission by any other person of an act of terrorism connected with the affairs of Northern Ireland; or

(b)   in securing the apprehension, prosecution or conviction of any other person for an offence involving the commission, preparation or instigation of such an act, and fails without reasonable excuse to disclose that information as soon as reasonably practicable—

(i)   in England and Wales, to a constable; or

(iii)   in Northern Ireland, to a constable or a member of Her Majesty's Forces.

(3)   Proceedings for an offence under this section may be taken, and the offence may for the purposes of those proceedings be treated as having been committed, in any place where the person to be charged is or has at any time been since he first knew or believed that the information might be of material assistance as mentioned in subsection (1) above.

18A. Failure to disclose knowledge or suspicion of financial assistance for terrorism

(1)   A person is guilty of an offence if—

(a)   he knows, or suspects, that another person is providing financial assistance for terrorism;

(b)   the information, or other matter, on which that knowledge or suspicion is based came to his attention in the course of his trade, profession, business or employment; and

(c)   he does not disclose the information or other matter to a constable as soon as is reasonably practicable after it comes to his attention.

(2)   Subsection (1) above does not make it an offence for a professional legal adviser to fail to disclose any information or other matter which has come to him in privileged circumstances.

(3)   It is a defence to a charge of committing an offence under this section that the person charged had a reasonable excuse for not disclosing the information or other matter in question.

(4)   Where a person discloses to a constable—

(a)   his suspicion or belief that another person is providing financial assistance for terrorism, or

(b)   any information or other matter on which that suspicion or belief is based; the disclosure shall not be treated as a breach of any restriction imposed by statute or otherwise.

(5)   Without prejudice to subsection (3) or (4) above, in the case of a person who was in employment at the relevant time, it is a defence to a charge of committing an offence under this section that he disclosed the information or other matter in question to the appropriate person in accordance with the procedure established by his employer for the making of such disclosures.

(6)   A disclosure to which subsection (5) above applies shall not be treated as a breach of any restriction imposed by statute or otherwise.

(7)   In this section 'providing financial assistance for terrorism' means doing any act which constitutes an offence under section 9, 10 or 11 above or, in the case of an act done otherwise than in the United Kingdom, which would constitute such an offence if done in the United Kingdom.

(8)   For the purposes of subsection (7) above, having possession of any property shall be taken to be doing an act in relation to it.

(9) For the purposes of this section, any information or other matter comes to a professional legal adviser in privileged circumstances if it is communicated, or given, to him—

(a) by, or by a representative of, a client of his in connection with the giving by the adviser of legal advice to the client;

(b) by, or by a representative of, a person seeking legal advice from the adviser; or

(c) by any person—

(i) in contemplation of, or in connection with, legal proceedings; and

(ii) for the purpose of those proceedings.

(10) No information or other matter shall be treated as coming to a professional legal adviser in privileged circumstances if it is communicated or given with a view to furthering any criminal purpose.

20. Interpretation

(1) In this Act—

'terrorism' means the use of violence for political ends, and includes any use of violence for the purpose of putting the public or any section of the public in fear.

POLICE ACT 1996

89. Assaults on constables

(1) Any person who assaults a constable in the execution of his duty, or a person assisting a constable in the execution of his duty, shall be guilty of an offence and liable on summary conviction to imprisonment for a term not exceeding six months or to a fine not exceeding level 5 on the standard scale or to both;

(2) Any person who resists or wilfully obstructs a constable in the execution of his duty, or a person assisting a constable in the execution of his duty shall be guilty of an offence and liable on summary conviction to imprisonment for a term not exceeding one month or to a fine not exceeding level 3 on the standard scale, or to both.

90. Impersonation, etc.

(1) Any person who with intent to deceive impersonates a member of a police force or special constable, or makes any statement or does any act calculated falsely to suggest that he is such a member or constable, shall be guilty of an offence and liable on summary conviction to imprisonment for a term not exceeding six months or to a fine not exceeding level 5 on the standard scale, or to both.

(2) Any person who, not being a constable, wears any article of police uniform in circumstances where it gives him an appearance so nearly resembling that of a member of a police force as to be calculated to deceive shall be guilty of an offence and liable on summary conviction to a fine not exceeding level 3 on the standard scale.

(3) Any person who, not being a member of a police force or special constable, has in his possession any article of police uniform shall, unless he proves that he obtained possession of that article lawfully and has possession of it for a lawful purpose, be guilty of an offence and liable on summary conviction to a fine not exceeding level 1 on the standard scale.

(4) In this section—

(a) 'article of police uniform' means any article of uniform or any distinctive badge or mark or document of identification usually issued to members of police forces or special constables, or anything having the appearance of such an article, badge, mark or document; and

(b) 'special constable' means a special constable appointed for a police area.

91. Causing disaffection

(1)   Any person who causes, or attempts to cause, or does any act calculated to cause, disaffection amongst the members of any police force, or induces or attempts to induce, or does any act calculated to induce, any member of a police force to withhold his services, shall be guilty of an offence and liable—

(a)   on summary conviction, to imprisonment for a term not exceeding six months or to a fine not exceeding the statutory maximum, or to both;

(b)   on conviction on indictment, to imprisonment for a term not exceeding two years or to a fine or to both.

(2)   This section applies to special constables appointed for a police area as it applies to members of a police force.

LICENSING ACT 1964

178.   Offences in relation to constables
[See page 112]

BAIL ACT 1976

6.   Offence of absconding by person released on bail

(1)   If a person who has been released on bail in criminal proceedings fails without reasonable cause to surrender to custody he shall be guilty of an offence.

(2)   If a person who—

(a)   has been released on bail in criminal proceedings, and

(b)   having reasonable cause therefor, has failed to surrender to custody,

fails to surrender to custody at the appointed place as soon after the appointed time as is reasonably practicable he shall be guilty of an offence.

(3)   It shall be for the accused to prove that he had reasonable cause for his failure to surrender to custody.

(4)   A failure to give to a person granted bail in criminal proceedings a copy of the record of the decision shall not constitute a reasonable cause for that person's failure to surrender to custody.

9.   Offence of agreeing to indemnify sureties in criminal proceedings

(1)   If a person agrees with another to indemnify that other against any liability which that other may incur as a surety to secure the surrender to custody of a person accused or convicted of or under arrest for an offence, he and that other person shall be guilty of an offence.

(2)   An offence under subsection (1) above is committed whether the agreement is made before or after the person to be indemnified becomes a surety and whether or not he becomes a surety and whether the agreement contemplates compensation in money or in money's worth.

11 INTERFERENCE WITH GOVERNMENTAL OR PUBLIC SERVICES

PUBLIC BODIES CORRUPT PRACTICES ACT 1889

1. Corruption in office a misdemeanour

(1) Every person who shall by himself or by or in conjunction with any other person, corruptly solicit or receive, or agree to receive, for himself, or for any other person, any gift, loan, fee, reward, or advantage whatever as an inducement to, or reward for, or otherwise on account of any member, officer, or servant of a public body as in this Act defined, doing or forbearing to do anything in respect of any matter or transaction whatsoever, actual or proposed, in which the said public body is concerned, shall be guilty of a misdemeanour.

(2) Every person who shall by himself or by or in conjunction with any other person corruptly give, promise, or offer any gift, loan, fee, reward, or advantage whatsoever to any person, whether for the benefit of that person or of another person, as an inducement to or reward for or otherwise on account of any member, officer, or servant of any public body as in this Act defined, doing or forbearing to do anything in respect of any matter or transaction whatsoever, actual or proposed, in which such public body as aforesaid is concerned, shall be guilty of a misdemeanour.

7. Interpretation

In this Act—

The expression 'public body' means any council of a county or county of a city or town, any council of a municipal borough, also any board, commissioners, select vestry, or other body which has power to act under and for the purposes of any Act relating to local government, or the public health, or to poor law or otherwise to administer money raised by rates in pursuance of any public general Act, but does not include any public body as above defined existing elsewhere than in the United Kingdom;

The expression 'public office' means any office or employment of a person as a member, officer, or servant of such public body;

The expression 'person' includes a body of persons, corporate or unincorporate;

The expression 'advantage' includes any office or dignity, and any forbearance to demand any money or money's worth or valuable thing, and includes any aid, vote, consent, or influence, or pretended aid, vote, consent, or influence, and also includes any promise or procurement of or agreement or endeavour to procure, or the holding out of any expectation of any gift, loan, fee, reward, or advantage, as before defined.

PREVENTION OF CORRUPTION ACT 1916

2. Presumption of corruption in certain cases

Where in any proceedings against a person for an offence under the Prevention of Corruption Act, 1906, or the Public Bodies Corrupt Practices Act, 1889, it is proved that any money, gift, or other consideration has been paid or given to or received by a person in the employment of His Majesty or any Government Department or a public body by or from a person, or agent of a person, holding or seeking to obtain a contract from His Majesty or any Government Department or public body, the money, gift, or consideration shall be deemed to have been paid or given and received corruptly as such inducement or reward as is mentioned in such Act unless the contrary is proved.

OFFICIAL SECRETS ACT 1911

1. Penalties for spying

(1) If any person for any purpose prejudicial to the safety or interests of the State—

    (a) approaches, inspects, passes over or is in the neighbourhood of, or enters any prohibited place within the meaning of this Act; or

    (b) makes any sketch, plan, model, or note which is calculated to be or might be or is intended to be directly or indirectly useful to an enemy; or

    (c) obtains, collects, records, or publishes, or communicates to any other person any secret official code word or pass word, or any sketch, plan, model, article, or note, or other document or information which is directly or indirectly useful to an enemy; he shall be guilty of felony . . .

(2) On a prosecution under this section, it shall not be necessary to show that the accused person was guilty of any particular act tending to show a purpose prejudicial to the safety or interests of the State, and, notwithstanding that no such act is proved against him, he may be convicted if, from the circumstances of the case, or his conduct, or his known character as proved, it appears that his purpose was a purpose prejudicial to the safety or interests of the State; and if any sketch, plan, model, article, note, document, or information relating to or used in any prohibited place within the meaning of this Act, or anything in such a place or any secret official code word or pass word, is made, obtained, collected, recorded, published, or communicated by any person other than a person acting under lawful authority, it shall be deemed to have been made, obtained, collected, recorded, published or communicated for a purpose prejudicial to the safety or interests of the State unless the contrary is proved.

3. Definition of prohibited place

For the purposes of this Act, the expression 'prohibited place' means—

    (a) any work of defence, arsenal, naval or air force establishment or station, factory, dockyard, mine, minefield, camp, ship, or aircraft belonging to or occupied by or on behalf of His Majesty, or any telegraph, telephone, wireless or signal station, or office so belonging or occupied, and any place belonging to or occupied by or on behalf of His Majesty and used for the purpose of building, repairing, making or storing any munitions of war, or any sketches, plans, models or documents relating thereto, or for the purpose of getting any metals, oil or minerals of use in time of war;

    (b) any place not belonging to His Majesty where any munitions of war, or any sketches, models, plans or documents relating thereto, are being made, repaired, gotten or stored under contract with, or with any person on behalf of, His Majesty, or otherwise on behalf of His Majesty; and

    (c) any place belonging to or used for the purposes of His Majesty which is for the time being declared by order of a Secretary of State to be a prohibited place for the purposes of this section on the ground that information with respect thereto, or damage thereto, would be useful to an enemy; and

(d) any railway, road, way, or channel, or other means of communication by land or water (including any works or structures being part thereof or connected therewith), or any place used for gas, water, or electricity works or other works for purposes of a public character, or any place where any munitions of war, or any sketches, models, plans, or documents relating thereto, are being made, repaired, or stored otherwise than on behalf of His Majesty, which is for the time being declared by order of a Secretary of State to be a prohibited place for the purposes of this section, on the ground that information with respect thereto, or the destruction or obstruction thereof, or interference therewith, would be useful to an enemy.

7. Penalty for harbouring spies

If any person knowingly harbours any person whom he knows, or has reasonable grounds for supposing, to be a person who is about to commit or who has committed an offence under this Act, or knowingly permits to meet or assemble in any premises in his occupation or under his control any such persons, or if any person having harboured any such person, or permitted to meet or assemble in any premises in his occupation or under his control any such person, wilfully omits or refuses to disclose to a superintendent of police any information which it is in his power to give in relation to any such person he shall be guilty of a misdemeanour . . .

OFFICIAL SECRETS ACT 1920

1. Unauthorised use of uniforms; falsification of reports, personation, and false documents

(1) If any person for the purpose of gaining admission, or of assisting any other person to gain admission, to a prohibited place within the meaning of the Official Secrets Act 1911 (hereinafter referred to as 'the principal Act'), or for any other purpose prejudicial to the safety or interests of the State within the meaning of the said Act—

(a) uses or wears, without lawful authority, any naval, military, air-force, police, or other official uniform, or any uniform so nearly resembling the same as to be calculated to deceive, or falsely represents himself to be a person who is or has been entitled to use or wear any such uniform; or

(b) orally, or in writing in any declaration or application, or in any document signed by him or on his behalf, knowingly makes or connives at the making of any false statement or any omission; or

(c) . . . tampers with any passport or naval, military, air-force, police, or official pass, permit, certificate, licence, or other document of a similar character (hereinafter in this section referred to as an official document), . . . or has in his possession any . . . forged, altered, or irregular official document; or

(d) personates, or falsely represents himself to be a person holding, or in the employment of a person holding office under His Majesty, or to be or not to be a person to whom an official document or secret official code word or pass word has been duly issued or communicated, or with intent to obtain an official document, secret official code word or pass word, whether for himself or any other person, knowingly makes any false statement; or

(e) uses, or has in his possession or under his control, without the authority of the Government Department, or the authority concerned, any die, seal, or stamp of or belonging to, or used, made or provided by any Government Department, or by any diplomatic, naval, military, or air-force authority appointed by or acting under the authority of His Majesty, or any die, seal or stamp so nearly resembling any such die, seal or stamp as to be calculated to deceive, or counterfeits any such die, seal or stamp, or uses, or has in his possession, or under his control, any such counterfeited die, seal or stamp;

he shall be guilty of a misdemeanour.

(2) If any person—

(a) retains for any purpose prejudicial to the safety or interests of the State any official document, whether or not completed or issued for use, when he has no right to retain it, or when it is contrary to his duty to retain it, or fails to comply with any directions issued by any Government Department or any person authorised by such department with regard to the return or disposal thereof; or

(b) allows any other person to have possession of any official document issued for his use alone, or communicates any secret official code word or pass word so issued, or, without lawful authority or excuse, has in his possession any official document or secret official code word or pass word issued for the use of some person other than himself, or on obtaining possession of any official document by finding or otherwise, neglects or fails to restore it to the person or authority by whom or for whom or for whose use it was issued, or to a police constable; or

(c) without lawful authority or excuse, manufactures or sells, or has in his possession for sale any such die, seal or stamp as aforesaid;

he shall be guilty of a misdemeanour.

(3) In the case of any prosecution under this section involving the proof of a purpose prejudicial to the safety or interests of the State, subsection (2) of section one of the principal Act shall apply in like manner as it applies to prosecutions under that section.

2. Communications with foreign agents to be evidence of commission of certain offences

(1) In any proceedings against a person for an offence under section one of the principal Act, the fact that he has been in communication with, or attempted to communicate with, a foreign agent, whether within or without the United Kingdom, shall be evidence that he has for a purpose prejudicial to the safety or interests of the State, obtained or attempted to obtain information which is calculated to be or might be or intended to be directly or indirectly useful to an enemy.

(2) For the purpose of this section, but without prejudice to the generality of the foregoing provision—

(a) A person shall, unless he proves the contrary, be deemed to have been in communication with a foreign agent if—

(i) He has, either within or without the United Kingdom, visited the address of a foreign agent or consorted or associated with a foreign agent; or

(ii) Either, within or without the United Kingdom, the name or address of, or any other information regarding a foreign agent has been found in his possession, or has been supplied by him to any other person, or has been obtained by him from any other person;

(b) The expression 'foreign agent' includes a person who is or has been or is reasonably suspected of being or having been employed by a foreign power either directly or indirectly for the purpose of committing an act, either within or without the United Kingdom, prejudicial to the safety or interests of the State, or who has or is reasonably suspected of having, either within or without the United Kingdom, committed, or attempted to commit, such an act in the interests of a foreign power;

(c) Any address, whether within or without the United Kingdom, reasonably suspected of being an address used for the receipt of communications intended for a foreign agent, or any address at which a foreign agent resides, or to which he resorts for the purpose of giving or receiving communications, or at which he carries on any business, shall be deemed to be the address of a foreign agent, and communications addressed to such an address to be communications with a foreign agent.

3. Interfering with officers of the police or members of His Majesty's forces
No person in the vicinity of any prohibited place shall obstruct, knowingly mislead or otherwise interfere with or impede the chief officer or a superintendent or other officer of police, or any member of His Majesty's forces engaged on guard, sentry, patrol, or other similar duty in relation to the prohibited place, and, if any person acts in contravention of, or fails to comply with, this provision, he shall be guilty of a misdemeanour.

7. Attempts, incitements, etc.
Any person who attempts to commit any offence under the principal Act or this Act, or solicits or incites or endeavours to persuade another person to commit an offence, or aids or abets and does any act preparatory to the commission of an offence under the principal Act or this Act, shall be guilty of a felony or a misdemeanour or a summary offence according as the offence in question is a felony, a misdemeanour or a summary offence, and on conviction shall be liable to the same punishment, and to be proceeded against in the same manner, as if he had committed the offence.

OFFICIAL SECRETS ACT 1989

1. Security and intelligence
  (1) A person who is or has been—
    (a) a member of the security and intelligence services; or
    (b) a person notified that he is subject to the provisions of this subsection,
is guilty of an offence if without lawful authority he discloses any information, document or other article relating to security or intelligence which is or has been in his possession by virtue of his position as a member of any of those services or in the course of his work while the notification is or was in force.

  (2) The reference in subsection (1) above to disclosing information relating to security or intelligence includes a reference to making any statement which purports to be a disclosure of such information or is intended to be taken by those to whom it is addressed as being such a disclosure.

  (3) A person who is or has been a Crown servant or government contractor is guilty of an offence if without lawful authority he makes a damaging disclosure of any information, document or other article relating to security or intelligence which is or has been in his possession by virtue of his position as such but otherwise than as mentioned in subsection (1) above.

  (4) For the purposes of subsection (3) above a disclosure is damaging if—
    (a) it causes damage to the work of, or of any part of, the security and intelligence services; or
    (b) it is of information or a document or other article which is such that its unauthorised disclosure would be likely to cause such damage or which falls within a class or description of information, documents or articles the unauthorised disclosure of which would be likely to have that effect.

  (5) It is a defence for a person charged with an offence under this section to prove that at the time of the alleged offence he did not know, and had no reasonable cause to believe, that the information, document or article in question related to security or intelligence or, in the case of an offence under subsection (2), that the disclosure would be damaging within the meaning of that subsection.

  (6) Notification that a person is subject to subsection (1) above shall be effected by a notice in writing served on him by a Minister of the Crown; and such a notice may be served if, in the Minister's opinion, the work undertaken by the person in

question is or includes work connected with the security and intelligence services and its nature is such that the interests of national security require that he should be subject to the provisions of that subsection.

(7) Subject to subsection (8) below, a notification for the purposes of subsection (1) above shall be in force for the period of five years beginning with the day on which it is served but may be renewed by further notices under subsection (6) above for periods of five years at a time.

(8) A notification for the purposes of subsection (1) above may at any time be revoked by a further notice in writing served by the Minister on the person concerned; and the Minister shall serve such a further notice as soon as, in his opinion, the work undertaken by that person ceases to be such as is mentioned in subsection (6) above.

(9) In this section 'security or intelligence' means the work of, or in support of, the security and intelligence services or any part of them, and references to information relating to security or intelligence include references to information held or transmitted by those services or by persons in support of, or of any part of, them.

2. Defence

(1) A person who is or has been a Crown servant or government contractor is guilty of an offence if without lawful authority he makes a damaging disclosure of any information, document or other article relating to defence which is or has been in his possession by virtue of his position as such.

(2) For the purposes of subsection (1) above a disclosure is damaging if—

(a) it damages the capability of, or of any part of, the armed forces of the Crown to carry out their tasks or leads to loss of life or injury to members of those forces or serious damage to the equipment or installations of those forces; or

(b) otherwise than as mentioned in paragraph (a) above, it endangers the interests of the United Kingdom abroad, seriously obstructs the promotion or protection by the United Kingdom of those interests or endangers the safety of British citizens abroad; or

(c) it is of information or of a document or article which is such that its unauthorised disclosure would be likely to have any of those effects.

(3) It is a defence for a person charged with an offence under this section to prove that at the time of the alleged offence he did not know, and had no reasonable cause to believe, that the information, document or article in question related to defence or that its disclosure would be damaging within the meaning of subsection (1) above.

(4) In this section 'defence' means—

(a) the size, shape, organisation, logistics, order of battle, deployment, operations, state of readiness and training of the armed forces of the Crown;

(b) the weapons, stores or other equipment of those forces and the invention, development, production and operation of such equipment and research relating to it;

(c) defence policy and strategy and military planning and intelligence;

(d) plans and measures for the maintenance of essential supplies and services that are or would be needed in time of war.

3. International relations

(1) A person who is or has been a Crown servant or government contractor is guilty of an offence if without lawful authority he makes a damaging disclosure of—

(a) any information, document or other article relating to international relations; or

(b) any confidential information, document or other article which was obtained from a State other than the United Kingdom or an international organisation,

being information or a document or article which is or has been in his possession by virtue of his position as a Crown servant or government contractor.

(2) For the purposes of subsection (1) above a disclosure is damaging if—

(a)   it endangers the interests of the United Kingdom abroad, seriously obstructs the promotion or protection by the United Kingdom of those interests or endangers the safety of British citizens abroad; or

(b)   it is of information or of a document or article which is such that its unauthorised disclosure would be likely to have any of those effects.

(3)   In the case of information or a document or article within subsection (1)(b) above—

(a)   the fact that it is confidential, or

(b)   its nature or contents,

may be sufficient to establish for the purposes of subsection (2)(b) above that the information, document or article is such that its unauthorised disclosure would be likely to have any of the effects there mentioned.

(4)   It is a defence for a person charged with an offence under this section to prove that at the time of the alleged offence he did not know, and had no reasonable cause to believe, that the information, document or article in question was such as is mentioned in subsection (1) above or that its disclosure would be damaging within the meaning of that subsection.

(5)   In this section 'international relations' means the relations between States, between international organisations or between one or more States and one or more such organisations and includes any matter relating to a State other than the United Kingdom or to an international organisation which is capable of affecting the relations of the United Kingdom with another State or with an international organisation.

(6)   For the purposes of this section any information, document or article obtained from a State or organisation is confidential at any time while the terms on which it was obtained require it to be held in confidence or while the circumstances in which it was obtained make it reasonable for the State or organisation to expect that it would be so held.

4.   Crime and special investigation powers

(1)   A person who is or has been a Crown servant or government contractor is guilty of an offence if without lawful authority he discloses any information, document or other article to which this section applies and which is or has been in his possession by virtue of his position as such.

(2)   This section applies to any information, document or other article—

(a)   the disclosure of which—

(i)   results in the commission of an offence; or

(ii)   facilitates an escape from legal custody or the doing of any other act prejudicial to the safekeeping of persons in legal custody; or

(iii)   impedes the prevention or detection of offences or the apprehension or prosecution of suspected offenders; or

(b)   which is such that its unauthorised disclosure would be likely to have any of those effects.

(3)   This section also applies to—

(a)   any information obtained by reason of the interception of any communication in obedience to a warrant issued under section 2 of the Interception of Communications Act 1985, any information relating to the obtaining of information by reason of any such interception and any document or other article which is or has been used or held for use in, or has been obtained by reason of, any such interception; and

(b)   any information obtained by reason of action authorised by a warrant issued under section 3 of the Security Service Act 1989 or under section 5 of the Intelligence Services Act 1994 or by an authorisation given under section 7 of that Act, any information relating to the obtaining of information by reason of any such action and any document or other article which is or has been used or held for use in, or has been otained by reason of, any such action.

(4) It is a defence for a person charged with an offence under this section in respect of a disclosure falling within subsection (2)(a) above to prove that at the time of the alleged offence he did not know, and had no reasonable cause to believe, that the disclosure would have any of the effects there mentioned.

(5) It is a defence for a person charged with an offence under this section in respect of any other disclosure to prove that at the time of the alleged offence he did not know, and had no reasonable cause to believe, that the information, document or article in question was information or a document or article to which this section applies.

(6) In this section 'legal custody' includes detention in pursuance of any enactment or any instrument made under an enactment.

5. Information resulting from unauthorised disclosures or entrusted in confidence

(1) Subsection (2) below applies where—

(a) any information, document or other article protected against disclosure by the foregoing provisions of this Act has come into a person's possession as a result of having been—

(i) disclosed (whether to him or another) by a Crown servant or government contractor without lawful authority; or

(ii) entrusted to him by a Crown servant or government contractor on terms requiring it to be held in confidence or in circumstances in which the Crown servant or government contractor could reasonably expect that it would be so held; or

(iii) disclosed (whether to him or another) without lawful authority by a person to whom it was entrusted as mentioned in sub-paragraph (ii) above; and

(b) the disclosure without lawful authority of the information, document or article by the person into whose possession it has come is not an offence under any of those provisions.

(2) Subject to subsections (3) and (4) below, the person into whose possession the information, document or article has come is guilty of an offence if he discloses it without lawful authority knowing, or having reasonable cause to believe, that it is protected against disclosure by the foregoing provisions of this Act and that it has come into his possession as mentioned in subsection (1) above.

(3) In the case of information or a document or article protected against disclosure by sections 1 to 3 above, a person does not commit an offence under subsection (2) above unless—

(a) the disclosure by him is damaging; and

(b) he makes it knowing, or having reasonable cause to believe, that it would be damaging;

and the question whether a disclosure is damaging shall be determined for the purposes of this subsection as it would be in relation to a disclosure of that information, document or article by a Crown servant in contravention of section 1(3), 2(1) or 3(1) above.

(4) A person does not commit an offence under subsection (2) above in respect of information or a document or other article which has come into his possession as a result of having been disclosed—

(a) as mentioned in subsection (1)(a)(i) above by a government contractor; or

(b) as mentioned in subsection (1)(a)(iii) above,

unless that disclosure was by a British citizen or took place in the United Kingdom, in any of the Channel Islands or in the Isle of Man or a colony.

(5) For the purposes of this section information or a document or article is protected against disclosure by the foregoing provisions of this Act if—

(a)   it relates to security or intelligence, defence or international relations within the meaning of section 1, 2 or 3 above or is such as is mentioned in section 3(1)(b) above; or

(b)   it is information or a document or article to which section 4 above applies; and information or a document or article is protected against disclosure by sections 1 to 3 above if it falls within paragraph (a) above.

(6)   A person is guilty of an offence if without lawful authority he discloses any information, document or other article which he knows, or has reasonable cause to believe, to have come into his possession as a result of a contravention of section 1 of the Official Secrets Act 1911.

6. Information entrusted in confidence to other States or international organisations

(1)   This section applies where—

    (a)   any information, document or other article which—

        (i)   relates to security or intelligence, defence or international relations; and

        (ii)   has been communicated in confidence by or on behalf of the United Kingdom to another State or to an international organisation,

has come into a person's possession as a result of having been disclosed (whether to him or another) without the authority of that State or organisation or, in the case of an organisation, of a member of it; and

(b)   the disclosure without lawful authority of the information, document or article by the person into whose possession it has come is not an offence under any of the foregoing provisions of this Act.

(2)   Subject to subsection (2) below, the person into whose possession the information, document or article has come is guilty of an offence if he makes a damaging disclosure of it knowing, or having reasonable cause to believe, that it is such as is mentioned in subsection (1) above, that it has come into his possession as there mentioned and that its disclosure would be damaging.

(3)   A person does not commit an offence under subsection (2) above if the information, document or article is disclosed by him with lawful authority or has previously been made available to the public with the authority of the State or organisation concerned or, in the case of an organisation, of a member of it.

(4)   For the purposes of this section 'security or intelligence', 'defence' and 'international relations' have the same meaning as in sections 1, 2 and 3 above and the question whether a disclosure is damaging shall be determined as it would be in relation to a disclosure of the information, document or article in question by a Crown servant in contravention of sections 1(3), 2(1) and 3(1) above.

(5)   For the purposes of this section information or a document or article is communicated in confidence if it is communicated on terms requiring it to be held in confidence or in circumstances in which the person communicating it could reasonably expect that it would be so held.

7. Authorised disclosures

(1)   For the purposes of this Act a disclosure by—

    (a)   a Crown servant; or

    (b)   a person, not being a Crown servant or government contractor, in whose case a notification for the purposes of section 1(1) above is in force,

is made with lawful authority if, and only if, it is made in accordance with his official duty.

(2)   For the purposes of this Act a disclosure by a government contractor is made with lawful authority if, and only if, it is made—

    (a)   in accordance with an official authorisation; or

    (b)   for the purposes of the functions by virtue of which he is a government contractor and without contravening an official restriction.

(3)   For the purposes of this Act a disclosure made by any other person is made with lawful authority if, and only if, it is made—

(a)   to a Crown servant for the purposes of his functions as such; or

(b)   in accordance with an official authorisation.

(4)   It is a defence for a person charged with an offence under any of the foregoing provisions of this Act to prove that at the time of the alleged offence he believed that he had lawful authority to make the disclosure in question and had no reasonable cause to believe otherwise.

(5)   In this section 'official authorisation' and 'official restriction' mean, subject to subsection (6) below, an authorisation or restriction duly given or imposed by a Crown servant or government contractor or by or on behalf of a prescribed body or a body of a prescribed class.

(6)   In relation to section 6 above 'official authorisation' includes an authorisation duly given by or on behalf of the State or organisation concerned or, in the case of an organisation, a member of it.

8.   Safeguarding of information

(1)   Where a Crown servant or government contractor, by virtue of his position as such, has in his possession or under his control any document or other article which it would be an offence under any of the foregoing provisions of this Act for him to disclose without lawful authority he is guilty of an offence if—

(a)   being a Crown servant, he retains the document or article contrary to his official duty; or

(b)   being a government contractor, he fails to comply with an official direction for the return or disposal of the document or article,

or if he fails to take such care to pevent the unauthorised disclosure of the document or article as a person in his position may reasonably be expected to take.

(2)   It is a defence for a Crown servant charged with an offence under subsection (1)(a) above to prove that at the time of the alleged offence he believed that he was acting in accordance with his official duty and had no reasonable cause to believe otherwise.

(3)   In subsections (1) and (2) above references to a Crown servant include any person, not being a Crown servant or government contractor, in whose case a notification for the purposes of section 1(1) above is in force.

(4)   Where a person has in his possession or under his control any document or other article which it would be an offence under section 5 above for him to disclose without lawful authority, he is guilty of an offence if—

(a)   he fails to comply with an official direction for its return or disposal; or

(b)   where he obtained it from a Crown servant or government contractor on terms requiring it to be held in confidence or in circumstances in which that servant or contractor could reasonably expect that it would be so held, he fails to take such care to prevent its unauthorised disclosure as a person in his position may reasonably be expected to take.

(5)   Where a person has in his possession or under his control any document or other article which it would be an offence under section 6 above for him to disclose without lawful authority, he is guilty of an offence if he fails to comply with an official direction for its return or disposal.

(6)   A person is guilty of an offence if he discloses any official information, document or other article which can be used for the purpose of obtaining access to any information, document or other article protected against disclosure by the foregoing provisions of this Act and the circumstances in which it is disclosed are such that it would be reasonable to expect that it might be used for that purpose without authority.

(7) For the purposes of subsection (6) above a person discloses information or a document or article which is official if—

(a) he has or has had it in his possession by virtue of his position as a Crown servant or government contractor; or

(b) he knows or has reasonable cause to believe that a Crown servant or government contractor has or has had it in his possession by virtue of his position as such.

(8) Subsection (5) of section 5 above applies for the purposes of subsection (6) above as it applies for the purposes of that section.

(9) In this section 'official direction' means a direction duly given by a Crown servant or government contractor or by or on behalf of a prescribed body or a body of a prescribed class.

12. 'Crown servant' and 'government contractor'

(1) In this Act 'Crown servant' means—

(a) a Minister of the Crown;

(b) a person appointed under section 8 of the Northern Ireland Constitution Act 1973 (the Northern Ireland Executive etc);

(c) any person employed in the civil service of the Crown, including Her Majesty's Diplomatic Service, Her Majesty's Overseas Civil Service, the civil service of Northern Ireland and the Northern Ireland Court Service;

(d) any member of the naval, military or air forces of the Crown, including any person employed by an association established for the purposes of the Reserve Forces Act 1980;

(e) any constable and any other person employed or appointed in or for the purposes of any police force (including a police force within the meaning of the Police Act (Northern Ireland) 1970);

(f) any person who is a member or employee of a prescribed body or a body of a prescribed class and either is prescribed for the purposes of this paragraph or belongs to a prescribed class of members or employees of any such body;

(g) any person who is the holder of a prescribed office or who is an employee of such a holder and either is prescribed for the purposes of this paragraph or belongs to a prescribed class of such employees.

(2) In this Act 'government contractor' means, subject to subsection (3) below, any person who is not a Crown servant but who provides, or is employed in the provision of, goods or services—

(a) for the purposes of any Minister or person mentioned in paragraph (a) or (b) of subsection (1) above, of any of the services, forces or bodies mentioned in that subsection or of the holder of any office prescribed under that subsection; or

(b) under an agreement or arrangement certified by the Secretary of State as being one to which the government of a State other than the United Kingdom or an international organisation is a party or which is subordinate to, or made for the purposes of implementing, any such agreement or arrangement.

(3) Where an employee or class of employees of any body, or of any holder of an office, is prescribed by an order made for the purposes of subsection (1) above—

(a) any employee of that body, or of the holder of that office, who is not prescribed or is not within the prescribed class; and

(b) any person who does not provide, or is not employed in the provision of, goods or services for the purposes of the performance of those functions of the body or the holder of the office in connection with which the employee or prescribed class of employees is engaged,

shall not be a government contractor for the purposes of this Act.

13. Other interpretation provisions

(1) In this Act—

'disclose' and 'disclosure', in relation to a document or other article, include parting with possession of it;

'international organisation' means, subject to subsections (2) and (3) below, an organisation of which only States are members and includes a reference to any organ of such an organisation;

'prescribed' means prescribed by an order made by the Secretary of State;

'State' includes the government of a State and any organ of its government and references to a State other than the United Kingdom include references to any territory outside the United Kingdom.

(2) In section 12(2)(b) above the reference to an international organisation includes a reference to any such organisation whether or not one of which only States are members and includes a commercial organisation.

(3) In determining for the purposes of subsection (1) above whether only States are members of an organisation, any member which is itself an organisation of which only States are members, or which is an organ of such an organisation, shall be treated as a State.

15. Acts done abroad

(1) Any act—
    (a) done by a British citizen or Crown servant; or
    (b) done by any person in any of the Channel Islands or the Isle of Man or any colony,
shall, if it would be an offence by that person under any provision of this Act other than section 8(1), (4) or (5) when done by him in the United Kingdom, be an offence under that provision.

INCITEMENT TO DISAFFECTION ACT 1934

1. Penalty on persons endeavouring to seduce members of His Majesty's forces from their duty or allegiance

If any person maliciously and advisedly endeavours to seduce any member of His Majesty's forces from his duty or allegiance to His Majesty, he shall be guilty of an offence under this Act.

2. Provisions for the prevention and detection of offences under this Act

(1) If any person, with intent to commit or to aid, abet, counsel, or procure the commission of an offence under section one of this Act, has in his possession or under his control any document of such a nature that the dissemination of copies thereof among members of His Majesty's forces would constitute such an offence, he shall be guilty of an offence under this Act.

FIRE SERVICES ACT 1947

30. Obstructing firemen

(2) Any person who wilfully obstructs or interferes with any member of a fire brigade maintained in pursuance of this Act who is engaged in operations for fire-fighting purposes shall be liable on summary conviction to a fine not exceeding [level 3 on the standard scale].

31. False alarms of fire

(1) Any person who knowingly gives or causes to be given a false alarm of fire to any fire brigade maintained in pursuance of this Act or to any member of such a brigade shall be liable on summary conviction to a fine not exceeding [level 4 on the standard scale] or to imprisonment for a term not exceeding three months or both such fine and such imprisonment.

POST OFFICE ACT 1953

59. Carelessness, negligence or misconduct of persons employed in carrying or delivering mail bags, postal packets, etc.

If any person employed to convey or deliver a mail bag, or a postal packet in course of transmission by post, or to perform any other duty in respect of a mail bag or such a postal packet—

(a)   without authority whilst so employed, or whilst the mail bag or postal packet is in his custody or possession, leaves it, or suffers any person, not being the person in charge thereof, to ride in the place appointed for the person in charge thereof in or upon any vehicle used for the conveyance thereof, or to ride in or upon a vehicle so used and not licensed to carry passengers, or upon a horse used for the conveyance on horseback thereof;

(b)   is guilty of any act of drunkenness whilst so employed;

(c)   is guilty of carelessness, negligence or other misconduct whereby the safety of the mail bag or postal packet is endangered;

(d)   without authority collects, receives, conveys or delivers a postal packet otherwise than in the ordinary course of post;

(e)   gives any false information of an assault or attempt at robbery upon him; or

(f)   loiters on the road or passage, or wilfully misspends his time so as to retard the progress or delay the arrival of a mail bag or postal packet in the course of transmission by post, or does not use due care and diligence safely to convey a mail bag or postal packet at the due rate of speed,

he shall be liable on summary conviction to a fine not exceeding level 2 on the standard scale.

CUSTOMS AND EXCISE MANAGEMENT ACT 1979

50. Penalty for improper importation of goods

(1)   Subsection (2) below applies to goods of the following descriptions, that is to say—

(a)   goods chargeable with a duty which has not been paid; and

(b)   goods the importation, landing or unloading of which is for the time being prohibited or restricted by or under any enactment.

(2)   If any person with intent to defraud Her Majesty of any such duty or to evade any such prohibition or restriction as is mentioned in subsection (1) above—

(a)   unships or lands in any port or unloads from any aircraft in the United Kingdom or from any vehicle in Northern Ireland any goods to which this subsection applies, or assists or is otherwise concerned in such unshipping, landing or unloading; or

(b)   removes from their place of importation or from any approved wharf, examination station, transit shed or customs and excise station any goods to which this subsection applies or assists or is otherwise concerned in such removal,

he shall be guilty of an offence under this subsection and may be detained.

(3)   If any person imports or is concerned in importing any goods contrary to any prohibition or restriction for the time being in force under or by virtue of any enactment with respect to those goods, whether or not the goods are unloaded, and does so with intent to evade the prohibition or restriction, he shall be guilty of an offence under this subsection and may be detained.

(7)   In any case where a person would, apart from this subsection, be guilty of—

(a)   an offence under this section in connection with the importation of goods contrary to a prohibition or restriction; and

(b)   a corresponding offence under the enactment or other instrument imposing the prohibition or restriction, being an offence for which a fine or other penalty is expressly provided by that enactment or other instrument, he shall not be guilty of the offence mentioned in paragraph (a) of this subsection.

170. Penalty for fraudulent evasion of duty, etc.

(1)   Without prejudice to any other provision of the Customs and Excise Acts 1979, if any person—

(a)   knowingly acquires possession of any of the following goods, that is to say—

(i)   goods which have been unlawfully removed from a warehouse or Queen's warehouse;

(ii)   goods which are chargeable with a duty which has not been paid;

(iii)   goods with respect to the importation or exportation of which any prohibition or restriction is for the time being in force under or by virtue of any enactment; or

(b)   is in any way knowingly concerned in carrying, removing, depositing, harbouring, keeping or concealing or in any manner dealing with any such goods, and does so with intent to defraud Her Majesty of any duty payable on the goods, or to evade any such prohibition or restriction with respect to the goods shall be guilty of an offence under this section and may be arrested.

(2)   Without prejudice to any other provision of the Customs and Excise Acts 1979, if any person is, in relation to any goods, in any way knowingly concerned in any fraudulent evasion or attempt at evasion—

(a)   of any duty chargeable on the goods;

(b)   of any prohibition or restriction for the time being in force with respect to the goods under or by virtue of any enactment; or

(c)   of any provision of the Customs and Excise Acts 1979 applicable to the goods, he shall be guilty of an offence under this section and may be arrested.

(5)   In any case where a person would, apart from this subsection, be guilty of—

(a)   an offence under this section in connection with a prohibition or restriction; and

(b)   a corresponding offence under the enactment or other instrument imposing the prohibition or restriction, being an offence for which a fine or other penalty is expressly provided by that enactment or other instrument,
he shall not be guilty of the offence mentioned in paragraph (a) of this subsection.

(6)   Where any person is guilty of an offence under this section, the goods in respect of which the offence was committed shall be liable to forfeiture.

12 PRELIMINARY OFFENCES

CRIMINAL ATTEMPTS ACT 1981

1. Attempting to commit an offence

(1) If, with intent to commit an offence to which this section applies, a person does an act which is more than merely preparatory to the commission of the offence, he is guilty of attempting to commit the offence.

(1A) Subject to section 8 of the Computer Misuse Act 1990 (relevance of external law), if this subsection applies to an act, what the person doing it had in view shall be treated as an offence to which this section applies.

(1B) Subsection (1A) above applies to an act if—

(a) it is done in England and Wales; and

(b) it would fall within subsection (1) above as more than merely preparatory to the commission of an offence under section 3 of the Computer Misuse Act 1990 but for the fact that the offence, if completed, would not be an offence triable in England and Wales.

(2) A person may be guilty of attempting to commit an offence to which this section applies even though the facts are such that the commission of the offence is impossible.

(3) In any case where —

(a) apart from this subsection a person's intention would not be regarded as having amounted to an intent to commit an offence: but

(b) if the facts of the case had been as he believed them to be, his intention would be so regarded, then, for the purposes of subsection (1) above, he shall be regarded as having had an intent to commit that offence.

(4) This section applies to any offence which, if it were completed, would be triable in England and Wales as an indictable offence, other than —

(a) conspiracy (at common law or under section 1 of the Criminal Law Act 1977 or any other enactment);

(b) aiding, abetting, counselling, procuring or suborning the commission of an offence;

(c) offences under section 4 (1) (assisting offenders) or 5 (1) (accepting or agreeing to accept consideration for not disclosing information about an arrestable offence) of the Criminal Law Act 1967.

1A. Extended jurisdiction in relation to certain attempts

(1) If this section applies to an act, what the person doing the act had in view shall be treated as an offence to which section 1(1) above applies.

(2) This section applies to an act if—

(a) it is done in England and Wales, and

(b) it would fall within section 1(1) above as more than merely preparatory to the commission of a Group A offence but for the fact that that offence, if completed, would not be an offence triable in England and Wales.

(3)   In this section 'Group A offence' has the same meaning as in Part 1 of the Criminal Justice Act 1993.

(4)   Subsection (1) above is subject to the provisions of section 6 of the Act of 1993 (relevance of external law).

(5)   Where a person does any act to which this section applies, the offence which he commits shall for all purposes be treated as the offence of attempting to commit the relevant Group A offence.

4.   Trial and penalties

(1)   A person guilty by virtue of section 1 above of attempting to commit an offence shall —

(a)   if the offence attempted is murder or any other offence the sentence for which is fixed by law, be liable on conviction on indictment to imprisonment for life; and

(b)   if the offence attempted is indictable but does not fall within paragraph (a) above, be liable on conviction on indictment to any penalty to which he would have been liable on conviction on indictment of that offence; and

(c)   if the offence attempted is triable either way, be liable on summary conviction to any penalty to which he would have been liable on summary conviction of that offence.

(2)   In any case in which a court may proceed to summary trial of an information charging a person with an offence and an information charging him with an offence under section 1 above of attempting to commit it or an attempt under a special statutory provision, the court may, without his consent, try the informations together.

(3)   Where, in proceedings against a person for an offence under section 1 above, there is evidence sufficient in law to support a finding that he did an act falling within subsection (1) of that section, the question whether or not his act fell within that subsection is a question of fact.

6.   Effect on common law

(1)   The offence of attempt at common law and any offence at common law of procuring materials for crime are hereby abolished for all purposes not relating to acts done before the commencement of this Act.

(2)   Except as regards offences committed before the commencement of this Act, references in any enactment passed before this Act which fall to be construed as references to the offence of attempt at common law shall be construed as references to the offence under section 1 above.

9.   Interference with vehicles

(1)   A person is guilty of the offence of vehicle interference if he interferes with a motor vehicle or trailer or with anything carried in or on a motor vehicle or trailer with the intention that any offence specified in subsection (2) below shall be committed by himself or some other person.

(2)   The offences mentioned in subsection (1) above are—

(a)   theft of the motor vehicle or trailer or part of it;

(b)   theft of anything carried in or on the motor vehicle or trailer; and

(c)   an offence under section 12(1) of the Theft Act 1968 (taking and driving away without consent);

and, if it is shown that a person accused of an offence under this section intended that one of those offences should be committed, it is immaterial that it cannot be shown which it was.

(3)   A person guilty of an offence under this section shall be liable on summary conviction to imprisonment for a term not exceeding three months or to a fine not exceeding £500 or to both.

(5)   In this section 'motor vehicle' and 'trailer' have the meanings assigned to them by section 190(1) of the Road Traffic Act 1972.

CRIMINAL LAW ACT 1977

1.   The offence of conspiracy

(1)   Subject to the following provisions of this Part of this Act, if a person agrees with any other person or persons that a course of conduct shall be pursued which, if the agreement is carried out in accordance with their intentions, either—

(a)   will necessarily amount to or involve the commission of any offence or offences by one or more parties to the agreement, or

(b)   would do so but for the existence of facts which render the commission of the offence or any offences impossible,

he is guilty of conspiracy to commit the offence or offences in question.

(1A)   Subject to section 8 of the Computer Misuse Act 1990 (relevance of external law), if this subsection applies to an agreement, this Part of this Act has effect in relation to it as it has effect in relation to an agreement falling within subsection (1) above.

(1B)   Subsection (1A) above applies to an agreement if—

(a)   a party to it, or a party's agent, did anything in England and Wales in relation to it before its formation; or

(b)   a party to it became a party in England and Wales (by joining it either in person or through an agent); or

(c)   a party to it, or a party's agent, did or omitted anything in England and Wales in pursuance of it;

and the agreement would fall within subsection (1) above as an agreement relating to the commission of a computer misuse offence but for the fact that the offence would not be an offence triable in England and Wales if commited in accordance with the parties' intentions.

(2)   Where liability for any offence may be incurred without knowledge on the part of the person committing it of any particular fact or circumstance necessary for the commission of the offence, a person shall nevertheless not be guilty of conspiracy to commit that offence by virtue of subsection (1) above unless he and at least one other party to the agreement intend or know that that fact or circumstance shall or will exist at the time when the conduct constituting the offence is to take place.

(4)   In this Part of this Act 'offence' means an offence triable in England and Wales, except that it includes murder notwithstanding that the murder in question would not be so triable if committed in accordance with the intentions of the parties to the agreement.

(5)   In the application of this Part of this Act to an agreement to which subsection (1A) above applies any reference to an offence shall be read as a reference to what would be the computer misuse offence in question but for the fact that it is not an offence triable in England and Wales.

(6)   In this section 'computer misuse offence' means an offence under the Computer Misuse Act 1990.

1A.   Extended jurisdiction over certain conspiracies

(1)   This Part of this Act has effect in relation to an agreement which falls within this section as it has effect in relation to one which falls within section 1(1) above.

(2)   An agreement falls within this section if—

(a)   a party to it, or a party's agent, did anything in England and Wales in relation to it before its formation, or

(b)   a party to it became a party in England and Wales (by joining it either in person or through an agent), or

(c)   a party to it, or a party's agent, did or omitted anything in England and Wales in pursuance of it,

and the agreement would fall within section 1(1) above as an agreement relating to the commission of a Group A offence but for that offence, if committed in accordance with the parties' intentions, not being an offence triable in England and Wales.

(3)   In subsection (2) above 'Group A offence' has the same meaning as in Part I of the Criminal Justice Act 1993.

(4)   Subsection (1) above is subject to the provisions of section 6 of the Act of 1993 (relevance of external law).

(5)   An offence which is an offence of conspiracy, by virtue of this section, shall be treated for all purposes as an offence of conspiracy to commit the relevant Group A offence.

2.   Exemptions from liability for conspiracy

(1)   A person shall not by virtue of section 1 above be guilty of conspiracy to commit any offence if he is an intended victim of that offence.

(2)   A person shall not by virtue of section 1 above be guilty of conspiracy to commit any offence or offences if the only other person or persons with whom he agrees are (both initially and at all times during the currency of the agreement) persons of any one or more of the following descriptions, that is to say —

   (a)   his spouse;

   (b)   a person under the age of criminal responsibility; and

   (c)   an intended victim of that offence or of each of those offences.

(3)   A person is under the age of criminal responsibility for the purposes of subsection (2) (b) above so long as it is conclusively presumed, by virtue of section 50 of the Children and Young Persons Act 1933, that he cannot be guilty of any offence.

3.   Penalties for conspiracy

(1)   A person guilty by virtue of section 1 above of conspiracy to commit any offence or offences shall be liable on conviction on indictment—

   (a)   in a case falling within subsection (2) or (3) below, to imprisonment for a term related in accordance with that subsection to the gravity of the offence or offences in question (referred to below in this section as the relevant offence or offences); and

   (b)   in any other case, to a fine.

Paragraph (b) above shall not be taken as prejudicing the application of section 30(1) of the Powers of Criminal Courts Act 1973 (general power of court to fine offender convicted on indictment) in a case falling within subsection (2) or (3) below.

(2)   Where the relevant offence or any of the relevant offences is an offence of any of the following descriptions, that is to say —

   (a)   murder, or any other offence the sentence for which is fixed by law;

   (b)   an offence for which a sentence extending to imprisonment for life is provided; or

   (c)   an indictable offence punishable with imprisonment for which no maximum term of imprisonment is provided,

the person convicted shall be liable to imprisonment for life.

(3)   Where in a case other than one to which subsection (2) above applies the relevant offence or any of the relevant offences is punishable with imprisonment, the person convicted shall be liable to imprisonment for a term not exceeding the maximum term provided for that offence or (where more than one such offence is in question) for any one of those offences (taking the longer or the longest term as the limit for the purposes of this section where the terms provided differ).

In the case of an offence triable either way the references above in this subsection to the maximum term provided for that offence are references to the maximum term so provided on conviction on indictment.

4. Restrictions on the institution of proceedings for conspiracy

(1) Subject to subsection (2) below proceedings under section 1 above for conspiracy to commit any offence shall not be instituted against any person except by or with the consent of the Director of Public Prosecutions if the offence or (as the case may be) each of the offences in question is a summary offence.

(2) In relation to the institution of proceedings under section 1 above for conspiracy to commit —

(a) an offence which is subject to a prohibition by or under any enactment on the institution of proceedings otherwise than by, or on behalf or with the consent of, the Attorney-General, or

(b) two or more offences of which at least one is subject to such a prohibition, subsection (1) above shall have effect with the substitution of a reference to the Attorney-General for the reference to the Director of Public Prosecutions.

(3) Any prohibition by or under any enactment on the institution of proceedings for any offence which is not a summary offence otherwise than by, or on behalf or with the consent of, the Director of Public Prosecutions or any other person shall apply also in relation to proceedings under section 1 above for conspiracy to commit that offence.

(4) Where —

(a) an offence has been committed in pursuance of any agreement; and

(b) proceedings may not be instituted for that offence because any time limit applicable to the institution of any such proceedings has expired,

proceedings under section 1 above for conspiracy to commit that offence shall not be instituted against any person on the basis of that agreement.

5. Abolitions, savings, transitional provisions, consequential amendment and repeals

(1) Subject to the following provisions of this section, the offence of conspiracy at common law is hereby abolished.

(2) Subsection (1) above shall not affect the offence of conspiracy at common law so far as relates to conspiracy to defraud.

(3) Subsection (1) above shall not affect the offence of conspiracy at common law if and in so far as it may be committed by entering into an agreement to engage in conduct which—

(a) tends to corrupt public morals or outrages public decency; but

(b) would not amount to or involve the commission of an offence if carried out by a single person otherwise than in pursuance of an agreement.

(6) The rules laid down by sections 1 and 2 above shall apply for determining whether a person is guilty of an offence of conspiracy under any enactment other than section 1 above, but conduct which is an offence under any such other enactment shall not also be an offence under section 1 above.

(7) Incitement to commit the offence of conspiracy (whether the conspiracy incited would be an offence at common law or under section 1 above or any other enactment) shall cease to be an offence.

(8) The fact that the person or persons who, so far as appears from the indictment on which any person has been convicted of conspiracy, were the only other parties to the agreement on which his conviction was based have been acquitted of conspiracy by reference to that agreement (whether after being tried with the person convicted or separately) shall not be a ground for quashing his conviction unless under all the circumstances of the case his conviction is inconsistent with the acquittal of the other person or persons in question.

(9) Any rule of law or practice inconsistent with the provisions of subsection (8) above is hereby abolished.

8. Trespassing with a weapon of offence
[See page 194]

TRADE UNION AND LABOUR RELATIONS (CONSOLIDATION) ACT 1992

242. Restriction of offence of conspiracy

(1) Where in pursuance of any such agreement as is mentioned in section 1(1) of the Criminal Law Act 1977 (which provides for the offence of conspiracy) the acts in question in relation to an offence are to be done in contemplation or furtherance of a trade dispute, the offence shall be disregarded for the purposes of that subsection if it is a summary offence which is not punishable with imprisonment.

244. Meaning of 'trade dispute'

(1) In this Part a 'trade dispute' means a dispute between workers and their employer which relates wholly or mainly to one or more of the following—

(a)   terms and conditions of employment, or the physical conditions in which any workers are required to work;

(b)   engagement or non-engagement, or termination or suspension of employment or the duties of employment, of one or more workers;

(c)   allocation of work or the duties of employment between workers or groups of workers;

(d)   matters of discipline;

(e)   a worker's membership or non-membership of a trade union;

(f)   facilities for officials of trade unions; and

(g)   machinery for negotiation or consultation, and other procedures, relating to any of the above matters, including the recognition by employers or employers' associations of the right of a trade union to represent workers in such negotiations of the right of a trade union to represent workers in such negotiation or consultation or in the carrying out of such procedures.

(2) A dispute between a Minister of the Crown and any workers shall, notwithstanding that he is not the employer of those workers, be treated as a dispute between those workers and their employer if the dispute relates to matters which—

(a)   have been referred for consideration by a joint body on which, by virtue of provision made by or under any enactment, he is represented, or

(b)   cannot be settled without him exercising a power conferred on him by or under an enactment.

(3) There is a trade dispute even though it relates to matters occurring outside the United Kingdom, so long as the person or persons whose actions in the United Kingdom are said to be in contemplation or furtherance of a trade dispute relating to matters occurring outside the United Kingdom are likely to be affected in respect of one or more of the matters specified in subsection (1) by the outcome of the dispute.

(4) An act, threat or demand done or made by one person or organisation against another which, if resisted, would have led to a trade dispute with that other, shall be treated as being done or made in contemplation of a trade dispute with that other, notwithstanding that because that other submits to the act or threat or accedes to the demand no dispute arises.

(5) In this section—

'employment' includes any relationship whereby one person personally does work or performs services for another; and

'worker', in relation to a dispute with an employer, means—

(a)   a worker employed by that employer; or

(b) a person who has ceased to be so employed if his employment was terminated in connection with the dispute or if the termination of his employment was one of the circumstances giving rise to the dispute.

CRIMINAL JUSTICE ACT 1987

12. Charges of and penalty for conspiracy to defraud

(1) If—

(a) a person agrees with any other person or persons that a course of conduct shall be pursued; and

(b) that course of conduct will necessarily amount to or involve the commission of any offence or offences by one or more of the parties to the agreement if the agreement is carried out in accordance with their intentions,

the fact that it will do so shall not preclude a charge of conspiracy to defraud being brought against any of them in respect of the agreement.

(3) A person guilty of conspiracy to defraud is liable on conviction on indictment to imprisonment for a term not exceeding 10 years or a fine or both.

CRIMINAL JUSTICE ACT 1993

5. Extended jurisdiction over conspiracies to defraud

(3) A person may be guilty of conspiracy to defraud if—

(a) a party to the agreement constituting the conspiracy, or a party's agent, did anything in England and Wales in relation to the agreement before its formation, or

(b) a party to it became a party in England and Wales (by joining it either in person or through an agent), or

(c) a party to it, or a party's agent, did or omitted anything in England and Wales in pursuance of it,

and the conspiracy would be triable in England and Wales but for the fraud which the parties to it had in view not being intended to take place in England and Wales.

6. Relevance of external law

(1) A person is guilty of an offence triable by virtue of section 1A of the Criminal Law Act 1977, or by virtue of section 5(3), only if the pursuit of the agreed course of conduct would at some stage involve—

(a) an act or omission by one or more of the parties, or

(b) the happening of some other event,

constituting an offence under the law in force where the act, omission or other event was intended to take place.

(2) A person is guilty of an offence triable by virtue of section 1A of the Criminal Attempts Act 1981, or by virtue of section 5(4), only if what he had in view would involve the commission of an offence under the law in force where the whole or any part of it was intended to take place.

(3) Conduct punishable under the law in force in any place is an offence under that law for the purposes of this section, however it is described in that law.

VAGRANCY ACT 1824

4. Persons committing certain offences shall be deemed rogues and vagabonds and may be imprisoned for three months

. . . Every person committing any of the offences herein-before mentioned, after having been convicted as an idle and disorderly person; . . . every person wandering abroad and lodging in any barn or outhouse, or in any deserted or unoccupied building, or in the open air, or under a tent, or in any cart or waggon, . . . and not giving a good account of himself or herself; . . . ; every person wilfully, openly, lewdly, and obscenely exposing his person . . . , with intent to insult any female; every person wandering abroad, and endeavouring by the exposure of wound or deformities to obtain or gather alms; every person going about as a gatherer or collector of alms, or endeavouring to procure charitable contributions of any nature or kind, under any false or fraudulent pretence; . . . ; every person being found in or upon any dwelling house, warehouse, coach-house, stable, or outhouse, or in any inclosed yard, garden, or area, for any unlawful purpose; . . . ; and every person apprehended as an idle and disorderly person, and violently resisting any constable, or other peace officer so apprehending him or her, and being subsequently convicted of the offence for which he or she shall have been so apprehended; shall be deemed a rogue and vagabond, within the true intent and meaning of this Act; and, subject to section 70 of the Criminal Justice Act 1982, it shall be lawful for any justice of the peace to commit such offender (being thereof convicted before him by the confession of such offender, or by the evidence on oath of one or more credible witness or witnesses,) to the house of correction . . . for any time not exceeding three calender months; . . .

OFFENCES AGAINST THE PERSON ACT 1861

4. Soliciting to commit murder
Whosoever shall solicit, encourage, persuade, or endeavour to persuade, or shall propose to any person, to murder any other person, whether he be a subject of Her Majesty or not, and whether he be within the Queen's dominions or not, shall be guilty of a misdemeanour, and being convicted thereof shall be liable to imprisonment for life.

21. Attempting to choke etc., in order to commit or assist in the committing of any indictable offence
[See pages 18]

22. Using chloroform etc., to commit or assist in committing any indictable offence
[See pages 18–19]

29. Causing gunpowder to explode, or sending to any person an explosive substance, or throwing corrosive fluid on a person, with intent to grievous bodily harm
Whosoever shall unlawfully and maliciously cause any gunpowder or other explosive substance to explode, or send or deliver to or cause to be taken or received by any person any explosive substance or any other dangerous or noxious thing, or put or lay at any place, or cast or throw at or upon or otherwise apply to any person, any corrosive fluid or any destructive or explosive substance, with intent in any of the cases aforesaid to burn, maim, disfigure, or disable any person, or to do some grievous bodily harm to any person, shall, whether any bodily injury be effected or not, be guilty of an offence, and being convicted thereof shall be liable, at the discretion of the court, to imprisonment for life.

30. Placing gunpowder near a building etc., with intent to do bodily injury to any person
Whosoever shall unlawfully and maliciously place or throw in, into, upon, against, or near any building, ship, or vessel any gunpowder or other explosive substance, with intent to do any bodily injury to any person, shall, whether or not any explosion take place, and whether or not any bodily injury be effected, be guilty of an offence, and being convicted thereof shall be liable, at the discretion of the court, to imprisonment for any term not exceeding fourteen years.

64. Making or having anything with intent to commit an offence in the Act
[See page 20]

EXPLOSIVE SUBSTANCES ACT 1883

2. Causing explosion likely to endanger life or property
[See page 96]

3. Attempt to cause explosion, or making or keeping explosive with intent to endanger life or property
Any person who in the United Kingdom or a dependency or (being a citizen of the United Kingdom and Colonies) elsewhere unlawfully and maliciously—

(a) does any act with intent to cause, or conspires to cause by an explosive substance, an explosion of a nature likely to endanger life or to cause serious injury to property, whether in the United Kingdom or the Republic of Ireland, or

(b) makes or has in his possession or under his control an explosive substance with intent by means thereof to endanger life, or cause serious injury to property whether in the United Kingdom or the Republic of Ireland, or to enable any other person so to do, shall, whether any explosion does or not take place, and whether any injury to person or property has been actually caused or not, be guilty of an offence and on conviction on indictment shall be liable to imprisonment for life, and the explosive substance shall be forfeited.

4. Making or possession of explosive under suspicious circumstances
(1) Any person who makes or knowingly has in his possession or under his control any explosive substance, under such circumstances as to give rise to a reasonable suspicion that he is not making it or does not have it in his possession or under his control for a lawful object, shall, unless he can show that he made it or had it in his possession or under his control for a lawful object, be guilty of felony, and, on conviction, shall be liable to penal servitude for a term not exceeding fourteen years, or to imprisonment for a term not exceeding two years with or without hard labour, and the explosive substance shall be forfeited.

5. Punishment of accessories
Any person who within or (being a subject of Her Majesty) without Her Majesty's dominions by the supply of or solicitation for money, the providing of premises, the supply of materials, or in any manner whatsoever, procures, counsels, aids, abets, or is accessory to, the commission of any crime under this Act, shall be guilty of felony, and shall be liable to be tried and punished for that crime, as if he had been guilty as a principal.

9. Definitions
(1) In this Act, unless the context otherwise requires—
The expression 'explosive substance' shall be deemed to include any materials for making any explosive substance; also any apparatus, machine, implement, or materials used, or intended to be used, or adapted for causing, or aiding in causing, any explosion in or with any explosive substance; also any part of any such apparatus, machine, or implement.

PREVENTION OF CRIME ACT 1953

1. Prohibition of the carrying of offensive weapons without lawful authority or reasonable excuse
(1) Any person who without lawful authority or reasonable excuse, the proof whereof shall lie on him, has with him in any public place any offensive weapon shall be guilty of an offence.

(2)   Where any person is convicted of an offence under subsection (1) of this section the court may make an order for the forfeiture or disposal of any weapon in respect of which the offence was committed.

(4)   In this section 'public place' includes any highway and any other premises or place to which at the material time the public have or are permitted to have access, whether on payment or otherwise; and 'offensive weapon' means any article made or adapted for use for causing injury to the person, or intended by the person having it with him for such use by him or by some other person.

RESTRICTION OF OFFENSIVE WEAPONS ACT 1959

1.   Penalties for offences in connection with dangerous weapons
(1)   Any person who manufactures, sells or hires or offers for sale or hire or exposes or has in his possession for the purpose of sale or hire, or lends or gives to any other person—

(a)   any knife which has a blade which opens automatically by hand pressure applied to a button, spring or other device in or attached to the handle of the knife, sometimes known as a 'flick knife' or 'flick gun'; or

(b)   any knife which has a blade which is released from the handle or sheath thereof by the force of gravity or the application of centrifugal force and which, when released, is locked into place by means of a button, spring, lever, or other device, sometimes known as a 'gravity knife'.
shall be guilty of an offence.

(2)   The importation of any such knife as is described in the foregoing subsection is hereby prohibited.

CRIMINAL JUSTICE ACT 1988

139.   Having article with blade or point in public place
(1)   Subject to subsections (4) and (5) below, any person who has an article to which this section applies with him in a public place shall be guilty of an offence.

(2)   Subject to subsection (3) below, this section applies to any article which has a blade or is sharply pointed except a folding pocketknife.

(3)   This section applies to a folding pocketknife if the cutting edge of its blade exceeds 3 inches.

(4)   It shall be a defence for a person charged with an offence under this section to prove that he had good reason or lawful authority for having the article with him in a public place.

(5)   Without prejudice to the generality of subsection (4) above, it shall be a defence for a person charged with an offence under this section to prove that he had the article with him—

(a)   for use at work;

(b)   for religious reasons; or

(c)   as part of any national costume.

(6)   A person guilty of an offence under subsection (1) above shall be liable—

(a)   on summary conviction, to imprisonment for a term not exceeding six months, or a fine not exceeding the statutory maximum, or both;

(b)   on conviction on indictment, to imprisonment for a term not exceeding two years, or a fine, or both.

(7)   In this section 'public place' includes any place to which at the material time the public have or are permitted access, whether on payment or otherwise.

139A. Offence of having article with blade or point (or offensive weapon) on school premises

(1) Any person who has an article to which section 139 of this Act applies with him on school premises shall be guilty of an offence.

(2) Any person who has an offensive weapon within the meaning of section 1 of the Prevention of Crime Act 1953 with him on school premises shall be guilty of an offence.

(3) It shall be a defence for a person charged with an offence under subsection (1) or (2) above to prove that he had good reason or lawful authority for having the article or weapon with him on the premises in question.

(4) Without prejudice to the generality of subsection (3) above, it shall be a defence for a person charged with an offence under subsection (1) or (2) above to prove that he had the article or weapon in question with him—

    (a) for use at work,

    (b) for educational purposes,

    (c) for religious reasons, or

    (d) as part of any national costume.

(6) In this section and section 139B, 'school premises' means land used for the purposes of a school excluding any land occupied solely as a dwelling by a person employed at the school; and 'school' has the meaning given by section 14(5) of the Further and Higher Education Act 1992.

141. Offensive weapons

(1) Any person who manufactures, sells or hires or offers for sale or hire, exposes or has in his possession for the purpose of sale or hire, or lends or gives to any other person, a weapon to which this section applies shall be guilty of an offence and liable on summary conviction to imprisonment for a term not exceeding six months or to a fine not exceeding level 5 on the standard scale or both.

(2) The Secretary of State may by order made by statutory instrument direct that this section shall apply to any description of weapon specified in the order except—

    (a) any weapon subject to the Firearms Act 1968; and

    (b) crossbows.

(3) A statutory instrument containing an order under this section shall not be made unless a draft of the instrument has been laid before Parliament and has been approved by a resolution of each House of Parliament.

(4) The importation of a weapon to which this section applies is hereby prohibited.

(5) It shall be a defence for any person charged in respect of any conduct of his relating to a weapon to which this section applies—

    (a) with an offence under subsection (1) above; or

    (b) with an offence under section 50(2) or (3) of the Customs and Excise Management Act 1979 (improper importation),

to prove that his conduct was only for the purposes of functions carried out on behalf of the Crown or of a visiting force.

(8) It shall be a defence for any person charged in respect of any conduct of his relating to a weapon to which this section applies—

    (a) with an offence under subsection (1) above; or

    (b) with an offence under section 50(2) or (3) of the Customs and Excise Management Act 1979,

to prove that the conduct in question was only for the purposes of making the weapon available to a museum or gallery to which this subsection applies.

(9) If a person acting on behalf of a museum or gallery to which subsection (8) above applies is charged with hiring or lending a weapon to which this section applies, it shall be a defence for him to prove that he had reasonable grounds for believing that the person to whom he lent or hired it would use it only for cultural, artistic or educational purposes.

(10) Subsection (8) above applies to a museum or gallery only if it does not distribute profits.

141A. Sale of knives and certain articles with blade or point to persons under sixteen

(1) Any person who sells to a person under the age of sixteen years an article to which this section applies shall be guilty of an offence and liable on summary conviction to imprisonment for a term not exceeding six months, or a fine not exceeding level 5 on the standard scale, or both.

(2) Subject to subsection (3) below, this section applies to—

    (a) any knife, knife blade or razor blade,

    (b) any axe, and

    (c) any other article which has a blade or which is sharply pointed and which is made or adapted for use for causing injury to the person.

(3) This section does not apply to any article described in—

    (a) section 1 of the Restriction of Offensive Weapons Act 1959,

    (b) an order made under section 141(2) of this Act, or

    (c) an order made by the Secretary of State under this section.

(4) It shall be a defence for a person charged with an offence under subsection (1) above to prove that he took all reasonable precautions and exercised all due diligence to avoid the commission of the offence.

KNIVES ACT 1997

1. Unlawful marketing of knives

(1) A person is guilty of an offence if he markets a knife in a way which—

    (a) indicates, or suggests, that it is suitable for combat; or

    (b) is otherwise likely to stimulate or encourage violent behaviour involving the use of the knife as a weapon.

(2) 'Suitable for combat' and 'violent behaviour' are defined in section 10.

(3) For the purposes of this Act, an indication or suggestion that a knife is suitable for combat may, in particular, be given or made by a name or description—

    (a) applied to the knife;

    (b) on the knife or on any packaging in which it is contained; or

    (c) included in any advertisement which, expressly or by implication, relates to the knife.

(4) For the purposes of this Act, a person markets a knife if—

    (a) he sells or hires it;

    (b) he offers, or exposes, it for sale or hire; or

    (c) he has it in his possession for the purpose of sale or hire.

(5) A person who is guilty of an offence under this section is liable—

    (a) on summary conviction to imprisonment for a term not exceeding six months or to a fine not exceeding the statutory maximum, or to both;

    (b) on conviction on indictment to imprisonment for a term not exceeding two years or to a fine, or to both.

2. Publications

(1) A person is guilty of an offence if he publishes any written, pictorial or other material in connection with the marketing of any knife and that material—

    (a) indicates, or suggests, that the knife is suitable for combat; or

    (b) is otherwise likely to stimulate or encourage violent behaviour involving the use of the knife as a weapon.

(2) A person who is guilty of an offence under this section is liable—

    (a) on summary conviction to imprisonment for a term not exceeding six months or to a fine not exceeding the statutory maximum, or to both;

(b)   on conviction on indictment to imprisonment for a term not exceeding two years or to a fine, or to both.

3.   Exempt trades

(1)   It is a defence for a person charged with an offence under section 1 to prove that—

    (a)   the knife was marketed—

        (i)   for use by the armed forces of any country;

        (ii)   as an antique or curio; or

        (iii)   as falling within such other category (if any) as may be prescribed;

    (b)   it was reasonable for the knife to be marketed in that way; and

    (c)   there were no reasonable grounds for suspecting that a person into whose possession the knife might come in consequence of the way in which it was marketed would use it for an unlawful purpose.

(2)   It is a defence for a person charged with an offence under section 2 to prove that—

    (a)   the material was published in connection with marketing a knife—

        (i)   for use by the armed forces of any country;

        (ii)   as an antique or curio; or

        (iii)   as falling within such other category (if any) as may be prescribed.

4.   Other defences

(1)   It is a defence for a person charged with an offence under section 1 to prove that he did not know or suspect, and had no reasonable grounds for suspecting, that the way in which the knife was marketed—

    (a)   amounted to an indication or suggestion that the knife was suitable for combat; or

    (b)   was likely to stimulate or encourage violent behaviour involving the use of the knife as a weapon.

(2)   It is a defence for a person charged with an offence under section 2 to prove that he did not know or suspect, and had no reasonable grounds for suspecting, that the material—

    (a)   amounted to an indication or suggestion that the knife was suitable for combat; or

    (b)   was likely to stimulate or encourage violent behaviour involving the use of the knife as a weapon.

(3)   It is a defence for a person charged with an offence under section 1 or 2 to prove that he took all reasonable precautions and exercised all due diligence to avoid committing the offence.

9.   Offences by bodies corporate

(1)   If an offence under this Act committed by a body corporate is proved—

    (a)   to have been committed with the consent or connivance of an officer, or

    (b)   to be attributable to any neglect on his part,

he as well as the body corporate is guilty of be offence and liable to be proceeded against and punished accordingly.

(2)   In subsection (1) 'officer', in relation to a body corporate, means a director, manager, secretary or other similar officer of the body, or a person purporting to act in any such capacity.

(3)   If the affairs of a body corporate are managed by its members, subsection (1) applies in relation to the acts and defaults of a member in connection with his functions of management as if he were a director of the body corporate.

10.   Interpretation

In this Act—

'the court' means—

(a)   in relation to England and Wales or Northern Ireland, the Crown Court or a magistrate's court;

'knife' means an instrument which has a blade or is sharply pointed;

'marketing' and related expressions are to be read with section 1(4);

'publication' includes a publication in electronic form and, in the case of a publication which is, or may be, produced from electronic data, any medium on which the data are stored;

'suitable for combat' means suitable for use as a weapon for inflicting injury on a person or causing a person to fear injury:

'violent behaviour' means an unlawful act inflicting injury on a person or causing a person to fear injury.

PREVENTION OF TERRORISM (TEMPORARY PROVISIONS) ACT 1989

16.   Possession of articles for suspected terrorist purposes

(1)   A person is guilty of an offence if he has any article in his possession in circumstances giving rise to a reasonable suspicion that the article is in his possession for a purpose connected with the commission, preparation or instigation of acts of terrorism to which this section applies.

(2)   The acts of terrorism which this section applies are—

(a)   acts of terrorism connected with the affairs of Northern Ireland; and

(b)   acts of terrorism of any other description except acts connected solely with the affairs of the United Kingdom or any part of the United Kingdom other than Northern Ireland.

(3)   It is a defence for a person charged with an offence under this section to prove that at the time of the alleged offence the article in question was not in his possession for such a purpose as is mentioned in subsection (1) above.

(4)   Where a person is charged with an offence under this section and it is proved that at the time of the alleged offence—

(a)   he and that article were both present in any premises; or

(b)   the article was in premises of which he was the occupier or which he habitually used otherwise than as a member of the public,

the court may accept the fact proved as sufficient evidence of his possessing that article at that time unless it is further proved that he did not at that time know of its presence in the premises in question, or, if he did know, that he had no control over it.

(6)   This section applies to vessels, aircraft and vehicles as it applies to premises.

16B.   Unlawful collection, etc of information

(1)   No person shall, without lawful authority or reasonable excuse (the proof of which lies on him)—

(a)   collect or record any information which is of such a nature as is likely to be useful to terrorists in planning or carrying out any act of terrorism to which this section applies; or

(b)   have in his possession any record or document containing any such information as is mentioned in paragraph (a) above.

(2)   The acts of terrorism to which this section applies are—

(a)   acts of terrorism connected with the affairs of Northern Ireland; and

(b)   acts of terrorism of any other description except acts connected solely with the affairs of the United Kingdom or any part of the United Kingdom other than Northern Ireland.

(3)   In subsection (1) above the reference to recording information includes a reference to recording it by means of photography or by any other means.

OFFICIAL SECRETS ACT 1920

7.   Attempts, incitements etc.
[See page 244]

THEFT ACT 1968

9.   Burglary
[See page 192]

10.   Aggravated burglary
[See page 192]

17.   False accounting
[See page 148]

20(1).   Suppression, etc., of documents
[See page 149]

21.   Blackmail
[See page 149]

25.   Going equipped for stealing, etc.
[See page 151]

FIREARMS ACT 1968

16.   Possession of firearm with intent to injure
[See page 101]

17.   Use of firearm to resist arrest
[See page 101]

18.   Carrying firearm with criminal intent
[See page 101]

CRIMINAL DAMAGE ACT 1971

3.   Possessing anything with intent to destroy or damage property
[See page 135]

FORGERY AND COUNTERFEITING ACT 1981

5.   Offences relating to money orders, share certificates, passports, etc.
[See page 171]

TELECOMMUNICATIONS ACT 1984

42A.   Possession or supply of anything for fraudulent purpose in connection with use of telecommunication system
[See pages 155–6]

COMPUTER MISUSE ACT 1990

2.   Unauthorised access with intent to commit or facilitate commission of further offences
[See page 138]

SOCIAL SECURITY ADMINISTRATION ACT 1992

111A.   Dishonest representations for obtaining benefit etc.

(1)   If a person dishonestly—

(a)   makes a false statement or representation;

(b)   produces or furnishes, or causes or allows to be produced or furnished, any document or information which is false in a material particular;

(c)   fails to notify a change of circumstances which regulations under this Act require him to notify; or

(d)   causes or allows another person to fail to notify a change of circumstances which such regulations require the other person to notify,

with a view to obtaining any benefit or other payment or advantage under the social security legislation (whether for himself or for some other person), he shall be guilty of an offence.

(2)   In this section 'the social security legislation' means the Acts to which section 110 above applies and the Jobseekers Act 1995.

(3)   A person guilty of an offence under this section shall be liable—

(a)   on summary conviction, to imprisonment for a term not exceeding six months, or to a fine not exceeding the statutory maximum, or to both; or

(b)   on conviction on indictment, to imprisonment for a term not exceeding seven years, or to a fine, or to both.

112.   Making false statements for the purpose of obtaining benefit

(1)   If a person for the purpose of obtaining any benefit or other payment under the legislation to which section 110 above applies whether for himself or some other person, or for any purpose connected with that legislation—

(a)   makes a statement or representation which he knows to be false; or

(b)   produces or furnishes or knowingly causes or knowingly allows to be produced or furnished any document or information which he knows to be false in any material particular;

he shall be guilty of a summary offence.

(1A)   If a person without reasonable excuse—

(a)   fails to notify a change of circumstances which regulations under this Act require him to notify; or

(b)   knowingly causes or knowingly allows another person to fail to notify a change of circumstances which such regulations require the other person to notify,

and he knows that he, or the other person, is required to notify the change of circumstances, he shall be guilty of an offence.

APPENDIX

'LEGISLATING THE CRIMINAL CODE'

DRAFT CRIMINAL LAW BILL 1993
(Law Commission Report No. 218)

PART II   GENERAL DEFENCES AND OTHER PROVISIONS

Preliminary

24. Application of this Part

The provisions of this Part apply in relation to all offences under the law of England and Wales, . . .

Duress

25. Duress by threats

(1)   No act of a person constitutes an offence if the act is done under duress by threats.

(2)   A person does an act under duress by threats if he does it because he knows or believes—

(a)   that a threat has been made to cause death or serious injury to himself or another if the act is not done, and

(b)   that the threat will be carried out immediately if he does not do the act or, if not immediately, before he or that other can obtain effective official protection, and

(c)   that there is no other way of preventing the threat being carried out,

and the threat is one which in all the circumstances (including any of his personal characteristics that affect its gravity) he cannot reasonably be expected to resist.

It is for the defendant to show that the reason for his act was such knowledge or belief as is mentioned in paragraphs (a) to (c).

(3)   This section applies in relation to omissions as it applies in relation to acts.

(4)   This section does not apply to a person who knowingly and without reasonable excuse exposed himself to the risk of the threat made or believed to have been made.

If the question arises whether a person knowingly and without reasonable excuse exposed himself to such a risk, it is for him to show that he did not.

26. Duress of circumstances

(1)   No act of a person constitutes an offence if the act is done under duress of circumstances.

(2)   A person does an act under duress of circumstances if—

(a)   he does it because he knows or believes that it is immediately necessary to avoid death or serious injury to himself or another, and

(b)   the danger that he knows or believes to exist is such that in all the circumstances (including any of his personal characteristics that affect its gravity) he cannot reasonably be expected to act otherwise.

It is for the defendant to show that the reason for his act was such knowledge or belief as is mentioned in paragraph (a).

(3)   This section applies in relation to omissions as it applies in relation to acts.

(4)   This section does not apply to a person who knowingly and without reasonable excuse exposed himself to the danger known or believed to exist.

If the question arises whether a person knowingly and without reasonable excuse exposed himself to that danger, it is for him to show that he did not.

(5)   This section does not apply to—

(a)   an act done in the knowledge or belief that a threat has been made to cause death or serious injury to himself or another (see section 25), or

(b)   the use of force within the meaning of section 27 or 28, or an act immediately preparatory to the use of force, for the purposes mentioned in section 27(1) or 28(1).

Self-defence, prevention of crime, etc.

27.   Justifiable use of force: protection of person or property, prevention of crime, etc.

(1)   The use of force by a person for any of the following purposes, if only such as is reasonable in the circumstances as he believes them to be, does not constitute an offence—

(a)   to protect himself or another from injury, assault or detention caused by a criminal act;

(b)   to protect himself or (with the authority of that other) another from trespass to the person;

(c)   to protect his property from appropriation, destruction or damage caused by a criminal act or from trespass or infringement;

(d)   to protect property belonging to another from appropriation, destruction or damage caused by a criminal act or (with the authority of the other) from trespass or infringement; or

(e)   to prevent crime or a breach of the peace.

(2)   The expressions 'use of force' and 'property' in subsection (1) are defined and extended by sections 29 and 30 respectively.

(3)   For the purposes of this section an act involves a 'crime' or is 'criminal' although the person committing it, if charged with an offence in respect of it, would be acquitted on the ground that—

(a)   he was under ten years of age, or

(b)   he acted under duress, whether by threats or of circumstances, or

(c)   his act was involuntary, or

(d)   he was in a state of intoxication, or

(e)   he was insane, so as not to be responsible, according to law, for the act.

(4)   The references in subsection (1) to protecting a person or property from anything include protecting him or it from its continuing; and the reference to preventing crime or a breach of the peace shall be similarly construed.

(5)   For the purposes of this section the question whether the act against which force is used is of a kind mentioned in any of paragraphs (a) to (e) of subsection (1) shall be determined according to the circumstances as the person using the force ('D') believes them to be.

In the following provisions of this section references to unlawful or lawful acts are to acts which are or are not of such a kind.

(6)   Where an act is lawful by reason only of a belief or suspicion which is mistaken, the defence provided by this section applies as in the case of an unlawful act, unless—

(a)   D knows or believes that the force is used against a constable or a person assisting a constable, and

(b)   the constable is acting in the execution of his duty,

in which case the defence applies only if D believes the force to be immediately necessary to prevent injury to himself or another.

(7)   The defence provided by this section does not apply to a person who causes conduct or a state of affairs with a view to using force to resist or terminate it.

But the defence may apply although the occasion for the use of force arises only because he does something he may lawfully do, knowing that such an occasion may arise.

28.   Justifiable use of force: effecting or assisting arrest

(1)   The use of force by a person in effecting or assisting in a lawful arrest, if only such as is reasonable in the circumstances as he believes them to be, does not constitute an offence.

(2)   The expression 'use of force' in subsection (1) is defined and extended by section 29.

(3)   For the purposes of this section the question whether the arrest is lawful shall be determined according to the circumstances as the person using the force believed them to be.

29.   Meaning of 'use of force' and related provisions

(1)   For the purposes of sections 27 and 28—

(a)   a person uses force in relation to another person or property not only where he applies force to, but also where he causes an impact on, the body of that person or that property;

(b)   a person shall be treated as using force in relation to another person if—

(i)   he threatens him with its use, or

(ii)   he detains him without actually using it; and

(c)   a person shall be treated as using force in relation to property if he threatens a person with its use in relation to property.

(2)   Those sections apply in relation to acts immediately preparatory to the use of force as they apply in relation to acts in which force is used.

(3)   A threat of force may be reasonable although the actual use of force would not be.

(4)   The fact that a person had an opportunity to retreat before using force shall be taken into account, in conjunction with other relevant evidence, in determining whether the use of force was reasonable.

30.   Meaning of 'property' and related provisions

(1)   For the purposes of section 27(1)(c) and (d) (justifiable use of force: protection of property) the expression 'property' means property of a tangible nature, whether real or personal, or any right, interest or privilege in or over any such property, whether created by grant, licence or otherwise.

The expression also includes—

(a)   money,

(b)   wild creatures which have been tamed or are ordinarily kept in captivity, and

(c)   any other wild creatures or their carcasses if, but only if, they have been reduced into possession which has not been lost or abandoned or are in the course of being reduced into possession,

but not mushrooms growing wild on any land or flowers, fruit or foliage of a plant growing wild on any land.

For this purpose 'mushroom' includes any fungus and 'plant' includes any shrub or tree.

(2)   Property shall be treated for the purposes of section 27(1)(c) and (d) as belonging to any person—

    (a)   having the custody or control of it,

    (b)   having in it any proprietary right or interest (not being an equitable interest arising only from an agreement to transfer or grant an interest), or

    (c)   having a charge on it;

and where a property is subject to a trust, the persons to whom it belongs shall be treated as including any person having a right to enforce the trust.

Property of a corporation sole shall be treated as belonging to the corporation notwithstanding a vacancy in the corporation.

34. Interpretation of Part II

In this Part—

    'fault', in relation to an offence, means an element of the offence consisting of either or both of the following—

        (a)   a state of mind with which a person acts, or

        (b)   a failure to comply with a standard of conduct,

and references to a person being at fault shall be construed accordingly; and 'injury' means—

        (a)   physical injury, including pain, unconsciousness, or any other impairment of a person's physical condition, or

        (b)   impairment of a person's mental health.

DRAFT INVOLUNTARY HOMICIDE BILL 1995
(Law Commission Report No. 237)

1. Reckless killing

    (1)   A person who by his conduct causes the death of another is guilty of reckless killing if—

        (a)   he is aware of a risk that his conduct will cause death or serious injury; and

        (b)   it is unreasonable for him to take that risk having regard to the circumstances as he knows or believes them to be.

    (2)   A person guilty of reckless killing is liable on conviction on indictment to imprisonment for life.

2. Killing by gross carelessness

    (1)   A person who by his conduct causes the death of another is guilty of killing by gross carelessness if—

        (a)   a risk that his conduct will cause death or serious injury would be obvious to a reasonable person in his position;

        (b)   he is capable of appreciating that risk at the material time; and

        (c)   either—

            (i)   his conduct falls far below what can reasonably be expected of him in the circumstances; or

            (ii)   he intends by his conduct to cause some injury or is aware of, and unreasonably takes, the risk that it may do so.

    (2)   There shall be attributed to the person referred to in subsection (1)(a) above—

        (a)   knowledge of any relevant facts which the accused is shown to have at the material time; and

        (b)   any skill or experience professed by him.

    (3)   In determining for the purposes of subsection (1)(c)(i) above what can reasonably be expected of the accused regard shall be had to the circumstances of which he can be expected to be aware, to any circumstances shown to be within his knowledge and to any other matter relevant for assessing his conduct at the material time.

    (4)   Subsection (1)(c)(ii) above applies only if the conduct causing, or intended to cause, the injury constitutes an offence.

(5) A person guilty of killing by gross carelessness is liable on conviction on indictment to imprisonment for a term not exceeding [   ] years.

3. Omissions causing death
A person is not guilty of an offence under sections 1 or 2 above by reason of an omission unless the omission is in breach of a duty at common law.

4. Corporate killing
(1) A corporation is guilty of corporate killing if—

(a) a management failure by the corporation is the cause or one of the causes of a person's death; and

(b) that failure constitutes conduct falling far below what can reasonably be expected of the corporation in the circumstances.

(2) For the purposes of subsection (1) above—

(a) there is a management failure by a corporation if the way in which its activities are managed or organised fails to ensure the health and safety of persons employed in or affected by those activities; and

(b) such a failure may be regarded as a cause of a person's death notwithstanding that the immediate cause is the act or omission of an individual.

(3) A corporation guilty of an offence under this section is liable on conviction on indictment to a fine.

(4) No individual shall be convicted of aiding, abetting, counselling or procuring an offence under this section but without prejudice to an individual being guilty of any other offence in respect of the death in question.

(5) This section does not preclude a corporation being guilty of an offence under section 1 or 2 above.

(6) This section applies if the injury resulting in death is sustained in England and Wales or—

(a) within the seaward limits of the territorial sea adjacent to the United Kingdom;

(b) on a British ship or vessel;

(c) on a British-controlled aircraft as defined in section 92 of the Civil Aviation Act 1982; or

(d) in any place to which an Order in Council under section 22(1) of the Oil and Gas (Enterprise) Act 1982 (criminal jurisdiction in relation to offshore activities).

(7) For the purposes of subsection (6)(b) and (c) above an injury sustained on a ship, vessel or aircraft shall be treated as including an injury sustained by a person who is then no longer on board, and who sustains the injury, in consequence of the wrecking of, or of some other mishap affecting, the ship, vessel or aircraft.

(8) In this section 'a corporation' does not include a corporation sole but includes any body corporate wherever incorporated.

5. Remedial orders against convicted corporation
(1) A court before which a corporation is convicted of corporate killing may, subject to subsection (2) below, order the corporation to take such steps, within such time, as the order specifies for remedying the failure in question and any matter which appears to the court to have resulted from the failure and been the cause or one of the causes of the death.

(2) No such order shall be made except on an application by the prosecution specifying the terms of the proposed order; and the order, if any, made by the court shall be on such terms (whether those proposed or others) as the court considers appropriate having regard to any representations made, and any evidence adduced, in relation to that matter by the prosecution or on behalf of the corporation.

(3) In subsection (2) above references to the prosecution include references to the Health and Safety Executive and to any other body or person designated for the

purposes of that subsection by the Secretary of State either generally or in relation to the case in question.

(4) The time specified by an order under subsection (1) above may be extended or further extended by order of the court on an application made before the end of that time or extended time, as the case may be.

(5) A corporation which fails to comply with an order under this section is guilty of an offence and liable—

(a) on conviction on indictment, to a fine;

(b) on summary conviction, to a fine not exceeding £20,000.

6. Alternative verdicts

(1) On an indictment for murder a person found not guilty of murder may be found guilty of reckless killing or killing by gross carelessness.

(2) On an indictment for reckless killing a person found not guilty of that offence may be found guilty of killing by gross carelessness.

(3) On an indictment for reckless killing, killing by gross carelessness or corporate killing a person found not guilty of that offence may be found guilty of an offence under section 2 or 3 of the Health and Safety at Work etc. Act 1974.

(4) Subsections (2) and (3) above are without prejudice to section 6(3) of the Criminal Law Act 1967 (alternative verdicts).

7. Abolition of involuntary manslaughter

The offence of manslaughter is abolished except for—

(a) the cases for which provision is made by sections 2(3) and 4 of the Homicide Act 1957 (cases which would be murder but for diminished responsibility or a suicide pact); and

(b) cases which would be murder but for provocation.

8. Supplementary provisions

(1) In this Act 'injury' means—

(a) physical injury, including pain, unconsciousness or other impairment of a person's physical condition; or

(b) impairment of a person's mental health.

(2) This Act has effect subject to any enactment or rule of law providing a defence, or providing lawful authority, justification or excuse for an act or omission.

(3) This Act has effect subject to the rules relating to the effect of intoxication on criminal liability.

[9. Consequential amendments]

[10. Commencement and saving]

[11. Short title and extent]

DRAFT OFFENCES AGAINST THE PERSON BILL 1998

(Home Office, *Violence — Reforming the Offences Against the Person Act 1861*
(February 1998))

Injury and assault

1. Intentional serious injury

(1) A person is guilty of an offence if he intentionally causes serious injury to another.

(2) A person is guilty of an offence if he omits to do an act which he has a duty to do at common law, the omission results in serious injury to another, and he intends the omission to have that result.

(3) An offence under this section is committed notwithstanding that the injury occurs outside England and Wales if the act causing injury is done in England and Wales or the omission resulting in injury is made there.

(4) A person guilty of an offence under this section is liable on conviction on indictment to imprisonment for life.

2. Reckless serious injury

(1) A person is guilty of an offence if he recklessly causes serious injury to another.

(2) An offence under this section is committed notwithstanding that the injury occurs outside England and Wales if the act causing injury is done in England and Wales.

(3) A person guilty of an offence under this section is liable—

(a) on conviction on indictment, to imprisonment for a term not exceeding 7 years;

(b) on summary conviction, to imprisonment for a term not exceeding 6 months or a fine not exceeding the statutory maximum or both.

3. Intentional or reckless injury

(1) A person is guilty of an offence if he intentionally or recklessly causes injury to another.

(2) An offence under this section is committed notwithstanding that the injury occurs outside England and Wales if the act causing injury is done in England and Wales.

(3) A person guilty of an offence under this section is liable—

(a) on conviction on indictment, to imprisonment for a term not exceeding 5 years;

(b) on summary conviction, to imprisonment for a term not exceeding 6 months or a fine not exceeding the statutory maximum or both.

4. Assault

(1) A person is guilty of an offence if—

(a) he intentionally or recklessly applies force to or causes an impact on the body of another, or

(b) he intentionally or recklessly causes the other to believe that any such force or impact is imminent.

(2) No such offence is committed if the force or impact, not being intended or likely to cause injury, is in the circumstances such as is generally acceptable in the ordinary conduct of daily life and the defendant does not know or believe that it is in fact unacceptable to the other person.

(3) A person guilty of an offence under this section is liable on summary conviction to imprisonment for a term not exceeding 6 months or a fine not exceeding level 5 on the standard scale or both.

5. Assault on a constable

(1) A person is guilty of an offence if he assaults—

(a) a constable acting in the execution of his duty, or

(b) a person assisting a constable acting in the execution of his duty.

(2) For the purposes of this section a person assaults if he commits the offence under section 4.

(3) A reference in this section to a constable acting in the execution of his duty includes a reference to a constable who is a member of a police force maintained in Scotland or Northern Ireland when he is executing a warrant, or otherwise acting in England or Wales, by virtue of an enactment conferring powers on him in England and Wales.

(4) For the purposes of subsection (3) each of the following is a police force—

(a) a police force within the meaning given by section 50 of the Police (Scotland) Act 1967;

(b) the Royal Ulster Constabulary and the Royal Ulster Constabulary Reserve.

(5) A person guilty of an offence under this section is liable on summary conviction to imprisonment for a term not exceeding 6 months or a fine not exceeding level 5 on the standard scale or both.

6. Causing serious injury to resist arrest etc.

(1) A person is guilty of an offence if he causes serious injury to another intending to resist, prevent or terminate the lawful arrest or detention of himself or a third person.

(2) The question whether the defendant believes the arrest or detention is lawful must be determined according to the circumstances as he believes them to be.

(3) A person guilty of an offence under this section is liable on conviction on indictment to imprisonment for life.

7. Assault to resist arrest etc.

(1) A person is guilty of an offence if he assaults another intending to resist, prevent or terminate the lawful arrest or detention of himself or a third person.

(2) The question whether the defendant believes the arrest or detention is lawful must be determined according to the circumstances as he believes them to be.

(3) For the purposes of this section a person assaults if he commits the offence under section 4.

(4) A person guilty of an offence under this section is liable—

    (a) on conviction on indictment, to imprisonment for a term not exceeding 2 years;

    (b) on summary conviction, to imprisonment for a term not exceeding 6 months or a fine not exceeding the statutory maximum or both.

Dangerous substances

8. Dangerous substances: intending or risking serious injury

(1) A person is guilty of an offence if he acts as mentioned in subsection (2) and—

    (a) he intends to cause serious injury, or

    (b) he is reckless whether serious injury is caused.

(2) A person acts as mentioned in this subsection if he—

    (a) causes an explosive substance to explode,

    (b) places a dangerous substance in any place,

    (c) delivers or sends a dangerous substance to a person,

    (d) throws a dangerous substance at or near a person, or

    (e) applies a dangerous substance to a person.

(3) For the purposes of subsection (2) a dangerous substance is an explosive substance of any other dangerous substance.

(4) In this section 'explosive substance' has the same meaning as in the Explosive Substances Act 1883.

(5) A person guilty of an offence under this section is liable on conviction on indictment to imprisonment for life.

9. Dangerous substances: intending or risking injury

(1) A person is guilty of an offence if he acts as mentioned in section 8(2) and—

    (a) he intends to cause injury, or

    (b) he is reckless whether injury is caused.

(2) A person guilty of an offence under this section is liable on conviction on indictment to imprisonment for a term not exceeding 14 years.

Other offences

10. Threats to kill or cause serious injury

(1) A person is guilty of an offence if he makes to another a threat to cause the death of, or serious injury to, that other or a third person, intending that other to believe that it will be carried out.

(2)   A person guilty of an offence under this section is liable—
    (a)   on conviction on indictment, to imprisonment for a term not exceeding 10 years;
    (b)   on summary conviction, to imprisonment for a term not exceeding 6 months or a fine not exceeding the statutory maximum or both.

11.   Administering a substance capable of causing injury

(1)   A person is guilty of an offence if—
    (a)   he administers a substance to another or causes it to be taken by him and (in either case) he does so intentionally or recklessly,
    (b)   he knows the substance is capable of causing injury to the other, and
    (c)   it is unreasonable to adminster the substance or cause it to be taken having regard to the circumstances as he knows or believes them to be.
(2)   A person guilty of an offence under this section is liable—
    (a)   on conviction on indictment, to imprisonment for a term not exceeding 5 years;
    (b)   on summary conviction, to imprisonment for a term not exceeding 6 months or a fine not exceeding the statutory maximum or both.

12.   Torture

(1)   A person is guilty of an offence if he intentionally inflicts severe pain or suffering on another and he does the act—
    (a)   in the performance or purported performance of his official duties as a public official, or
    (b)   at the instigation or with the consent or acquiescence of a public official who is performing or purporting to perform his official duties.
(2)   A person is guilty of an offence if—
    (a)   he omits to do an act which he has a duty to do at common law.
    (b)   he makes the omission as mentioned in subsection (1)(a) or (b).
    (c)   the omission results in the infliction of severe pain or suffering on another, and
    (d)   he intends the omission to have that result.
(3)   The following are immaterial—
    (a)   the nationality of the persons concerned;
    (b)   whether anything occurs in the United Kingdom or elsewhere;
    (c)   whether the pain or suffering is physical or mental.
(4)   References in this section to an official include references to a person acting in an official capacity.
(5)   Proceedings for an offence under this section may be instituted only by or with the consent of the Attorney General.
(6)   A person guilty of an offence under this section is liable on conviction on indictment to imprisonment for life.

13.   Causing danger on railways

(1)   A person is guilty of an offence if he intentionally or recklessly causes danger to a person who is on a railway or is being carried on a railway.
(2)   A person is guilty of an offence if he omits to do an act which he has a duty to do at common law, the omission results in danger to a person who is on a railway or is being carried on a railway, and he intends the omission to have that result or is reckless whether it will have that result.
(3)   A person guilty of an offence under this section is liable—
    (a)   on conviction on indictment, to imprisonment for a term not exceeding 2 years;
    (b)   on sumary conviction, to imprisonment for a term not exceeding 6 months or a fine not exceeding the statutory maximum or both.

Meaning of fault terms and of injury

14. Meaning of fault terms

(1)   A person acts intentionally with respect to a result if—

(a)   it is his purpose to cause it, or

(b)   although it is not his purpose to cause it he knows that it would occur in the ordinary course of events if he were to succeed in his purpose of causing some other result.

(2)   A person acts recklessly with respect to a result if he is aware of a risk that it will occur and it is unreasonable to take that risk having regard to the circumstances as he knows or belies them to be.

(3)   A person intends an omission to have a result if—

(a)   it is his purpose that the result will occur, or

(b)   although it is not his purpose that the result will occur, he knows that it would occur in the ordinary course of events if he were to succeed in his purpose that some other result will occur.

(4)   A person is reckless whether an omission will have a result if he is aware of a risk that the result will occur and it is unreasonable to take that risk having regard to the circumstances as he knows or believes them to be.

(5)   Related expressions must be construed accordingly.

(6)   This section has effect for the purposes of this Act.

15. Meaning of injury

(1)   In this Act 'injury' means—

(a)   physical injury, or

(b)   mental injury.

(2)   Physical injury does not include anything caused by disease but (subject to that) it includes pain, unconsciousness and any other impairment of a person's physical condition.

(3)   Mental injury does not include anything caused by disease but (subject to that) it includes any impairment of a person's mental health.

(4)   In its application to section 1 this section applies without the exceptions relating to things caused by disease.

Matters affecting liability

16. Supervening fault

(1)   Where it is an offence under this Act to be at fault in causing a result by an act and a person lacks the fault required when he does an act that may cause or does cause the result, he nevertheless commits the offence if—

(a)   being aware that he has done the act and that the result may occur or (as the case may be) has occurred and may continue, and

(b)   with the fault required,

he falls to take reasonable steps to prevent the result occurring or continuing and it does occur or continue.

(2)   Where it is an offence under this Act to be at fault in causing a result by an omission and a person lacks the fault required when he makes an omission that may cause or does cause the result, he nevertheless commits the offence if—

(a)   being aware that he has made the omission and that the result may occur or (as the case may be) has occurred and may continue, and

(b)   with the fault required,

he fails to take reasonable steps to prevent the result occurring or continuing and it does occur or continue.

(3)   For the purposes of this section fault is intention or recklessness, and references to a person being at fault must be construed accordingly.

(4)   Common law rules relating to matters provided for in this section do not apply to offences under this Act.

17. Transferred fault

(1)   This section applies in determining whether a person is guilty of an offence under this Act.

(2)   A person's intention, or awareness of a risk, that his act will cause a result in relation to a person capable of being the victim of the offence must be treated as an intention or (as the case may be) awareness of a risk that his act will cause that result in relation to any other person affected by his act.

(3)   A person 's intention, or awareness of a risk, that his omission will have a result in relation to a person capable of being the victim of the offence must be treated as an intention or (as the case may be) awareness of a risk that his omission will have that result in relation to any other person affected as a result of his omission.

(4)   Common law rules relating to matters provided for in this section do not apply to offences under this Act.

18. General defences etc.

(1)   The provisions of this Act have effect subject to any enactment or rule of law providing—

   (a)   a defence, or

   (b)   lawful authority, justification or excuse for an act or omission.

(2)   In the application of subsection (1) to section 12 'lawful authority, justification or excuse' means—

   (a)   in relation to pain or suffering inflicted in the United Kingdom, lawful authority, justification or excuse under the law of the part of the United Kingdom where it was inflicted;

   (b)   in relation to pain or suffering inflicted outside the United Kingdom by (or as a result of an omission by) a United Kingdom official acting under the law of the United Kingdom or any part of the United Kingdom, lawful authority, justification or excuse under that law;

   (c)   in any other case, lawful authority, justification or excuse under the law of the place where the pain or suffering was inflicted.

(3)   The reference in this section to an official includes a reference to a person acting in an official capacity.

19. Effect of voluntary intoxication

(1)   For the purposes of this Act a person who was voluntarily intoxicated at any material time must be treated—

   (a)   as having been aware of any risk of which he would have been aware had he not been intoxicated, and

   (b)   as having known or believed in any circumstances which he would have known or believed in had he not been intoxicated.

(2)   Whether a person is voluntarily intoxicated for this purpose must be determined in accordance with the following provisions.

(3)   A person is voluntarily intoxicated if—

   (a)   he takes an intoxicant otherwise than properly for a medicinal purpose,

   (b)   he is aware that it is or way be an intoxicant, and

   (c)   he takes it in such a quantity as impairs his awareness or understanding.

(4)   An intoxicant, although taken for a medicinal purpose, is not properly so taken if—

   (a)   the intoxicant is not taken on medical advice, and the taker is aware that the taking may result in his doing an act or making an omission capable of constituting an offence of the kind in question, or

(b) the intoxicant is taken on medical advice, but the taker fails then or afterwards to comply with any forming condition forming part of the advice and he is aware that the failure may result in his doing an act or making an omission capable of constituting an offence of the kind in question.

(5) Intoxication must be presumed to have been voluntary unless there is adduced such evidence as might lead the court or jury to conclude that there is a reasonable possibility that the intoxication was involuntary.

(6) An intoxicant is any alcohol, drug or other thing which, when taken into the body, may impair the awareness or understanding of the person taking it.

(7) A person must be treated as taking an intoxicant if he permits it to be administered to him.

20. Attempts

(1) This section applies for the purpose of deciding whether a person is guilty under section 1 of the Criminal Attempts Act 1981 of attempting to commit an offence under this Act.

(2) For that purpose a person acts with intent with respect to a result if—

(a) it is his purpose to cause it, or

(b) although it is not his purpose to cause it, he knows that it would occur in the ordinary course of events if he were to succeed in his purpose of causing some other result.

Charges and verdicts

21. Charging more than one offence

For the purposes of the rules against charging more than one offence in the same count or information, each of sections 1 to 13 creates one offence.

22. Alternative verdicts

(1) For the purposes of the application of section 6(3) of the Criminal Law Act 1967 (alternative verdicts) to the trial of a person on indictment for any offence under this Act, an allegation in the indictment of intention includes an allegation of recklessness.

(2) If on the trial on indictment of a person charged with an offence under section 1, 2, 3, 6 or 7 the jury find him not guilty of the offence charged, they may (without prejudice to section 6(3) of the Criminal Law Act 1967) find him guilty of an offence under section 4.

(3) If on the summary trial of a person charged with an offence under section 2 the magistrates' court find him not guilty of that offence, they may find him guilty of an offence under section 3 or 4.

(4) If on the summary trial of a person charged with an offence under section 3, 5 or 7 the magistrates' court find him not guilty of that offence, they may find him guilty of an offence under section 4.

(5) If—

(a) on the summary trial of a person charged with an offence under section 2 the magistrates' court convict him of that offence and make no decision whether he is guilty of an offence under section 3 or 4, and

(b) he appeals to the Crown Court against the conviction,

the Crown Court may reverse the conviction and find him guilty of an offence under section 3 or 4.

(6) If—

(a) on the summary trial of a person charged with an offence under section 3, 5 or 7 the magistrates' court convict him of that offence and make no decision whether he is guilty of an offence under section 4, and

(b) he appeals to the Crown Court against the conviction,

the Crown Court may reverse the conviction and find him guilty of an offence under section 4.

Amendments etc.

23. Abolition of certain common law offences
The following common law offences are abolished—
    (a)   common assault;
    (b)   battery;
    (c)   mayhem.

[24. Amendments and repeals.]

General

[25. Extent.]

[26. Commencement.]

[27 Citation.]

INDEX

Video Recordings Act 1984
  ss. 1–3, 7, 9–12, 14A, 16, 22
   219–223
War Crimes Act 1991
  s.1 **13**

Water Resources Act 1991
  ss. 85, 89 **133–134**
Weights and Measures Act 1985
  ss. 28–37, 82 **180–185**
Wild Mammals (Protection) Act 1996
  ss. 1–3 **132–133**

BLACKSTONE'S STATUTES

TITLES IN THE SERIES

Company Law
Contract, Tort & Restitution
Public Law Statutes
Employment Law Statutes
Criminal Law Statutes
Evidence Statutes
Family Law Statutes
Land Law Statutes
Commercial and Consumer Law Statutes
English Legal System Statutes
EC Legislation
International Law Documents
Landlord and Tenant Statutes
Medical Law Statutes
Planning Law Statutes
Intellectual Property Statutes
Environmental Law Statutes
International Human Rights Documents
Property Law Statutes